The Complete SLOW COOKER Cookbook

1000 Recipes For Easy & Delicious Crock Pot Homemade Meals

Patrick Jones

CONTENTS

STEWS & CHILIS 40

CHICKEN RECIPES **66**

PORK RECIPES 90

FISH & SEAFOOD **123**

DESKERTS 128

INTRODUCTION

This cookbook has been put together as a simple and understandable guide for you as you explore the use of a slow cooker. It is my goal that you will be able to make some lip-licking, drool-worthy but healthy meals while cooking with as little heat as possible.

I put in the effort to ensure that the ingredients used are very easy to find and the processes very easy to follow.

Cooking with the slow cooker requires a longer amount of time for cooking than most cooking appliances, and this is simply because it cooks with as little heat as possible. However, the results are one of the best that you will encounter in your world of cooking.

With this, I wish you a good time making dishes that will create lasting memories for you and your family.

WHAT IS A SLOW COOKER?

It is an electronic cooking appliance that cooks food slowly at a given temperature for a long period, which works by locking up the heat in its ceramic pot and sustaining a steady temperature within the pot to cook ingredients slowly.

Slow cookers cook foods with as little indirect heat as possible, making it one of the best and healthiest cooking methods. Direct heat kills most of the nutrients in foods that the slow cooker seeks to avoid through cooking.

Cooking with it requires a lot of patience and less interruption; a lot of time will need to be invested into this worthy process while also ensuring to keep the lid closed at most times during the cook to prevent heat from escaping from the pot.

WHAT ARE THE BENEFITS OF A SLOW COOKER?

The benefits of a slow cooker are endless, but I would take time to elaborate on a few important ones below:

- **Energy-Savers**

As compared to an electric oven, the slow cooker consumes a lesser amount of electricity. A standard oven uses about 4000 watts of electricity, while a slow cooker uses just 300 watts. Now that is some cut on electricity right there!

- **Easier meal preparations**

Anyone can master meals with the slow cooker which is because all that is required of you is to toss in all the ingredients of a recipe mostly at the same time, leave it to cook until the cooking time is over, and voila, you have one good bunch of a delicious meal for your table.

- **Safe to Use**

Slow cookers are very safe to use because they are designed to be left unattended for a long time. Foods cooked in slow cookers have a minimal chance of getting burnt because they do not have any contact with direct heat and are cooked at a controlled temperature.

- **Healthy Meals**

Foods that are cooked on low heat and slowly tend to retain more vitamins while serving it with the gravy that is yielded from it also helps to increase the nutritional content and flavor that comes with slow cooking it.

HOW TO USE A SLOW COOKER

Here is how to use a slow cooker in a few steps!

1. Start by always preheating your slow cooker for 15 to 20 minutes before beginning the cook.

2. Prepare your ingredients in good time before the cooking begins, as you will mostly be tossing them into the pot for a one-pot cook. Cut vegetables into larger pieces, and brown your meat in a skillet before placing it in the slow cooker. Also, avoid sautéing vegetables in the slow cooker but rather do this on a stovetop before transferring them to the slow cooker.

3. There are three cooking settings on a slow cooker, i.e., HIGH, LOW, and WARM settings. Set the slow cooker to LOW if you want the food to cook for longer hours, and place the HIGH set if you wish to cook for shorter hours. The WARM setting is for keeping the food warm when not ready to serve.

4. After cooking, allow your slow cooker to cool down completely before cleaning.

5. Clean the pot with warm water and soap, wipe the base with a soft napkin dipped in warm water and allow it to dry.

NOTE! Some Slow Cooker models may have slightly different functions or buttons. Always check the manufacturer's manual before using any setting on your slow cooker.

MORNING RECIPES

Healthy Spinach Quiche

Serves: 6 | Total Time: 5 hours 15 minutes

1 tbsp olive oil	1 cup shredded mozzarella
4 eggs, beaten	3 cups spinach, torn
2 cups ham cubes	2 tbsp parsley, chopped
1 cup heavy cream	Salt and pepper to taste

Grease your Slow Cooker with olive oil. Add the eggs, heavy cream, mozzarella cheese, spinach, ham, parsley, salt, and pepper to a large bowl and stir to combine. Pour the mixture into the slow cooker. Cover with the lid and cook on Low for 5 hours. When done, let the quiche sit for 15 minutes before serving. Enjoy!

Morning Egg & Bacon Casserole

Serves: 4 | Total Time: 4 hours 15 minutes

1 (1-lb) package frozen hash browns	
8 oz bacon, chopped	½ cup milk
1 tbsp olive oil	Salt and pepper to taste
⅓ cup scallions, minced	½ cup hot sauce
4 large eggs	1 cup shredded cheddar

Warm the olive oil in a skillet over medium heat and cook the bacon for 5 minutes until crispy. Remove to your Slow Cooker. In a large bowl, whisk together the eggs and milk and season with salt and pepper.

Pour the mixture into the slow cooker. Add the hash browns, scallions, hot sauce, and cheese and stir. Cover with the lid and cook on Low for 4 hours or until the potatoes are cooked through, and the eggs are set.

Hard-Boiled Eggs

Serves: 6 | Total Time: 2 hours 45 minutes

6 large eggs	1 tbsp white vinegar

Arrange the eggs in an even layer on the bottom of your Slow Cooker without stacking. Cover them with enough water. Add the vinegar. Cover the cooker and cook for 2 ½ hours on High. Gently place the eggs in a bowl of ice water to cool for at least 10 minutes and stop the cooking. Serve sliced into wedges.

Honey Baked Oatmeal

Serves: 4 | Total Time: 3 hours 15 minutes

2 tbsp butter, melted	½ cup honey
1 egg	1 tsp baking powder
¾ cup milk	½ tsp salt
2 cups quick-cooking oats	

Grease your Slow Cooker with butter. In a medium bowl, beat the egg with salt. Add the milk, oats, honey, and baking powder and mix well. Pour the mixture into the cooker. Cover and cook on Low for 3 hours or until tender. Serve and enjoy!

Cheddar & Egg Bake

Serves: 6 | Total Time: 4 hours 15 minutes

1 tbsp olive oil	6 large eggs
3 bread slices, cubed	3 cups milk
1 ½ cups shredded cheddar	½ tsp mustard powder
4 oz ham, cubed	Salt and pepper to taste

Grease your Slow Cooker with olive oil. Add the bread cubes, cheese, and ham and stir to combine. In a bowl, whisk together the eggs, milk, mustard powder, salt, and pepper. Pour over the bread mixture. Cover and cook on Low for 4 hours. Turn off the cooker and let it rest for 10 minutes before serving.

Breakfast Millet with Raspberries

Serves: 4 | Total Time: 8 hours 15 minutes

1 cup millet	½ tsp ground cinnamon
2 cups water	½ tsp ground ginger
2 cups coconut milk	¼ tsp vanilla extract
½ teaspoon sea salt	½ cup fresh raspberries

Place the millet, water, coconut milk, salt, cinnamon, ginger, and vanilla in your Slow Cooker and stir well. Cover the cooker and cook on Low for 8 hours. Stir in the raspberries before serving.

Mushroom & Spinach Frittata

Serves: 4 | Total Time: 3 hours 20 minutes

1 tbsp butter, melted	2 green onions, sliced
6 large eggs	1 tsp garlic powder
2 tbsp buttermilk	Salt and pepper to taste
1 cup mushrooms, sliced	1 cup shredded cheddar
1 cup spinach, torn	

Grease a baking dish with butter. Beat the eggs in a large bowl. Stir in salt and pepper, buttermilk, mushrooms, spinach, green onions, cheese, and garlic powder. Pour the mixture into the baking dish. Place the dish in your Slow Cooker. Cover and cook on Low for 3 hours or until set. Turn off the cooker and allow the frittata to cool for 10 minutes. Serve sliced into wedges.

Lemon-Honey Porridge

Serves: 6 | Total Time: 8 hours 5 minutes

4 cups milk	1 tsp ground cinnamon
3 cups apple juice	¼ cup honey
2 ¼ cups coconut flour	1 tsp lemon zest

Place milk, apple juice, coconut flour, cinnamon, lemon zest, and honey in your Slow Cooker. Stir to combine. Cover and cook on Low for 8 hours. Serve.

Breakfast Coconut Quinoa with Blueberries

Serves: 4 | Total Time: 3 hours 15 minutes

¾ cup quinoa, rinsed	1 (13.5-oz) can coconut milk
¼ cup shredded coconut	2 cups fresh blueberries
1 tbsp maple syrup	1 tsp lemon zest

Mix the quinoa, coconut, lemon zest, and maple syrup in your Slow Cooker. Pour the coconut milk over the quinoa. Cover and cook on Low for 3 hours. Fluff the quinoa with a fork, then scoop it into serving bowls. Top with blueberries and serve.

Chive & Gruyère Omelet

Serves: 6 | Total Time: 4 hours 15 minutes

1 tbsp olive oil	1 lb Gruyère cheese, grated
6 large eggs	Salt and pepper to taste
½ cup milk	2 tbsp chives, chopped

Grease your Slow Cooker with olive oil. Whisk together the eggs, milk, cheese, chives, salt, and pepper in a medium bowl. Pour the mixture into the slow cooker. Cover and cook on Low for 4 hours until the eggs are set. Turn off the cooker and serve.

Chorizo & Cheese Egg Scramble

Serves: 6 | Total Time: 4 hours 15 minutes

1 tbsp olive oil	½ cup heavy cream
½ lb chorizo sausage, sliced	½ tsp oregano
12 large eggs	Salt and pepper to taste
1 lb mozzarella, shredded	

Grease your Slow Cooker with olive oil. Add chorizo, eggs, cheese, heavy cream, oregano, salt, and pepper and stir to mix well. Cover and cook on Low for 4 hours until the eggs are set. Scramble the eggs with a fork and serve.

Apple Steel-Cut Oatmeal

Serves: 4 | Total Time: 4 hours 10 minutes

1 Granny Smith apple, peeled, cored, and chopped	
1 cup steel-cut oats	1 tsp ground cinnamon
1 tbsp butter, melted	½ tsp salt
4 cups water	½ cup milk
¼ cup brown sugar	2 tbsp walnuts, chopped

Place the steel-cut oats and butter in your Slow Cooker and stir to coat. Add the water, brown sugar, cinnamon, and salt. Cover and cook on Low for 4 hours.

Add in the chopped apple and walnuts and divide between 4 serving bowls. Serve with a splash of milk.

Morning Granola

Serves: 6 | Total Time: 6 hours 10 minutes

2 tbsp olive oil	1 tsp cinnamon
2 cups almonds	½ tsp salt
½ cup pepitas	¼ tsp nutmeg
¼ cup coconut flakes	¼ cup coconut oil, melted
½ cup dried berries	1 tsp vanilla
¼ cup chia seeds	

Grease the bottom and sides of your Slow Cooker with olive oil. Add in the almonds, pepitas, coconut flakes, dried berries, chia seeds, cinnamon, salt, and nutmeg.

In a medium bowl, whisk the coconut oil with vanilla. Pour the mixture into the cooker and stir, making sure all the ingredients are moistened. Cover and cook on Low for 6 hours. Turn off the cooker and let it cool completely. Store the granola in an airtight container in the refrigerator for up to 14 days.

Classic French Toast Casserole

Serves: 6 | Total Time: 4 hours 15 minutes + soaking time

6 large eggs	1 French loaf bread, cubed
2 cups milk	½ stick butter, softened
1 tsp ground nutmeg	½ cup brown sugar
½ tsp vanilla extract	2 tbsp powdered sugar
1 ½ tsp cinnamon, divided	

Arrange the bread cubes in your Slow Cooker. Beat the eggs, milk, vanilla, ground nutmeg, and ½ teaspoon of cinnamon in a large bowl. Pour the mixture over the bread cubes, pressing down to make sure all the bread is submerged. Cover and refrigerate for at least 4 hours.

Mix the butter, brown sugar, and remaining cinnamon in a bowl. Scatter the topping over the bread mixture. Cook on Low for 4 hours. Turn off the cooker and let it rest for 15 minutes. Dust with powdered sugar and serve.

Authentic Huevos Rancheros

Serves: 6 | Total Time: 4 hours 15 minutes

1 ½ cups Cotija cheese, crumbled	
1 (28-oz) can diced tomatoes	1 jalapeño pepper, minced
1 cup tomato sauce	1 tbsp cumin
2 tbsp extra-virgin olive oil	½ tsp chili powder
½ onion, chopped	Salt and pepper to taste
1 red bell pepper, chopped	6 eggs

Pour the diced tomatoes, tomato sauce, olive oil, onion, bell pepper, jalapeño pepper, cumin, chili powder, salt, pepper, and cheese into your Slow Cooker. Stir to mix well. Cover and cook on Low for 4 hours. With a wooden spoon, make 6 small holes in the sauce. Crack one egg into each hole. Cover and cook on High for an additional 10-20 minutes. Serve immediately.

Veggie Omelet

Serves: 4 | Total Time: 4 hours 15 minutes

1 tbsp olive oil	1 red bell pepper, sliced
6 eggs	1 cup broccoli florets
¼ tsp chili powder	¼ tsp garlic powder
1 garlic clove, minced	Salt and pepper to taste
1 yellow onion, chopped	½ cup milk

Grease your Slow Cooker with olive oil. In a mixing bowl, combine milk, salt, eggs, garlic powder, pepper, and chili powder. Whisk until well blended.

Place the broccoli florets, onion, garlic, peppers in the cooker and gently stir in the egg mixture. Place the lid on your cooker and set it on Low for 2 hours. When the dish is done, the eggs will be cooked through. Serve.

Tater Tot Egg Bake

Serves: 6 | Total Time: 8 hours 5 minutes

1 tbsp olive oil	12 eggs
1 (30-oz) pkg Tater Tots	1 cup milk
2 cups cheddar, grated	4 tbsp flour
2 onions, chopped	1 tsp salt
6 oz Canadian bacon, diced	½ tsp pepper
¼ cup Parmesan, grated	2 green onions, chopped

Grease your Slow Cooker with olive oil. Place bacon, onions, tater tots, and cheeses in three layers, be sure to end with a layer of cheese.

Whisk eggs, milk, flour, salt, and pepper in a mixing bowl. Pour this mixture over the layers in your slow cooker. Cover with lid and cook on Low for 8 hours. Turn off the cooker. Sprinkle with chopped green onions over the top and serve warm.

Quinoa Energy Bars

Serves: 4 | Total Time: 4 hours 15 minutes

1 cup vanilla almond milk	1/3 cup almonds, chopped
2 tbsp maple syrup	½ cup raisins
2 tbsp almond butter	1/3 cup quinoa, uncooked
½ tsp cinnamon	2 tbsp chia seeds
2 large eggs	1/3 cup dry apples, chopped

Lightly spray your Slow Cooker with cooking spray and line it with parchment paper. Grease the parchment paper with cooking spray. Place the almond butter and maple syrup in a mixing bowl. Melt in microwave for 20 seconds or until butter is creamy. Stir with a whisk.

Whisk the almond milk and cinnamon with the butter. Whisk the eggs. Add into the bowl the remaining ingredients and mix well. Carefully pour the mixture into the cooker and cook on Low for 4 hours. Place in the fridge and allow bars to set and then cut and serve them.

Vanilla Bean Oats

Serves: 6 | Total Time: 4 hours 10 minutes

1 cup steel-cut oats	2 tbsp ground flaxseed
2 cups water	2 tsp cinnamon
2 cups vanilla almond milk	2 tbsp maple syrup
2 vanilla bean pods	

Lightly coat the inside of your cooker with some oil. Mix the milk, water, and oats in your Slow Cooker. Carefully scrape out the inside of vanilla beans and add to the mixture along with the syrup, cinnamon, and flaxseed. Cover and cook on Low for 4 hours. Stir and then divide amongst serving bowls. Serve with fresh fruit if desired.

Berry Clafoutis

Serves: 6 | Total Time: 4 hours 15 minutes

1 ½ cups fresh berries	2/3 cups milk
1 tsp butter	¼ tsp lemon zest
2 eggs	2 tbsp Confectioner's sugar
½ cup sugar	½ cup flour

Coat the inside of your Slow Cooker with butter and some flour. Gently pour the blueberries into the cooker. Add the sugar, eggs, and remaining flour to a mixing bowl and whisk together. Add the milk and lemon zest Whisk well until the mixture is smooth.

Pour the mixture into the cooker but do not stir the mix. Put the lid on your cooker and cook on High for 4 hours. The dish is ready when the center is set and the edges are lightly browned. Serve warm with a sprinkling of confectioner's sugar on top.

Breakfast Sweet Potatoes with Sausage

Serves: 6 | Total Time: 4 hours 10 minutes

1 lb breakfast sausage, cooked and sliced into chunks
6 sweet potatoes, peeled and chopped into chunks

1 yellow onion, chopped	½ cup black olives, sliced
2 tbsp olive oil	2 tbsp parsley, chopped
Salt and pepper to taste	½ cup water

Place the sweet potatoes, onion, and water in your Slow Cooker. Stir in the olives, salt, and pepper. It should be at least half covered by water. Layer the sausage on top of the mixture. Drizzle with olive oil. Cover with lid and cook for 4 hours on Low. Turn off the cooker and garnish with parsley to serve!

Cheesy Breakfast Potatoes

Serves: 6 | Total Time: 4 hours 15 minutes

3 russet potatoes, peeled and diced
1 (10.75-oz) can cream of chicken soup (condensed)
10 oz smoked chicken sausage, sliced

1 green bell pepper, diced	¼ tsp oregano, dried
1 red bell pepper, diced	½ cup sour cream
2 tbsp parsley, chopped	1 ½ cups cheddar, shredded
Salt and pepper to taste	1 onion, diced
¼ tsp basil, dried	

Combine the potatoes, chicken sausage, peppers, sour cream, onion, basil, oregano, and cheese. Slowly add in the chicken soup along with salt and pepper as needed. Cover and cook on Low for 4 hours. Top with parsley.

Thyme Pork Meatloaf

Serves: 4 | Total Time: 8 hours 20 minutes

1 lb ground pork	1 carrot, grated
1 cup breadcrumbs	2 tsp dried thyme
½ cup milk	1 tsp garlic powder
1 egg, beaten	Salt and pepper to taste
1 onion, grated	1 tbsp olive oil

In a bowl, place the ground pork, milk, egg, onion, carrot, breadcrumbs, thyme, garlic powder, salt, and pepper. Using your hands, mix to combine.

Press the mixture into a lightly greased loaf pan that fits inside your slow cooker insert. Cover the top of the pan with aluminum foil. Place the pan in the cooker. Cover and cook on Low for 8 hours and serve.

SOUPS

Beef & Millet Soup

Serves: 6 | Total Time: 8 hours 15 minutes

1 ½ lb beef chuck roast, cut into bite-size pieces

6 cups beef broth	1 bay leaf
1 tbsp tomato paste	1 tsp onion powder
2 cups frozen mirepoix	1 tsp garlic powder
⅔ cup millet	¾ tsp dried thyme
1 cup sliced mushrooms	Salt and pepper to taste

Combine all the ingredients in your Slow Cooker and stir. Cover with the lid and cook on Low for 8 hours. Discard the bay leaf. Serve and enjoy!

Greek-Style Chicken & Lentil Soup

Serves: 6 | Total Time: 6 hours 15 minutes

1 lb boneless, skinless chicken thighs

1 cup brown lentils	¼ cup Greek yogurt
1 yellow onion, thinly sliced	½ tsp dried oregano
2 garlic cloves, minced	Salt and pepper to taste
5 cups chicken broth	2 tbsp parsley, chopped
2 egg yolks	

Combine the onion, lentils, chicken, garlic, and chicken broth in your Slow Cooker. Cover and cook on Low for 6 hours. Transfer the chicken to a cutting board. Shred the chicken with two forks and return it to the slow cooker. In a small bowl, whisk together the egg yolks, yogurt, and oregano. Stir the mixture into the slow cooker. Adjust the seasoning with salt and pepper. Garnish with parsley and serve warm.

Broccoli Cheese Soup

Serves: 6 | Total Time: 8 hours 15 minutes

½ tsp red pepper flakes	¼ tsp dried thyme
2 cups chicken broth	Salt and pepper to taste
1 lb potatoes, peeled	1 lb broccoli florets
1 yellow onion, diced	½ cup shredded Cheddar
2 scallions, minced	½ cup milk
1 tsp garlic powder	1 tbsp butter

Place the broth, potatoes, onion, scallions, garlic powder, and thyme in your Slow Cooker. Season with salt and pepper. Cover and cook on Low for 8 hours. When ready, transfer the soup to a food processor and blend until smooth. Add three-quarters of the broccoli. Pulse three or four times to get the soup to your desired consistency.

Pour the soup back into the Slow Cooker. Add the cheddar cheese, milk, butter, and remaining broccoli and stir. Cover and cook on High and for a few minutes until warmed through. Sprinkle with red pepper flakes and serve.

Tomato Black Bean Soup

Serves: 6 | Total Time: 6 hours 15 minutes

1 can (15 oz) black beans	1 garlic clove, chopped
1 red onion, chopped	1 parsnip, diced

1 celery stalk, sliced	½ tsp dried oregano
1 red bell pepper, diced	1 tsp Cajun seasoning
1 green bell pepper, diced	2 tbsp chopped cilantro
1 jalapeno, chopped	4 cups chicken stock
2 tbsp olive oil	1 cup tomato paste
1 tsp dried thyme	2 cups water
½ tsp dried basil	Salt and pepper to taste

Warm the olive oil in a skillet over medium heat. Place onion, garlic, parsnip, and bell peppers and cook for 5 minutes until softened, stirring frequently. Add everything to your Slow Cooker. Add celery, jalapeño, thyme, basil, oregano, cajun seasoning, chicken stock, tomato paste, water, black beans, salt, and black pepper. Cover with the lid and cook for 6 hours on Low. When done, remove the lid, stir in cilantro, and serve immediately.

Mixed Lentil Soup with Garlicky Tomato

Serves: 6 | Total Time: 6 hours 30 minutes

SOUP:

½ cup tomato sauce	1 carrot, diced
½ cup red lentils, rinsed	1 red bell pepper, diced
½ cup green lentils, rinsed	1 bay leaf
1 shallot, chopped	2 cups chicken stock
1 celery stalk, sliced	Salt and pepper to taste

TOPPING:

2 peeled tomatoes, diced	2 tbsp chopped parsley
3 garlic cloves, chopped	Salt and pepper to taste
1 tbsp olive oil	

Mix lentils, shallot, celery, carrot, bell pepper, tomato sauce, bay leaf, 4 cups of water, chicken stock, salt, and pepper in your Slow Cooker. Cover and cook for 6 hours on Low. When done, remove the lid.

In a bowl, combine garlic, parsley, tomatoes, salt, pepper, and olive oil. To serve, divide the soup between bowls and top each with topping mixture and serve.

Vegan Soup

Serves: 6 | Total Time: 4 hours 15 minutes

1 can (15 oz) white bean	1 lime, juiced
1 can (15 oz) cannellini beans	1 avocado, peeled and sliced
1 cup diced tomatoes	2 tbsp chopped cilantro
1 sweet onion, chopped	½ tsp chili powder
1 garlic clove, chopped	½ tsp cumin powder
1 carrot, diced	2 cups vegetable stock
1 celery stalk, sliced	1 tbsp olive oil
1 red bell pepper, diced	Salt and pepper to taste

Warm the olive oil in a skillet over medium heat. Place onion, carrot, garlic, and celery and cook for 5 minutes until softened. Add everything to your Slow Cooker. Add in bell pepper, chili powder, cumin, vegetable stock, beans, tomatoes, 2 cups of water, salt, and pepper.

Cover with the lid and cook for 4 hours on Low. When done, remove the lid, divide between bowls and top with cilantro and avocado. Sprinkle with lime juice and serve.

Tangy Chicken Soup

Serves: 4 | Total Time: 5 hours 15 minutes

1 cup marinated artichoke hearts, chopped
2 chicken breasts, cubed
2 tbsp fresh oregano
4 cups chicken broth
¼ tsp sugar
¼ tsp onion powder
¼ tsp lemon pepper
¼ tsp ground coriander
¼ tsp garlic powder
¼ tsp black pepper
¼ cup white wine vinegar
1 onion, coarsely chopped
1 cup white wine
3 potatoes, roughly diced
5 baby carrots, diced
Juice of 1 lemon
3 garlic cloves, minced
1 tbsp oregano, dried

Put all of the ingredients in the slow cooker. Cover and cook soup on high, then adjust the setting to low and cook for 5 hours. Before serving, break the chicken breasts into bite-size pieces. Enjoy!

Creamy Butternut Squash Soup

Serves: 6 | Total Time: 4 hours 15 minutes

2 cups butternut squash cubed
2 parsnips, cubed
1 celery root, peeled, cubed
1 potato, peeled and cubed
1 sweet onion, chopped
2 garlic cloves, chopped
¼ tsp cumin powder
2 tbsp olive oil
2 cups chicken stock
Salt and pepper to taste
1 pinch cayenne pepper

Warm the olive oil in a skillet over medium heat. Place onion and garlic and cook for 2-3 minutes until softened. Transfer it into your Slow Cooker. Add in parsnip, butternut squash, celery, potato, 3 cups of water, chicken stock, cayenne pepper, cumin, salt, and black pepper. Cover with the lid and cook for 4 hours on Low. When done, remove the lid, blend it with an immersion blender until purée, and serve warm.

Tangy White Bean Soup

Serves: 6 | Total Time: 4 hours 15 minutes

1 can (15 oz) white beans
1 sweet onion, chopped
2 garlic cloves, chopped
½ celery root, peeled, cubed
1 parsnip, diced
2 cups chicken stock
3 cups water
1 tbsp olive oil
½ tsp dried thyme
Salt and pepper to taste

Warm the olive oil in a skillet over medium heat. Place onion, garlic, celery, and parsnip and cook for 5 minutes until softened. Add everything to your Slow Cooker. Add in beans, chicken stock, water, thyme, salt, and pepper. Cover with the lid and cook for 4 hours on Low. When done, remove the lid, blend it with an immersion blender until smooth, and serve immediately.

Potato & Bacon Soup

Serves: 6 | Total Time: 1 hour 45 minutes

1 lb potatoes, peeled, cubed
6 bacon slices, chopped
1 sweet onion, chopped
1 parsnip, diced
½ celery root, cubed
1 tbsp olive oil
2 cups chicken stock
Salt and pepper to taste

Warm the olive oil in a skillet over medium heat. Place bacon and cook until crispy. Set aside. Put bacon fat, onion, potatoes, parsnip, celery, chicken stock, 3 cups of water, salt, and pepper in your Slow Cooker. Cover with the lid and cook for 1 hour and 15 minutes on High. When done, remove the lid, blend it with an immersion blender until smooth, and serve topped with bacon.

Tomato White Bean Soup with Ham

Serves: 6 | Total Time: 2 hours 15 minutes

1 can (15 oz) white beans
4 oz ham, diced
1 sweet onion, chopped
2 garlic cloves, chopped
1 yellow bell pepper, diced
1 red bell pepper, diced
1 carrot, diced
1 cup diced tomatoes
1 tbsp olive oil
2 cups chicken stock
3 cups water
Salt and pepper to taste

Warm the olive oil in a skillet over medium heat. Place ham and cook for 2 minutes. Add in onion and garlic and cook for 2 more minutes. Add everything to your Slow Cooker. Add in bell peppers, carrot, tomatoes, beans, chicken stock, water, salt, and pepper. Cover with the lid and cook for 2 hours on High. When done, remove the lid and serve warm.

Bean & Corn Soup

Serves: 6 | Total Time: 4 hours 15 minutes

2 cups cooked pinto beans
½ cup canned sweet corn
1 red onion, chopped
2 red bell peppers, diced
1 garlic clove, chopped
½ tsp chili powder
½ tsp cumin powder
1 lb butternut squash cubes
2 tbsp olive oil
4 cups chicken stock
2 tbsp tomato paste
1 bay leaf
1 thyme sprig
Salt and pepper to taste

Warm the olive oil in a skillet over medium heat. Place onion and cook for 2 minutes until softened. Transfer it to your Slow Cooker. Add in bell peppers, garlic, chili powder, cumin powder, squash, beans, corn, 2 cups of water, stock, tomato paste, bay leaf, thyme, salt, and pepper. Cover with the lid and cook for 4 hours on Low. When done, remove the lid and serve immediately.

Nona Chicken Soup

Serves: 6 | Total Time: 6 hours 15 minutes

1 red bell pepper, diced
1 can (15 oz) cannellini beans
2 chicken breasts, cubed
1 shallot, chopped
1 carrot, diced
1 parsnip, diced
1 celery stalk, sliced
1 can diced tomatoes
2 cups chicken stock
2 tbsp canola oil
2 cups water
Salt and pepper to taste
1 tsp dried Italian herbs
2 oz Parmesan shavings

Warm the canola oil in a skillet over medium heat. Place chicken and cook for 2 minutes until golden brown on all sides. Add it to your Slow Cooker. Add shallot, carrot, parsnip, celery, bell peppers, beans, tomatoes, chicken stock, water, Italian herbs, and Parmesan shavings.

Vegetable & Bean Soup

Serves: 6 | Total Time: 7 hours 15 minutes

1 red bell pepper, diced	4 cups water
2 tomatoes, diced	2 tbsp tomato paste
½ lb black beans, rinsed	½ tsp cumin powder
1 sweet onion, chopped	¼ tsp chili powder
2 carrots, diced	1 bay leaf
1 parsnip, diced	Salt and pepper to taste
1 celery stalk, diced	2 tbsp chopped cilantro
2 cups chicken stock	½ cup sour cream

Mix beans, stock, water, onion, carrots, parsnip, celery, bell peppers, tomatoes, tomato paste, cumin powder, chili powder, bay leaf, salt, and pepper in your Slow Cooker. Cover with the lid and cook for 7 hours on Low. When done, remove the lid, stir in cilantro, and serve warm topped with sour cream.

Pork Sausages & White Bean Soup

Serves: 6 | Total Time: 3 hours 15 minutes

1 can (15 oz) white beans	1 carrot, diced
2 bacon slices, chopped	1 parsnip, diced
4 pork sausages, sliced	1 celery stalk, sliced
1 sweet onion, chopped	1 can diced tomatoes
1 garlic clove, chopped	2 cups chicken stock
½ tsp dried rosemary	4 cups water
½ tsp dried thyme	Salt and pepper to taste

Place a skillet over medium heat. Add bacon and cook for 2-3 minutes until crisp. Transfer it to your Slow Cooker. Add in onion, garlic, rosemary, thyme, sausages, carrot, parsnip, celery, tomatoes, beans, chicken stock, water, salt, and pepper. Cover with the lid and cook for 3 hours on High. When done, remove the lid and serve.

Mixed Bean Cream Soup

Serves: 6 | Total Time: 4 hours 30 minutes

1 can (15 oz) black beans	2 cups chicken stock
1 can (15 oz) kidney beans	1 cup diced tomatoes
1 can (15 oz) pinto beans	2 tbsp olive oil
2 sweet onions, chopped	1 lime, juiced
2 garlic cloves, minced	½ cup sour cream
2 red bell peppers, diced	2 tbsp chopped parsley
2 carrots, diced	Salt and pepper to taste

Warm the olive oil in a skillet over medium heat. Place the onions, garlic, bell peppers, and carrot and cook for 5 minutes. Add everything to your Slow Cooker. Add in beans, stock, 4 cups of water, tomatoes, salt, and pepper. Cover with the lid and cook for 4 hours on Low. When done, remove the lid, stir in lime juice, and serve warm topped with sour cream and parsley.

Potato & Sweet Corn Soup

Serves: 6 | Total Time: 6 hours 15 minutes

4 peeled potatoes, cubed	2 shallots, chopped
1 can (15 oz) sweet corn	2 cups chicken stock
1 celery stalk, sliced	Salt and pepper to taste

Mix shallots, potatoes, celery, corn, chicken stock, 4 cups of water, salt, and pepper in your Slow Cooker. Cover and cook for 6 hours on Low. When done, remove the lid, reserve some corn and blend the soup until smooth. Divide between bowls, top with reserved corn and serve.

Holiday Pozole with Black Beans

Serves: 6 | Total Time: 6 hours 15 minutes

1 can (15 oz) black beans	1 tbsp canola oil
1 lb pork tenderloin, cubed	½ tsp cumin powder
1 sweet onion, chopped	½ tsp dried oregano
2 garlic cloves, chopped	½ tsp dried basil
1 can sweet corn	¼ tsp chili powder
1 cup diced tomatoes	4 cups chicken stock
1 jalapeno pepper, chopped	2 cups water
2 limes, juiced	Salt and pepper to taste

Warm the canola oil in a skillet over medium heat. Place pork and cook for 5 minutes on all sides. Transfer it to your Slow Cooker. Add onion, garlic, cumin powder, oregano, basil, chili powder, beans, corn, tomatoes, jalapeño, chicken stock, water, salt, and pepper. Cover with the lid and cook for 6 hours on Low. When done, remove the lid, stir in lime juice and serve.

Beef & Sweet Onion Soup

Serves: 6 | Total Time: 7 hours 15 minutes

2 carrots, sliced	1 cup beef stock
1 lb beef roast, cubed	1 cup red wine
1 sweet onion, chopped	2 tbsp olive oil
1 garlic clove, chopped	½ tsp dried thyme
1 celery stalk, sliced	1 bay leaf
1 can diced tomatoes	Salt and pepper to taste

Warm the olive oil in a skillet over medium heat. Place beef roast and cook for 5 minutes on all sides. Transfer it to your Slow Cooker. Add onion, garlic, carrots, celery, tomatoes, beef stock, wine, 4 cups of water, thyme, bay leaf, salt, and pepper. Cover with the lid and cook for 7 hours on Low. When done, remove the lid and serve.

Easy Lentil & Bacon Soup

Serves: 6 | Total Time: 4 hours 15 minutes

1 cup dried lentils, rinsed	1 cup diced tomatoes
1 carrot, diced	2 cups chicken stock
4 bacon slices, chopped	1 lime, juiced
1 sweet onion, chopped	2 tbsp chopped parsley
2 garlic cloves, chopped	1 tsp curry powder
1 celery stalk, sliced	¼ tsp ground ginger
1 parsnip, diced	Salt and pepper to taste

Place a skillet over medium heat. Add the bacon and cook for 2-3 minutes until crisp. Transfer it to your Slow Cooker. Add in onion, garlic, lentils, carrot, celery, parsnip, tomatoes, stock, 4 cups of water, curry powder, ginger, salt, and pepper. Cover with the lid and cook for 4 hours on Low. When done, remove the lid, stir in lime juice and parsley, and serve warm.

Bacon & Beef Tomato Soup

Serves: 6 | Total Time: 8 hours 15 minutes

2 sweet onions, chopped	1 cup beef stock
2 peeled tomatoes, diced	2 tbsp olive oil
2 bacon slices, chopped	Salt and pepper to taste
2 lb beef roast, cubed	1 thyme sprig
2 cups tomato sauce	1 rosemary sprig

Warm the olive oil in a skillet over medium heat. Place bacon and cook until crisp. Add in beef roast and cook for 5 minutes on all sides. Transfer it to your Slow Cooker. Add onions, tomatoes, tomato sauce, beef stock, 3 cups of water, thyme, rosemary, salt, and pepper. Cover with the lid and cook for 8 hours on Low. When done, remove the lid and serve immediately.

Butternut Squash Curry

Serves: 6 | Total Time: 2 hours 15 minutes

1 lb butternut squash cubes	1 tbsp olive oil
1 shallot, chopped	½ tsp grated ginger
2 garlic cloves, minced	2 cups chicken stock
1 tbsp curry paste	1 cup coconut milk
1 tsp brown sugar	1 tbsp tomato paste
1 tsp Worcestershire sauce	Salt and pepper to taste

Warm the olive oil in a skillet over medium heat. Place shallot, garlic, ginger, and curry paste and cook for 1 minute. Add everything to your Slow Cooker. Add in sugar, Worcestershire sauce, squash, chicken stock, 2 cups of water, coconut milk, tomato paste, salt, and pepper. Cover with the lid and cook for 2 hours on High. When done, remove the lid, blend it with an immersion blender until smooth, and serve warm.

Traditional Onion Soup

Serves: 6 | Total Time: 1 hour 45 minutes

4 sweet onions, sliced	1 tbsp red wine vinegar
4 cups beef stock	Salt and pepper to taste
2 cups water	1 thyme sprig
2 tbsp butter	1 rosemary sprig
1 tsp brown sugar	Toasted bread for serving
1 tbsp canola oil	2 tbsp grated Gruyere cheese

Melt butter and canola oil in a skillet over medium heat. Place onion and cook for 10-12 minutes until caramelized, stirring sugar by half. Transfer it to your Slow Cooker. Add in beef stock, water, vinegar, thyme, rosemary, salt, and pepper. Cover with the lid and cook for 1 hour and 30 minutes on High. When done, remove the lid, divide between bowls and top with toasted bread and grated cheese. Serve immediately.

Potato Cream Soup with Bacon

Serves: 6 | Total Time: 6 hours 30 minutes

1 (10.5-oz) can condensed chicken soup	
2 peeled potatoes, cubed	1 ½ cups half and half
6 bacon slices, chopped	1 tbsp chopped parsley
1 sweet onion, chopped	Salt and pepper to taste

Place a skillet over medium heat. Add bacon and cook until crisp. Transfer it to your Slow Cooker. Add in onion, chicken soup, potatoes, 4 cups of water, salt, and pepper. Cover with the lid and cook for 4 hours on Low. Put in half and half and cook for 2 hours on Low. When done, remove the lid, stir in parsley and serve warm.

Spicy Seafood Soup

Serves: 6 | Total Time: 6 hours 15 minutes

½ lb fresh shrimps, peeled and deveined	
½ lb cod fillets, cubed	½ cup tomato sauce
1 sweet onion, chopped	1 lime, juiced
1 fennel bulb, sliced	2 tbsp olive oil
4 garlic cloves, chopped	1 tsp dried oregano
4 peeled tomatoes, diced	1 tsp dried basil
1 bay leaf	1 pinch chili powder
1 cup dry white wine	Salt and pepper to taste

Warm the olive oil in a skillet over medium heat. Cook onion, fennel, and garlic for 5 minutes until softened. Remove to your Slow Cooker. Add in wine, tomato sauce, 2 cups of water, oregano, basil, chili powder, tomatoes, and bay leaf. Cover and cook for 1 hour on High.

Put in cod, shrimp, lime juice, salt, and pepper and cook for another 5 hours on Low. When done, remove the lid and serve immediately.

Barley & Beef Soup

Serves: 6 | Total Time: 6 hours 15 minutes

2 peeled tomatoes, diced	2 tbsp olive oil
1 lb beef roast, cubed	½ cup uncooked barley
1 sweet onion, chopped	½ tsp dried oregano
1 carrot, sliced	1 tsp dried basil
1 parsnip, sliced	½ tsp dried thyme
2 cups beef stock	Salt and pepper to taste

Warm the olive oil in a skillet over medium heat. Place beef roast and cook for 5-6 minutes on all sides. Transfer it to your Slow Cooker. Add in onion, carrot, parsnip, tomatoes, beef stock, 3 cups of water, barley, oregano, basil, thyme, salt, and pepper. Cover with the lid and cook for 6 hours on Low. Serve warm.

Herbed Sausage & Zucchini Soup

Serves: 6 | Total Time: 2 hours 15 minutes

2 zucchinis, cubed	2 cups vegetable stock
2 peeled potatoes, cubed	2 tbsp chopped parsley
1 lb Italian sausages, sliced	½ tsp dried oregano
2 celery stalks, sliced	½ tsp dried basil
2 yellow bell peppers, diced	¼ tsp garlic powder
2 carrots, sliced	Salt and pepper to taste
1 shallot, chopped	

Mix sausages, celery, zucchinis, potatoes, bell peppers, carrots, shallots, 3 cups of water, stock, oregano, basil, garlic powder, salt, and pepper in your Slow Cooker. Cover with the lid and cook for 2 hours on High. When done, remove the lid, stir in parsley and serve warm.

Lentil Soup with Ham

Serves: 6 | Total Time: 1 hour 45 minutes

4 oz ham, diced	1 ½ cups chicken stock
1 cup dried lentils, rinsed	½ tsp dried oregano
1 carrot, diced	½ tsp dried basil
1 celery stalk, sliced	1 tbsp olive oil
1 shallot, chopped	2 cups water
½ cup tomato sauce	Salt and pepper to taste

Mix the olive oil, ham, carrot, celery, shallot, oregano, basil, lentils, water, tomato sauce, chicken stock, salt, and pepper in your Slow Cooker. Cover with the lid and cook for 1 hour and 30 minutes on High. When done, remove the lid and serve immediately.

Sausage Soup with Split Peas

Serves: 6 | Total Time: 6 hours 15 minutes

1 sweet onion, chopped	1 red chili, chopped
2 carrots, diced	1 lemon, juiced
1 cup split peas, rinsed	½ tsp dried oregano
4 Italian sausages, sliced	2 tbsp tomato paste
1 celery stalk, diced	2 tbsp chopped parsley
1 garlic clove, chopped	Salt and pepper to taste

Mix split peas, 6 cups of water, sausages, onion, carrots, celery, garlic, red chili, oregano, tomato paste, salt, and pepper in your Slow Cooker. Cover with the lid and cook for 6 hours on Low. When done, remove the lid, stir in lemon juice and parsley and serve warm.

Tomato Soup with Beef & Bean

Serves: 6 | Total Time: 7 hours 15 minutes

1 can (15 oz) black beans	4 cups water
1 can (15 oz) cannellini beans	2 cups beef stock
1 lb beef, cubed	1 avocado, sliced
1 onion, chopped	½ cup sour cream
1 garlic clove, chopped	2 tbsp taco seasoning
1 cup canned corn	1 jalapeno pepper, chopped
1 cup tomato sauce	1 tbsp olive oil
1 cup dark beer	Salt and pepper to taste

Warm the olive oil in a skillet over medium heat. Place onion, beef, and garlic and cook for 2 minutes. Transfer everything to your Slow Cooker. Add beans, corn, tomato sauce, beer, taco seasoning, jalapeño, water, beef stock, salt, and pepper. Cover with the lid and cook for 6 hours on Low. When done, remove the lid, divide between bowls and top with sour cream and avocado slices. Serve.

Rustic Bean Soup

Serves: 6 | Total Time: 6 hours 15 minutes

1 cup sweet corn	2 tbsp olive oil
1 shallot, chopped	½ tsp chili powder
½ lb ground chicken	½ tsp cumin powder
1 can (15 oz) white beans	½ tsp coriander seeds
1 can diced tomatoes	Salt and pepper to taste
1 jalapeno pepper, chopped	2 cups chicken stock
2 garlic cloves, chopped	1 lime, juiced

Warm the olive oil in a skillet over medium heat. Place chicken and cook for 5 minutes until no longer pink, stirring often. Add it to your Slow Cooker.

Add in beans, tomatoes, corn, shallot, jalapeño, garlic, chili powder, cumin, coriander, chicken stock, 3 cups of water, salt, and pepper. Cover with the lid and cook for 6 hours on Low. When done, remove the lid, stir in lime juice and serve warm.

Rice & Chicken Soup

Serves: 6 | Total Time: 7 hours 15 minutes

2 red bell peppers, diced	1 can diced tomatoes
1 celery stalk, sliced	4 cups water
1 sweet onion, chopped	2 cups chicken stock
2 chicken breasts, cubed	2 /3 cup white rice, rinsed
2 carrots, diced	2 tbsp canola oil
1 parsnip, diced	Salt and pepper to taste

Warm the canola oil in a skillet over medium heat. Place chicken and cook for 5 minutes until golden on all sides. Add it to your Slow Cooker. Add in carrots, bell peppers, celery, onion, parsnip, tomatoes, water, chicken stock, rice, salt, and pepper. Cover with the lid and cook for 7 hours on Low. When done, remove the lid and serve.

Tuscan Soup

Serves: 6 | Total Time: 6 hours 30 minutes

1 can diced tomatoes	2 tbsp chopped parsley
1 can cannellini beans	½ tsp dried oregano
½ lb Italian sausages, sliced	½ tsp dried basil
1 sweet onion, chopped	¼ cup dry white wine
2 garlic cloves, chopped	2 cups chicken stock
1 red bell pepper, diced	½ cup short pasta
1 carrot, diced	Salt and pepper to taste

Mix sausages, onion, garlic, bell pepper, carrot, oregano, basil, tomatoes, beans, wine, 3 cups of water, and chicken stock in your Slow Cooker. Cover with the lid and cook for 1 hour on High. Put in pasta, salt, and pepper and cook for another 5 hours on High. When done, remove the lid and serve warm topped with parsley.

Divine Fish Soup

Serves: 6 | Total Time: 6 hours 15 minutes

1 chipotle pepper, chopped	1 lemon, juiced
1 carrot, diced	3 salmon fillets, cubed
1 sweet onion, chopped	3 cod fillets, cubed
1 red bell pepper, diced	3 tbsp canola oil
1 celery stalk, diced	2 tbsp chopped parsley
1 cup diced tomatoes	Salt and pepper to taste

Warm the canola oil in a skillet over medium heat. Place onion and cook for 2 minutes until softened. Add it to your Slow Cooker. Add in bell pepper, chipotle, carrot, celery, tomatoes, lemon juice, salmon, cod, parsley, 6 cups of water, salt, and pepper. Cover with the lid and cook for 6 hours on Low. When done, remove the lid and serve warm.

Fantastic Hungarian Borscht

Serves: 6 | Total Time: 8 hours 15 minutes

2 peeled potatoes, cubed	1 cup vegetable stock
1 sweet onion, chopped	½ tsp cumin seeds
1 lb beef roast, cubed	1 tsp red wine vinegar
2 beets, peeled and cubed	1 tsp honey
1 can diced tomatoes	½ tsp dried dill
2 tbsp tomato paste	1 tsp dried parsley
2 tbsp canola oil	Salt and pepper to taste

Warm the canola oil in a skillet over medium heat. Place beef roast and cook for 2-3 minutes until golden on all sides. Add it to your Slow Cooker. Add in beets, tomatoes, potatoes, onion, tomato paste, 5 cups of water, stock, cumin seeds, vinegar, honey, dill, parsley, salt, and pepper. Cover with the lid and cook for 8 hours on Low. When done, remove the lid and serve immediately.

Rich Barley Soup

Serves: 6 | Total Time: 6 hours 15 minutes

2 cups spinach, chopped	2 cups vegetable stock
1 shallot, chopped	2 tbsp olive oil
1 garlic clove, chopped	1 tsp dried oregano
1 carrot, diced	1 tsp dried basil
1 celery stalk, diced	2 /3 cup pearl barley
2 red bell peppers, diced	1 lemon, juiced
2 peeled tomatoes, diced	Salt and pepper to taste

Warm the olive oil in a skillet over medium heat. Place shallot, garlic, carrot, celery, and bell peppers and cook for 5 minutes until softened. Remove to your Slow Cooker. Add in tomatoes, vegetable stock, oregano, basil, barley, 4 cups of water, spinach, lemon juice, salt, and pepper. Cover with the lid and cook for 6 hours on Low. When done, remove the lid and serve immediately.

Farmhouse Soup

Serves: 6 | Total Time: 6 hours 15 minutes

1 can (15 oz) black beans	1 tbsp olive oil
1 shallot, chopped	½ tsp chili powder
1 carrot, diced	½ tsp cumin powder
2 jalapeno peppers, minced	½ cup diced tomatoes
2 cups chicken stock	Salt and pepper to taste
4 cups water	½ cup sour cream

Mix the olive oil, shallot, carrot, jalapeño, chicken stock, beans, water, chili powder, cumin, tomatoes, salt, and pepper in your Slow Cooker. Cover with the lid and cook for 6 hours on Low. When done, remove the lid and serve warm topped with sour cream.

Cabbage Soup with Beef Roast

Serves: 6 | Total Time: 7 hours 30 minutes

1 can (15 oz) diced tomatoes	2 cups beef stock
½ lb beef roast, cubed	2 cups water
1 sweet onion, chopped	2 tbsp olive oil
1 carrot, grated	½ tsp cumin seeds
½ cabbage head, shredded	Salt and pepper to taste

Warm the olive oil in a skillet over medium heat. Place beef roast and cook for 5-6 minutes on all sides. Add it to your Slow Cooker. Add in onion, carrot, cabbage, tomatoes, beef stock, water, cumin seeds, salt, and pepper. Cover with the lid and cook for 7 hours on Low. When done, remove the lid and serve warm.

Vegetable Soup with Beef Roast

Serves: 6 | Total Time: 7 hours 15 minutes

2 peeled potatoes, cubed	5 oz cauliflower florets
½ lb beef roast, cubed	1 cup diced tomatoes
1 celery stalk, sliced	2 tbsp canola oil
1 sweet onion, chopped	½ tsp dried basil
1 carrot, sliced	2 cups beef stock
1 garlic clove, chopped	Salt and pepper to taste

Warm the canola oil in a skillet over medium heat. Place beef roast and cook for 2-3 minutes on all sides. Transfer it to your Slow Cooker. Add in celery, onion, carrot, garlic, cauliflower, potatoes, tomatoes, basil, beef stock, 4 cups of water, salt, and pepper. Cover with the lid and cook for 7 hours on Low. When done, remove the lid and serve immediately.

Fiery Chicken Soup

Serves: 6 | Total Time: 6 hours 30 minutes

1 can (4 oz) green chile, chopped	
1 can (15 oz) diced tomatoes	4 cups water
1 can (15 oz) sweet corn	1 tbsp olive oil
2 shallots, chopped	½ tsp cumin powder
2 garlic cloves, chopped	½ tsp chili powder
1 chicken breast, diced	1 bay leaf
2 cups chicken stock	Salt and pepper to taste

Warm the olive oil in a skillet over medium heat. Place the shallots, garlic, and chicken and cook for 5 minutes. Transfer everything to your Slow Cooker and add the remaining ingredients. Cook for 6 hours on Low. Serve.

Tomato Cabbage Soup with Ham Bone

Serves: 6 | Total Time: 7 hours 15 minutes

1 can diced tomatoes	6 cups beef stock
1 ham bone	1 bay leaf
1 sweet onion, chopped	1 thyme sprig
1 cabbage head, shredded	1 lemon, juiced
2 tbsp tomato paste	Salt and pepper to taste

Mix ham bone, onion, cabbage, tomato paste, tomatoes, beef stock, salt, pepper, bay leaf, and thyme in your Slow Cooker. Cover with the lid and cook for 7 hours on Low. Stir in lemon juice and serve warm.

Nordic Potato Soup

Serves: 6 | Total Time: 6 hours 15 minutes

4 peeled potatoes, cubed	2 cups chicken stock
2 tbsp olive oil	½ cup heavy cream
2 leeks, sliced	1 thyme sprig
1 tbsp all-purpose flour	Salt and pepper to taste

Warm the olive oil in a skillet over medium heat. Place leeks and cook for 5 minutes until softened. Add in flour and cook for 1 more minute. Transfer everything to your Slow Cooker. Add the stock, 4 cups of water, potatoes, thyme, salt, and pepper. Cover with the lid and cook for 6 hours on Low. When done, stir in heavy cream and blend it with an immersion blender until creamy. Serve.

Spooky Soup

Serves: 6 | Total Time: 3 hours 30 minutes

2 large sweet peeled potatoes, cubed
1 shallot, chopped
2 carrots, sliced   1 bay leaf
½ celery stalk   2 tbsp olive oil
2 oranges, juiced   1 tsp pumpkin seeds oil
1 tsp orange zest   2 tbsp pumpkin seeds
6 cups chicken stock   ½ cinnamon stalk
    Salt and pepper to taste

Warm the olive oil in a skillet over medium heat. Place shallot and carrots and cook for 2-3 minutes. Transfer everything to your Slow Cooker. Add celery, sweet potatoes, orange juice, orange zest, stock, bay leaf, salt, pepper, and cinnamon stalk. Cover with the lid and cook for 2 hours on High. Then cook for 1 hour on Low.

When done, remove the lid, discard the cinnamon stick and bay leaf and blend it with an immersion blender until smooth. Divide between bowls, drizzle with pumpkin oil and top with pumpkin seeds to serve.

Bacon & Lima Bean Soup

Serves: 6 | Total Time: 7 hours 15 minutes

4 cups frozen lima beans   1 can diced tomatoes
2 shallots, chopped   2 cups vegetable stock
2 bacon slices, chopped   4 cups water
2 carrots, diced   1 bay leaf
2 peeled potatoes, cubed   Salt and pepper to taste
1 celery stalk, sliced   1 tbsp chopped cilantro

Mix bacon, lima beans, shallots, carrots, potatoes, celery, tomatoes, vegetable stock, water, bay leaf, salt, and pepper in your Slow Cooker. Cover with the lid and cook for 7 hours on Low. Top with cilantro and serve.

Tangy Broccoli Cream Soup

Serves: 6 | Total Time: 2 hours 15 minutes

10 oz broccoli florets   ½ tsp dried oregano
2 peeled potatoes, cubed   2 tbsp olive oil
2 shallots, chopped   3 cups chicken stock
2 garlic cloves, chopped   3 cups water
½ tsp dried basil   Salt and pepper to taste

Warm the olive oil in a skillet over medium heat. Place shallots and garlic and cook for 2-3 minutes until softened. Transfer everything to your Slow Cooker. Add in broccoli, potatoes, chicken stock, water, basil, oregano, salt, and pepper. Cover with the lid and cook for 2 hours on High. When done, remove the lid, blend it with an immersion blender until creamy, and serve.

Harvest Soup

Serves: 6 | Total Time: 7 hours 15 minutes

1 (14.5-oz) can fire-roasted tomatoes, chopped
2 peeled potatoes, cubed   ½ cup sweet corn
1 lb ground beef   2 tbsp canola oil
2 shallots, chopped   4 cups water
1 carrot, sliced   2 cups chicken stock
2 cups chopped okra   1 lemon, juiced
½ cup green peas   Salt and pepper to taste

Warm the canola oil in a skillet over medium heat. Place ground beef and cook for 2-3 minutes, stirring often. Add it to your Slow Cooker. Add in shallots, carrot, tomatoes, okra, green peas, potatoes, corn, water, chicken stock, lemon juice, salt, and pepper. Cover with the lid and cook for 7 hours on Low. Serve warm.

Chicken Noodle Soup

Serves: 6 | Total Time: 8 hours 15 minutes

1 (10.5-oz) can condensed chicken soup
6 oz egg noodles   1 cup green peas
2 chicken breasts, cubed   1 celery stalk, sliced
2 tbsp all-purpose flour   2 cups chicken stock
2 shallots, chopped   Salt and pepper to taste

Dust chicken breasts with salt, pepper, and flour. Place seasoned chicken, shallots, celery, chicken soup, 4 cups of water, chicken stock, green peas, salt, pepper, and noodles in your Slow Cooker. Cover with the lid and cook for 8 hours on Low. Serve warm.

Corn & Bacon Soup

Serves: 4 | Total Time: 5 hours 30 minutes

2 bacon slices, chopped   1 garlic clove, chopped
3 cups frozen corn   2 tbsp olive oil
4 cups chicken stock   ¼ tsp chili powder
1 shallot, chopped   Salt and pepper to taste

Warm the olive oil in a skillet over medium heat, place garlic, shallot, and bacon, and cook until golden brown on all sides. Transfer everything to your Slow Cooker. Add in corn, chicken stock, chili powder, salt, and pepper. Cover and cook for 5 hours on Low. When done, blend it with an immersion blender until smooth, and serve.

Sweet Corn & Potato Chowder with Ham

Serves: 6 | Total Time: 4 hours 15 minutes

1 (10.5-oz) can condensed chicken soup
4 peeled potatoes, cubed   1 tbsp olive oil
1 cup diced ham   ½ tsp celery seeds
1 cup sweet corn   ½ tsp cumin seeds
1 sweet onion, chopped   Salt and pepper to taste

Combine olive oil, onion, chicken soup, 4 cups of water, potatoes, ham, corn, celery seeds, cumin seeds, salt, and pepper in your Slow Cooker. Cover with the lid and cook for 4 hours on High. Serve warm.

Kielbasa Soup with Spinach

Serves: 6 | Total Time: 6 hours 15 minutes

1 sweet onion, chopped	2 red bell peppers, diced
2 carrots, diced	2 peeled potatoes, cubed
½ lb kielbasa sausages, sliced	2 cups chicken stock
½ lb spinach, torn	4 cups water
1 parsnip, diced	1 lemon, juiced
1 garlic clove, chopped	Salt and pepper to taste

Mix sausages, onion, carrots, parsnip, garlic, bell peppers, potatoes, chicken stock, water, spinach, lemon juice, salt, and pepper in your Slow Cooker. Cover with the lid and cook for 6 hours on Low. When done, remove the lid and serve immediately.

Spicy Curry Corn Chowder

Serves: 6 | Total Time: 8 hours 15 minutes

1 can (15 oz) sweet corn	½ chili pepper, chopped
2 peeled potatoes, cubed	1 ½ cups whole milk
1 sweet onion, chopped	¼ tsp cumin seeds
2 garlic cloves, chopped	Salt and pepper to taste
4 cups chicken stock	

Mix onion, garlic, chicken stock, corn, potatoes, chili pepper, milk, cumin seeds, salt, and pepper in your Slow Cooker. Cover with the lid and cook for 8 hours on Low. When done, remove the lid and serve immediately.

Parmesan Cauliflower Cream Soup

Serves: 6 | Total Time: 3 hours 15 minutes

1 head cauliflower, cut into florets	
1 (10.5-oz) can condensed cream of chicken soup	
2 peeled potatoes, cubed	½ cup grated Parmesan
1 sweet onion, chopped	1 tbsp canola oil
2 garlic cloves, chopped	Salt and pepper to taste

Warm the canola oil in a skillet over medium heat. Place onion and cook for 2 minutes. Transfer it to your Slow Cooker. Add in garlic, cauliflower, potatoes, chicken soup, 3 cups of water, salt, and pepper. Cover with the lid and cook for 3 hours on High. When done, remove the lid, blend it with an immersion blender until smooth and serve topped with Parmesan cheese.

Easy Stroganoff Soup

Serves: 6 | Total Time: 8 hours 15 minutes

1 (10.5-oz) can condensed cream of mushroom soup	
2 lb beef roast, cubed	4 cups chicken stock
1 sweet onion, chopped	1 cup water
2 tbsp all-purpose flour	½ cup sour cream
2 tbsp canola oil	Salt and pepper to taste

Dust beef roast with salt, pepper, and flour. Warm canola oil in a skillet over medium heat. Place beef and cook for 2-3 minutes on all sides. Add it to your Slow Cooker. Add in onion, mushroom soup, chicken stock, water, sour cream, salt, and pepper. Cover with the lid and cook for 8 hours on Low. Serve immediately.

The Ultimate Minestrone Soup

Serves: 6 | Total Time: 6 hours 15 minutes

4 sun-dried tomatoes, chopped	
2 carrots, diced	4 cups vegetable stock
2 celery stalks, diced	1 tsp dried oregano
2 garlic cloves, chopped	1 thyme sprig
1 sweet onion, chopped	1 bay leaf
4 peeled tomatoes, diced	1 can red beans
2 tbsp tomato paste	1 cup small pasta
1 zucchini, cubed	Salt and pepper to taste
1 cup frozen green peas	2 tbsp chopped parsley
2 cups water	Grated Parmesan for serving

Mix the tomatoes, tomato paste, sun-dried tomatoes, water, vegetable stock, carrots, celery, garlic, onion, zucchini, green peas, oregano, thyme, bay leaf, beans, pasta, salt, and pepper in your Slow Cooker. Cover with the lid and cook for 6 hours on Low. When done, remove the lid and serve warm topped with Parmesan cheese and parsley.

Salty Pumpkin Soup

Serves: 6 | Total Time: 5 hours 15 minutes

1 peeled pumpkin, cubed	2 tbsp olive oil
1 shallot, chopped	½ cinnamon stick
2 carrots, sliced	1 star anise
2 garlic cloves, chopped	½ tsp cumin powder
2 cups chicken stock	¼ tsp chili powder
1 thyme sprig	Salt and pepper to taste

Warm the olive oil in a skillet over medium heat. Place shallot, carrots, and garlic and cook until softened. Transfer everything to your Slow Cooker. Add pumpkin, stock, 4 cups of water, thyme, salt, pepper, cinnamon stick, star anise, cumin, and chili powder. Cover with the lid and cook for 5 hours on Low. When done, remove the lid, discard cinnamon, thyme, and star anise and blend the soup with an immersion blender until smooth. Serve.

Root Soup

Serves: 6 | Total Time: 6 hours 30 minutes

2 carrots, sliced	1 peeled parsnip, sliced
1 sweet onion, chopped	1 celery root, cubed
1 celery stalk, sliced	2 cups vegetable stock
½ head cabbage, shredded	4 cups water
1 cup diced tomatoes	1 lemon, juiced
¼ cup white rice, rinsed	Salt and pepper to taste

Mix onion, carrots, celery, cabbage, parsnip, celery, vegetable stock, water, tomatoes, rice, lemon juice, salt, and pepper in your Slow Cooker. Cover with the lid and cook for 6 hours on Low. Serve warm.

Bean Soup with Kale & Kielbasa

Serves: 6 | Total Time: 6 hours 15 minutes

1 red bell pepper, diced	1 sweet onion, chopped
1 can (15 oz) white beans	1 carrot, diced
½ lb kielbasa sausages, sliced	1 parsnip, diced

1 cup diced tomatoes	½ tsp dried oregano
½ lb kale, shredded	½ tsp dried basil
2 cups chicken stock	Salt and pepper to taste

Mix sausages, onion, carrot, parsnip, bell pepper, beans, tomatoes, kale, chicken stock, 4 cups of water, basil, oregano, salt, and pepper in your Slow Cooker. Cover with the lid and cook for 6 hours on Low. When done, remove the lid and serve immediately.

Basil Salmon Cream Soup

Serves: 6 | Total Time: 4 hours 15 minutes

1 lb salmon fillets, cubed	½ tsp dried oregano
1 red bell pepper, diced	½ tsp dried basil
1 shallot, chopped	2 cups milk
1 garlic clove, chopped	4 cups water
1 celery stalk, sliced	1 lemon, juiced
1 carrot, sliced	1 tsp lemon zest
1 parsnip, sliced	Salt and pepper to taste

Mix shallot, garlic, celery,m carrot, parsnip, bell pepper, oregano, basil, milk, water, lemon juice, and lemon zest in your Slow Cooker. Cover with the lid and cook for 1 hour on High. Put in salmon, salt, and pepper and cook for 3 hours on Low. Serve immediately.

Maine Soup

Serves: 6 | Total Time: 2 hours 15 minutes

1 bunch of asparagus, trimmed and chopped	
1 (6-oz) can crab meat	2 cups chicken stock
1 shallot, chopped	4 cups water
1 celery stalk, sliced	1 tbsp olive oil
1 cup green peas	Salt and pepper to taste

Warm the olive oil in a skillet over medium heat. Place shallot and celery and cook for 2 minutes until softened. Transfer everything to your Slow Cooker. Add in asparagus, green peas, stock, water, salt, and pepper.

Cover with the lid and cook for 2 hours on High. When done, remove the lid, blend it with an immersion blender until creamy. Top with crab meat and serve immediately.

Cheesy Broccoli Cream Soup

Serves: 6 | Total Time: 4 hours 15 minutes

1 (10.5-oz) can condensed chicken soup	
10 oz broccoli florets	2 tbsp olive oil
1 peeled potato, cubed	½ tsp dried oregano
1 shallot, chopped	1 cup grated Cheddar soup
2 garlic cloves, chopped	Salt and pepper to taste

Warm the olive oil in a skillet over medium heat. Place shallot and garlic and cook for 5 minutes until softened. Transfer everything to your Slow Cooker. Add in broccoli, potato, chicken soup, 4 cups of water, oregano, cheddar soup, salt, and pepper.

Cover with the lid and cook for 4 hours on Low. When done, remove the lid, blend it with an immersion blender until purée and serve. Enjoy!

Great Ham & Bean Soup

Serves: 6 | Total Time: 6 hours 15 minutes

2 cans (15-oz) white beans	1 cup diced ham
1 yellow bell pepper, diced	2 cups chicken stock
1 sweet onion, chopped	2 tbsp olive oil
1 garlic clove, chopped	2 tbsp chopped parsley
1 celery stalk, diced	Salt and pepper to taste

Warm the olive oil in a skillet over medium heat. Place onion, garlic, celery, and bell pepper and cook for 5 minutes until softened. Remove to your Slow Cooker. Add in ham, beans, chicken stock, 4 cups of water, salt, and pepper. Cover with the lid and cook for 6 hours on Low. Top with parsley and serve.

Southern Pumpkin Soup

Serves: 4 | Total Time: 6 hours 30 minutes

2 cups pumpkin cubes	2 cups vegetable stock
1 sweet onion, chopped	2 cups water
1 red bell pepper, diced	1 bunch kale, shredded
½ red chili, chopped	½ tsp cumin seeds
2 tbsp olive oil	Salt and pepper to taste

Mix onion, bell pepper, red chili, olive oil, pumpkin, vegetable stock, water, kale, cumin seeds, salt, and pepper in your Slow Cooker. Cover with the lid and cook for 6 hours on Low. Serve immediately.

Ham Soup with Vegetables

Serves: 4 | Total Time: 8 hours 30 minutes

2 carrots, sliced	1 celery stalk, sliced
2 lb peeled potatoes, cubed	½ tsp dried oregano
2 cups diced ham	½ tsp dried basil
1 sweet onion, chopped	2 cups chicken stock
1 garlic clove, chopped	2 cups water
1 leek, sliced	Salt and pepper to taste

Mix ham, onion, garlic, leek, celery, carrots, potatoes, oregano, basil, chicken stock, water, salt, and pepper in your Slow Cooker. Cover with the lid and cook for 8 hours on Low. Serve immediately.

Bacon & Potato Soup

Serves: 6 | Total Time: 6 hours 30 minutes

4 peeled potatoes, cubed	1 tbsp olive oil
4 bacon slices, chopped	¼ tsp cayenne pepper
1 celery stalk, sliced	¼ tsp smoked paprika
2 cups chicken stock	1 thyme sprig
1 bay leaf	1 rosemary sprig
4 leeks, sliced	Salt and pepper to taste

Warm the olive oil in a skillet over medium heat. Place bacon and cook until crisp. Add in leeks and cook for 5 minutes until softened. Transfer everything to your Slow Cooker. Add celery, potatoes, chicken stock, 4 cups of water, bay leaf, cayenne pepper, paprika, thyme, rosemary, salt, and pepper. Cover with the lid and cook for 6 hours on Low. Serve warm.

Tomato Quinoa Soup

Serves: 6 | Total Time: 6 hours 30 minutes

4 roasted red bell peppers, chopped
½ cup red quinoa, rinsed
½ cup tomato paste
1 shallot, chopped
1 garlic clove, chopped
2 cups vegetable stock
4 cups water
½ tsp dried oregano
½ tsp dried basil
1 pinch cayenne pepper
Salt and pepper to taste

Mix shallot, garlic, bell peppers, tomato paste, vegetable stock, water, quinoa, oregano, basil, cayenne pepper, salt, and pepper in your Slow Cooker. Cover with the lid and cook for 6 hours on Low. Serve immediately.

Picante Quinoa Soup

Serves: 6 | Total Time: 3 hours 15 minutes

½ cup quinoa, rinsed
1 can (15 oz) red beans
2 shallots, chopped
1 carrot, diced
½ peeled celery root, diced
1 can diced tomatoes
4 cups water
2 cups chicken stock
½ tsp chili powder
Salt and pepper to taste
2 tbsp chopped cilantro
Sour cream for serving

Mix the shallots, carrot, celery, tomatoes, quinoa, beans, water, chicken stock, chili powder, salt, and pepper in your Slow Cooker. Cover with the lid and cook for 3 hours on High. When done, remove the lid and serve topped with sour cream and cilantro.

Smoked Red Pepper Chowder

Serves: 6 | Total Time: 8 hours 15 minutes

1 red bell pepper, diced
2 peeled potatoes, cubed
1 shallot, chopped
2 cups frozen sweet corn
2 cups chicken stock
4 cups water
2 tbsp olive oil
¼ tsp smoked paprika
¼ tsp cumin powder
Salt and pepper to taste

Warm the olive oil in a skillet over medium heat. Place shallot and cook until softened. Transfer it to your Slow Cooker. Add bell pepper, potatoes, corn, chicken stock, water, paprika, cumin, salt, and pepper. Cover with the lid and cook for 8 hours on Low. When done, remove the lid, transfer it into a blender, and pulse until purée. Serve warm.

Tortellini Mushroom Soup

Serves: 4 | Total Time: 6 hours 15 minutes

1 (10.5-oz) can condensed cream of mushroom soup
½ lb mushrooms, sliced
7 oz cheese tortellini
1 shallot, chopped
1 garlic clove, chopped
3 cups chicken stock
1 cup water
½ tsp dried oregano
½ tsp dried basil
1 cup evaporated milk
Salt and pepper to taste

Mix shallot, garlic, mushrooms, mushroom soup, chicken stock, water, oregano, basil, milk, cheese tortellini, salt, and pepper in your Slow Cooker. Cover with the lid and cook for 6 hours on Low. Serve warm.

Vegetarian Dumplings

Serves: 4 | Total Time: 8 hours 15 minutes

2 shallots, chopped
2 garlic cloves, chopped
2 lb peeled tomatoes, cubed
1 carrot, sliced
1 peeled celery root, cubed
1 egg
2 cups chicken stock
2 tbsp olive oil
1 tsp canola oil
4 tsp all-purpose flour
½ tsp dried oregano
½ tsp dried basil
½ red chili, sliced
1 tbsp brown sugar
1 tsp balsamic vinegar
Salt and pepper to taste

Warm the olive oil in a skillet over medium heat. Place shallot and garlic and cook for 5 minutes until softened. Transfer everything to your Slow Cooker. Add tomatoes, carrot, celery, chicken stock, 2 cups of water, oregano, basil, red chili, brown sugar, vinegar, salt, and pepper. Cover with the lid and cook for 6 hours on Low.

When done, remove the lid, blend it with an immersion blender until purée. In a bowl, combine egg, canola oil, flour, and salt to taste. Make small pieces out of the mixture and place them into the soup. Cover with the lid and cook for 2 hours on Low. Serve immediately.

Vegetarian Curry

Serves: 6 | Total Time: 6 hours 30 minutes

10 oz cauliflower florets
2 peeled potatoes, cubed
½ head cabbage, shredded
2 peeled tomatoes, diced
1 sweet onion, chopped
4 garlic cloves, chopped
2 tbsp olive oil
1 tsp grated ginger
1 cup green peas
2 tbsp red curry paste
2 cups vegetable stock
4 cups water
½ lemongrass talk, crushed
Salt and pepper to taste

Warm the olive oil in a skillet over medium heat. Place onion and garlic and cook for 5 minutes. Add in ginger and curry paste and cook for 2 more minutes. Transfer everything to your Slow Cooker. Add in cauliflower, potatoes, cabbage, tomatoes, green peas, vegetable stock, water, lemongrass, salt, and pepper. Cover with the lid and cook for 6 hours on Low. When done, remove the lid and serve immediately.

Easy French Bouillabaisse

Serves: 4 | Total Time: 6 hours 30 minutes

1 lb haddock fillets, cubed
2 peeled potatoes, cubed
1 shallot, chopped
2 garlic cloves, chopped
1 red bell pepper, diced
1 carrot, diced
1 fennel bulb, sliced
1 cup diced tomatoes
4 cups vegetable stock
1 celery stalk, sliced
½ lemon, juiced
1 tbsp chopped parsley
Salt and pepper to taste

Mix shallot, garlic, bell pepper, carrot, fennel, tomatoes, vegetable stock, potatoes, celery, lemon juice, salt, and pepper in your Slow Cooker. Cover with the lid and cook for 1 hour on High. Put in haddock fillets and cook for 5 hours on Low. When done, remove the lid, top with parsley, and serve warm.

Chicken & White Bean Soup

Serves: 6 | Total Time: 7 hours 30 minutes

2 cans (15 oz) white beans	1 parsnip, diced
1 lb ground chicken	2 cups chicken stock
1 yellow bell pepper, diced	2 tbsp olive oil
2 carrots, diced	½ tsp chili powder
1 celery stalk, diced	Salt and pepper to taste

Warm the olive oil in a skillet over medium heat. Place ground chicken and cook for 5 minutes, stirring frequently. Transfer it to your Slow Cooker. Add in bell pepper, carrots, celery, parsnip, beans, chicken stock, 4 cups of water, chili powder, salt, and pepper. Cover with the lid and cook for 7 hours on Low. When done, remove the lid and serve warm.

Lemony Veggie Soup

Serves: 6 | Total Time: 8 hours 30 minutes

1 lb mushrooms, chopped	1 zucchini, cubed
2 peeled potatoes, cubed	2 cups vegetable stock
2 peeled tomatoes, diced	1 lemon, juiced
1 sweet onion, chopped	1 tbsp chopped dill
1 garlic clove, chopped	4 cups water
1 yellow bell pepper, diced	½ cup tomato sauce
2 tbsp olive oil	Salt and pepper to taste

Warm the olive oil in a skillet over medium heat. Place onion, garlic, and bell pepper and cook for 5 minutes until softened. Transfer everything to your Slow Cooker. Add mushrooms, zucchini, potatoes, tomatoes, vegetable stock, water, tomato sauce, salt, and pepper. Cover with the lid and cook for 8 hours on Low. When done, remove the lid, stir in lemon juice and dill and serve chilled.

Sweet Potato Curry

Serves: 4 | Total Time: 7 hours 30 minutes

2 sweet peeled potatoes, cubed

8 oz cauliflower florets	½ tsp cumin powder
1 sweet onion, chopped	¼ tsp chili powder
2 garlic cloves, chopped	1 cup coconut milk
1 tsp grated ginger	3 cups vegetable stock
2 tbsp red curry paste	Salt and pepper to taste
2 tbsp olive oil	½ lemongrass stalk

Warm the olive oil in a skillet over medium heat. Place onion, garlic, ginger, and curry paste and cook for 2-3 minutes until softened. Transfer everything to your Slow Cooker. Add in cauliflower, sweet potatoes, cumin, chili powder, coconut milk, vegetable stock, lemongrass, salt, and pepper. Cover with the lid and cook for 7 hours on Low. When done, remove the lid, discard lemongrass and blend it with an immersion blender until smooth. Serve.

Country Soup

Serves: 4 | Total Time: 3 hours 30 minutes

2 large sweet peeled potatoes, cubed

1 ½ cups diced ham	
1 sweet onion, chopped	1 carrot, diced
	1celery stalk, diced
1 parsnip, diced	1 bay leaf
2 cups chicken stock	1 thyme sprig
2 cups water	Salt and pepper to taste

Mix ham, onion, carrot, celery, parsnip, sweet potatoes, chicken stock, water, bay leaf, thyme, salt, and pepper in your Slow Cooker. Cover with the lid and cook for 3 hours on High. Serve warm.

Bean & Pumpkin Soup

Serves: 6 | Total Time: 6 hours 15 minutes

1 can diced tomatoes	¼ tsp grated ginger
1 can (15 oz) black beans	½ cinnamon stick
2 cups pumpkin cubes	¼ tsp cumin powder
2 shallots, chopped	2 tbsp tomato paste
2 garlic cloves, chopped	3 cups vegetable stock
1 red chili, chopped	1 bay leaf
2 tbsp olive oil	Salt and pepper to taste

Warm the olive oil in a skillet over medium heat. Place shallots, garlic, ginger, and red chili and cook for 3-4 minutes. Transfer everything to your Slow Cooker. Add in tomato paste, tomatoes, beans, pumpkin, 3 cups of water, vegetable stock, bay leaf, cinnamon stick, cumin, salt, and pepper. Cover with the lid and cook for 6 hours on Low. When done, remove the lid and serve.

Pasta e Fagioli

Serves: 6 | Total Time: 8 hours 30 minutes

1 cup fusilli pasta	1 cup tomato sauce
1 sweet onion, chopped	2 cups chicken stock
2 garlic cloves, chopped	1 bay leaf
2 red bell peppers, diced	2 tbsp olive oil
2 zucchinis, sliced	½ tsp dried basil
1 can white beans	1 tsp dried oregano
2 peeled tomatoes, diced	Salt and pepper to taste

Warm the olive oil in a skillet over medium heat. Place the onion, garlic, bell peppers, and zucchinis and cook for 5 minutes, stirring often. Transfer everything to your Slow Cooker. Add in beans, tomatoes, tomato sauce, chicken stock, 4 cups of water, bay leaf, basil, oregano, fusilli, salt, and pepper. Cover with the lid and cook for 8 hours on Low. Serve warm.

Mushroom Soup with Black Beans

Serves: 6 | Total Time: 6 hours 30 minutes

1 can (15 oz) black beans	2 cups vegetable stock
½ lb mushrooms, sliced	2 tbsp chopped parsley
1 shallot, chopped	½ tsp mustard seeds
2 garlic cloves, chopped	½ tsp cumin seeds
1 can fire-roasted tomatoes	Salt and pepper to taste

Mix shallot, garlic, beans, mushrooms, tomatoes, vegetable stock, 4 cups of water, mustard seeds, cumin seeds, salt, and pepper in your Slow Cooker. Cover with the lid and cook for 6 hours on Low. When done, remove the lid, top with parsley, and serve.

Chicken Soup

Serves: 4 | Total Time: 8 hours 15 minutes

2 peeled potatoes, cubed	1 cup tomato sauce
8 chicken drumsticks	1 bay leaf
1 sweet onion, chopped	2 tbsp canola oil
2 garlic cloves, chopped	1 tsp garam masala
1 cup coconut milk	½ lemongrass stalk, crushed
2 cups chicken stock	½ tsp cumin seeds
2 cups water	Salt and pepper to taste

Warm the canola oil in a skillet over medium heat. Place chicken drumsticks and cook for 5 minutes until golden brown on all sides. Transfer them to your Slow Cooker. Add in onion, garlic, garam masala, potatoes, coconut milk, chicken stock, water, tomato sauce, bay leaf, lemongrass, cumin seeds, salt, and pepper. Cover with the lid and cook for 8 hours on Low. When done, remove the lid and serve warm.

Norwegian Soup

Serves: 6 | Total Time: 2 hours 15 minutes

3 salmon fillets, cubed	2 cups vegetable stock
1 sweet onion, chopped	4 cups water
1 garlic clove, chopped	1 lemon, juiced
1 celery stalk, sliced	1 orange, juiced
1 small fennel bulb, sliced	½ tsp grated orange zest
1 cup diced tomatoes	Salt and pepper to taste

Mix onion, garlic, celery, fennel, tomatoes, vegetable stock, water, lemon juice, orange juice, orange zest, salt, pepper, and salmon in your Slow Cooker. Cover with the lid and cook for 2 hours on High. When done, remove the lid and serve warm.

Mexican Beef Soup

Serves: 6 | Total Time: 8 hours 30 minutes

10 oz canned tomatillos, rinsed and chopped	
1 can (15 oz) black beans	1 bay leaf
1 can fire-roasted tomatoes	1 thyme sprig
½ lb beef roast, cubed	5 cups water
1 dried ancho chili, chopped	Salt and pepper to taste
1 jalapeno pepper, chopped	2 tbsp chopped cilantro
1 cup beef stock	Sour cream for serving

Mix beef roast, tomatillos, ancho chili, jalapeño, beans, tomatoes, beef stock, water, bay leaf, thyme, salt, and pepper in your Slow Cooker. Cover with the lid and cook for 8 hours on Low. When done, remove the lid, top with sour cream and cilantro, and serve.

Turkey Curry

Serves: 4 | Total Time: 6 hours 30 minutes

2 carrots, diced	1 tsp grated ginger
1 sweet onion, chopped	1 cup coconut milk
1 ½ lb turkey breast, cubed	3 cups chicken stock
1 celery stalk, sliced	1 cup water
2 garlic cloves, chopped	1 tbsp curry powder
2 tbsp olive oil	Salt and pepper to taste

Warm the olive oil in a skillet over medium heat. Place turkey and cook for 5 minutes until golden. Transfer it to your Slow Cooker. Add carrots, onion, celery, garlic, ginger, coconut milk, chicken stock, water, curry powder, salt, and pepper. Cover with the lid and cook for 6 hours on Low. When done, remove the lid and serve.

Cream of Mushroom Soup

Serves: 4 | Total Time: 6 hours 15 minutes

1 (10.5-oz) can condensed cream of mushroom soup	
4 Portobello mushrooms, sliced	
1 shallot, chopped	½ tsp cumin seeds
2 garlic cloves, chopped	1 tbsp chopped parsley
1 cup diced tomatoes	1 tbsp chopped cilantro
1 tbsp tomato paste	Salt and pepper to taste
2 cups chicken stock	

Mix mushrooms, shallot, garlic, tomatoes, tomato paste, chicken stock, mushroom soup, cumin seeds, salt, and pepper in your Slow Cooker. Cover with the lid and cook for 6 hours on Low. When done, remove the lid, stir in parsley and cilantro and serve warm.

Healthful Pork Soup

Serves: 6 | Total Time: 8 hours 15 minutes

2 yellow bell peppers, diced	1 celery stalk, sliced
2 cups frozen sweet corn	½ tsp cumin seeds
½ lb pork roast, cubed	½ red chili, sliced
1 sweet onion, chopped	2 cups chicken stock
2 bacon slices, chopped	2 tbsp chopped cilantro
1 garlic clove, chopped	4 cups water
2 carrots, sliced	Salt and pepper to taste

Place a skillet over medium heat. Add pork roast, onion, bacon, and garlic and cook for 5 minutes, stirring frequently. Transfer everything to your Slow Cooker. Add carrots, celery, bell peppers, corn, cumin seeds, red chili, chicken stock, water, salt, and pepper. Cover with the lid and cook for 8 hours on Low. When done, remove the lid, top with cilantro, and serve.

Quinoa Bowl with Mixed Beans

Serves: 6 | Total Time: 7 hours 30 minutes

2 carrots, diced	½ tsp cumin seeds
2 sweet onions, chopped	½ tsp chili powder
2 garlic cloves, chopped	4 cups chicken stock
1 celery stalk, sliced	1 rosemary sprig
½ cup dried black beans	1 thyme sprig
¼ cup dried kidney beans	¼ cup red quinoa, rinsed
¼ cup cannellini beans	½ cup tomato sauce
2 tbsp olive oil	Salt and pepper to taste

Warm the olive oil in a skillet over medium heat. Place onion and garlic and cook for 2 minutes until softened. Transfer everything to your Slow Cooker. Add in celery, carrots, beans, cumin seeds, chili powder, chicken stock, 2 cups of water, rosemary, thyme, quinoa, tomato sauce, salt, and pepper. Cover with the lid and cook for 7 hours on Low. When done, remove the lid and serve warm.

Cream of Cauliflower Soup

Serves: 4 | Total Time: 6 hours 30 minutes

1 cauliflower head, cut into florets
2 peeled potatoes, cubed
1 sweet onion, chopped
1 celery stalk, sliced
2 garlic cloves, chopped
1 tbsp red curry paste
2 cups vegetable stock
2 tbsp olive oil
¼ tsp cumin powder
1 pinch red pepper flakes
Salt and pepper to taste

Warm the olive oil in a skillet over medium heat. Place onion, garlic, and celery and cook for 6 minutes until softened. Remove to your Slow Cooker. Add in curry paste, cauliflower, potatoes, vegetable stock, 2 cups of water, cumin, red pepper flakes, salt, and pepper. Cover and cook for 6 hours on Low. When done, blend the soup with an immersion blender until purée and serve.

African Lentil Soup

Serves: 6 | Total Time: 6 hours 15 minutes

1 cup red lentils
1 sweet onion, chopped
2 garlic cloves, chopped
2 carrots, diced
1 parsnip, diced
1 cup chopped cauliflower
2 tbsp olive oil
½ tsp cumin powder
¼ tsp turmeric powder
½ tsp ground coriander
3 cups chicken stock
2 tbsp tomato paste
2 tbsp lemon juice
Salt and pepper to taste

Warm the olive oil in a skillet over medium heat. Place onion, garlic, carrots, and parsnip and cook for 5 minutes. Transfer everything to your Slow Cooker. Add in cauliflower, cumin, turmeric, coriander, 3 cups of water, chicken stock, lentils, tomato paste, lemon juice, salt, and pepper. Cover with the lid and cook for 6 hours on Low. When done, remove the lid and serve warm.

Overwarming Chicken Soup

Serves: 6 | Total Time: 6 hours 15 minutes

1 chicken breast (bone-in)
1 cup chicken stock
2 carrots, diced
1 sweet onion, chopped
1 parsnip, diced
½ peeled celery root, diced
1 cup sour cream
2 egg yolks
4 garlic cloves, minced
2 tbsp chopped parsley
5 cups water
Salt and pepper to taste

Mix chicken breasts, chicken stock, water, carrots, onion, parsnip, celery, salt, and pepper in your Slow Cooker. Cover with the lid and cook for 6 hours on Low. When done, remove the lid and transfer the chicken to a plate and shred it. In a bowl, combine sour cream, egg yolks, and garlic. Pour it into the pot and toss to combine. Stir in parsley and shredded chicken. Serve right away.

Original Salmon Soup

Serves: 6 | Total Time: 5 hours 15 minutes

2 salmon fillets, cubed
1 carrot, diced
1 shallot, chopped
1 garlic clove, sliced
1 fennel bulb, sliced
1 celery stalk, sliced
1 lemon, juiced
Salt and pepper to taste

Mix shallot, garlic, fennel, carrot, celery, lemon juice, salmon, 6 cups of water, salt, and pepper in your Slow Cooker. Cover with the lid and cook for 5 hours on Low. When done, remove the lid and serve warm.

Japanese Mushroom Soup

Serves: 6 | Total Time: 7 hours 30 minutes

2 oz dried shiitake mushrooms
½ head green cabbage, shredded
1 can (8 oz) bamboo shoots
1 lb mushrooms, sliced
2 carrots, sliced
1 sweet onion, chopped
14 oz tofu, cubed
2 cups chicken stock
4 cups water
1 tsp grated ginger
½ tsp chili flakes
2 tbsp soy sauce
2 tbsp rice vinegar
2 green onions, sliced

In a bowl with boiling water, put shiitake mushrooms and let soak for 10 minutes. Cut into pieces and place them into your Slow Cooker. Add in mushrooms, bamboo shoots, carrots, onion, tofu, cabbage, ginger, chili flakes, chicken stock, water, soy sauce, and vinegar. Cover with the lid and cook for 7 hours on Low. When done, remove the lid, stir in green onions and serve warm.

Pork & Bacon Soup

Serves: 4 | Total Time: 7 hours 30 minutes

1 red bell pepper, diced
1 carrot, sliced
1 parsnip, diced
1 peeled green apple, diced
½ lb pork roast, cubed
2 bacon slices, chopped
1 shallot, chopped
1 garlic clove, chopped
1 cup applesauce
2 cups chicken stock
2 cups water
1 cup fire-roasted tomatoes
1 bay leaf
1 thyme sprig
Salt and pepper to taste
1 tsp apple cider vinegar

Place a skillet over medium heat. Add pork roast and bacon and cook until golden brown on all sides. Transfer everything to your Slow Cooker. Add in shallot, garlic, bell pepper, carrot, parsnip, green apple, applesauce, chicken stock, water, tomatoes, bay leaf, thyme, vinegar, salt, and pepper. Cover with the lid and cook for 7 hours on Low. When done, remove the lid and serve warm.

Amazing Chicken Stock

Serves: 6 | Total Time: 9 hours

1 whole chicken, cut into smaller pieces
2 onions, halved
1 parsnip
1 peeled celery root, sliced
2 carrots, cut in half
1 bay leaf
1 rosemary sprig
1 thyme sprig
Salt and pepper to taste

Preheat the oven to 400°F. Line a baking sheet with parchment paper. Sprinkle chicken with salt and pepper, place it in the oven, and bake for 40 minutes. Transfer the chicken to your Slow Cooker. Add in carrots, parsnip, celery, onions, 6 cups of water, bay leaf, rosemary, thyme, salt, and pepper. Cover with the lid and cook for 8 hours on Low. When done, remove the lid and use right away or store it in the fridge or freezer.

Spinach Tortellini Soup with Turkey

Serves: 6 | Total Time: 8 hours 30 minutes

2 peeled tomatoes, diced	1 red bell pepper, diced
10 oz spinach tortellini	2 cups chicken stock
1 lb turkey breast, cubed	2 tbsp olive oil
2 carrots, sliced	½ tsp dried oregano
1 celery stalk, sliced	Salt and pepper to taste
1 parsnip, sliced	1 lemon, juiced

Warm the olive oil in a skillet over medium heat. Place turkey and cook until golden brown on all sides. Transfer it to your Slow Cooker. Add in carrots, celery, parsnip, bell pepper, tomatoes, spinach tortellini, chicken stock, 4 cups of water, oregano, lemon juice, salt, and pepper. Cover with the lid and cook for 8 hours on Low. When done, remove the lid and serve warm.

Chicken Soup with Vegetables

Serves: 6 | Total Time: 7 hours 30 minutes

1 (10.5-oz) can condensed cream of chicken soup	
1 sweet onion, chopped	1 celery stalk, diced
1 garlic clove, chopped	1 red bell pepper, diced
2 carrots, diced	1 cup diced tomatoes
2 chicken breasts, cubed	1 lemon, juiced
1 cup chicken stock	1 tbsp chopped parsley
1 parsnip, diced	Salt and pepper to taste

Mix chicken breasts, onion, garlic, carrots, parsnip, celery, bell pepper, tomatoes, chicken stock, 5 cups of water, chicken soup, lemon juice, parsley, salt, and pepper in your Slow Cooker. Cover with the lid and cook for 7 hours on Low. Serve warm.

Chickpea Soup with Summer Squash

Serves: 6 | Total Time: 2 hours 30 minutes

2 summer squashes, cubed	1 cup diced tomatoes
1 can (15 oz) chickpeas	1 bay leaf
3 cups chicken stock	1 thyme sprig
1 sweet onion, chopped	1 lemon, juiced
1 garlic clove, chopped	1 tbsp chopped cilantro
1 carrot, diced	1 tbsp chopped parsley
1 celery stalk, sliced	Salt and pepper to taste

Mix onion, garlic, carrot, celery, squash, chickpeas, chicken stock, 3 cups of water, tomatoes, bay leaf, thyme, salt, and pepper in your Slow Cooker. Cover with the lid and cook for 2 hours on High. When done, remove the lid, stir in lemon juice, parsley, and cilantro and serve.

Chickpea & Lamb Soup

Serves: 6 | Total Time: 7 hours 30 minutes

1 cup fire-roasted tomatoes	½ tsp cumin powder
1 cup canned chickpeas	½ tsp chili powder
1 lb lamb shoulder	2 tbsp canola oil
2 cups chicken stock	½ tsp dried sage
4 cups water	½ tsp dried oregano
1 thyme sprig	Salt and pepper to taste
1 tsp turmeric powder	1 lemon, juiced

Rub lamb shoulder with salt, pepper, turmeric, cumin, and chili powder. Warm the canola oil in a skillet over medium heat. Place lamb and cook for 2-3 minutes on all sides. Transfer it to your Slow Cooker. Add in chicken stock, water, tomatoes, chickpeas, thyme, sage, oregano, lemon juice, salt, and pepper. Cover with the lid and cook for 7 hours on Low. Serve warm.

Moroccan Chicken Soup

Serves: 6 | Total Time: 6 hours 15 minutes

1 lb peeled potatoes, cubed	1 leek, sliced
2 garlic cloves, chopped	2 cups chicken stock
¼ lb dried chickpeas, rinsed	4 cups water
2 chicken breasts, cubed	2 tbsp canola oil
1 chorizo link, sliced	½ tsp dried marjoram
2 carrots, diced	Salt and pepper to taste
1 celery stalk	2 tbsp chopped cilantro

Warm the canola oil in a skillet over medium heat. Place chicken and chorizo and cook for 5 minutes on all sides. Transfer everything to your Slow Cooker. Add in chickpeas, carrots, celery, potatoes, garlic, leek, chicken stock, water, marjoram, salt, and pepper. Cover with the lid and cook for 6 hours on Low. When done, remove the lid, stir in cilantro and serve warm.

Beef Hungarian Goulash

Serves: 6 | Total Time: 8 hours 30 minutes

2 red bell peppers, diced	1 cup beef stock
1 lb peeled potatoes, cubed	5 cups water
2 sweet onions, chopped	2 tbsp canola oil
1 lb beef roast, cubed	2 tbsp tomato paste
2 carrots, diced	½ tsp cumin seeds
½ celery stalk, diced	½ tsp smoked paprika
1 cup diced tomatoes	Salt and pepper to taste

Warm the canola oil in a skillet over medium heat. Place beef roast and cook for 5 minutes on all sides. Add in onion and cook for 2 more minutes. Transfer everything to your Slow Cooker. Add in carrots, celery, bell peppers, potatoes, tomato paste, tomatoes, beef stock, water, cumin seeds, paprika, salt, and pepper. Cover with the lid and cook for 8 hours on Low. Serve warm.

Sloopy Joe Soup

Serves: 6 | Total Time: 8 hours 30 minutes

2 jalapenos, chopped	2 red bell peppers, diced
1 cup fire-roasted tomatoes	½ tsp cumin powder
1 ½ lb beef roast	½ tsp dried oregano
1 sweet onion, chopped	½ tsp dried basil
2 garlic cloves, chopped	½ tsp chili powder
2 carrots, sliced	2 cups chicken stock
2 celery stalks, sliced	Salt and pepper to taste

Mix the beef, onion, garlic, carrots, celery, bell peppers, cumin, oregano, basil, chili powder, chicken stock, 6 cups of water, jalapeños, tomatoes, salt, and pepper. Cover with the lid and cook for 8 hours on Low. When done, remove the lid, shred beef and serve warm.

Edamame & Vegetable Soup

Serves: 6 | Total Time: 6 hours 30 minutes

½ head cauliflower, cut into florets
½ head broccoli, cut into florets
2 peeled tomatoes, cubed
1 carrot, sliced
1 sweet onion, chopped
1 garlic clove, chopped
1 zucchini, cubed
1 yellow squash, cubed
1 celery stalk, sliced

½ cup edamame
2 cups chicken stock
4 cups water
1 lemon, juiced
1 tbsp chopped parsley
2 tbsp olive oil
Salt and pepper to taste

Mix the onion, garlic, olive oil, zucchini, squash, cauliflower, broccoli, tomatoes, carrot, celery, edamame, chicken stock, water, salt, and pepper in your Slow Cooker. Cover with the lid and cook for 6 hours on Low. When done, remove the lid, stir in lemon juice and parsley and serve warm.

Belgian Fish Soup

Serves: 6 | Total Time: 3 hours 30 minutes

1 lb salmon fillets, cubed
2 haddock fillets, cubed
1 shallot, chopped
2 garlic cloves, chopped
1 tbsp olive oil

4 ripe tomatoes, pureed
6 cups vegetable stock
1 bay leaf
1 lemon, juiced
Salt and pepper to taste

Warm the olive oil in a skillet over medium heat. Place shallot and garlic and cook for 2 minutes until softened. Transfer everything to your Slow Cooker. Add in tomatoes, vegetable stock, bay leaf, lemon juice, salt, and pepper. Cover with the lid and cook for 1 hour on High. Put in salmon and haddock fillets and cook for 2 hours on High. When done, remove the lid and serve warm.

Roasted Mushroom Soup with Beef

Serves: 6 | Total Time: 8 hours 30 minutes

1 lb mushrooms, sliced
1 can fire-roasted tomatoes
1 lb beef roast, cubed
1 sweet onion, chopped
2 garlic cloves, chopped

2 cups beef stock
1 thyme sprig
2 tbsp canola oil
½ tsp caraway seeds
Salt and pepper to taste

Warm the canola oil in a skillet over medium heat. Place beef roast and cook for 8 minutes on all sides. Transfer it to your Slow Cooker. Add in onion, garlic, mushrooms, tomatoes, beef stock, 4 cups of water, thyme, caraway seeds, salt, and pepper. Cover with the lid and cook for 8 hours on Low. Serve warm.

Chicken Soup with Sweet Potatoes

Serves: 6 | Total Time: 6 hours 15 minutes

1 lb sweet peeled potatoes, cubed
1 can fire-roasted tomatoes
2 chicken breasts, cubed
2 shallots, chopped
1 celery stalk, sliced
1 cup chicken stock

2 tbsp olive oil
½ tsp cumin seeds
¼ tsp caraway seeds
1 thyme sprig
Salt and pepper to taste

Warm the olive oil in a skillet over medium heat. Place chicken, shallots, and celery and cook for 2-3 minutes until softened. Transfer everything to your Slow Cooker. Add in tomatoes, sweet potatoes, chicken stock, 6 cups of water, cumin seeds, caraway seeds, thyme, salt, and pepper. Cover with the lid and cook for 6 hours on Low. When done, remove the lid and serve warm.

Winter Pork Soup

Serves: 6 | Total Time: 7 hours 15 minutes

4 bacon slices, chopped
1 can fire-roasted tomatoes
1 lb pork roast, cubed
2 carrots, diced
1 celery stalk, sliced
2 red bell peppers, diced
2 peeled potatoes, cubed
1 sweet potato, cubed

2 cups chicken stock
1 tbsp all-purpose flour
1 tsp dried oregano
1 tsp cumin powder
½ tsp smoked paprika
¼ tsp cinnamon powder
4 cups water
Salt and pepper to taste

Rub pork roast with salt, pepper, flour, oregano, cumin, paprika, and cinnamon.

Place a skillet over medium heat. Add bacon and cook for 2-3 minutes until crisp. Add in pork and cook for 2-3 minutes. Transfer everything to your Slow Cooker. Add in tomatoes, carrots, celery, bell peppers, potatoes, sweet potatoes, chicken stock, water, salt, and pepper. Cover with the lid and cook for 7 hours on Low. When done, remove the lid and serve warm.

Herbed Quinoa Soup with Parmesan

Serves: 6 | Total Time: 3 hours 30 minutes

1 cup grated Parmesan
2 chicken breasts, cubed
2/3 cup quinoa, rinsed
1 sweet onion, chopped
1 garlic clove, chopped
1 cup diced tomatoes

2 cups chicken stock
2 tbsp olive oil
½ tsp dried oregano
½ tsp dried basil
4 cups water
Salt and pepper to taste

Warm the olive oil in a skillet over medium heat. Place chicken and cook until golden brown on all sides. Transfer it to your Slow Cooker. Add in quinoa, oregano, basil, onion, garlic, tomatoes, chicken stock, water, salt, and pepper. Cover with the lid and cook for 3 hours on High. When done, remove the lid, divide between bowls and serve topped with Parmesan cheese.

Comfy Swedish Soup

Serves: 6 | Total Time: 6 hours 15 minutes

1 sweet onion, chopped
2 carrots, diced
2 cups yellow split peas
2 cups chicken stock
4 cups water

1 celery stalk, diced
2 cups diced ham
½ tsp dried oregano
½ tsp dried marjoram
Salt and pepper to taste

Mix split peas, chicken stock, water, onion, carrots, celery, ham, oregano, marjoram, salt, and pepper in your Slow Cooker. Cover with the lid and cook for 6 hours on Low. When done, remove the lid and serve warm.

Barley & Chicken Soup

Serves: 6 | Total Time: 6 hours 30 minutes

2 peeled tomatoes, diced	2 cups chicken stock
2 peeled potatoes, cubed	2 tbsp olive oil
3 chicken breasts, cubed	1 tsp dried oregano
1 sweet onion, chopped	½ tsp paprika
2 carrots, sliced	2 tbsp chopped parsley
2 celery stalks, sliced	4 cups water
½ cup pearl barley	Salt and pepper to taste

Warm the olive oil in a skillet over medium heat. Place chicken and cook for 2-3 minutes until golden brown. Remove to your Slow Cooker. Add in oregano, paprika, onion, carrots, celery, tomatoes, potatoes, barley, chicken stock, water, salt, and pepper. Cover with the lid and cook for 6 hours on Low. Top with parsley and serve.

Lentil & Sausage Soup

Serves: 4 | Total Time: 6 hours 15 minutes

2 links smoked sausages, sliced	
1 cup red lentils	2 cups water
1 sweet onion, chopped	½ tsp smoked paprika
2 carrots, diced	1 bay leaf
½ cup green lentils	1 thyme sprig
1 cup fire-roasted tomatoes	1 lemon, juiced
2 cups chicken stock	Salt and pepper to taste

Mix sausages, onion, carrots, lentils, chicken stock, water, paprika, bay leaf, thyme, lemon juice, tomatoes, salt, and pepper in your Slow Cooker. Cover with the lid and cook for 6 hours on Low. When done, remove the lid and serve warm. Enjoy!

Cream of Broccoli Soup with Cheese

Serves: 4 | Total Time: 2 hours 30 minutes

4 cups chicken stock	2 tbsp butter
5 oz broccoli florets	1 cup grated cheddar cheese
1 sweet onion, chopped	1 cup grated Monterey Jack
1 garlic clove, chopped	½ cup grated Parmesan
1 tbsp all-purpose flour	Salt and pepper to taste
1 ½ cups evaporated milk	

Melt butter in a skillet over medium heat. Place onion and garlic and cook for 2 minutes until softened. Add in flour and cook for 1 more minute. Transfer everything to your Slow Cooker. Add in milk, chicken stock, broccoli, cheeses, salt, and pepper. Cover with the lid and cook for 2 hours on High. When done, remove the lid and serve.

Shrimp Curry

Serves: 6 | Total Time: 6 hours 15 minutes

1 lb fresh shrimps, peeled and deveined	
½ head cauliflower, cut into florets	
2 cups cherry tomatoes, halved	
2 cups chicken stock	4 cups water
2 tbsp olive oil	2 tbsp lemon juice
2 shallots, chopped	1 tbsp red curry paste
1 carrot, sliced	Salt and pepper to taste

Mix olive oil, shallots, carrot, cauliflower, tomatoes, chicken stock, water, lemon juice, curry paste, salt, and pepper in your Slow Cooker and put shrimps on top. Cover with the lid and cook for 2 hours on High. When done, remove the lid and serve immediately.

Chili Cabbage Soup with Chorizo

Serves: 6 | Total Time: 7 hours 15 minutes

1 head green cabbage, shredded	
4 chorizo sausage, sliced	4 cups water
1 cup fire-roasted tomatoes	¼ tsp cumin seeds
2 sweet onions, chopped	¼ tsp chili powder
1 thyme sprig	Salt and pepper to taste
2 cups chicken stock	

Mix chorizo, onions, cabbage, tomatoes, thyme, chicken stock, water, cumin seeds, chili powder, salt, and pepper in your Slow Cooker. Cover with the lid and cook for 7 hours on Low. Serve warm.

Special Edamame Soup

Serves: 4 | Total Time: 2 hours 15 minutes

1 peeled potato, cubed	2 garlic cloves, chopped
1 peeled celery root, cubed	Salt and pepper to taste
1 lb frozen edamame	3 cups chicken stock
1 tbsp olive oil	¼ tsp dried oregano
2 shallots, chopped	¼ tsp dried marjoram

Warm the olive oil in a skillet over medium heat. Place shallots and garlic and cook for 2 minutes until softened. Transfer everything to your Slow Cooker. Add in potato, celery, edamame, chicken stock, 1 cup of water, oregano, marjoram, salt, and pepper. Cover with the lid and cook for 2 hours on High. Serve immediately.

Edamame Soup with Pork Roast

Serves: 6 | Total Time: 6 hours 15 minutes

1 peeled potato, diced	1 celery root, diced
½ lb pork roast, cubed	1 red bell pepper, diced
1 sweet onion, chopped	2 cups edamame
1 garlic clove, chopped	2 cups chicken stock
2 carrots, sliced	2 tbsp chopped parsley
1 parsnip, diced	Salt and pepper to taste

Mix pork roast, onion, garlic, carrots, parsnip, celery, bell pepper, edamame, potato, chicken stock, 4 cups of water, salt, and pepper in your Slow Cooker. Cover and cook for 6 hours on Low. Stir in parsley and serve.

Rich Bean Medley

Serves: 6 | Total Time: 8 hours 30 minutes

1 can fire-roasted tomatoes	¼ cup dried kidney beans
2 red bell peppers, diced	¼ cup cannellini beans
2 sweet onions, chopped	½ cup dried white beans
2 carrots, diced	¼ cup dried chickpeas
1 celery stalk, sliced	2 cups chicken stock
1 parsnip, diced	1 bay leaf
¼ cup dried black beans	Salt and pepper to taste

Stir onions, carrots, celery, parsnip, bell peppers, beans, chickpeas, tomatoes, chicken stock, 4 cups of water, bay leaf, salt, and pepper in your Slow Cooker. Cover with the lid and cook for 8 hours on Low. When done, remove the lid and serve warm.

Fresh Roasted Tomato Soup

Serves: 4 | Total Time: 5 hours

2 lb heirloom tomatoes, halved

1 carrot, sliced	1 tsp dried oregano
½ peeled celery root, cubed	2 tbsp olive oil
2 red onions, halved	3 cups vegetable stock
4 garlic cloves	Salt and pepper to taste

Preheat the oven to 400°F. Line a baking sheet with parchment paper. Stir tomatoes, onions, garlic, and oregano on the sheet, sprinkle with salt and pepper and bake for 30 minutes. Transfer everything to your Slow Cooker. Add in olive oil, stock, 1 cup of water, carrot, celery, salt, and pepper. Cover with the lid and cook for 4 hours on Low. When done, remove the lid, blend it with an immersion blender until creamy, and serve warm.

Country-Style Bacon Soup

Serves: 6 | Total Time: 6 hours 30 minutes

2 lb peeled potatoes, cubed	1 celery stalk, sliced
1 cup diced bacon	2 cups chicken stock
1 sweet onion, chopped	¼ tsp cumin seeds
1 garlic clove, chopped	4 cups water
1 carrot, diced	Salt and pepper to taste

Place a skillet over medium heat. Add bacon and cook until golden brown on all sides. Transfer it to your Slow Cooker. Add in onion, garlic, carrot, celery, potatoes, chicken stock, water, cumin seeds, salt, and pepper. Cover with the lid and cook for 6 hours on Low. When done, remove the lid and serve immediately.

Haddock Soup with Bacon

Serves: 6 | Total Time: 2 hours 15 minutes

2 peeled potatoes, diced	2 cups milk
½ lb haddock fillets, cubed	4 cups water
2 bacon slices, chopped	2 cups frozen sweet corn
1 sweet onion, chopped	Salt and pepper to taste

Place a skillet over medium heat. Add bacon and cook until crisp. Transfer it to your Slow Cooker. Add in onion, milk, corn, potatoes, haddock fillets, salt, and pepper. Cover with the lid and cook for 2 hours on High. When done, remove the lid and serve warm.

Quick Lentil Soup

Serves: 4 | Total Time: 2 hours 15 minutes

4 carrots, sliced	2 tbsp olive oil
1 shallot, chopped	1 thyme sprig
1 small fennel bulb, sliced	1 rosemary sprig
½ cup red lentils	¼ tsp cumin powder
2 cups chicken stock	Salt and pepper to taste

Warm the olive oil in a skillet over medium heat. Place shallot and carrots and cook for 5 minutes until softened. Transfer everything to your Slow Cooker. Add in fennel, lentils, stock, 2 cups of water, cumin, thyme, rosemary, salt, and pepper. Cover and cook for 2 hours on High. When done, discard thyme and rosemary and blend it with an immersion blender until purée. Serve.

Rumford's Soup

Serves: 6 | Total Time: 8 hours 30 minutes

4 peeled potatoes, cubed	1 medium onion, chopped
1 cup baby carrots, halved	½ cup pearl barley, rinsed
1 cup frozen sweet corn	2 cups beef stock
1 cup fire-roasted tomatoes	4 cups water
4 bacon slices, chopped	½ tsp dried basil
1 lb beef steak, cubed	½ tsp dried oregano
½ tsp smoked paprika	Salt and pepper to taste

Place a skillet over medium heat. Add bacon and cook until crisp. Add in beef steak and cook for 5 minutes until golden brown on all sides. Transfer everything to your Slow Cooker. Add in paprika, onion, potatoes, carrots, corn, tomatoes, barley, beef stock, water, basil, oregano, salt, and pepper. Cover with the lid and cook for 8 hours on Low. Serve right away.

Tuscan Soup

Serves: 4 | Total Time: 4 hours 15 minutes

½ head cauliflower, cut into florets

1 head broccoli, cut into florets

1 sweet onion, chopped	2 cups vegetable stock
1 garlic clove, chopped	2 cups water
1 tsp dried oregano	2 tbsp Italian pesto
2 tbsp olive oil	Salt and pepper to taste

Warm the olive oil in a skillet over medium heat. Place onion and garlic and cook for 2 minutes until softened. Transfer everything to your Slow Cooker. Add in cauliflower, broccoli, oregano, stock, water, Italian pesto, salt, and pepper. Cover with the lid and cook for 4 hours on Low. When done, remove the lid, blend it with an immersion blender until smooth, and serve.

Tasty Pork Soup

Serves: 6 | Total Time: 6 hours 30 minutes

1 sweet onion, chopped	¼ cup white rice
2 celery stalks, sliced	½ tsp dried oregano
1 carrot, sliced	½ tsp dried basil
1 fennel bulb, sliced	2 cups chicken stock
1 cup diced tomatoes	4 cups water
1 lb ground pork	Salt and pepper to taste

Stir onion, celery, carrot, fennel, tomatoes, chicken stock, water, salt, and pepper in your Slow Cooker. In a bowl, combine ground pork, rice, oregano, basil, salt, and pepper. Make small balls out of the mixture and place them into the pot. Cover with the lid and cook for 6 hours on Low. Serve warm.

Lemony Chicken Soup with Chickpeas

Serves: 6 | Total Time: 6 hours 30 minutes

1 lb peeled potatoes, diced	2 cups chicken stock
1 can (15 oz) chickpeas	1 cup buttermilk
2 chicken breasts, cubed	2 tbsp lemon juice
2 tbsp olive oil	1 tsp dried tarragon
2 shallots, chopped	Salt and pepper to taste

Warm the olive oil in a skillet over medium heat. Place chicken and cook until golden brown on all sides. Transfer it to your Slow Cooker. Add in shallots, potatoes, chickpeas, chicken stock, 4 cups of water, lemon juice, tarragon, salt, and pepper. Cover with the lid and cook for 6 hours on Low. When done, remove the lid, put in buttermilk, and serve right away.

Italian White Bean Soup with Chicken

Serves: 6 | Total Time: 6 hours 15 minutes

1 can (15 oz) white beans	1 celery stalk, sliced
1 chicken breast, cubed	2 tbsp Italian pesto
1 shallot, chopped	½ cup chopped parsley
1 garlic clove, chopped	Salt and pepper to taste
1 parsnip, diced	

Mix chicken, shallot, garlic, beans, parsnip, celery, Italian pesto, parsley, 6 cups of water, salt, and pepper in your Slow Cooker. Cover with the lid and cook for 6 hours on Low. When done, remove the lid and serve warm.

Tomato Chickpea Soup

Serves: 6 | Total Time: 6 hours 15 minutes

1 carrot, diced	2 cups chicken stock
1 red bell pepper, diced	2 tbsp tomato paste
1 cup dried chickpeas	2 tbsp chopped parsley
1 shallot, chopped	2 tbsp chopped cilantro
1 celery stalk, sliced	1 tbsp chopped dill
1 fennel bulb, chopped	Salt and pepper to taste

Mix chickpeas, shallot, carrot, bell pepper, celery, fennel, chicken stock, 4 cups of water, tomato paste, salt, and pepper in your Slow Cooker. Cover with the lid and cook for 6 hours on Low. When done, remove the lid, stir in parsley, cilantro, and dill serve warm.

Mexican Lentil Soup

Serves: 6 | Total Time: 6 hours 15 minutes

½ cup red lentils, rinsed	½ tsp cumin powder
2 cups chicken stock	¼ tsp chili powder
1 cup green lentils, rinsed	½ tsp dried oregano
4 cups water	1 celery stalk, chopped
2 tbsp lemon juice	1 shallot, chopped
1 tbsp chopped parsley	Salt and pepper to taste

Mix lentils, chicken stock, water, cumin, chili powder, oregano, celery, shallot, salt, and pepper in your Slow Cooker. Cover with the lid and cook for 6 hours on Low. When done, remove the lid, stir in lemon juice and parsley and serve immediately.

Herbed Chicken & White Bean Soup

Serves: 6 | Total Time: 6 hours 15 minutes

1 can (15 oz) white beans	½ tsp cumin seeds
2 chicken breasts, cubed	¼ tsp cayenne pepper
1 large onion, chopped	½ tsp dried oregano
2 garlic cloves, chopped	½ tsp dried basil
2 cups chicken stock	6 cups water
1 parsnip, diced	1 bay leaf
2 tbsp olive oil	Salt and pepper to taste

Warm the olive oil in a skillet over medium heat. Place chicken and cook until golden brown on all sides. Transfer it to your Slow Cooker. Add in onion, garlic, chicken stock, parsnip, cumin seeds, cayenne pepper, oregano, basil, beans, water, bay leaf, salt, and pepper. Cover with the lid and cook for 6 hours on Low. When done, remove the lid and serve warm.

Gnocchi Soup with Chicken

Serves: 6 | Total Time: 6 hours 15 minutes

1 (10.5-oz) can condensed cream of mushroom soup
6 chicken thighs, without skin

8 oz gnocchi	1 cup frozen green peas
2 carrots, sliced	2 cups chicken stock
1 sweet onion, chopped	1 thyme sprig
1 garlic clove, chopped	1 rosemary sprig
1 celery stalk, sliced	Salt and pepper to taste

Mix onion, garlic, chicken thighs, carrots, celery, green peas, gnocchi, mushroom soup, chicken stock, 4 cups of water, thyme, rosemary, salt, and pepper in your Slow Cooker. Cover with the lid and cook for 6 hours on Low. When done, remove the lid and serve warm.

Cheese Tortellini Soup with Beef

Serves: 6 | Total Time: 8 hours 30 minutes

8 oz cheese tortellini	2 tbsp olive oil
1 lb beef roast, cubed	½ tsp dried basil
1 large onion, chopped	¼ cup kidney beans, rinsed
1 carrot, sliced	2 cups beef stock
1 celery stalk, sliced	½ cup dark beer
2 garlic cloves, chopped	1 bay leaf
1 cup diced tomatoes	Salt and pepper to taste

Warm the olive oil in a skillet over medium heat. Place beef roast and cook for 5 minutes until golden brown on all sides. Transfer it to your Slow Cooker. Add in onion, carrot, celery, garlic, tomatoes, basil, cheese tortellini, beans, beef stock, beer, 4 cups of water, bay leaf, salt, and pepper. Cover with the lid and cook for 8 hours on Low. When done, remove the lid and serve warm.

Cheese Tortellini Soup

Serves: 6 | Total Time: 8 hours 30 minutes

1 (3.5-lb) whole chicken, cut into smaller pieces

10 oz cheese tortellini	1 parsnip, halved
1 carrot, halved	6 cups water
1 celery stalk, halved	Salt and pepper to taste

Mix chicken, carrot, celery, parsnip, and water in your Slow Cooker. Season yo taste. Cover with the lid and cook for 6 hours on Low. Put in cheese tortellini and cook for 2 hours on High. When done, remove the lid and serve warm.

Rice Chicken Soup

Serves: 6 | Total Time: 6 hours 15 minutes

2 peeled potatoes, cubed	1 yellow bell pepper, diced
2 chicken sausages, sliced	1 cup diced tomatoes
1 shallot, chopped	¼ cup jasmine rice
1 carrot, sliced	2 cups chicken stock
1 celery stalk, sliced	Salt and pepper to taste

Mix sausages, shallot, carrot, celery, bell pepper, tomatoes, potatoes, rice, chicken stock, 4 cups of water, salt, and pepper in your Slow Cooker. Cover with the lid and cook for 6 hours on Low. Serve warm.

Chicken & Sweet Potato Soup with Spinach

Serves: 6 | Total Time: 3 hours 30 minutes

4 cups spinach, torn	2 tbsp olive oil
2 sweet potatoes, cubed	½ tsp dried oregano
2 cups chicken stock	½ tsp dried basil
1 shallot, chopped	1 tbsp chopped parsley
1 garlic clove, chopped	4 cups water
½ lb ground chicken	Salt and pepper to taste

Warm the olive oil in a skillet over medium heat. Place ground chicken, shallot, and garlic and cook for 5 minutes, stirring often. Transfer everything to your Slow Cooker. Add in sweet potatoes, chicken stock, water, salt, and pepper. Cover with the lid and cook for 2 hours on High. Put in spinach, oregano, basil, and parsley and cook for another 1 hour on High. Serve warm.

Spinach & Sweet Potato Lentils

Serves: 6 | Total Time: 3 hours 15 minutes

2 sweet potatoes, cubed	1 sweet onion, chopped
4 cups spinach, shredded	6 cups chicken stock
1 cup green lentils, rinsed	1 bay leaf
1 celery stalk, sliced	1 thyme sprig
1 carrot, sliced	Salt and pepper to taste

Mix lentils, celery, carrot, onion, sweet potatoes, chicken stock, bay leaf, thyme, salt, and pepper in your Slow Cooker. Cover with the lid and cook for 2 hours on High. Put in spinach and cook for 1 hour on High. When done, remove the lid and serve warm.

Kale Soup

Serves: 6 | Total Time: 2 hours 15 minutes

1 lb peeled potatoes, cubed	½ cup diced tomatoes
¼ lb kale, chopped	2 cups chicken stock
1 shallot, chopped	4 cups water
1 garlic clove, chopped	¼ tsp chili flakes
1 celery stalk, sliced	2 tbsp lemon juice
2 carrots, sliced	Salt and pepper to taste

Mix shallot, garlic, celery, carrots, potatoes, tomatoes, kale, chicken stock, water, chili flakes, lemon juice, salt, and pepper in your Slow Cooker. Cover with the lid and cook for 2 hours on High. Serve warm.

Spinach Soup with Croutons

Serves: 4 | Total Time: 2 hours 15 minutes

10 oz one-day old bread, cubed	
1 lb fresh spinach, shredded	2 cups chicken stock
½ tsp dried oregano	1 lemon, juiced
1 shallot, chopped	3 tbsp olive oil
4 garlic cloves, chopped	1 tsp dried basil
½ cup half and half	1 tsp dried marjoram
½ celery stalk, sliced	Salt and pepper to taste

Stir spinach, oregano, shallot, garlic, celery, 2 cups of water, stock, lemon juice, salt, and pepper in your Slow Cooker. Cover with the lid and cook for 2 hours on High.

Meanwhile, preheat the oven to 375°F. Line a baking sheet with parchment paper. Place bread cubes in the sheet, sprinkle with olive oil, salt, pepper, basil, and marjoram, and bake for 10-12 minutes until golden.

When the soup is ready, pour in half and half and blend it with an immersion blender until smooth. Serve topped with herbed croutons.

Aunt's Minestrone

Serves: 6 | Total Time: 6 hours 30 minutes

2 potatoes, diced	1 carrot, diced
2 cups chicken stock	1 cup diced tomatoes
1 shallot, chopped	1 tsp Italian herbs
1 garlic clove, chopped	4 cups water
1 celery stalk, sliced	1 cup farfalle pasta
1 red bell pepper, diced	Salt and pepper to taste

Stir shallot, garlic, celery, bell pepper, carrot, tomatoes, potatoes, Italian herbs, chicken stock, water, pasta, salt, and pepper in your Slow Cooker. Cover with the lid and cook for 6 hours on Low. When done, remove the lid and serve warm.

Spinach Ravioli Soup with Chicken

Serves: 6 | Total Time: 6 hours 15 minutes

1 (10.5-oz) can condensed mushroom soup	
8 oz spinach ravioli	5 cups chicken stock
1 chicken breast, diced	1 tbsp olive oil
2 shallots, chopped	2 cups sliced mushrooms
2 garlic cloves, chopped	1 cup water
2 cups tomato sauce	Salt and pepper to taste

Warm the olive oil in a skillet over medium heat. Place chicken and cook for 5 minutes until golden brown on all sides. Transfer it to your Slow Cooker. Add in shallots, garlic, tomato sauce, chicken stock, mushroom soup, sliced mushrooms, water, spinach ravioli, salt, and pepper. Cover with the lid and cook for 6 hours on Low. When done, remove the lid and serve warm.

Cheesy Beef Soup

Serves: 6 | Total Time: 6 hours 30 minutes

2 peeled potatoes, cubed
2 carrots, diced
4 bacon slices, chopped
1 lb ground beef
1 sweet onion, chopped
1 celery stalk, sliced
1 cup diced tomatoes
½ tsp dried thyme
½ tsp dried oregano
1 cup cream cheese
2 cups beef stock
4 cups water
Salt and pepper to taste
Processed cheese for serving

Place a skillet over medium heat. Add bacon and cook until crisp. Add in ground beef and cook for 2-3 minutes, stirring often. Transfer everything to your Slow Cooker. Add in onion, carrots, celery, potatoes, tomatoes, thyme, oregano, cream cheese, beef stock, water, salt, and pepper. Cover with the lid and cook for 6 hours on Low. When done, remove the lid, top with cheese, and serve.

Favorite Tomato Soup

Serves: 4 | Total Time: 6 hours 30 minutes

1 ½ lb fresh tomatoes, peeled and cubed
½ red chili, minced
2 red onions, sliced
1 tsp dried basil
1 celery stalk, sliced
2 tbsp olive oil
4 cups vegetable stock
½ cup half and half
Salt and pepper to taste

Warm the olive oil in a skillet over medium heat. Place onions and cook for 5 minutes until softened. Transfer them to your Slow Cooker. Add in basil, tomatoes, celery, red chili, vegetable stock, salt, and pepper. Cover with the lid and cook for 6 hours on Low. When done, remove the lid, pour in half and half, and blend it with an immersion blender until creamy. Serve right away.

Parmesan Chicken Soup

Serves: 6 | Total Time: 8 hours 15 minutes

1 celery root, cubed
2 peeled potatoes, cubed
8 chicken thighs
1 sweet onion, chopped
1 celery stalk, sliced
1 carrot, sliced
1 can diced tomatoes
2 cups chicken stock
4 cups water
2 tbsp chopped parsley
Salt and pepper to taste
Parmesan shavings for serving

Mix chicken thighs, onion, celery, carrot, celery root, potatoes, tomatoes, chicken stock, water, salt, and pepper in your Slow Cooker. Cover with the lid and cook for 8 hours on Low. When done, remove the lid, stir in parsley and serve topped with Parmesan shavings.

Chicken Coconut Soup

Serves: 6 | Total Time: 6 hours 30 minutes

2 cups coconut milk
8 chicken thighs
2 celery stalks, sliced
1 sweet onion, chopped
1 cup green peas
2 cups chicken stock
2 cups water
1 lemongrass stalk, crushed
1 tsp grated ginger
1 tsp fish sauce
2 tbsp soy sauce
1 tbsp brown sugar
1 lime, juiced
Salt and pepper to taste

Stir chicken thighs, celery, onion, ginger, fish sauce, soy sauce, brown sugar, lime juice, coconut milk, chicken stock, water, lemongrass, green peas, salt, and pepper in your Slow Cooker. Cover with the lid and cook for 6 hours on Low. Serve warm.

Comfortable Chicken Soup with Wild Rice

Serves: 6 | Total Time: 6 hours 30 minutes

1 lb chicken breasts, cubed
1 celery stalk, sliced
2 carrots, sliced
3/4 cup wild rice, rinsed
1 sweet onion, chopped
6 cups chicken stock
½ tsp dried oregano
1 tbsp butter
½ cup half and half
Salt and pepper to taste

Mix rice, chicken breasts, celery, carrots, onion, chicken stock, oregano, butter, half and half, salt, and pepper in your Slow Cooker. Cover with the lid and cook for 6 hours on Low. When done, remove the lid and serve warm.

Lasagna-Style Beef Soup

Serves: 6 | Total Time: 8 hours 30 minutes

1 ½ cups pasta shells
1 lb ground beef
1 sweet onion, chopped
2 garlic cloves, chopped
1 ½ cups tomato sauce
1 cup diced tomatoes
2 cups beef stock
4 cups water
2 tbsp olive oil
1 tsp dried oregano
Salt and pepper to taste
Grated cheddar for serving

Warm the olive oil in a skillet over medium heat. Place ground beef and cook for 5 minutes. Remove to your Slow Cooker. Add in onion, garlic, oregano, tomato sauce, tomatoes, beef stock, water, pasta, salt, and pepper. Cover with the lid and cook for 8 hours on Low. Top with cheddar cheese and serve.

Veggie & Bean Soup with Bacon

Serves: 6 | Total Time: 6 hours 30 minutes

2 ripe tomatoes, peeled and diced
1 large sweet onion, chopped
½ cup white beans, rinsed
1 cup diced bacon
2 carrots, diced
1 celery stalk, diced
4 cups water
2 cups chicken stock
1 thyme sprig
Salt and pepper to taste

Place a skillet over medium heat. Add bacon and cook until golden brown on all sides. Transfer it to your Slow Cooker. Add in onion, carrots, celery, tomatoes, beans, water, stock, thyme, salt, and pepper. Cover with the lid and cook for 6 hours on Low. When done, remove the lid and serve immediately.

Simple Chicken Soup

Serves: 6 | Total Time: 7 hours 30 minutes

¼ cup all-purpose flour
1 cup chicken stock
4 chicken thighs
¼ tsp garlic powder
1 pinch chili flakes
Salt and pepper to taste

Place the chicken thighs and 6 cups of water in your Slow Cooker. Cover with the lid and cook for 6 hours on Low. When done, remove the lid, transfer the chicken to a plate and shred it.

In a bowl, whisk flour, chicken stock, garlic powder, chili flakes, salt, and pepper. Pour it into the pot among shredded chicken and cover it with the lid. Cook for 1 hour on High. When done, remove the lid and serve warm.

Strong Bacon Chowder

Serves: 6 | Total Time: 6 hours 15 minutes

½ lb peeled potatoes, cubed
4 bacon slices, chopped
½ cup grits
2 cups chicken stock
½ celery stalk, sliced
1 carrot, diced
1 parsnip, diced
1 cup diced tomatoes
½ tsp dried thyme
½ tsp dried oregano
Salt and pepper to taste

Place a skillet over medium heat. Add bacon and cook until crisp. Transfer it to your Slow Cooker. Add in grits, chicken stock, water, potatoes, celery, carrot, parsnip, tomatoes, thyme, oregano, salt, and pepper. Cover with the lid and cook for 6 hours on Low. When done, remove the lid and serve immediately.

Tex-Mex Soup

Serves: 6 | Total Time: 6 hours 30 minutes

2 chicken breasts, cut into strips
1 can (15 oz) pinto beans
1 can (15 oz) black beans
1 cup diced tomatoes
½ cup canned corn
1 large onion, chopped
2 garlic cloves, chopped
1 cup dark beer
1 tbsp taco seasoning
2 cups chicken stock
4 cups water
Salt and pepper to taste
Tortilla chips for serving

Stir chicken breasts, onion, garlic, beans, tomatoes, corn, beer, taco seasoning, chicken stock, water, salt, and pepper in your Slow Cooker. Cover with the lid and cook for 6 hours on Low. Serve topped with tortilla chips.

Garlic Soup with Cheddar

Serves: 6 | Total Time: 2 hours 15 minutes

3 cups grated cheddar
8 garlic cloves, chopped
2 cups chicken stock
¼ cup white wine
4 cups water
2 tbsp olive oil
1 tsp cumin seeds
1 tsp mustard seeds
2 tbsp all-purpose flour
Salt and pepper to taste

Warm the olive oil in a skillet over medium heat. Cook the garlic for 1-2 minutes. Add in cumin seeds and mustard seeds and cook for 1 more minute. Put in the flour and stir for 1 more minute.

Transfer everything to your Slow Cooker. Add in chicken stock, wine, water, cheddar cheese, salt, and pepper. Cover with the lid and cook for 2 hours on High. When done, remove the lid and serve warm.

Ground Chicken & Kale Soup

Serves: 6 | Total Time: 6 hours 30 minutes

6 oz spinach tortellini
½ lb ground chicken
¼ cup white rice
1 garlic clove, chopped
1 celery stalk, sliced
1 carrot, sliced
1 shallot, chopped
1 tbsp chopped parsley
2 cups chicken stock
Salt and pepper to taste

Stir the chicken stock, 4 cups of water, celery, carrot, shallot, salt, and pepper in your Slow Cooker. In a bowl, combine ground chicken, rice, garlic, parsley, salt, and pepper. Make small balls out of the mixture and place them into the pot. Put in spinach tortellini, cover with the lid and cook for 6 hours on Low. Serve warm.

Basil Bean Soup with Kale

Serves: 6 | Total Time: 8 hours 30 minutes

1 bunch kale, shredded
1 ½ cups white beans, rinsed
1 sweet onion, chopped
2 carrots, diced
1 celery stalk, sliced
1 bay leaf
1 tsp dried oregano
2 cups chicken stock
4 cups water
1 tsp dried basil
Salt and pepper to taste
1 lemon, juiced

Mix beans, onion, carrots, celery, oregano, chicken stock, water, bay leaf, basil, salt, and pepper in your Slow Cooker. Cover with the lid and cook for 4 hours on Low. Put in kale and lemon juice and cook for 4 hours on Low. When done, remove the lid and serve warm.

Home Chicken Soup with Noodles

Serves: 6 | Total Time: 8 hours 30 minutes

1 (3.5-oz) whole chicken, cut into pieces
6 oz egg noodles
2 carrots, cut into sticks
1 celery stalk, sliced
4 peeled potatoes, cubed
2 garlic cloves, chopped
Salt and pepper to taste
1 whole onion
1 bay leaf

Mix chicken, carrots, celery, potatoes, 6 cups of water, noodles, garlic, onion, bay leaf, salt, and pepper in your Slow Cooker. Cover with the lid and cook for 8 hours on Low. When done, remove the lid and serve right away.

Mediterranean Bean Soup

Serves: 6 | Total Time: 6 hours 30 minutes

2 cups spinach, shredded
1 cup dried white beans
2 cups chicken stock
1 carrot, diced
1 celery stalk, diced
4 garlic cloves, chopped
2 tbsp tomato paste
1 bay leaf
1 tsp dried oregano
1 tsp dried basil
½ lemon, juiced
Salt and pepper to taste

Stir beans, chicken stock, 4 cups of water, carrot, celery, garlic, tomato paste, bay leaf, oregano, basil, lemon juice, salt, and pepper in your Slow Cooker. Cover with the lid and cook for 4 hours on Low. Put in spinach and cook for 2 hours on Low. Serve warm.

STEWS & CHILIS

Beef & Bacon Mushroom Stew

Serving Size: 6 | Total Time: 8 hours 10 minutes

1 tbsp olive oil	2 carrots, chopped
2 lb beef stew meat, cubed	1 onion, diced
8 oz bacon, chopped	2 garlic cloves, minced
2 cups beef broth	1 tsp dried rosemary
4 mushrooms, sliced	Salt and pepper to taste

Warm the olive oil in a skillet over medium heat. Add the bacon and fry for 5 minutes until crispy. Stir in beef, onion, carrots, garlic, and mushrooms and sauté for 5-6 minutes. Season with rosemary, salt, and pepper. Transfer the contents to your Slow Cooker and pour in the broth. Stir to mix well. Cook on Low for 8 hours. Serve warm.

Harissa Chicken Stew

Serving Size: 6 | Total Time: 8 hours 10 minutes

2 lb boneless, skinless chicken thighs, trimmed of excess fat

4 cups chicken broth	½ tsp dried thyme
2 cups frozen mirepoix	4 russet potatoes, peeled
3 tbsp harissa paste	1 cup frozen peas
1 tsp garlic powder	Salt and pepper to taste

Place the broth, mirepoix, harissa paste, garlic powder, thyme, and salt in your Slow Cooker and stir to combine. Add the potatoes and chicken. Cover and cook on Low for 8 hours. When ready, transfer the potatoes to a plate. Mash two of them with a fork and cut the remaining into cubes. Add all potatoes back to the cooker. Place the chicken on the cutting board and shred it with two forks. Return the chicken to the Slow Cooker too. Stir to combine. Add the peas and let them rest for 5 minutes until heated through. Serve and enjoy!

Seafood Stew

Serving Size: 6 | Total Time: 8 hours 15 minutes

8 oz cremini mushrooms, halved
6 oz boneless, skinless haddock fillet, cut into 1-inch pieces
6 oz boneless, skinless salmon fillet, cut into 1-inch pieces
8 oz mussels, cleaned and debearded

6 cups chicken stock	3 carrots, chopped
1 lb pearl onions, peeled	Salt and pepper to taste
3 Roma tomatoes, chopped	1 lemon, juiced and zested
1 celeriac bulb, cubed	1 tbsp flour
1 fennel bulb, chopped	8 oz cooked shrimp
2 celery stalks, chopped	2 tbsp chopped dill

Place the pearl onions, mushrooms, tomatoes, celeriac, fennel, celery, carrots, salt, and pepper in your Slow Cooker and top with 5 cups of the chicken stock. Cover and cook on Low for 7 ½ hours. In a small bowl, whisk together the lemon juice, remaining stock, and flour and stir the mixture in the Slow Cooker. Add the haddock, salmon, shrimp, and mussels. Set the Slow Cooker to High and cook for 30 more minutes until the fish is cooked. Top with dill and lemon zest just before serving.

Classic Beef Stroganoff

Serving Size: 4 | Total Time: 8 hours 15 minutes

2 lb beef chuck roast, cut into bite-size pieces
2 yellow onions, cut into very thin half-moons
1 lb white button mushrooms, sliced

1 tsp paprika	1 tbsp all-purpose flour
2 garlic cloves, pressed	2 tbsp dry white wine
1 cup beef broth	2 cups cooked white rice
1 ½ cups sour cream	Salt and pepper to taste

Place the onions, garlic, mushrooms, and beef in your Slow Cooker. Sprinkle with paprika, salt, and pepper. Pour the beef broth and white wine over the top.

Cover and cook on Low for 8 hours. In a small bowl, whisk together the flour and sour cream. Stir the sour cream mixture into the stew. Set the slow cooker to High and cook with the lid off for 8-10 minutes until the sauce thickens. Serve the beef stroganoff over the rice.

Homestyle Pork Stew

Serving Size: 6 | Total Time: 8 hours

1 ½ lb boneless pork loin roast, cut into 1-inch pieces
3 leeks (white part only), chopped

1 yellow onion, chopped	¾ tsp dried thyme
1 lb peeled potatoes, cubed	Salt and pepper to taste
4 cups chicken broth	3 tbsp all-purpose flour
1 tsp dried sage	3 tbsp butter, melted

Mix together the pork, leeks, onion, potatoes, broth, sage, thyme, salt, and pepper in your Slow Cooker. Cover and cook on Low for 7 hours.

In a small bowl, whisk together the flour and butter. Stir in the slow cooker. Cover and set to High. Let the stew thicken for about 30 minutes. Ladle into bowls and serve.

Chicken & Poblano Stew

Serving Size: 6 | Total Time: 8 hours 10 minutes

1 ½ lb boneless, skinless chicken thighs, cut into 1-inch pieces

2 chopped poblano peppers	1 cup chicken broth
2 oz bacon, chopped	2 garlic cloves, pressed
8 oz mushrooms, chopped	1 tsp dried oregano
1 (16-oz) can diced tomatoes	Salt and pepper to taste
1 onion, chopped	1 tsp cayenne pepper
2 carrots, chopped	2 tbsp chopped cilantro

Combine chicken thighs, poblano peppers, bacon, mushrooms, tomatoes, onion, carrots, broth, garlic, oregano, cayenne pepper, salt, and pepper in your Slow Cooker. Cover and cook on Low for 8 hours. Top with cilantro and serve.

Mixed Mushroom Stew

Serving Size: 4 | Total Time: 8 hours 15 minutes

4 Portobello mushrooms, stems and gills removed, chopped
4 oz Chanterelle mushrooms, sliced
4 oz cremini mushrooms, quartered
8 oz button mushrooms, quartered

4 cups vegetable stock
1 tbsp porcini powder
½ tbsp flour
1 tbsp Dijon mustard
2 carrots, chopped
1 red onion, chopped
1 tsp dried rosemary
1 tsp dried thyme
1 tsp garlic powder
Salt and pepper to taste
Pinch red pepper flakes
2 tbsp chopped parsley

Combine the mushrooms, carrots, onion, rosemary, thyme, garlic powder, salt, pepper, and red pepper flakes in your Slow Cooker. Whisk the vegetable stock with porcini powder, flour, and Dijon mustard in a bowl. Stir the mixture in the Slow Cooker. Cover and cook on Low for 8 hours. Sprinkle parsley and serve.

Moroccan Lamb Stew

Serving Size: 6 | Total Time: 8 hours 20 minutes

2 lb boneless leg of lamb, cut into 1-inch pieces
1 orange, juiced and zested
1 tbsp flour
2 onions, chopped
2 carrots, chopped
1 (14-oz) can diced tomatoes
1 cup chopped dried dates
1 tsp garlic powder
1 tsp ground ginger
1 tsp ground cumin
½ tsp red pepper flakes
Salt and pepper to taste
3 tbsp chopped parsley

Whisk together the orange juice, orange zest, and flour in your Slow Cooker. Add the lamb, onions, carrots, tomatoes, dates, garlic powder, ginger, cumin, pepper flakes, salt, and pepper. Cover and cook on Low for 8 hours. Sprinkle with parsley and serve.

Fall Vegetable Stew

Serving Size: 6 | Total Time: 8 hours 15 minutes

1 acorn squash, peel and seeds removed, cubed
4 cups vegetable stock
1 tbsp flour
1 lb baby carrots
1 lb parsnips, chopped
1 sweet potato, cubed
8 shallots, quartered
4 garlic cloves, minced
2 tbsp olive oil
1 tsp dried thyme
1 tsp dried rosemary
Salt and pepper to taste
2 tbsp chopped parsley

Whisk together the flour and vegetable stock in your Slow Cooker. Add the squash, carrots, parsnips, sweet potato, shallots, garlic, olive oil, thyme, rosemary, salt, and pepper. Cover and cook on Low for 8 hours. Sprinkle parsley just before serving.

Thai Chicken Stew

Serves: 6 | Total Time: 4 hours 15 minutes

2 chicken breasts, cut into strips
2 red bell peppers, sliced
2 heirloom tomatoes, diced
2 cups button mushrooms
2 zucchinis, sliced
4 garlic cloves, minced
1 leek, sliced
1 tbsp red Thai curry paste
1 cup coconut milk
½ cup vegetable stock
Salt and pepper to taste

In your Slow Cooker, mix the chicken, zucchinis, bell peppers, tomatoes, mushrooms, garlic, leek, curry paste, coconut milk, vegetable stock, salt, and pepper. Cover with the lid and cook for 4 hours on Low. Serve warm.

Cajun Jambalaya

Serving Size: 6 | Total Time: 8 hours 20 minutes

1 lb medium shrimp, peeled and deveined
1 lb andouille sausage, sliced
2 (14-oz) cans diced tomatoes
2 cups vegetable stock
1 green bell pepper, chopped
1 red bell pepper, chopped
2 large carrots, chopped
1 onion, chopped
2 jalapeño peppers, minced
1 tsp smoked paprika
1 tsp garlic powder
1 tsp Cajun seasoning mix
Salt and pepper to taste
1 cup basmati rice
⅛ tsp cayenne pepper

Combine the shrimp, sausage, tomatoes, stock, bell peppers, carrots, onion, jalapeños, paprika, garlic powder, Cajun seasoning, salt, black pepper, rice, and cayenne in your Slow Cooker. Cover and cook on Low for 8 hours.

Chicken & Bell Pepper Cacciatore

Serving Size: 6 | Total Time: 8 hours 20 minutes

1 yellow bell pepper, chopped
1 green bell pepper, chopped
1 red bell pepper, chopped
1 onion, chopped
2 (14-oz) cans diced tomatoes
¼ cup capers, drained
2 tsp Italian seasoning
1 tsp garlic powder
Salt and pepper to taste
Pinch red pepper flakes
¾ cup chicken broth
1 tbsp flour
8 chicken thighs
¼ cup chopped fresh basil
7 oz pitted black olives
2 tbsp basil, chopped

Place bell peppers, onion, tomatoes, capers, Italian seasoning, garlic powder, salt, pepper, olives, and pepper flakes in your Slow Cooker; stir to combine. In a small bowl, whisk together the broth and flour. Pour the mixture into the Slow Cooker. Top with the chicken thighs, pressing them into the vegetable mixture. Cover and cook on Low for 8 hours. Top with basil and serve.

Tasty White Bean Stew

Serves: 6 | Total Time: 6 hours 30 minutes

1 can (28 oz) diced tomatoes
1 tsp Worcestershire sauce
1 red onion, chopped
2 garlic cloves, chopped
1 ½ cups white beans, soaked
3 cups vegetable stock
1 bay leaf
1 thyme sprig
1 rosemary sprig
Salt and pepper to taste

Stir onion, garlic, tomatoes, Worcestershire sauce, beans, vegetable stock, bay leaf, thyme, rosemary, salt, and pepper in your Slow Cooker. Cover with the lid and cook for 6 hours on Low. Serve immediately.

Wine Mushroom & Chicken Stew

Serves: 6 | Total Time: 6 hours 30 minutes

4 garlic cloves, minced
4 cups sliced mushrooms
6 chicken thighs
1 large onion, chopped
½ cup red wine
1 cup chicken stock
1 thyme sprig
Salt and pepper to taste

Toss chicken, onion, garlic, mushrooms, wine, chicken stock, thyme, salt, and pepper in your Slow Cooker. Cover with the lid and cook for 6 hours on Low. Serve.

Cauliflower & Chicken Stew

Serves: 6 | Total Time: 6 hours 15 minutes

1 (10.5-oz) can condensed cream of chicken soup
½ head cauliflower, cut into florets

3 chicken breasts, cubed	1 cup vegetable stock
2 potatoes, cubed	2 tbsp olive oil
1 celery stalk, sliced	Salt and pepper to taste
1 shallot, sliced	

Warm the olive oil in a pan over medium heat. Cook the chicken for 2-3 minutes until golden on all sides. Transfer it to your Slow Cooker. Add in chicken soup, celery, shallot, cauliflower, potatoes, vegetable stock, salt, and pepper. Cover with the lid and cook for 6 hours on Low. When done, remove the lid and serve warm.

Herbed Chicken Stew

Serves: 6 | Total Time: 8 hours 15 minutes

1 ½ cups apple cider	1 tsp dried oregano
1 whole chicken, cubed	1 tsp cumin powder
1 tsp dried thyme	Salt and pepper to taste

Dust chicken with thyme, oregano, cumin, salt, and pepper. Place it into your Slow Cooker and pour in apple cider. Cover with the lid and cook for 8 hours on Low. Serve warm with your desired side dish.

Sweet Potato & Chicken Stew

Serves: 6 | Total Time: 3 hours 15 minutes

2 lb sweet potatoes, peeled and cubed

2 chicken breasts, cubed	½ tsp garlic powder
2 shallots, chopped	1 pinch cinnamon powder
2 tbsp butter	1 ½ cups vegetable stock
½ tsp cumin powder	Salt and pepper to taste

Melt butter in a pan over medium heat, place chicken and shallots and cook for 5 minutes. Transfer everything to your Slow Cooker. Add in sweet potatoes, cumin, garlic powder, cinnamon powder, stock, salt, and pepper. Cover with the lid and cook for 3 hours on High. When done, remove the lid and serve warm.

Hot Soy Beef Stew

Serves: 6 | Total Time: 8 hours 15 minutes

1 lb baby carrots	3 tbsp soy sauce
1 lb beef roast, cubed	1 tbsp brown sugar
1 large onion, chopped	1 tsp hot sauce
4 garlic cloves, minced	1 cup diced tomatoes
½ cup tomato juice	Salt and pepper to taste
2 tbsp canola oil	Cooked rice for serving
1 tsp sesame oil	

Warm canola oil in a pan over medium heat. Place the beef and cook for 2-3 minutes until golden on all sides. Transfer it to your Slow Cooker. Add in sesame oil, carrots, onion, garlic, tomato juice, soy sauce, sugar, hot sauce, tomatoes, salt, and pepper. Cover with the lid and cook for 8 hours on Low. Serve over cooked rice.

Coconut Chicken & Chickpea Stew

Serves: 6 | Total Time: 6 hours 30 minutes

½ head cauliflower, cut into florets

1 can (15-oz) chickpeas	1 cup coconut milk
2 red bell peppers, diced	1 cup chicken stock
2 cups fresh spinach, torn	2 tbsp canola oil
2 chicken breasts, cubed	1 tsp turmeric powder
1 cup tomato sauce	Salt and pepper to taste

Sprinkle chicken breasts with turmeric, salt, and pepper. Warm canola oil in a pan over medium heat. Place the chicken and cook for 2-3 minutes until golden brown on all sides. Transfer it to your Slow Cooker.

Add in cauliflower, chickpeas, bell peppers, tomato sauce, coconut milk, chicken stock, and spinach and season with salt and pepper to taste. Cover with the lid and cook for 6 hours on Low. Serve right away.

Spicy Chicken Stew with Spinach

Serves: 6 | Total Time: 6 hours 30 minutes

6 chicken thighs, boneless	2 tbsp canola oil
3 cups spinach, chopped	¼ tsp cumin powder
2 potatoes, cubed	¼ tsp chili powder
¼ cup chopped cilantro	¼ tsp all-spice powder
¼ cup chopped parsley	Salt and pepper to taste
1 cup vegetable stock	

Warm canola oil in a pan over medium heat. Add the chicken and cook until golden brown on all sides. Transfer it to your Slow Cooker. Put in cilantro, parsley, spinach, potatoes, vegetable stock, cumin, chili powder, all-spice powder, salt, and pepper. Cover with the lid and cook for 6 hours on Low. Serve warm and enjoy!

Garden Chicken Stew

Serves: 6 | Total Time: 8 hours 30 minutes

3 chicken breasts, cubed	4 potatoes, cubed
1 onion, chopped	2 cups chicken stock
2 carrots, sliced	2 tbsp canola oil
2 celery stalks, sliced	1 tsp dried oregano
2 ripe tomatoes, diced	½ tsp dried basil
1 can (15 oz) white beans	Salt and pepper to taste
1 cup tomato sauce	

In your Slow Cooker, add canola oil, chicken, onion, carrots, celery, tomatoes, beans, chicken stock, oregano, basil, tomato sauce, potatoes, salt, and pepper, and stir. Cover with the lid and cook for 8 hours on Low. Serve.

Mediterranean Chicken Stew

Serves: 6 | Total Time: 6 hours 15 minutes

6 chicken thighs	12 pitted Kalamata olives
4 garlic cloves, minced	2 tbsp tomato paste
1 shallot, chopped	½ cup tomato sauce
¼ cup dry white wine	2 tbsp olive oil
1 can (28 oz) diced tomatoes	¼ tsp chili powder
½ cup pitted black olives	Salt and pepper to taste

Mix the olive oil, chicken, garlic, shallot, wine, tomato paste, tomato sauce, chili powder, tomatoes, olives, salt, and pepper in your Slow Cooker. Cover with the lid and cook for 6 hours on Low. Serve immediately.

Cheesy Chicken & Mushroom Stew

Serves: 6 | Total Time: 6 hours 15 minutes

2 chicken breasts, cubed	1 cup vegetable stock
2 garlic cloves, minced	2 tbsp canola oil
1 shallot, chopped	1 thyme sprig
4 cups button mushrooms	Salt and pepper to taste
1 cup cream cheese	

Warm the canola oil in a pan over medium heat. Place the chicken and cook for 5 minutes until golden brown on all sides. Transfer it to your Slow Cooker. Add garlic, shallot, mushrooms, cream cheese, stock, thyme, salt, and pepper. Cover with the lid and cook for 6 hours on Low. When done, remove the lid and serve warm.

Chicken Stew with Bacon

Serves: 6 | Total Time: 6 hours 30 minutes

6 bacon slices, chopped	2 cups sliced mushrooms
1 sweet onion, chopped	¼ cup dry white wine
6 chicken thighs	1 cup vegetable stock
2 garlic cloves, chopped	½ cup heavy cream
2 large carrots, sliced	1 thyme sprig
2 celery stalks, sliced	1 rosemary sprig
1 cup green peas	Salt and pepper to taste

Warm a pan over medium heat, place bacon and cook until crispy. Transfer it to your Slow Cooker. Put in chicken, onion, garlic, carrots, celery, green peas, mushrooms, wine, vegetable stock, heavy cream, thyme, rosemary, salt, and pepper. Cover with the lid and cook for 6 hours on Low. Serve warm.

Roasted Chickpea & Chicken Stew

Serves: 6 | Total Time: 8 hours 15 minutes

2 sweet potatoes, peeled and cubed	
2 carrots, sliced	½ tsp cumin powder
6 chicken drumsticks	½ tsp chili powder
1 celery stalk, sliced	½ tsp dried oregano
1 onion, chopped	1 can fire-roasted tomatoes
4 garlic cloves, chopped	1 cup vegetable stock
1 can (15 oz) chickpeas	Salt and pepper to taste

Stir carrots, celery, onion, garlic, sweet potatoes, chickpeas, cumin, chili powder, oregano, tomatoes, chicken, vegetable stock, salt, and pepper in your Slow Cooker. Cover with the lid and cook for 8 hours on Low. When done, remove the lid and serve immediately.

Chicken Glazed with Soy Sauce

Serves: 6 | Total Time: 8 hours 15 minutes

½ cup tomato sauce	2 tbsp brown sugar
6 chicken thighs	1 tsp chili powder
½ cup soy sauce	

Mix the chicken, soy sauce, sugar, chili powder, and tomato sauce in your Slow Cooker. Cover with the lid and cook for 8 hours on Low. Serve warm.

Spring Mediterranean Beef Stew

Serves: 6 | Total Time: 7 hours 15 minutes

2 ripe tomatoes, diced	2 tbsp tomato paste
2 zucchinis, cubed	½ cup fresh orange juice
2 lb beef sirloin, cubed	1 tsp dried oregano
1 sweet onion, chopped	½ tsp dried basil
4 garlic cloves, minced	Salt and pepper to taste
4 red bell peppers, diced	1 bay leaf
1 cup tomato sauce	1 thyme sprig
2 tbsp canola oil	1 rosemary sprig

Warm canola oil in a pan over medium heat. Place the beef and cook for 5 minutes until golden on all sides. Transfer it to your Slow Cooker. Add in onion, garlic, tomatoes, zucchinis, bell peppers, tomato sauce, tomato paste, orange juice, oregano, basil, bay leaf, thyme, rosemary, salt, and pepper. Cover with the lid and cook for 8 hours on Low. Serve warm and enjoy!

Root Vegetable & Beef Stew

Serves: 6 | Total Time: 7 hours 15 minutes

1 ½ lb beef roast, cubed	1 ½ cups beef stock
1 onion, chopped	2 tbsp canola oil
1 celery stalk, sliced	2 tbsp all-purpose flour
2 carrots, sliced	1 bay leaf
2 parsnips, sliced	1 thyme sprig
4 potatoes, cubed	Salt and pepper to taste
1 cup diced tomatoes	

Rub beef roast with flour. Warm the canola oil in a pan over medium heat. Place the beef and cook until golden on all sides, 5 minutes. Transfer it to your Slow Cooker. Add in onion, celery, carrots, parsnips, potatoes, tomatoes, beef stock, bay leaf, thyme, salt, and pepper. Cover with the lid and cook for 7 hours on Low. Serve.

Tuscan Pork Stew

Serves: 6 | Total Time: 6 hours 15 minutes

1 lb porcini mushrooms, chopped	
2 lb pork tenderloin, cubed	10 pitted black olives, sliced
6 garlic cloves, minced	1 celery stalk, sliced
2 shallots, chopped	½ cup fire-roasted tomatoes
2 carrots, sliced	1 tbsp canola oil
1 parsnip, diced	2 bay leaves
½ cup vegetable stock	1 thyme sprig
½ cup red wine	Salt and pepper to taste
1 cup tomato sauce	

Warm the canola oil in a pan over medium heat. Put the pork and cook until golden on all sides. Transfer it to your Slow Cooker. Add in garlic, shallots, carrots, parsnip, mushrooms, vegetable stock, wine, tomato sauce, olives, celery, tomatoes, bay leaves, thyme, salt, and pepper. Cover with the lid and cook for 6 hours on Low. Serve.

Winter Pork Stew

Serves: 6 | Total Time: 6 hours 30 minutes

2 red apples, peeled and cubed
1 ½ lb potatoes, cubed
2 ripe tomatoes, cubed   1 cup chicken stock
2 lb pork shoulder, cubed   2 tbsp canola oil
4 garlic cloves, chopped   1 tsp dried rosemary
1 large onion, chopped   1 tsp dried thyme
1 lb butternut squash cubes   2 bay leaves
1 carrot, sliced   Salt and pepper to taste

Warm the canola oil in a pan over medium heat. Place the pork and cook until golden on all sides. Transfer it to your Slow Cooker. Put in garlic, onion, butternut squash, apples, carrots, potatoes, tomatoes, rosemary, thyme, bay leaves, chicken stock, salt, and pepper. Cover with the lid and cook for 6 hours on Low. Serve immediately.

Delicious Chicken Stew with Onions

Serves: 6 | Total Time: 6 hours 30 minutes

2 chicken breasts, cubed   ¼ cup dry white wine
4 bacon slices, chopped   1 can fire-roasted tomatoes
2 red bell peppers, sliced   2 tbsp canola oil
3 large onions, sliced   ½ tsp dried thyme
1 celery stalk, sliced   Salt and pepper to taste

Warm canola oil in a pan over medium heat. Put the bacon and cook until crispy. Add in onions and cook for 10 minutes until soft and begin to caramelize. Transfer everything to your Slow Cooker. Add in chicken, celery, bell peppers, wine, tomatoes, thyme, salt, and pepper. Cover with the lid and cook for 6 hours on Low. Serve.

Rich Chicken Stew with Sweet Potatoes

Serves: 4 | Total Time: 4 hours 15 minutes

1 chicken breast, cut into strips
2 large sweet potatoes, peeled and cubed
1 cup coconut milk   ½ cinnamon stick
½ cup chicken stock   ¼ tsp cumin seeds
1-star anise   1 rosemary sprig
2 tbsp olive oil   Salt and pepper to taste

In your Slow Cooker, put chicken, olive oil, sweet potatoes, coconut milk, chicken stock, star anise, cinnamon stick, cumin seeds, rosemary, salt, and pepper and mix. Cover with the lid and cook for 4 hours on Low. When done, remove the lid and serve warm.

Jerk Beef & Bean Stew

Serves: 6 | Total Time: 8 hours 30 minutes

2 sweet potatoes, peeled and cubed
1 can (15 oz) white beans   1 cup green peas
1 large zucchini, cubed   1 ½ cups beef stock
2 lb beef roast, cubed   ½ tsp chili powder
1 large onion, chopped   1 tsp dried oregano
2 carrots, sliced   1 tsp jerk seasoning
1 cup frozen corn   Salt and pepper to taste
1 cup diced tomatoes   Sour cream for serving

Mix the beef roast, onion, carrots, beans, zucchini, sweet potatoes, corn, tomatoes, green peas, chili powder, oregano, jerk seasoning, beef stock, salt, and pepper in your Slow Cooker. Cover with the lid and cook for 8 hours on Low. Drizzle with sour cream and serve.

Roasted Beef Stew with Croutons

Serves: 6 | Total Time: 5 hours 15 minutes

2 carrots, sliced   1 poblano pepper, chopped
8 oz bread croutons   1 cup beef stock
1 lb ground beef   1 cup chopped mushrooms
1 shallot, chopped   2 celery stalks, chopped
2 garlic cloves, chopped   2 tbsp canola oil
1 can fire-roasted tomatoes   Salt and pepper to taste

Warm canola oil in a pan over medium heat. Add the beef and cook for 2-3 minutes until golden on all sides. Transfer it to your Slow Cooker. Add in shallot, garlic, tomatoes, poblano pepper, stock, mushrooms, celery, carrots, salt, pepper, and scatter with bread croutons. Cover with the lid and cook for 5 hours on Low. Serve.

Cajun Sirloin & Potato Stew

Serves: 6 | Total Time: 6 hours 30 minutes

1 ½ lb potatoes, cubed   1 tsp garlic powder
1 ½ lb beef sirloin, cubed   ¼ tsp chili powder
4 bacon slices, chopped   1 tbsp apple cider vinegar
2 tbsp canola oil   Salt and pepper to taste
1 tbsp Cajun seasoning

Warm canola oil in a pan over medium heat. Put the beef and bacon and cook for 5 minutes until the meat begins to golden on all sides and the bacon is crispy. Transfer everything to your Slow Cooker. Add in cajun seasoning, garlic powder, chili powder, vinegar, potatoes, salt, and pepper. Cover and cook for 6 hours on Low. Serve.

Beef & Vegetable Stew

Serves: 6 | Total Time: 7 hours 15 minutes

2 red bell peppers, sliced   2 bay leaves
2 yellow bell peppers, sliced   1 thyme sprig
2 lb beef roast, cubed   2 tbsp canola oil
1 cup tomato sauce   1 tsp cayenne pepper
2 cups cherry tomatoes   Salt to taste

Warm canola oil in a pan over medium heat. Add the beef and cook for 5 minutes until golden on all sides. Transfer it to your Slow Cooker. Put in bell peppers, tomato sauce, tomatoes, bay leaves, thyme, cayenne pepper, and salt. Cover with the lid and cook for 7 hours on Low. When done, remove the lid and serve warm.

Pork & Mushroom Stew with Cheddar

Serves: 6 | Total Time: 5 hours 30 minutes

2 large onions, sliced   2 tbsp canola oil
1 ½ lb ground pork   ½ cup hot ketchup
1 carrot, grated   Salt and pepper to taste
1 cup chopped mushrooms   2 cups grated cheddar

Warm canola oil in a pan over medium heat. Sauté the onions for 10 minutes until it begins to caramelize. Transfer them to your Slow Cooker. Add in ground pork, carrot, mushrooms, ketchup, salt, and pepper. Scatter with cheddar cheese on top. Cover with the lid and cook for 5 hours on Low. Serve immediately.

Mushroom & Beef Stew

Serves: 6 | Total Time: 6 hours 15 minutes

2 tbsp canola oil	½ cup white wine
4 garlic cloves, chopped	2 tbsp all-purpose flour
2 cups chopped mushrooms	2 tbsp Dijon mustard
2 lb beef roast, cubed	1 rosemary sprig
1 cup beef stock	Salt and pepper to taste

Sprinkle beef roast with salt, pepper, and flour. Warm canola oil in a pan over medium heat. Add the beef and cook for 2-3 minutes until golden on all sides. Transfer it to your Slow Cooker. Add in garlic, mushrooms, beef stock, wine, mustard, rosemary, salt, and pepper. Cover with the lid and cook for 6 hours on Low. Serve warm.

Tomato Beef Roast Stew

Serves: 6 | Total Time: 5 hours 30 minutes

2 lb small new potatoes, washed and cleaned	
2 carrots, diced	1 cup beef stock
2 lb beef roast, cubed	1 cup tomato sauce
1 large onion, chopped	1 bay leaf
2 red bell peppers, diced	1 thyme sprig
1 celery stalk, chopped	Salt and pepper to taste
2 tbsp canola oil	

Warm canola oil in a pan over medium heat. Place the beef and cook for 2-3 minutes until golden on all sides. Transfer it to your Slow Cooker. Put in onion, bell peppers, carrots, celery, potatoes, beef stock, tomato sauce, bay leaf, thyme, salt, and pepper. Cover with the lid and cook for 5 hours on Low. Serve warm.

Bean & Pork Stew with Bacon

Serves: 6 | Total Time: 7 hours 15 minutes

1 ½ lb pork shoulder, cubed	1 tsp cumin seeds
2 sweet onions, chopped	½ tsp ground coriander
4 bacon slices, chopped	1 tsp white wine vinegar
½ lb dried black beans	2 cups chicken stock
4 garlic cloves, chopped	Salt and pepper to taste

Mix the beans, pork, onions, bacon, garlic, cumin seeds, coriander, wine vinegar, chicken stock, salt, and pepper in your Slow Cooker. Cover with the lid and cook for 7 hours on Low. Serve immediately.

Beef & Red Potato Stew

Serves: 6 | Total Time: 5 hours 15 minutes

4 garlic cloves, minced	1 sweet onion, sliced
2 lb red potatoes, cubed	1 leek, sliced
2 lb beef roast, cubed	1 tbsp soy sauce
1 celery stalk, sliced	1 tbsp brown sugar

1 tbsp dried rosemary	1 tsp Worcestershire sauce
1 cup diced tomatoes	1 bay leaf
1 cup beef stock	Salt and pepper to taste
1 tbsp Dijon mustard	

Combine beef roast, celery, onion, leek, garlic, potatoes, mustard, Worcestershire sauce, soy sauce, sugar, rosemary, tomatoes, beef stock, bay leaf, salt, and pepper in your Slow Cooker. Cover with the lid and cook for 5 hours on Low. Serve immediately.

Chili Pork Stew

Serves: 6 | Total Time: 5 hours 15 minutes

1 jar roasted bell pepper, drained and chopped	
2 lb pork tenderloin, cubed	1 cup tomato sauce
4 garlic cloves, chopped	2 tbsp canola oil
1 large onion, chopped	½ tsp red pepper flakes
1 cup chicken stock	Salt and pepper to taste

Warm canola oil in a pan over medium heat. Place the pork and cook for 2-3 minutes until golden on all sides. Transfer it to your Slow Cooker. Add in bell pepper, garlic, onion, red pepper flakes, chicken stock, tomato sauce, salt, and pepper. Cover with the lid and cook for 5 hours on Low. Serve warm.

Pork Sausage & Lentil Stew

Serves: 6 | Total Time: 6 hours 15 minutes

1 onion, finely chopped	1 cup diced tomatoes
2 carrots, diced	3 cups chicken stock
1 lb pork sausages, sliced	1 bay leaf
1 celery stalk, diced	1 chipotle pepper, chopped
2 garlic cloves, chopped	2 tbsp chopped parsley
1 cup red lentils	1 tbsp tomato paste
1 cup brown lentils	Salt and pepper to taste

In your Slow Cooker, add sausages, onion, carrots, celery, garlic, lentils, tomatoes, tomato paste, chicken stock, bay leaf, chipotle pepper, salt, and pepper, and stir. Cover with the lid and cook for 6 hours on Low. When done, remove the lid and sprinkle with parsley to serve.

Meat Lover Stew

Serves: 6 | Total Time: 6 hours 30 minutes

2 lb potatoes, cubed	2 red bell peppers, diced
2 ripe tomatoes, diced	1 tbsp tomato paste
6 bacon slices, chopped	2 cups chicken stock
2 lb pork shoulder, cubed	2 bay leaves
1 chorizo, sliced	1 tbsp canola oil
1 onion, finely chopped	¼ tsp cayenne pepper
2 garlic cloves, chopped	Salt and pepper to taste

Warm canola oil in a pan over medium heat. Place the bacon and cook until crispy. Add in pork and cook for 2-3 minutes until golden on all sides. Transfer everything to your Slow Cooker. Add in chorizo, onion, garlic, bell peppers, tomatoes, potatoes, tomato paste, chicken stock, bay leaves, cayenne pepper, salt, and pepper. Cover with the lid and cook for 6 hours on Low. Serve immediately.

Potato & Bacon Stew

Serves: 6 | Total Time: 6 hours 30 minutes

2 sweet potatoes, peeled and cubed
1 lb Yukon gold potatoes, peeled and cubed

1 cup diced bacon	½ tsp cumin seeds
1 large onion, chopped	½ tsp chili powder
2 carrots, diced	1 cup diced tomatoes
1 celery stalk, diced	Salt and pepper to taste
2 red bell peppers, diced	2 cups chicken stock

Warm a pan over medium heat, place bacon and cook until crispy. Transfer it to your Slow Cooker. Put in onion, carrots, celery, bell peppers, sweet potatoes, potatoes, cumin seeds, chili powder, tomatoes, chicken stock, salt, and pepper. Cover with the lid and cook for 6 hours on Low. Serve warm.

Chipotle Pork & Bean Stew

Serves: 6 | Total Time: 10 hours 15 minutes

2 carrots, sliced	1 celery stalk, sliced
1 onion, chopped	1 can fire-roasted tomatoes
1 lb dried navy beans, rinsed	2 chipotle peppers, chopped
1 cup red beans, soaked	1 cup chicken stock
2 lb pork shoulder, cubed	Salt and pepper to taste
½ cup diced bacon	

Mix the pork, bacon, celery, carrots, onion, beans, tomatoes, chipotle peppers, chicken stock, salt, and pepper in your Slow Cooker. Cover with the lid and cook for 10 hours on Low. Serve immediately.

Pork & Chorizo Stew

Serves: 6 | Total Time: 3 hours 15 minutes

1 chorizo link, chopped	½ cup wild rice
1 can (15 oz) red beans	1 tbsp canola oil
1 red onion, chopped	1 ½ cups chicken stock
1 lb ground pork	Salt and pepper to taste
1 cup green peas	1 lemon for serving
½ cup frozen sweet corn	

Warm canola oil in a pan over medium heat. Place the ground pork and cook for 10 minutes, stirring often. Transfer it to your Slow Cooker. Add the chorizo, beans, onion, green peas, corn, rice, stock, salt, and pepper. Cover with the lid and cook for 3 hours on High. When done, remove the lid and serve drizzled with lemon juice.

Pork Stew with Red Cole Slaw

Serves: 6 | Total Time: 4 hours 15 minutes

1 head red cabbage, shredded

1 large onion, chopped	1 tbsp maple syrup
4 garlic cloves, minced	1 tsp chili powder
1 ½ lb pork roast, cubed	¼ cup apple cider vinegar
2 tbsp canola oil	Salt and pepper to taste

Stir cabbage, pork roast, canola oil, onion, garlic, maple syrup, chili powder, apple cider vinegar, salt, and pepper in your Slow Cooker. Cook for 4 hours on Low. Serve.

Pork & White Bean Stew

Serves: 4 | Total Time: 4 hours 15 minutes

1 shallot, chopped	1 cup diced tomatoes
1 garlic clove, chopped	2 thyme sprigs
1 lb pork tenderloin, cubed	2 tbsp canola oil
1 can (15 oz) white beans	1 cup chicken stock
1 celery stalk, sliced	Salt and pepper to taste

Warm canola oil in a pan over medium heat. Place the pork and cook for 2-3 minutes until golden brown on all sides. Transfer it to your Slow Cooker. Put in beans, celery, shallot, garlic, tomatoes, thyme, chicken stock, salt, and pepper. Cover with the lid and cook for 4 hours on Low. When done, remove the lid and serve warm.

Tomato Veggie Stew

Serves: 6 | Total Time: 6 hours 30 minutes

½ head cauliflower, cut into florets

1 carrot, sliced	1 zucchini, cubed
1 sweet onion, chopped	1 cup cherry tomatoes, halved
4 garlic cloves, chopped	½ cup tomato sauce
2 red bell peppers, diced	2 cups vegetable stock
2 tbsp olive oil	1 bay leaf
1 parsnip, cubed	Salt and pepper to taste

Warm the olive oil in a pan over medium heat. Place onion and garlic and cook for 2 minutes until softened. Add everything to your Slow Cooker. Add in cauliflower, bell peppers, carrot, parsnip, zucchini, cherry tomatoes, tomato sauce, vegetable stock, bay leaf, salt, and pepper. Cover with the lid and cook for 6 hours on Low. Serve.

Simple Zucchini Stew

Serves: 4 | Total Time: 1 hour 45 minutes

1 shallot, chopped	1 bay leaf
1 garlic clove, chopped	½ cup Vegetable stock
2 large zucchinis, cubed	1 tbsp olive oil
2 ripe tomatoes, diced	Salt and pepper to taste

Mix the olive oil, shallot, garlic, zucchinis, tomatoes, bay leaf, vegetable stock, salt, and pepper in your Slow Cooker. Cover with the lid and cook for 1 ½ hours on High. When done, remove the lid and serve warm.

Roasted Tomato Chili

Serves: 6 | Total Time: 7 hours 30 minutes

2 tomatoes, diced	2 tbsp tomato paste
1 carrot, diced	1 cup black beans, soaked
2 red onions, chopped	2 cups vegetable stock
2 garlic cloves, chopped	1 cup water
1 red bell pepper, diced	1 bay leaf
1 celery stalk, diced	1 thyme sprig
1 cup fire-roasted tomatoes	Salt and pepper to taste

Mix the onions, garlic, bell pepper, carrot, celery, tomatoes, roasted tomatoes, tomato paste, black beans, vegetable stock, water, bay leaf, thyme, salt, and pepper in your Slow Cooker. Cook for 7 hours on Low. Serve.

Two-Beans Stew

Serves: 6 | Total Time: 3 hours 15 minutes

1 can (15 oz) black beans
1 cup canned corn, drained
1 shallot, chopped
1 garlic clove, chopped
1 green onion, chopped
½ cup pearl barley

1 ½ cups vegetable stock
½ cup diced tomatoes
¼ tsp chili powder
¼ tsp cumin powder
2 tbsp chopped cilantro
Salt and pepper to taste

Stir shallot, garlic, black beans, corn, pearl barley, vegetable stock, tomatoes, chili powder, cumin, salt, and pepper in your Slow Cooker. Cover with the lid and cook for 3 hours on High. When done, remove the lid and mix in cilantro and green onion before serving.

Curried Sweet Potato Chili

Serves: 6 | Total Time: 5 hours 30 minutes

1 ½ lb sweet potatoes, peeled and cubed
1 can (15 oz) black beans
2 shallots, chopped
1 garlic clove, chopped
½ tsp curry powder
1 carrot, diced

½ tsp chili powder
2 tbsp olive oil
2 cups vegetable stock
2 tbsp tomato paste
Salt and pepper to taste

Warm the olive oil in a pan over medium heat. Place the shallots and garlic and cook for 2 minutes. Add everything to your Slow Cooker. Put in curry powder, carrot, sweet potatoes, black beans, chili powder, vegetable stock, tomato paste, salt, and pepper. Cover with the lid and cook for 5 hours on Low. Serve right away.

Sweet Black Bean Chili

Serves: 6 | Total Time: 8 hours 30 minutes

1 red bell pepper, diced
1 large carrot, diced
2 tbsp olive oil
2 red onions, chopped
4 garlic cloves, chopped
½ tsp chili powder
½ tsp cumin powder

1 tbsp cocoa powder
2 tbsp tomato paste
½ cinnamon stick
1 bay leaf
2 cups dried black beans
2 cups vegetable stock
Salt and pepper to taste

Warm the olive oil in a pan over medium heat. Add the onions and garlic and cook for 5 minutes until softened. Add everything to your Slow Cooker. Put in chili powder, cumin, bell pepper, carrot, cocoa powder, tomato paste, cinnamon stick, bay leaf, black beans, vegetable stock, 3 cups of water, salt, and pepper. Cover with the lid and cook for 8 hours on Low. Serve warm.

Butternut Squash Chili

Serves: 6 | Total Time: 6 hours 15 minutes

1 large onion, chopped
2 garlic cloves, chopped
1 lb butternut squash cubes
2 cans (15-oz) pinto beans,
1 cup canned corn, drained
2 tbsp tomato paste
½ cup tomato sauce

1 cup vegetable stock
½ tsp chili powder
1 bay leaf
1 thyme sprig
1 lime, sliced
Salt and pepper to taste

Stir butternut squash, beans, corn, onion, garlic, tomato paste, tomato sauce, vegetable stock, chili powder, bay leaf, thyme, salt, and pepper in your Slow Cooker. Cover with the lid and cook for 6 hours on Low. When done, remove the lid and top with lime slices to serve.

Tuscan Vegetarian Stew

Serves: 6 | Total Time: 6 hours 30 minutes

5 roasted red bell peppers, chopped
1 large onion, chopped
1 eggplant, peeled, cubed
4 garlic cloves, minced
2 zucchinis, cubed
2 cups okra
1 carrot, sliced
1 tomato, diced
1 cup tomato sauce

2 tbsp olive oil
1 cup vegetable stock
¼ cup golden raisins
½ tsp cumin powder
½ tsp turmeric powder
1 pinch red pepper flakes
½ tsp dried basil
Salt and pepper to taste

Warm the olive oil in a pan over medium heat. Add onion and garlic and cook for 2 minutes until softened. Add everything to your Slow Cooker. Add in eggplants, bell peppers, zucchinis, okra, carrot, tomato, tomato sauce, vegetable stock, raisins, cumin, turmeric, red pepper flakes, basil, salt, and pepper. Cover with the lid and cook for 6 hours on Low. Serve immediately.

Quinoa Chili

Serves: 6 | Total Time: 6 hours 30 minutes

1 can (15 oz) black beans
2 poblano peppers, diced
1 shallot, chopped
2 garlic cloves, chopped
½ cup quinoa, rinsed
2 tbsp olive oil

2 cups vegetable stock
1 cup diced tomatoes
1 tbsp tomato paste
¼ tsp cumin powder
Salt and pepper to taste
2 tbsp chopped cilantro

Warm the olive oil in a pan over medium heat. Sauté the shallot and garlic for 2 minutes until softened. Add everything to your Slow Cooker. Put in beans, poblano peppers, quinoa, vegetable stock, tomatoes, tomato paste, cumin, salt, and pepper. Cover with the lid and cook for 6 hours on Low. Top with cilantro to serve.

Butternut Squash & Parsnip Chili

Serves: 6 | Total Time: 4 hours 30 minutes

1 lb butternut squash cubes
1 green apple, peeled, diced
1 sweet onion, chopped
3 parsnips, diced
1 cup diced tomatoes
2 tbsp olive oil
½ tsp cumin powder

½ tsp ground coriander
½ tsp fennel seeds
1 pinch chili powder
1 thyme sprig
Salt and pepper to taste
Plain yogurt for serving

Warm the olive oil in a pan over medium heat. Place onion and parsnip and cook for 5 minutes until softened. Add everything to your Slow Cooker. Put in butternut squash, apple, tomatoes, cumin, coriander, fennel seeds, chili powder, thyme, salt, and pepper. Cover with the lid and cook for 4 hours on Low. Top with yogurt to serve.

Indian Lentil Stew

Serves: 6 | Total Time: 2 hours 15 minutes

1 large onion, chopped
2 garlic cloves, chopped
1 carrot, diced
1 cup red lentils, rinsed
½ cup green lentils, rinsed
1 cup diced tomatoes
1 celery stalk, diced
1 jalapeno, chopped
¼ tsp cumin powder
¼ tsp garam masala
2 cups vegetable stock
Salt and pepper to taste

Stir lentils, tomatoes, onion, garlic, carrot, celery, jalapeño, cumin, garam masala, vegetable stock, salt, and pepper in your Slow Cooker. Cover with the lid and cook for 2 hours on High. Serve immediately.

Black Bean & Lentil Stew with Chipotle

Serves: 6 | Total Time: 6 hours 30 minutes

2/3 cup brown lentils
2 shallots, chopped
4 garlic cloves, chopped
2 carrots, diced
1 chipotle pepper, chopped
1 can (15 oz) black beans
2 tbsp olive oil
1 cup diced tomatoes
2 cups vegetable stock
¼ tsp chili powder
¼ tsp cumin powder
Salt and pepper to taste

Warm the olive oil in a pan over medium heat. Sauté the shallots and garlic for 2 minutes until softened. Add everything to your Slow Cooker. Add in carrots, chipotle pepper, beans, lentils, tomatoes, stock, chili powder, cumin, salt, and pepper. Cook for 6 hours on Low. Serve.

Amazing Lentil Stew with Cauliflower

Serves: 6 | Total Time: 6 hours 15 minutes

1 small head cauliflower, cut into florets
½ cup red lentils, rinsed
1 cup diced tomatoes
1 shallot, chopped
2 garlic cloves, chopped
1 celery stalk, sliced
1 carrot, sliced
2 cups vegetable stock
1 bay leaf
¼ tsp cumin powder
1 pinch cayenne pepper
Salt and pepper to taste

Mix the shallot, garlic, celery, carrot, cauliflower, lentils, vegetable stock, tomatoes, bay leaf, cumin, cayenne pepper, salt, and pepper in your Slow Cooker. Cover with the lid and cook for 6 hours on Low. When done, remove the lid and serve immediately.

Potato Stew with Leeks

Serves: 6 | Total Time: 4 hours 30 minutes

2 carrots, diced
1 ½ lb potatoes, cubed
2 tbsp olive oil
2 leeks, sliced
2 celery stalks, sliced
2 tbsp tomato paste
½ cup diced tomatoes
1 bay leaf
1 thyme sprig
Salt and pepper to taste

Warm the olive oil in a pan over medium heat. Put the leeks and cook for 5 minutes until softened. Add them to your Slow Cooker. Add in celery, carrots, potatoes, tomato paste, tomatoes, bay leaf, thyme, salt, and pepper. Cover with the lid and cook for 4 hours on Low. Serve.

Bombay Lentil Stew

Serves: 6 | Total Time: 4 hours 15 minutes

1 large potato, cubed
1 shallot, chopped
3 garlic cloves, chopped
1 cup red lentils, rinsed
½ cup brown lentils, rinsed
1 cup tomato sauce
2 cups vegetable stock
½ cup coconut milk
½ tsp cumin powder
Salt and pepper to taste

Combine the lentils, tomato sauce, vegetable stock, potato, shallot, garlic, cumin, salt, pepper, and coconut milk in your Slow Cooker. Cover with the lid and cook for 4 hours on Low. Serve immediately.

Rice & Green Peas Stew with Olives

Serves: 6 | Total Time: 6 hours 15 minutes

2 garlic cloves, chopped
1 shallot, chopped
3 cups vegetable stock
½ cup green peas
1 zucchini, cubed
½ cup Kalamata olives, sliced
2 tbsp olive oil
½ tsp dried oregano
½ tsp dried basil
½ tsp dried marjoram
1 ½ cups white rice
½ lemon, juiced
2 tbsp chopped parsley
Salt and pepper to taste

Warm the olive oil in a pan over medium heat. Put the garlic and shallot and cook for 2 minutes. Add everything to your Slow Cooker. Put in oregano, basil, marjoram, rice, stock, green peas, zucchini, kalamata olives, salt, and pepper. Cover with the lid and cook for 6 hours on Low. Scatter with lemon juice and parsley and serve.

Basil Bell Pepper Chili

Serves: 6 | Total Time: 6 hours 15 minutes

4 roasted red bell peppers, chopped
2 ripe tomatoes, diced
1 can (15 oz) cannellini beans
2 garlic cloves, chopped
1 shallot, chopped
½ cup tomato sauce
1 cup vegetable stock
½ tsp dried basil
1 pinch cumin powder
2 tbsp chopped parsley
Salt and pepper to taste

Stir beans, bell peppers, garlic, shallot, tomatoes, tomato sauce, vegetable stock, basil, cumin, salt, and pepper in your Slow Cooker. Cover with the lid and cook for 6 hours on Low. Top with parsley and serve.

Farmer Stew

Serves: 6 | Total Time: 7 hours 30 minutes

2 cups sliced mushrooms
2 cups chopped okra
1 cup frozen green peas
1 onion, chopped
2 garlic cloves, chopped
½ tsp smoked paprika
1 cup canned corn, drained
1 zucchini, cubed
2 tbsp tomato paste
1 cup diced tomatoes
1 can (15 oz) black beans
½ tsp dried oregano
Salt and pepper to taste

Mix the onion, garlic, paprika, corn, mushrooms, okra, green peas, zucchini, tomato paste, tomatoes, beans, oregano, salt, and pepper in your Slow Cooker. Cover with the lid and cook for 7 hours on Low. Serve warm.

Mushroom Chili with Lentils

Serves: 6 | Total Time: 6 hours 15 minutes

2 garlic cloves, chopped	1 cup diced tomatoes
1 lb mushrooms, sliced	½ cup dried red lentils
1 shallot, chopped	½ cup pearl barley, rinsed
1 celery stalk, sliced	2 cups vegetable stock
1 bay leaf	Salt and pepper to taste

Stir mushrooms, shallot, garlic, celery, lentils, pearl barley, vegetable stock, bay leaf, tomatoes, salt, and pepper in your Slow Cooker. Cover with the lid and cook for 6 hours on Low. Serve warm.

Divine Vegan Chili

Serves: 8 | Total Time: 6 hours 30 minutes

1 can (15 oz) chickpeas	2 red bell peppers, diced
1 can (15 oz) black beans	2 tbsp olive oil
2 shallots, chopped	1 celery stalk, diced
4 garlic cloves, chopped	1 tsp chili powder
2 cups cauliflower florets	1 cup tomato sauce
1 zucchini, cubed	2 cups vegetable stock
1 can fire-roasted tomatoes	Salt and pepper to taste
1 cup canned corn, drained	Sour cream for serving

Warm the olive oil in a pan over medium heat. Place shallots and garlic and cook for 2-3 minutes until softened. Add everything to your Slow Cooker. Put in cauliflower, zucchini, chickpeas, beans, tomatoes, corn, bell peppers, celery, chili powder, tomato sauce, vegetable stock, salt, and pepper. Cover with the lid and cook for 6 hours on Low. Serve topped with sour cream.

Chickpea, Bell Pepper & Zucchini Stew

Serves: 6 | Total Time: 6 hours 30 minutes

2 ripe tomatoes, diced	1 zucchini, sliced
1 ½ cups tomato sauce	1 ½ cups vegetable stock
1 ½ cups chickpeas, rinsed	1 pinch chili powder
1 large onion, chopped	½ tsp cumin powder
2 red bell peppers, diced	Salt and pepper to taste

Mix the chickpeas, onion, bell peppers, zucchini, tomatoes, tomato sauce, vegetable stock, chili powder, cumin, salt, and pepper in your Slow Cooker. Cover with the lid and cook for 6 hours on Low. Serve warm.

Chili Butternut Squash & Apple Stew

Serves: 6 | Total Time: 6 hours 15 minutes

1 carrot, sliced	1 celery stalk, sliced
2 ripe tomatoes, diced	¼ tsp cumin powder
1 lb butternut squash cubes	1 pinch chili powder
1 shallot, chopped	½ cup tomato sauce
2 garlic cloves, chopped	½ cup vegetable stock
2 apples, peeled and diced	Salt and pepper to taste

Stir butternut squash, shallot, garlic, apples, celery, carrot, tomatoes, cumin, tomato sauce, chili powder, vegetable stock, salt, and pepper in your Slow Cooker. Cover with the lid and cook for 6 hours on Low. Serve warm.

Vegetable Stew

Serves: 8 | Total Time: 7 hours 30 minutes

2 large onions, sliced	2 tbsp olive oil
1 zucchini, sliced	1 ½ cups tomato sauce
2 carrots, sliced	¼ tsp garlic powder
1 eggplant, peeled and sliced	½ tsp dried oregano
2 potatoes, peeled, sliced	½ tsp dried marjoram
4 ripe tomatoes, sliced	Salt and pepper to taste
2 cups canned chickpeas	

Rub olive oil in your Slow Cooker and put onions, zucchini, carrots, eggplant, potatoes, chickpeas, and tomatoes. In a bowl, combine tomato sauce, garlic powder, oregano, marjoram, salt, and pepper and pour it over the vegetables. Cook for 7 hours on Low. Serve.

Spicy Sweet Potato Chili with Oats

Serves: 6 | Total Time: 6 hours 15 minutes

2 large sweet potatoes, peeled and cubed	
1 can pinto beans, drained	½ tsp dried oregano
1 shallot, chopped	¼ cup oat groats
2 garlic cloves, chopped	2 cups vegetable stock
1 tbsp olive oil	Salt and pepper to taste
¼ tsp chipotle powder	

Mix the sweet potatoes, olive oil, beans, shallot, garlic, chipotle powder, oregano, oats, vegetable stock, salt, and pepper in your Slow Cooker. Cover with the lid and cook for 6 hours on Low. Serve immediately.

Sweet Potato & Peanut Butter Stew

Serves: 6 | Total Time: 6 hours 30 minutes

1 ½ lb sweet potatoes, peeled and cubed	
1 can diced tomatoes	1 tsp grated ginger
1 onion, chopped	1 pinch chili powder
2 garlic cloves, chopped	4 cups fresh spinach
1 cup vegetable stock	2 tbsp chopped peanuts
2 tbsp peanut butter	Salt and pepper to taste

Stir onion, garlic, sweet potatoes, tomatoes, vegetable stock, peanut butter, ginger, chili powder, spinach, salt, and pepper in your Slow Cooker. Cover with the lid and cook for 6 hours on Low. Top with peanuts and serve.

Creamy Corn Chili

Serves: 6 | Total Time: 6 hours 15 minutes

2 jalapeno peppers, minced	¼ cup cold butter, cubed
1 can fire-roasted tomatoes	¼ tsp cumin powder
1 can (15 oz) black beans	½ tsp baking powder
1 can (10 oz) sweet corn	½ cup chilled buttermilk
½ cup all-purpose flour	Salt and pepper to taste

Mix the beans, corn, jalapeño peppers, tomatoes, salt, and pepper in your Slow Cooker.

In a bowl, combine flour, butter, cumin, and baking powder. Pour in buttermilk and, using a fork, whisk quickly. Top the veggies with this batter. Cover with the lid and cook for 6 hours on Low. Serve right away.

Bell Pepper & Quinoa Chili with Chipotle

Serves: 6 | Total Time: 8 hours 15 minutes

3 garlic cloves, chopped
2 red bell peppers, diced
1 lb black beans, soaked
2/3 cup quinoa, rinsed
2 shallots, chopped
½ tsp cumin powder
½ tsp coriander powder
½ tsp mustard seeds
1 cinnamon stick
1 dried chipotle pepper
2 cups vegetable stock
5 cups water
1 cup diced tomatoes
Salt and pepper to taste

Mix the beans, quinoa, shallots, garlic, bell peppers, cumin, coriander, mustard seeds, cinnamon stick, chipotle pepper, vegetable stock, water, tomatoes, salt, and pepper in your Slow Cooker. Cover with the lid and cook for 8 hours on Low. Discard the cinnamon stick and chipotle pepper and serve right away.

Apple & Butternut Squash Chili with Rice

Serves: 6 | Total Time: 6 hours 15 minutes

1 can (15 oz) black beans
1 lb butternut squash cubes
1 shallot, chopped
1 celery stalk, sliced
2 carrots, diced
1 red apple, cored and diced
4 garlic cloves, chopped
1 tsp chili powder
½ tsp cumin powder
2 cups vegetable stock
1 cup coconut milk
2 tbsp tomato paste
1 bay leaf
Salt and pepper to taste
3 cups cooked rice
2 tbsp chopped cilantro

Stir shallot, celery, carrots, apple, garlic, beans, butternut squash, chili powder, cumin, vegetable stock, coconut milk, tomato paste, bay leaf, salt, and pepper in your Slow Cooker. Cover with the lid and cook for 6 hours on Low. Serve over cooked rice and sprinkle with cilantro.

Bulgur & Mushroom Chili

Serves: 6 | Total Time: 8 hours 15 minutes

1 cup diced tomatoes
1 can (15 oz) black beans
1 can (15 oz) kidney beans
1 cup bulgur wheat
1 large onion, chopped
2 cups sliced mushrooms
1 red bell pepper, diced
2 garlic cloves, chopped
2 cups vegetable stock
1 tbsp brown sugar
1 tsp apple cider vinegar
1 tsp chili powder
Salt and pepper to taste
1 thyme sprig

Mix the bulgur, onion, mushrooms, bell pepper, garlic, vegetable stock, tomatoes, beans, sugar, vinegar, chili powder, thyme, salt, and pepper in your Slow Cooker. Cover with the lid and cook for 8 hours on Low. Serve.

Creamy Lentil Stew with Spinach

Serves: 6 | Total Time: 6 hours 15 minutes

1 cup red lentils, rinsed
1 cup diced tomatoes
1 shallot, chopped
4 garlic cloves, chopped
2 tbsp tomato paste
½ tsp cumin powder
½ tsp coriander seeds
½ tsp turmeric powder
¼ tsp chili powder
¼ tsp garam masala
1 ½ cups vegetable stock
½ cup coconut cream
1 thyme sprig
Salt and pepper to taste

Mix the shallot, garlic, tomato paste, cumin, coriander seeds, turmeric, chili powder, garam masala, lentils, tomatoes, vegetable stock, coconut cream, thyme, salt, and pepper in your Slow Cooker. Cover with the lid and cook for 6 hours on Low. Serve warm.

Hot Cauliflower Chili

Serves: 6 | Total Time: 6 hours 15 minutes

1 head cauliflower, cut into florets
1 can (15 oz) cannellini beans
1 can fire-roasted green chilies, chopped
1 onion, chopped
1 can diced tomatoes
1 tsp hot sauce
½ cup tomato sauce
1 tsp cumin powder
Salt and pepper to taste
2 tbsp grated cheddar

Stir cauliflower, onion, tomatoes, green chilies, hot sauce, tomato sauce, cumin, beans, salt, and pepper in your Slow Cooker. Cover with the lid and cook for 6 hours on Low. Serve topped with grated cheddar.

Coconut Butternut Squash Stew

Serves: 6 | Total Time: 6 hours 30 minutes

2 ripe tomatoes, cubed
1 lb butternut squash cubes
2 shallots, sliced
2 garlic cloves, chopped
1 celery stalk, sliced
1 carrot, sliced
1 cup tomato sauce
1 cup coconut milk
2 tbsp olive oil
¼ tsp fennel seeds
½ tsp cumin seeds
1 thyme sprig
Salt and pepper to taste

Warm the olive oil in a pan over medium heat. Place shallots and garlic and cook for 2 minutes until softened. Add everything to your Slow Cooker. Add in celery, carrot, tomatoes, butternut squash, tomato sauce, coconut milk, fennel seeds, cumin seeds, thyme, salt, and pepper. Cover and cook for 6 hours on Low. Serve.

Spinach & Black-Eyed Pea Stew

Serves: 6 | Total Time: 8 hours 15 minutes

2 cups black-eyed peas, soaked
1 cup diced tomato
2 cups baby spinach
2 carrots, diced
2 red bell peppers, diced
½ tsp grated ginger
2 cups water
2 cups vegetable stock
2 garlic cloves, minced
2 tbsp tomato paste
Salt and pepper to taste

In your Slow Cooker, put black-eyed peas, carrots, bell peppers, ginger, water, vegetable stock, garlic, tomato paste, tomato, spinach, salt, and pepper and stir. Cover with the lid and cook for 8 hours on Low. Serve.

Portobello & Sweet Potato Stew

Serves: 6 | Total Time: 6 hours 30 minutes

2 sweet potatoes, peeled and cubed
4 Portobello mushrooms, sliced
1 large onion, chopped
2 garlic cloves, minced
2 large carrots, sliced
2 parsnips, diced
2 red potatoes, cubed
1 cup diced tomatoes

2 tbsp olive oil	1 bay leaf
½ cup red wine	1 thyme sprig
1 ½ cups vegetable stock	Salt and pepper to taste

Warm the olive oil in a pan over medium heat. Sauté the onion and garlic for 2 minutes until softened. Add everything to your Slow Cooker. Add in carrots, parsnips, sweet potatoes, potatoes, tomatoes, mushrooms, wine, vegetable stock, bay leaf, thyme, salt, and pepper. Cover with the lid and cook for 6 hours on Low. Serve.

Leek & Fave Bean Stew

Serves: 6 | Total Time: 7 hours 15 minutes

1 carrot, sliced	1 celery stalk, sliced
1 can diced tomatoes	1 bay leaf
1 lb frozen fava beans	1 cup vegetable stock
2 leeks, sliced	1 thyme sprig
1 shallot, chopped	¼ tsp cumin seeds
1 garlic clove, chopped	Salt and pepper to taste

Mix the fava beans, leeks, shallot, garlic, celery, carrot, tomatoes, bay leaf, vegetable stock, thyme, cumin seeds, salt, and pepper in your Slow Cooker. Cover with the lid and cook for 7 hours on Low. Serve warm.

Roasted Eggplant & Pepper Stew with Tofu

Serves: 6 | Total Time: 6 hours 30 minutes

1 eggplant, peeled and cubed	2 tbsp olive oil
2 red bell peppers, diced	1 tbsp tomato paste
1 cup fire-roasted tomatoes	1 ¼ cups vegetable stock
6 oz firm tofu, cubed	1 thyme sprig
1 sweet onion, chopped	Salt and pepper to taste
3 garlic cloves, chopped	

Warm the olive oil in a pan over medium heat. Add the tofu and cook until golden brown on all sides. Transfer it to your Slow Cooker. Add in onion, garlic, eggplant, bell peppers, tomatoes, tomato paste, vegetable stock, thyme, salt, and pepper. Cook for 6 hours on Low. Serve.

Zesty Chili

Serves: 6 | Total Time: 6 hours 45 minutes

2 large onions, chopped	1 orange, zested and juiced
2 garlic cloves, minced	1 tsp lemon zest
1 red bell pepper, diced	1 tsp cumin seeds
1 red chili, chopped	1 tsp dried oregano
1 cup black beans, soaked	1 tsp dried thyme
2 cups vegetable stock	Salt and pepper to taste

In your Slow Cooker, put beans, vegetable stock, orange zest, orange juice, lemon zest, onions, garlic, bell pepper, red chili, cumin seeds, oregano, thyme, salt, and pepper and stir. Cook for 6 ½ hours on Low. Serve warm.

Savory Red Lentil Stew

Serves: 6 | Total Time: 3 hours 15 minutes

1 cup red lentils	2 garlic cloves, chopped
1 large onion, chopped	½ tsp cumin powder

¼ tsp chili powder	2 cups vegetable stock
½ tsp grated ginger	2 tbsp olive oil
½ tsp coriander seeds	½ cup tomato sauce
½ tsp turmeric powder	Salt and pepper to taste

Warm the olive oil in a pan over medium heat. Stir-fry the onion and garlic for 2 minutes until softened. Add in cumin, chili powder, ginger, coriander seeds, and turmeric and cook for 30 seconds until release flavor. Add everything to your Slow Cooker. Add in lentils, vegetable stock, tomato sauce, salt, and pepper. Cover with the lid and cook for 3 hours on High. Serve warm.

Authentic Indian Lentil Stew

Serves: 6 | Total Time: 4 hours 15 minutes

1 cup diced tomatoes	½ tsp garam masala
1 cup red lentils	1 tsp brown sugar
6 garlic cloves, chopped	2 tbsp tomato paste
1 onion, chopped	1 bay leaf
1 cup vegetable stock	1 thyme sprig
1 cup coconut milk	Salt and pepper to taste
½ tsp grated ginger	

In your Slow Cooker, add lentils, garlic, onion, ginger, garam masala, sugar, tomato paste, vegetable stock, tomatoes, coconut milk, bay leaf, thyme, salt, and pepper and stir. Cover with the lid and cook for 4 hours on Low. When done, remove the lid and serve.

Jerk Sweet Potato & Red Bean Chili

Serves: 6 | Total Time: 8 hours 15 minutes

2 large sweet potatoes, peeled and cubed	
1 cup diced tomatoes	¼ tsp cayenne pepper
2 cups vegetable stock	½ tsp dried thyme
1 cup red beans, soaked	1 tsp jerk seasoning
1 large red onion, chopped	2 tbsp tomato paste
3 garlic cloves, minced	Salt and pepper to taste
½ tsp cumin powder	2 tbsp chopped cilantro

In your Slow Cooker, mix beans, onion, garlic, and sweet potatoes. Sprinkle with cumin, cayenne pepper, thyme, jerk seasoning, tomato paste, tomatoes, vegetable stock, salt, and pepper and toss to combine. Cover with the lid and cook for 8 hours on Low. Stir in cilantro and serve.

Butternut Squash Stew with Tofu

Serves: 6 | Total Time: 6 hours 30 minutes

8 oz firm tofu, cubed	½ tsp grated ginger
2 carrots, sliced	1 lemongrass stalk, crushed
1 lb butternut squash cubes	¼ tsp cumin seeds
2 tbsp olive oil	½ tsp turmeric powder
1 pinch chili powder	Salt and pepper to taste

Warm the olive oil in a pan over medium heat. Add the tofu and cook until golden and crispy on all sides. Transfer it to your Slow Cooker. Put in carrots, butternut squash, chili powder, ginger, lemongrass, cumin seeds, turmeric, salt, and pepper. Cover and cook for 6 hours on Low. When done, remove the lid and serve warm.

Collard Green Chili

Serves: 6 | Total Time: 6 hours 15 minutes

1 bunch collard greens, torn
2 garlic cloves, chopped
1 cup black beans, soaked
½ cup tomato sauce

2 cups vegetable stock
1 tbsp olive oil
Salt and pepper to taste
1 tbsp chopped cilantro

Mix the olive oil, garlic, beans, tomato sauce, vegetable stock, collard greens, salt, and pepper in your Slow Cooker. Cover with the lid and cook for 6 hours on Low. Serve warm topped with cilantro.

Quinoa & Lentil Stew

Serves: 6 | Total Time: 7 hours 15 minutes

1 large sweet potato, peeled and cubed
1 turnip, peeled and cubed
2 shallots, chopped
2 garlic cloves, chopped
½ cup red quinoa, rinsed

½ cup red lentils, rinsed
3 cups vegetable stock
½ tsp turmeric powder
½ tsp garam masala
2 tbsp olive oil
Salt and pepper to taste

Mix the olive oil, shallots, garlic, quinoa, lentils, sweet potato, turnip, turmeric, garam masala, vegetable stock, salt, and pepper in your Slow Cooker. Cover with the lid and cook for 7 hours on Low. Serve warm.

Citrus Portobello Chili

Serves: 6 | Total Time: 8 hours 30 minutes

4 Portobello mushrooms, sliced
1 cup diced tomatoes
4 garlic cloves, chopped
½ lb dried black beans
½ tsp mustard seeds
½ tsp chili powder
¼ tsp cardamom powder
2 tbsp olive oil

2 shallots, chopped
2 cups vegetable stock
2 cups water
1 bay leaf
1 thyme sprig
Salt and pepper to taste
1 lime for serving

Warm the olive oil in a pan over medium heat. Add shallots and garlic and cook for 2 minutes until softened. Add everything to your Slow Cooker. Add in beans, mustard seeds, chili powder, cardamom, mushrooms, tomatoes, stock, water, bay leaf, thyme, salt, and pepper.

Cover with the lid and cook for 8 hours on Low. When done, remove the lid and serve sprinkled with lime juice.

Cavolo Nero, Fennel & Leek Chili

Serves: 6 | Total Time: 6 hours 15 minutes

1 fennel bulb, sliced
1 red bell pepper, sliced
2 cans (15-oz) white beans
1 bunch of cavolo nero, torn
1 shallot, chopped
2 garlic cloves, minced

1 leek, sliced
½ cup vegetable stock
1 cup diced tomatoes
½ tsp dried oregano
½ tsp dried basil
Salt and pepper to taste

In your Slow Cooker, mix beans, cavolo nero, shallot, garlic, leek, fennel, bell pepper, vegetable stock, tomatoes, oregano, basil, salt, and pepper. Cover with the lid and cook for 6 hours on Low. Serve right away.

Mushroom & Barley Stew with Pine Nuts

Serves: 6 | Total Time: 7 hours 15 minutes

1 cup diced tomatoes
1 zucchini, diced
2 red bell peppers, diced
2 cups sliced mushrooms
1 cup pearl barley
1 onion, finely chopped
4 garlic cloves, chopped

1 tsp dried oregano
1 tsp dried basil
2 cups vegetable stock
2 tbsp pine nuts
2 tbsp chopped parsley
1 tbsp chopped cilantro
Salt and pepper to taste

Toss barley, onion, garlic, oregano, basil, tomatoes, zucchini, bell peppers, mushrooms, vegetable stock, pine nuts, parsley, cilantro, salt, and pepper in your Slow Cooker. Cover with the lid and cook for 7 hours on Low. When done, remove the lid and serve warm.

Chickpea & Squash Stew

Serves: 6 | Total Time: 6 hours 30 minutes

1 cup diced tomatoes
1 cup chickpeas, soaked
1 lb grated butternut squash
½ tsp cumin seeds

¼ tsp mustard seeds
2 cups vegetable stock
1 bay leaf
Salt and pepper to taste

Add chickpeas, butternut squash, cumin seeds, mustard seeds, vegetable stock, tomatoes, bay leaf, salt, and pepper in your Slow Cooker and stir. Cover with the lid and cook for 6 hours on Low. Serve warm.

Cheddar Tricolor Chili

Serves: 6 | Total Time: 8 hours 30 minutes

1 can fire-roasted tomatoes
2 sweet onions, chopped
4 garlic cloves, chopped
1 celery stalk, sliced
1 carrot, diced
1 cup dried black beans
1 cup kidney beans

2 tbsp olive oil
½ cup red beans
2 bay leaves
2 cups vegetable stock
2 cups water
Salt and pepper to taste
1 cup grated cheddar

Warm the olive oil in a pan over low heat, place onions, garlic, celery, and carrot and cook for 5 minutes until softened. Add everything to your Slow Cooker. Add in beans, tomatoes, bay leaves, vegetable stock, water, salt, and pepper. Cook for 8 hours on Low. Scatter with cheddar cheese and serve.

Lentil & Sweet Potato Stew

Serves: 4 | Total Time: 2 hours 15 minutes

2 large sweet potatoes, peeled and cubed
2 large carrots, sliced
½ cup red lentils
2 ripe tomatoes, diced
1 ½ cups vegetable stock
2 tbsp olive oil

¼ tsp cumin seeds
¼ tsp fennel seeds
¼ tsp garlic powder
¼ tsp onion powder
Salt and pepper to taste

Mix the olive oil, carrots, sweet potatoes, lentils, tomatoes, vegetable stock, cumin seeds, fennel seeds, garlic powder, onion powder, salt, and pepper in your Slow Cooker. Cook for 2 hours on High. Serve warm.

Tofu & Mushroom Stew

Serves: 6 | Total Time: 6 hours 30 minutes

12 oz firm tofu, cubed	½ cup tomato sauce
1 large onion, chopped	2 tbsp soy sauce
4 garlic cloves, minced	2 tbsp olive oil
2 large carrots, sliced	½ tsp dried sage
2 celery stalks, sliced	1 cup vegetable stock
2 cups sliced mushrooms	Salt and pepper to taste

FOR THE DUMPLING

¼ cup whole milk	½ tsp baking soda
2 eggs	¼ cup cold butter, cubed
1 cup all-purpose flour	

Warm the olive oil in a pan over medium heat. Add the tofu cubes and cook them until golden and crusty on all sides. Transfer it to your Slow Cooker. Add in onion, garlic, soy sauce, carrots, celery, mushrooms, tomato sauce, sage, vegetable stock, salt, and pepper.

In a bowl, whisk flour, eggs, baking soda, butter, and salt until sandy. Stir in milk until lightly smooth and pour it over the veggies. Cover with the lid and cook for 6 hours on Low. When done, remove the lid and serve warm.

Lemony Mediterranean Stew

Serves: 6 | Total Time: 6 hours 30 minutes

4 sun-dried tomatoes, chopped

2 zucchinis, cubed	2 tbsp olive oil
1 large onion, chopped	2 tbsp tomato paste
2 carrots, sliced	1 tbsp lemon juice
2 red bell peppers, diced	1 ½ cups vegetable stock
2 ripe tomatoes, diced	Salt and pepper to taste
½ cup pitted black olives	2 tbsp pesto sauce

Warm the olive oil in a pan over medium heat. Sauté the carrots, onion, and bell peppers for 5 minutes, stirring often until softened. Add everything to your Slow Cooker. Add in tomatoes, sun-dried tomatoes, zucchinis, olives, tomato paste, lemon juice, stock, salt, and pepper.

Cover with the lid and cook for 6 hours on Low. When done, remove the lid and serve topped with pesto sauce.

Jalapeño Garden Chili

Serves: 6 | Total Time: 8 hours 30 minutes

½ head cauliflower, cut into florets
1 head broccoli, cut into florets

1 large carrot, sliced	2 red bell peppers, diced
1 can (15 oz) kidney beans	1 can fire-roasted tomatoes
2 potatoes, peeled, cubed	1 cup vegetable stock
1 cup frozen corn	1 tsp chili powder
2 shallots, chopped	½ tsp dried oregano
4 garlic cloves, chopped	Salt and pepper to taste
2 jalapeno peppers, minced	

Mix the shallots, garlic, beans, corn, broccoli, cauliflower, jalapeño peppers, bell peppers, carrot, tomatoes, vegetable stock, potatoes, chili powder, oregano, salt, and pepper in your Slow Cooker. Cover with the lid and cook for 8 hours on Low. Serve warm.

Feta Chickpea Stew

Serves: 6 | Total Time: 8 hours 15 minutes

2 carrots, diced	1 pinch chili powder
1 large onion, chopped	2 cups chickpeas, soaked
2 heirloom tomatoes, diced	2 cups vegetable stock
1 celery stalk, diced	Salt and pepper to taste
1 tsp dried oregano	8 oz feta cheese for servings

Mix the chickpeas, onion, carrots, celery, oregano, chili powder, tomatoes, vegetable stock, salt, and pepper in your Slow Cooker. Cook for 8 hours on Low. Serve topped with feta cheese.

Okra & Black-Eyed Peas

Serves: 6 | Total Time: 6 hours 15 minutes

2 cups dried black eyes peas, rinsed

2 large onions, chopped	2 cups water
2 red bell peppers, diced	1 cup tomato sauce
1 celery stalk, sliced	2 cups chopped okra
1 jalapeno peppers, minced	Salt and pepper to taste

Mix the black-eyed peas, water, tomato sauce, onions, okra, bell peppers, celery, jalapeño peppers, salt, and pepper in your Slow Cooker. Cover with the lid and cook for 6 hours on Low. Serve warm.

Three Lentil Stew

Serves: 6 | Total Time: 6 hours 15 minutes

1 onion, finely chopped	½ tsp cumin seeds
2 carrots, diced	½ tsp mustard seeds
1 celery stalk, diced	½ tsp fennel seeds
2 cups cauliflower florets	1 thyme sprig
½ cup red lentils	¼ tsp chili powder
½ cup brown lentils	½ tsp ground ginger
½ cup green lentils	Salt and pepper to taste

Mix the lentils, onion, carrots, celery, cauliflower, cumin seeds, mustard seeds, fennel seeds, thyme, chili powder, ginger, salt, and pepper in your Slow Cooker. Cover with the lid and cook for 6 hours on Low. Serve right away.

Chipotle Quinoa Chili

Serves: 6 | Total Time: 8 hours 15 minutes

2 chipotle peppers, chopped	1 celery stalk, diced
4 garlic cloves, chopped	2 tbsp chopped parsley
2 red bell peppers, diced	½ tsp cumin powder
2 cups dried black beans	¼ cup red quinoa, rinsed
4 cups vegetable stock	¼ tsp chili powder
1 can fire-roasted tomatoes	Salt and pepper to taste

In your Slow Cooker, stir beans, vegetable stock, tomatoes, chipotle peppers, garlic, celery, bell peppers, cumin, quinoa, chili powder, salt, and pepper. Cover with the lid and cook for 8 hours on Low. When done, remove the lid and sprinkle with parsley to serve.

SNACKS & APPETIZERS

Eggplant Caviar

Serves: 6 | Total Time: 6 hours 15 minutes

2 large eggplants
Salt and pepper to taste
4 tbsp lemon juice
1 tsp dried oregano
4 tbsp olive oil
6 cloves garlic, minced
½ cup yogurt
½ cup onion, chopped
1 cup tomato, chopped

Use a fork to poke the eggplant all over, then place it in your Slow Cooker. Cover with cooker lid, then cook on Low for 6 hours. Slice the eggplant in half and spoon out the pulp into a bowl. Mash the pulp and combine it with onion, yogurt, tomato, garlic, olive oil, and oregano. Mix well. Season with lemon juice, pepper, and salt. Serve the dish with pita or bread wedges.

Italian Mushrooms

Serves: 4 | Total Time: 4 hours 15 minutes

8 large mushrooms
1 cup marinara sauce
3 tsp Parmesan cheese,
Sea salt and pepper to taste
¼ lb ground sausage
1 clove garlic, finely diced
1/8 cup onion, diced
½ tablespoon coconut oil

Clean the mushrooms, then cut off stems. Set aside the caps on a paper towel. Mince the stems in a bowl.

In a skillet over medium heat, add the oil. Sauté garlic, onion, and minced mushroom stems until softened. Place the sausage in skillet, then cook until browned. Add the sausage mixture into a mixing bowl, and add the Parmesan cheese, salt, and pepper. Mix well.

Carefully spoon the sausage mixture into the mushroom caps. Pour the marinara sauce into your Slow Cooker and place mushrooms into the pot. Cover with sauce. Cook on high for 4 hours. Serve and enjoy!

Little Smokies

Serves: 4 | Total Time: 4 hours 10 minutes

14 oz little smokies
½ cup brown sugar
1 onion, diced
½ cup ketchup

Place all the ingredients in your Slow Cooker. Stir to coat sausage. Close the cooker lid. Set the heat setting on Low, then cook for 4 hours. Serve sausage on toothpicks as a tasty appetizer, and enjoy!

Chicken Livers Wrapped in Bacon

Serves: 6 | Total Time: 3 hours 30 minutes

2 lb chicken livers
Bacon slices as needed

Place the bacon slices on a flat surface. Top each bacon with a liver slice and wrap them. Place them into your Slow Cooker. Cover with the lid and cook for 3 hours on High. When done, remove the lid and serve warm.

BBQ Chicken Drumsticks

Serves: 6 | Total Time: 4 hours 10 minutes

2 lb chicken drumsticks
2 tsp garlic, minced
1/8 tsp black pepper
¼ cup honey
2 tbsp chili sauce
1 ¼ cups barbecue sauce

Place the drumsticks on a broiler pan, leaving space in between them. Preheat broiler, then place drumsticks about 6-inches away from heat. Broil for 10 minutes, turning them numerous times to brown them evenly.

Place drumsticks into your Slow Cooker. Add chili sauce, barbecue sauce, honey, garlic, and pepper in a bowl. Mix well. Pour the mixture over drumsticks in the cooker. Cook on Low for 4 hours. Serve and enjoy!

BBQ Kielbasa Sausages

Serves: 6 | Total Time: 6 hours 15 minutes

1 cup BBQ sauce
2 lb kielbasa sausages
½ cup brown sugar
1 tsp horseradish sauce
½ tsp black pepper
¼ tsp cumin powder

Place the kielbasa sausages, brown sugar, BBQ sauce, horseradish, black pepper, and cumin in your Slow Cooker. Sprinkle with salt to taste. Cover with the lid and cook for 6 hours on Low. When done, remove the lid and serve warm or chilled.

Mini Meatballs with Cranberry Sauce

Serves: 6 | Total Time: 6 hours 30 minutes

1 lb ground beef
2 lb ground pork
4 garlic cloves, minced
1 shallot, chopped
1 egg
1 cup BBQ sauce
¼ cup breadcrumbs
2 tbsp chopped parsley
1 tbsp chopped cilantro
½ tsp chili powder
2 tbsp cranberry sauce
½ cup tomato sauce
1 tsp red wine vinegar
Salt and pepper to taste

Mix the cranberry sauce, BBQ sauce, tomato sauce, vinegar, salt, and pepper in your Slow Cooker. Combine ground pork, ground beef, garlic, shallot, egg, breadcrumbs, parsley, cilantro, and chili powder in a bowl. Sprinkle with salt and pepper to taste.

Make balls out of the mixture and place them into the pot. Cover and cook for 6 hours on Low. When done, remove the lid and serve with cocktail skewers.

Easy Sausage Spread

Serves: 6 | Total Time: 6 hours 15 minutes

1 lb spicy pork sausages
1 lb fresh pork sausages
1 cup cream cheese
1 can diced tomatoes
2 poblano peppers, minced

Place the pork sausages, cream cheese, tomatoes, and poblano peppers in your Slow Cooker and stir. Cover with the lid and cook for 6 hours on Low. When done, remove the lid and serve warm or chilled.

Hawaiian Meatballs

Serves: 6 | Total Time: 7 hours 30 minutes

1 can pineapple chunks (keep the juices)
2 poblano peppers, minced   2 lb ground pork
4 garlic cloves, minced   1 lb ground beef
¼ cup brown sugar   1 tsp dried basil
2 tbsp soy sauce   1 egg
2 tbsp cornstarch   ¼ cup breadcrumbs
1 tbsp lemon juice   Salt and pepper to taste

Combine the pineapple, poblano peppers, brown sugar, soy sauce, cornstarch, and lemon juice in your Slow Cooker. In a bowl, mix ground pork, ground beef, garlic, basil, egg, breadcrumbs, salt, and pepper. Make small balls out of the mixture and place them into the pot. Cover with the lid and cook for 7 hours on Low. When done, remove the lid and serve warm or chilled.

Cajun Seasoned Peanuts

Serves: 6 | Total Time: 2 hours 15 minutes

2 lb raw, whole peanuts   ½ tsp garlic powder
¼ cup coconut oil   1 tbsp Cajun seasoning
¼ cup brown sugar   ½ tsp red pepper flakes

Mix the peanuts, brown sugar, garlic powder, Cajun seasoning, red pepper flakes, and coconut oil in your Slow Cooker. Cover with the lid and cook for 2 hours on High. When done, remove the lid and serve chilled.

Beefy Cheese Dip

Serves: 6 | Total Time: 3 hours 15 minutes

1 lb grated cheddar   ½ cup white wine
2 lb ground beef   1 poblano pepper, chopped
½ cup cream cheese

Place ground beef, cheddar, cream cheese, white wine, and poblano peppers in your Slow Cooker and stir. Cover with the lid and cook for 3 hours on High. When done, remove the lid and serve warm.

Cheesy Ham Dip

Serves: 6 | Total Time: 4 hours 15 minutes

1 (14-oz) can condensed cream of mushroom soup
1 (14-oz) can condensed onion soup
1 cup cream cheese   2 cups grated Swiss cheese
1 lb ham, diced   ½ tsp chili powder

Mix the ham, cream cheese, mushroom soup, onion soup, Swiss cheese, and chili powder in your Slow Cooker. Cover with the lid and cook for 4 hours on Low. When done, remove the lid and serve warm

Marinated Mushrooms

Serves: 6 | Total Time: 8 hours 15 minutes

1 cup soy sauce   ½ cup brown sugar
2 lb mushrooms   ¼ cup rice vinegar
1 cup water   ½ tsp chili powder

Mix the mushrooms, soy sauce, water, brown sugar, rice vinegar, and chili powder in your Slow Cooker. Cover with the lid and cook for 8 hours on Low. When done, remove the lid and let cool before serving.

Chili Black Bean Dip

Serves: 6 | Total Time: 4 hours 15 minutes

1 can black beans, drained   ½ tsp chili powder
2 lb ground beef   2 cups grated cheddar
1 can diced tomatoes   Salt and pepper to taste
2 poblano peppers, minced

Mix the ground beef, black beans, tomatoes, poblano peppers, chili powder, and cheddar cheese in your Slow Cooker. Sprinkle with salt and pepper to taste. Cover with the lid and cook for 4 hours on High. When done, remove the lid and serve warm.

Tangy Buffalo Wings

Serves: 6 | Total Time: 8 hours 15 minutes

4 lb chicken wings   1 tsp onion powder
¼ cup butter, melted   1 tsp garlic powder
1 cup BBQ sauce   ½ tsp cumin powder
1 tbsp Worcestershire sauce   ½ tsp cinnamon powder
1 tsp dried oregano   1 tsp hot sauce
1 tsp dried basil   1 tsp salt

Place the butter, chicken wings, BBQ sauce, Worcestershire sauce, oregano, basil, onion powder, garlic powder, cumin, cinnamon, hot sauce, and salt in your Slow Cooker and toss until everything well coated. Cover with the lid and cook for 8 hours on Low. When done, remove the lid and serve warm or chilled.

Chinese Five-Spice Chicken Wings

Serves: 6 | Total Time: 7 hours 15 minutes

4 lb chicken wings   1 tbsp five-spice powder
2 tbsp butter   1 tsp salt
½ cup plum sauce   ½ tsp chili powder
½ cup BBQ sauce

Place the butter, plum sauce, BBQ sauce, five-spice powder, salt, and chili powder in your Slow Cooker. Add the chicken wings and toss until everything is well coated. Cover with the lid and cook for 7 hours on Low. When done, remove the lid and serve warm or chilled.

Mexican Beef Sauce

Serves: 6 | Total Time: 6 hours 15 minutes

2 shallots, chopped   1 tsp chili powder
2 lb ground beef   1 can diced tomatoes
4 garlic cloves, minced   1 can sweet corn, drained
2 tbsp Mexican seasoning   2 cups grated cheddar

Mix the ground beef, Mexican seasoning, chili powder, tomatoes, shallots, garlic, sweet corn, and cheddar cheese in your Slow Cooker. Cover with the lid and cook for 6 hours on Low. When done, remove the lid and serve.

Spicy Chorizo Cheddar Dip

Serves: 6 | Total Time: 6 hours 15 minutes

1 can diced tomatoes
8 chorizo links, diced
1 chili pepper, chopped
1 cup cream cheese
2 cups grated cheddar
¼ cup white wine

Combine chorizo, tomatoes, chili pepper, cream cheese, cheddar cheese, and white wine in your Slow Cooker. Cover with the lid and cook for 6 hours on Low. Serve.

Chicken & Salsa Verde Dip

Serves: 6 | Total Time: 4 hours 15 minutes

1 lb ground chicken
2 shallots, chopped
2 tbsp olive oil
2 cups salsa verde
1 cup cream cheese
2 cups grated cheddar
2 poblano peppers, minced
1 tbsp Worcestershire sauce
4 garlic cloves, minced
¼ cup chopped cilantro
Salt and pepper to taste

Mix ground chicken, olive oil, shallots, salsa verde, cream cheese, cheddar, poblano peppers, Worcestershire sauce, garlic, and cilantro in your Slow Cooker. Sprinkle with salt and pepper to taste. Cover with the lid and cook for 4 hours on Low. When done, remove the lid and serve.

Swiss Cheese with Caramelized Onions

Serves: 6 | Total Time: 4 hours 30 minutes

1 cup beef stock
4 red onions, sliced
2 tbsp butter
1 tbsp canola oil
1 tsp dried thyme
½ cup white wine
2 garlic cloves, chopped
2 cups grated Swiss cheese
1 tbsp cornstarch
Salt and pepper to taste

Melt butter and canola oil in a skillet over medium heat. Add in onions and cook until it begins to caramelize. Transfer them into your Slow Cooker among beef stock, thyme, white wine, garlic, Swiss cheese, and cornstarch. Sprinkle with salt and pepper to taste. Cover with the lid and cook for 4 hours on Low. When done, remove the lid and serve warm with vegetable sticks.

Juicy Meatballs

Serves: 6 | Total Time: 8 hours 15 minutes

2 garlic cloves, minced
1 shallot, chopped
2 lb ground beef
½ cup oat flour
½ tsp cumin powder
½ tsp chili powder
1 egg
½ cup molasses
¼ cup soy sauce
2 tbsp lime juice
½ cup beef stock
1 tbsp Worcestershire sauce
Salt and pepper to taste

Mix the molasses, soy sauce, lime juice, beef stock, and Worcestershire sauce in your Slow Cooker. In a bowl, Combine the ground beef, garlic, shallot, oat flour, cumin, chili powder, egg, salt, and pepper. Make small balls out of the mixture and place them into the pot. Cover with the lid and cook for 8 hours on Low. When done, remove the lid and serve warm or chilled.

Sausages with Bourbon Glaze

Serves: 6 | Total Time: 4 hours 15 minutes

½ cup apricot preserves
2 lb small sausage links
¼ cup maple syrup
2 tbsp Bourbon

Mix the sausages, apricot preserves, maple syrup, and bourbon in your Slow Cooker. Cover with the lid and cook for 4 hours on Low. When done, remove the lid and serve warm or chilled with cocktail skewers.

Sunday Night Snacks

Serves: 6 | Total Time: 1 hour 45 minutes

4 cups cereals
4 cups crunchy cereals
½ cup butter, melted
2 cups mixed nuts
1 cup mixed seeds
2 tbsp Worcestershire sauce
1 tsp hot sauce
1 tsp salt
½ tsp cumin powder

Place butter, cereals, crunchy cereals, mixed nuts, mixed seeds, Worcestershire sauce, hot sauce, salt, and cumin in your Slow Cooker and toss to combine. Cover with the lid and cook for 11/2 hours on High. When done, remove the lid and serve chilled.

Delicious Crab Dip

Serves: 6 | Total Time: 2 hours 15 minutes

1 cup canned sweet corn
½ cup apricot preserves
2 tbsp butter
2 red bell peppers, diced
2 poblano peppers, minced
1 cup sour cream
1 can crab meat, drained
1 tsp Worcestershire sauce
1 tsp hot sauce
1 cup grated cheddar cheese

Combine the butter, sweet corn, bell peppers, apricot preserves, poblano peppers, sour cream, crabmeat, Worcestershire sauce, hot sauce, and cheddar cheese in your Slow Cooker. Cover with the lid and cook for 2 hours on Low. When done, remove the lid and serve warm or chilled.

Chicken Wings with Blue Cheese Sauce

Serves: 6 | Total Time: 7 hours 15 minutes

½ cup buffalo sauce
3 lb chicken wings
½ cup spicy tomato sauce
1 tbsp tomato paste
2 tbsp apple cider vinegar
1 tbsp Worcestershire sauce
1 cup sour cream
2 oz blue cheese, crumbled
1 thyme sprig

Place buffalo sauce, tomato sauce, vinegar, Worcestershire sauce, tomato paste, sour cream, blue cheese, and thyme in your Slow Cooker. Add in chicken wings and toss until well coated. Cover with the lid and cook for 7 hours on Low. When done, remove the lid and serve warm.

Spiced Potatoes

Serves: 6 | Total Time: 2 hours 15 minutes

2 garlic cloves, chopped
3 lb small new potatoes
¼ cup chicken stock
1 rosemary sprig, chopped

1 shallot, sliced
1 tsp smoked paprika
1 tsp salt
¼ tsp ground black pepper

Mix potatoes, rosemary, shallot, garlic, smoked paprika, salt, black pepper, and chicken stock in your Slow Cooker. Cover with the lid and cook for 2 hours on High. When done, remove the lid and serve warm or chilled.

Spinach & Crab Dip

Serves: 6 | Total Time: 2 hours 15 minutes

2 garlic cloves, chopped
1 lb fresh spinach, chopped
1 can crab meat, drained
2 shallots, chopped
2 jalapeno peppers, minced
1 cup grated Parmesan
½ cup whole milk
1 cup sour cream
1 cup cream cheese
1 cup grated cheddar cheese
1 tbsp sherry vinegar

Mix crabmeat, spinach, shallots, jalapeño peppers, Parmesan, milk, sour cream, cream cheese, cheddar cheese, sherry vinegar, and garlic in your Slow Cooker. Cover with the lid and cook for 2 hours on High. Serve warm or chilled with vegetable sticks if desired.

Dijon Bacon Dip

Serves: 6 | Total Time: 4 hours 15 minutes

1 sweet onion, chopped
10 bacon slices, chopped
1 cup cream cheese
1 tsp Worcestershire sauce
1 tsp Dijon mustard
1 cup grated Gruyere
½ cup whole milk
Salt and pepper to taste

Mix bacon, onions, Worcestershire sauce, mustard, cream cheese, Gruyere, and milk in your Slow Cooker. Sprinkle with salt and pepper to taste. Cover with the lid and cook for 4 hours on Low. Serve with biscuits if desired.

Blue Cheese & Artichoke Dip

Serves: 6 | Total Time: 6 hours 15 minutes

1 jar artichoke hearts, drained and chopped
2 garlic cloves, chopped
2 sweet onions, chopped
1 red chili, chopped
1 cup cream cheese
1 cup heavy cream
2 oz blue cheese, crumbled
2 tbsp chopped cilantro

Combine the onions, red chili, garlic, artichoke hearts, cream cheese, heavy cream, and blue cheese in your Slow Cooker. Cover with the lid and cook for 6 hours on Low. Stir in cilantro and serve warm or chilled.

Citrus Lamb Bites

Serves: 6 | Total Time: 7 hours 15 minutes

2 garlic cloves, minced
3 lb ground lamb
1 shallot, chopped
1 tbsp lemon zest
¼ tsp five-spice powder
½ tsp cumin powder
¼ tsp chili powder
½ cup raisins, chopped
1 tsp dried mint
1 red chili, chopped
2 cups tomato sauce
1 lemon, juiced
1 bay leaf
1 thyme sprig
Salt and pepper to taste

Combine the tomato sauce, lemon juice, bay leaf, thyme, and red chili in your Slow Cooker. In a bowl, mix ground lamb, shallot, garlic, lemon zest, five-spice powder, cumin, chili powder, raisins, mint, salt, and pepper. Make small balls out of the mixture and place them into the pot. Cover with the lid and cook for 7 hours on Low. When done, remove the lid and serve warm or chilled.

Bean Hummus with Caramelized Onions

Serves: 6 | Total Time: 8 hours 15 minutes

1 lb white beans, soaked
4 garlic cloves, minced
2 large sweet onions, sliced
2 tbsp canola oil
2 cups water
2 cups chicken stock
1 bay leaf
1 thyme sprig
Salt and pepper to taste

Place white beans, garlic, water, chicken stock, bay leaf, and thyme in your Slow Cooker. Cover with the lid and cook for 8 hours on Low. When done, remove the lid, strain the beans, reserving ¼ cup, and discard bay leaf and thyme. Remove the beans and reserved liquid into a blender and pulse until smooth. Sprinkle with salt and pepper to taste. Transfer it into a bowl. Warm canola oil in a skillet over medium heat. Place the onions and cook for 10 minutes until it begins to caramelize. Serve the beans topped with caramelized onions.

Beer & Cheddar Fondue

Serves: 6 | Total Time: 2 hours 15 minutes

2 cups grated cheddar
4 tbsp butter
1 shallot, chopped
2 garlic cloves, minced
2 tbsp all-purpose flour
2 poblano peppers, minced
1 cup milk
1 cup light beer
½ tsp chili powder

Melt butter in a skillet over medium heat. Add the shallot and garlic and cook for 2 minutes. Stir in flour and cook for 2 more minutes. Pour in milk and cook for 5 minutes until it thickens, stirring often. Add to into your Slow Cooker. Place in poblano peppers, beer, cheddar, and chili powder. Cover with the lid and cook for 2 hours on High. When done, remove the lid and serve warm with biscuits or salty snacks.

Artichokes Stuffed with Anchovies

Serves: 6 | Total Time: 6 hours 15 minutes

6 fresh artichokes
2 tbsp olive oil
6 anchovy fillets, chopped
4 garlic cloves, minced
1 cup breadcrumbs
1 tbsp chopped parsley
¼ cup white wine
Salt and pepper to taste

Cut stems of each artichoke, place them onto a flat surface, cut the top and trim outer leaves, cleaning the center. Combine the anchovy fillets, garlic, olive oil, breadcrumbs, parsley, salt, and pepper in a bowl. Top each artichoke with the anchovy mixture and place them into your Slow Cooker. Pour in white wine. Cover with the lid and cook for 6 hours on Low. Serve warm.

Greek-Style Beef Dip

Serves: 6 | Total Time: 6 hours 15 minutes

1 lb ground beef	½ cup black olives, chopped
2 garlic cloves, chopped	½ tsp dried oregano
2 tbsp canola oil	1 tsp dried basil
2 shallots, chopped	¼ cup white wine
4 ripe tomatoes, diced	½ cup tomato sauce
16 Kalamata olives, chopped	Salt and pepper to taste

Warm the canola oil in a skillet over medium heat, put ground beef, and cook for 5 minutes. Add in shallots and garlic and cook for 5 more minutes. Transfer them to your Slow Cooker. Stir in tomatoes, Kalamata olives, black olives, oregano, basil, white wine, and tomato sauce. Sprinkle with salt and pepper to taste. Cover with the lid and cook for 6 hours on Low. Serve warm.

Bourbon Black Beans with Bacon

Serves: 6 | Total Time: 6 hours 15 minutes

2 shallots, sliced	1 tbsp brown sugar
6 bacon slices	1 tbsp molasses
2 cans black beans, drained	½ tsp chili powder
1 garlic cloves, chopped	1 tbsp apple cider vinegar
1 cup red salsa	2 tbsp Bourbon
½ cup beef stock	Salt and pepper to taste

Place a skillet over medium heat. Add the bacon and cook until crispy. Add it to your Slow Cooker. Add in black beans, shallots, garlic, red salsa, beef stock, brown sugar, molasses, chili powder, vinegar, bourbon, salt, and pepper. Cover and cook for 6 hours on Low. When done, remove the lid, mash the beans and serve.

Balsamic Chicken Wings

Serves: 6 | Total Time: 7 hours 15 minutes

¼ cup maple syrup	1 tbsp Dijon mustard
3 lb chicken wings	1 tsp Worcestershire sauce
1 tsp garlic powder	½ cup tomato sauce
1 tsp chili powder	1 tsp salt
2 tbsp balsamic vinegar	

Mix chicken wings, maple syrup, garlic powder, chili powder, balsamic vinegar, mustard, Worcestershire sauce, tomato sauce, and salt in your Slow Cooker and toss to well coated. Cover with the lid and cook for 7 hours on Low. Serve warm or chilled.

Meatballs in Chipotle Sauce

Serves: 6 | Total Time: 7 hours 30 minutes

2 shallots, chopped	2 cups BBQ sauce
3 lb ground pork	1 bay leaf
2 garlic cloves, minced	¼ cup cranberry sauce
2 chipotle peppers, chopped	Salt and pepper to taste

Mix the BBQ sauce, cranberry sauce, bay leaf, salt, and pepper in your Slow Cooker. In a bowl, combine the ground pork, garlic, shallots, chipotle peppers, salt, and pepper. Shape balls out of the mixture.

Place them into the pot. Cover with the lid and cook for 7 hours on Low. Serve with cocktail skewers if desired.

Sausages with Spicy BBQ Sauce

Serves: 6 | Total Time: 2 hours 15 minutes

2 chipotle peppers in adobo sauce	
3 lb small smoked sausages	¼ cup white wine
1 cup BBQ sauce	Salt and pepper to taste
1 tbsp tomato paste	

Mix the sausages, BBQ sauce, chipotle peppers, tomato paste, and white wine in your Slow Cooker. Sprinkle with salt and pepper to taste. Cover with the lid and cook for 2 hours on High. Serve warm and enjoy!

Chicken & Bell Pepper Bites with Cheese

Serves: 6 | Total Time: 6 hours 15 minutes

1 cup cream cheese	1 cup shredded mozzarella
4 chicken breasts, cubed	¼ tsp chili powder
¼ cup all-purpose flour	Salt and pepper to taste
2 roasted red bell peppers	

In a blender, mix cream cheese, bell peppers, chili powder, salt, and pepper and pulse until smooth. Pour it into your Slow Cooker. Add in chicken, flour, and mozzarella. Cover with the lid and cook for 6 hours on Low. When done, remove the lid and serve warm or chilled.

Ground Pork & Ham Dip

Serves: 6 | Total Time: 6 hours 15 minutes

1 lb ground pork	1 cup tomato sauce
2 garlic cloves, chopped	½ cup chili sauce
2 cups diced ham	½ cup cranberry sauce
1 shallot, chopped	Salt and pepper to taste
1 tsp Dijon mustard	

Place a skillet over medium heat. Add the ground pork, and cook for 5 minutes, stirring often. Add it to your Slow Cooker. Add in ham, shallot, garlic, mustard, tomato sauce, chili sauce, and cranberry sauce. Sprinkle with salt and pepper to taste. Cover with the lid and cook for 6 hours on Low. Serve warm or chilled.

Italian Salami Dip

Serves: 6 | Total Time: 6 hours 15 minutes

½ lb salami, diced	2 cups tomato sauce
1 onion, chopped	½ cup grated Parmesan
1 lb spicy sausages, sliced	1 cup shredded mozzarella
1 red bell pepper, diced	½ tsp dried basil
1 yellow bell pepper, sliced	½ tsp dried oregano
2 garlic cloves, minced	

Place the sausages, salami, red bell pepper, yellow bell pepper, onion, garlic, tomato sauce, Parmesan, mozzarella, basil, and oregano in your Slow Cooker. Cover with the lid and cook for 6 hours on Low. When done, remove the lid and serve warm.

Cheese & Bacon Crab Dip

Serves: 6 | Total Time: 2 hours 15 minutes

1 can crab meat, drained and shredded
1 lb bacon, diced
1 cup cream cheese   1 tsp Worcestershire sauce
½ cup grated Parmesan   1 tsp Dijon mustard
   1 tsp hot sauce

Place a skillet over medium heat. Add the bacon and cook for 5 minutes. Add it to your Slow Cooker. Mix in cream cheese, Parmesan cheese, Worcestershire sauce, mustard, crabmeat, and hot sauce. Cover with the lid and cook for 2 hours on High. Serve warm or chilled.

Hot BBQ Meatballs

Serves: 8 | Total Time: 7 hours 30 minutes

1 lb ground turkey   1 thyme sprig
2 lb ground pork   2 cups cranberry sauce
1 egg   1 cup BBQ sauce
½ cup breadcrumbs   1 tsp hot sauce
1 shallot, chopped   Salt and pepper to taste
½ tsp ground cloves

Mix the cranberry sauce, BBQ sauce, and hot sauce, and thyme in your Slow Cooker. In a bowl, Combine the ground pork, ground turkey, egg, breadcrumbs, shallot, cloves, salt, and pepper. Form small balls out of the mixture and place them into the pot. Cover with the lid and cook for 7 hours on Low. Serve warm.

Cheesy Mushroom Dip

Serves: 6 | Total Time: 4 hours 15 minutes

1 can condensed cream of mushroom soup
1 lb wild mushrooms, chopped
1 cup white wine   1 tsp dried tarragon
1 cup cream cheese   ½ tsp dried oregano
1 cup heavy cream   Salt and pepper to taste
½ cup grated Parmesan

Mix mushrooms, mushroom soup, white wine, cream cheese, heavy cream, Parmesan, tarragon, and oregano in your Slow Cooker. Sprinkle with salt and pepper to taste. Cover with the lid and cook for 4 hours on Low. When done, remove the lid and serve warm or chilled.

Chicken & Corn Taquitos

Serves: 6 | Total Time: 6 hours 30 minutes

4 chicken breasts, cooked and diced
12 taco-sized flour tortillas   ½ tsp cumin powder
1 cup cream cheese   4 garlic cloves, minced
2 jalapeno peppers, minced   2 cups grated cheddar
½ cup canned sweet corn

Combine chicken, cream cheese, jalapeño pepper, garlic, cumin, corn, and cheddar in a bowl. Lay flour tortillas onto a flat surface and fill each tortilla with chicken mixture. Wrap each tortilla into a roll and place them into your Slow Cooker. Cover with the lid and cook for 6 hours on Low. When done, remove the lid and serve.

Chilaquiles with Carne Asada

Serves: 6 | Total Time: 8 hours 30 minutes

2 cups grated Monterey jack cheese
2 lb flanks steak   1 tsp garlic powder
6 oz tortillas chips   1 cup dark beer
2 tbsp canola oil   1 cup red salsa
1 tsp smoked paprika   1 can sweet corn, drained
½ tsp chili powder   1 tsp salt
2 tbsp brown sugar   Sour cream for serving
1 tsp cumin powder   2 tbsp chopped cilantro

In a bowl, Combine the salt, paprika, chili powder, brown sugar, cumin, and garlic powder. Put in flank steak and rub it until well coated. Warm canola oil in a skillet over medium heat. Place the steak and sear for 4-5 minutes on all sides. Add it to your Slow Cooker and pour in dark beer. Cover and cook for 6 hours on Low.

When done, remove the lid, remove the meat and cut it into thin slices. Clean the pot, put tortilla chips on the bottom, pour red salsa over, and top with steak slices, corn, and Monterey Jack. Cover with the lid and cook for 2 hours on Low. When done, remove the lid and serve topped with sour cream and cilantro.

Cheddar Corn Dip

Serves: 6 | Total Time: 2 hours 15 minutes

1 lb ground beef   1 cup diced tomatoes
1 shallot, chopped   ½ cup black olives, chopped
2 cups grated cheddar   1 tsp dried oregano
1 can sweet corn, drained   ½ tsp chili powder
1 can kidney beans, drained   ½ tsp cumin powder
½ cup beef stock   ¼ tsp garlic powder
2 tbsp olive oil   Tortilla chips for serving

Warm olive oil in a skillet over medium heat, place ground beef, and cook for 5-7 minutes, stirring often. Place the cooked beef, shallot, corn, kidney beans, beef stock, tomatoes, black olives, oregano, chili powder, cumin, garlic powder, cheddar, salt, and pepper in your Slow Cooker. Cover with the lid and cook for 2 hours on High. Serve warm with tortilla chips, if you like.

Cranberry & Caramelized Onion Dip

Serves: 6 | Total Time: 6 hours 15 minutes

1 cup frozen cranberries   2 tbsp brown sugar
4 red onions, sliced   1 tsp orange zest
1 apple, peeled and diced   1 bay leaf
¼ cup balsamic vinegar   1 thyme sprig
¼ cup fresh orange juice   1 tsp salt
2 tbsp olive oil

Warm the olive oil in a skillet over medium heat, place onions, and cook for 10 minutes until it begins to caramelize. Place caramelized onions, apples, cranberries, balsamic vinegar, orange juice, brown sugar, orange zest, bay leaf, thyme, and salt in your Slow Cooker. Cover with the lid and cook for 6 hours on Low. When done, remove the lid and serve chilled.

Jalapeño Tomato Sauce

Serves: 6 | Total Time: 3 hours

2 shallots, chopped	½ tsp dried mint
4 ripe tomatoes, sliced	1 jalapeno pepper, chopped
1 bay leaf	1 can black beans, drained
2 tbsp olive oil	¼ cup chicken stock
1 tsp dried basil	Salt and pepper to taste

Preheat the oven to 350°F. Place tomato slices in a baking sheet and sprinkle with salt, pepper, mint, and olive oil. Put it in the oven and bake for 35 minutes until it begins to caramelize. Put caramelized tomato, basil, shallots, jalapeño, black beans, chicken stock, and bay leaf in your Slow Cooker. Cover with the lid and cook for 2 hours on High. When done, remove the lid and serve warm.

Tasty Cheeseburger Dip

Serves: 6 | Total Time: 6 hours 15 minutes

2 lb ground beef	1 tbsp Dijon mustard
4 garlic cloves, chopped	2 tbsp pickle relish
1 tbsp canola oil	1 cup shredded cheese
2 sweet onions, chopped	1 cup grated cheddar
½ cup tomato sauce	

Warm the canola oil in a skillet over medium heat. Place ground beef and cook for 5 minutes. Add it to your Slow Cooker. Mix in onions, garlic, tomato sauce, mustard, pickle relish, cheese, and cheddar. Cover with the lid and cook for 6 hours on Low. Serve.

Chicken & Mozzarella Appetizer

Serves: 6 | Total Time: 7 hours 30 minutes

4 tomatoes, sliced	¼ tsp chili powder
4 chicken breasts, cubed	4 large tortillas
1 tsp dried basil	2 cups shredded mozzarella
1 tsp dried oregano	Salt and pepper to taste
1 cup cream cheese	

Combine the chicken, basil, oregano, cream cheese, chili powder, salt, and pepper in a bowl. Place everything into your Slow Cooker. Add in tomato slices, top with tortillas, and finally scatter with mozzarella. Cover with the lid and cook for 7 hours on Low. When done, remove the lid and let it cool before slicing. Serve right away.

Cheese Dip with Green Veggies

Serves: 6 | Total Time: 2 hours 15 minutes

1 jar artichoke hearts	½ cup grated Parmesan
10 oz spinach, torn	½ cup feta, crumbled
1 cup chopped parsley	½ tsp onion powder
1 cup cream cheese	¼ tsp garlic powder
1 cup sour cream	

Stir spinach, artichoke hearts, parsley, cream cheese, sour cream, Parmesan, feta cheese, onion powder, and garlic powder in your Slow Cooker. Cover with the lid and cook for 2 hours on High. When done, remove the lid and serve warm with crusty bread if desired.

Thai Chicken Drumsticks

Serves: 6 | Total Time: 7 hours 15 minutes

3 lb chicken drumsticks	¼ cup honey
2 tbsp tomato paste	1 tsp rice vinegar
½ tsp sesame oil	½ tsp dried Thai basil
¼ cup soy sauce	

Place chicken, soy sauce, honey, rice vinegar, sesame oil, tomato paste, and Thai basil in your Slow Cooker and toss until everything is coated. Cover with the lid and cook for 7 hours on Low. Serve warm or chilled.

Indian Chicken Wings

Serves: 6 | Total Time: 7 hours 15 minutes

2 shallots, chopped	½ cup coconut milk
3 lb chicken wings	½ tsp dried basil
1 cup tomato sauce	Salt and pepper to taste
¼ cup red curry paste	

Mix chicken wings, tomato sauce, curry paste, coconut milk, shallots, basil in your Slow Cooker and toss until well coated. Sprinkle with salt and pepper to taste. Cover with the lid and cook for 7 hours on Low. Serve warm.

Rosemary Potatoes with Bacon

Serves: 6 | Total Time: 3 hours 15 minutes

12 slices bacon, chopped	1 rosemary sprig
3 lb new potatoes, halved	Salt and pepper to taste
2 tbsp white wine	

Put potatoes, white wine, and rosemary in your Slow Cooker. Sprinkle with salt and pepper to taste and top with bacon. Cover with the lid and cook for 3 hours on High. When done, remove the lid and serve warm.

Cheddar Black Beans

Serves: 6 | Total Time: 6 hours 15 minutes

1 cup chopped green chiles	1 tsp dried oregano
1 ½ cups grated cheddar	½ tsp cumin powder
1 (14-oz) can black beans	1 cup light beer
½ cup red salsa	Salt and pepper to taste

Stir black beans, green chilies, red salsa, oregano, cumin, beer, and cheddar in your Slow Cooker. Sprinkle with salt and pepper to taste. Cover with the lid and cook for 6 hours on Low. When done, remove the lid and serve.

Cheesy-Artichoke Sauce

Serves: 6 | Total Time: 4 hours 15 minutes

1 jar artichoke hearts, chopped	
1 shallot, chopped	1 cup grated Swiss cheese
2 cups shredded mozzarella	½ tsp dried thyme
1 cup grated Parmesan	¼ tsp chili powder

Stir artichoke hearts, shallot, mozzarella, Parmesan, Swiss cheese, thyme, and chili powder in your Slow Cooker. Cover with the lid and cook for 4 hours on Low. Serve.

Chili Enchilada Chicken Dip

Serves: 6 | Total Time: 6 hours 15 minutes

2 garlic cloves, chopped	1 red bell pepper, diced
1 ½ cups grated cheddar	2 tomatoes, diced
1 lb ground chicken	1 cup tomato sauce
½ tsp chili powder	Salt and pepper to taste
1 shallot, chopped	

Mix ground chicken, chili powder, shallot, garlic, bell pepper, tomatoes, tomato sauce, salt, pepper, and cheddar cheese in your Slow Cooker. Cover with the lid and cook for 6 hours on Low. When done, remove the lid and serve warm with tortilla chips.

Healthy Peanuts

Serves: 6 | Total Time: 7 hours 15 minutes

2 lb whole peanuts	Salt to taste

Mix the peanuts, salt, and 4 cups of water in your Slow Cooker. Cover with the lid and cook for 7 hours on Low. When done, remove the lid and let cool before serving.

Mushroom & Cheese Dip

Serves: 6 | Total Time: 4 hours 15 minutes

1 can condensed cream of mushroom soup	
1 lb mushrooms, chopped	½ tsp chili powder
1 tsp Worcestershire sauce	1 cup grated cheddar cheese
¼ cup evaporated milk	1 cup grated Swiss cheese

Combine the mushroom soup, mushrooms, Worcestershire sauce, evaporated milk, and chili powder in your Slow Cooker. Scatter with grated cheeses. Cover with the lid and cook for 4 hours on Low. Serve warm.

Rich Taco Dip

Serves: 6 | Total Time: 6 hours 15 minutes

2 cups Velveeta cheese, shredded	
2 lb ground beef	½ cup beef stock
2 tbsp canola oil	1 cup tomato sauce
1 can black beans, drained	1 tbsp taco seasoning

Warm the canola oil in a skillet over medium heat. Place in ground beef and cook for 10 minutes, stirring often. Add it to your Slow Cooker. Add in black beans, beef stock, tomato sauce, taco seasoning, and Velveeta cheese. Cover with the lid and cook for 6 hours on Low. When done, remove the lid and serve warm.

Carrot Sticks with Maple Glaze

Serves: 6 | Total Time: 6 hours 15 minutes

3 lb baby carrots	1/8 tsp pumpkin pie spices
4 tbsp butter, melted	1 tsp salt
3 tbsp maple syrup	

Put baby carrots in your Slow Cooker. Stir in butter, maple syrup, pumpkin spice, and salt until well coated. Cover with the lid and cook for 6 hours on Low. Serve.

Hoisin-Glazed Mushrooms

Serves: 6 | Total Time: 2 hours 15 minutes

2 lb fresh mushrooms	¼ cup soy sauce
2 garlic cloves, minced	½ tsp red pepper flakes
¼ cup hoisin sauce	

In a bowl, Combine the hoisin sauce, soy sauce, garlic, and red pepper flakes. Place mushrooms in your Slow Cooker and sprinkle with the sauce, toss to combine. Cover with the lid and cook for 2 hours on High. When done, remove the lid and let cool before serving.

South American Dip

Serves: 6 | Total Time: 2 hours 15 minutes

1 can black beans, drained	½ tsp chili powder
1 can diced tomatoes	½ cup beef stock
1 can red beans, drained	1 ½ cups grated cheddar
½ tsp cumin powder	Salt and pepper to taste

Mix black beans, red beans, tomatoes, cumin, chili powder, and beef stock in your Slow Cooker. Sprinkle with salt and pepper to taste and top with grated cheddar. Cover with the lid and cook for 2 hours on High. Serve.

Sweet & Spicy Pecans

Serves: 6 | Total Time: 3 hours 15 minutes

2 lb pecans	1 tsp dried thyme
½ cup butter, melted	¼ tsp cayenne pepper
1 tsp chili powder	½ tsp garlic powder
1 tsp smoked paprika	2 tbsp honey
1 tsp dried basil	

Place pecans, butter, chili powder, paprika, basil, thyme, cayenne pepper, garlic powder, and honey in your Slow Cooker and toss until everything is coated. Cook for 3 hours on High. Let cool before serving.

Traditional Swiss Cheese Fondue

Serves: 6 | Total Time: 4 hours 15 minutes

1 cup grated cheddar	2 cups grated Swiss cheese
1 garlic cloves	2 tbsp cornstarch
2 cups dry white wine	1 pinch nutmeg

Rub with a garlic clove the pot of your Slow Cooker. Put in white wine, Swiss cheese, cheddar, cornstarch, and nutmeg. Cover with the lid and cook for 4 hours on Low. Serve warm with vegetable sticks if desired.

Irresistible Dates Rolled in Bacon

Serves: 6 | Total Time: 1 hour 45 minutes

12 bacon slices	12 almonds
12 dates, pitted	

Fill each date with an almond, wrap them with a bacon slice, and place them into your Slow Cooker. Cover with the lid and cook for 1 ¼ hours on High. When done, remove the lid and serve warm or chilled.

Gingery Chicken Bites

Serves: 6 | Total Time: 7 hours 15 minutes

4 garlic cloves, minced
4 chicken breasts, cubed
2 sweet onions, sliced
2 tbsp olive oil
1 tsp grated ginger
½ tsp cinnamon powder
1 tsp smoked paprika
1 tsp cumin powder
1 cup chicken stock
½ lemon, juiced
Salt and pepper to taste

Stir olive oil, chicken, onions, ginger, garlic, cinnamon, paprika, cumin, chicken stock, and lemon juice in your Slow Cooker. Sprinkle with salt and pepper to taste. Cover with the lid and cook for 7 hours on Low. Serve.

Jalapeño Bacon & Corn Dip

Serves: 6 | Total Time: 2 hours 15 minutes

3 cans sweet corn, drained
4 bacon slices, chopped
4 jalapeno peppers, minced
1 cup sour cream
1 cup grated cheddar cheese
½ cup cream cheese
1 pinch nutmeg
2 tbsp chopped cilantro

Mix bacon, corn, jalapeños, sour cream, cheddar, cream cheese, and nutmeg in your Slow Cooker. Cover with the lid and cook for 2 hours on High. When done, remove the lid, stir in cilantro and serve warm. Store it in a container in the fridge for up to 2 days.

Emmental & Tahini Dip

Serves: 6 | Total Time: 2 hours 15 minutes

¼ cup grated Emmental cheese
½ cup tahini paste
1 cup whole milk
1/8 tsp garlic powder
½ tsp cumin powder
¼ lb grated Gruyere
Salt and pepper to taste
1 pinch of nutmeg

Stir tahini paste, milk, garlic powder, cumin, Gruyere, Emmental, and nutmeg in your Slow Cooker. Sprinkle with salt and pepper to taste. Cover with the lid and cook for 2 hours on High. Serve warm.

Salty Mix Snacks

Serves: 6 | Total Time: 2 hours 15 minutes

4 cups pretzels
1 cup peanuts
1 cup pecans
¼ cup butter, melted
1 cup crispy rice cereals
1 tsp Worcestershire sauce
1 tsp salt
1 tsp garlic powder

Place the pretzels, peanuts, pecans, and rice cereals in your Slow Cooker. Sprinkle with melted butter, Worcestershire sauce, salt, and garlic powder, and toss until well coated. Cover with the lid and cook for 2 hours on High, stirring once. Let cool before serving.

Homemade Pulled Pork

Serves: 6 | Total Time: 8 hours 15 minutes

2 garlic cloves, minced
2 shallots, sliced
2 lb boneless pork shoulder
2 tbsp honey

¼ cup balsamic vinegar
¼ cup hoisin sauce
1 tbsp Dijon mustard
¼ cup chicken stock
2 tbsp soy sauce

Stir honey, balsamic vinegar, hoisin sauce, mustard, chicken stock, garlic, shallots, and soy sauce in your Slow Cooker. Put in pork shoulder and toss until well coated. Cover with the lid and cook for 8 hours on Low. When done, remove the lid, shred the meat and serve warm.

Chicken & Olive Dip

Serves: 6 | Total Time: 3 hours 10 minutes

1 lb ground chicken
1 green bell pepper, diced
10 Kalamata olives, chopped
10 green olives, chopped
10 black olives, chopped
1 cup green salsa
½ cup chicken stock
2 tbsp olive oil
1 cup grated cheddar cheese
½ cup shredded mozzarella

Stir olive oil, ground chicken, bell pepper, Kalamata olives, black olives, green olives, green salsa, chicken stock, cheddar, and mozzarella in your Slow Cooker. Cover with the lid and cook for 3 hours on High. When done, remove the lid and serve warm.

Chili Monterey Jack Fondue

Serves: 6 | Total Time: 4 hours 15 minutes

2 cups grated Monterey Jack cheese
½ cup grated Parmesan
1 garlic clove
1 cup white wine
1 red chili, minced chopped
1 tbsp cornstarch
½ cup milk
1 pinch nutmeg
Salt and pepper to taste

Rub with a garlic clove the pot of your Slow Cooker. Add in white wine, Monterey Jack, Parmesan, red chili, cornstarch, milk, nutmeg, salt, and pepper. Cover with the lid and cook for 4 hours on Low. When done, remove the lid and serve warm with breadsticks or vegetables.

Classic Hummus

Serves: 6 | Total Time: 6 hours 15 minutes

2 cups chickpeas, soaked
2 tbsp olive oil
5 cups water
1 bay leaf
1 lemon, juiced
¼ cup tahini paste
1 pinch red pepper flakes
Salt and pepper to taste

Place the chickpeas, water, bay leaf, salt, and pepper in your Slow Cooker. Cover and cook for 6 hours on Low. When done, remove the lid and transfer everything to a blender. Add in lemon juice, tahini paste, olive oil, and red pepper flakes and pulse until smooth. Serve chilled.

Hot Pimiento & Olive Dip

Serves: 6 | Total Time: 2 hours 15 minutes

¼ lb grated pepper Jack cheese
½ lb grated cheddar cheese
½ cup sour cream
½ cup green olives, sliced
2 tbsp diced pimientos
1 tsp hot sauce
¼ tsp garlic powder
¼ tsp onion powder

Stir cheddar, Jack cheese, sour cream, green olives, pimientos, hot sauce, garlic powder, and onion powder in your Slow Cooker. Cover with the lid and cook for 2 hours on High. When done, remove the lid and serve warm with vegetable sticks or breadsticks.

Hummus with Roasted Peppers

Serves: 6 | Total Time: 2 hours 15 minutes

4 roasted red bell peppers, drained
4 garlic cloves, minced
1 shallot, chopped
2 cans chickpeas, drained

2 tbsp olive oil
2 tbsp lemon juice
Salt and pepper to taste

Put bell peppers, chickpeas, ½ cup of water, shallot, and garlic in your Slow Cooker. Sprinkle with salt and pepper to taste. Cover and cook for 2 hours on High. When done, remove the lid and Add it to a blender. Add in lemon juice and olive oil and pulse until smooth. Serve cool or store it in a container in the fridge.

Vegetarian Caviar

Serves: 6 | Total Time: 3 hours 15 minutes

2 garlic cloves, minced
2 peeled eggplants, cubed
1 tsp dried basil
1 tsp dried oregano

1 lemon, juiced
4 tbsp olive oil
Salt and pepper to taste

Mix the eggplants, olive oil, basil, and oregano in your Slow Cooker. Sprinkle with salt and pepper. Cover with the lid and cook for 3 hours on High. When done, remove the lid and mix in lemon juice, garlic, salt, and pepper. Using a potato masher, mash it and serve chilled.

Pepper & Sausage Appetizer

Serves: 6 | Total Time: 6 hours 15 minutes

4 roasted bell peppers, chopped
6 fresh pork sausages, skins removed
1 cup grated provolone cheese
1 can fire-roasted tomatoes   2 tbsp olive oil
1 poblano pepper, chopped   Salt and pepper to taste
1 shallot, chopped

Warm the olive oil in a skillet over medium heat. Place the sausages and cook for 5 minutes, stirring often. Place cooked sausages, tomatoes, bell peppers, poblano pepper, shallot, Provolone, salt, and pepper in your Slow Cooker. Cover with the lid and cook for 6 hours on Low. When done, remove the lid and serve warm or chilled.

Thyme Brie with Cranberry Sauce

Serves: 6 | Total Time: 2 hours 15 minutes

½ cup cranberry sauce   ½ tsp dried thyme
1 wheel of Brie

Pour cranberry sauce in your Slow Cooker. Add in thyme and Brie cheese. Cover with the lid and cook for 2 hours on Low. When done, remove the lid and serve warm with breadsticks or tortilla chips.

Parmesan Artichoke Bread Pudding

Serves: 6 | Total Time: 6 hours 30 minutes

4 oz. spinach, chopped
½ cup grated Parmesan
6 cups bread cubes
6 artichoke hearts, chopped
4 eggs
½ cup sour cream

1 cup milk
1 tbsp chopped parsley
2 tbsp olive oil
½ tsp dried oregano
½ tsp dried basil
Salt and pepper to taste

Mix the bread cubes, artichoke hearts, Parmesan, spinach, olive oil and parsley in your Slow Cooker. In a bowl, Combine the eggs, sour cream, milk, oregano, basil, salt, and pepper. Pour it over the bread mixture and press it until it absorbs the liquid. Cover with the lid and cook for 6 hours on Low. When done, remove the lid and serve warm or chilled.

Oregano Potatoes

Serves: 6 | Total Time: 6 hours 15 minutes

3 lb small new potatoes, washed
4 bacon slices, chopped
2 green onions, chopped
1 tsp dried oregano
1 shallot, chopped
2 garlic cloves, chopped

2 tbsp olive oil
1 cup sour cream
2 tbsp chopped parsley
Salt and pepper to taste

Mix potatoes, bacon, oregano, shallot, olive oil, and garlic in your Slow Cooker. Sprinkle with salt and pepper to taste. Cover with the lid and cook for 6 hours on Low. Mix in sour cream, green onions, and parsley and serve.

Mouth-Watering Potatoes with Bacon

Serves: 6 | Total Time: 3 hours 15 minutes

6 slices bacon, chopped
2 lb new potatoes, halved
1 tsp dried rosemary

¼ cup chicken stock
Salt and pepper to taste

Place a skillet over medium heat. Add the bacon, and cook until crispy, stirring frequently. Place the potatoes, bacon and its fat, rosemary, salt, pepper, and chicken stock in your Slow Cooker. Cover with the lid and cook for 3 hours on High. Serve warm.

Italian Sausage & Cheese Dip

Serves: 6 | Total Time: 4 hours 15 minutes

½ lb fresh Italian sausages, skins removed
1 cup tomato sauce
1 cup cottage cheese
1 cup grated mozzarella
2 tbsp olive oil
½ cup grated Parmesan

1 cup grated cheddar cheese
½ tsp dried thyme
½ tsp dried basil
Salt and pepper to taste

Warm olive oil in a skillet over medium heat, place the sausages, and cook for 5 minutes, stirring often. Remove into your Slow Cooker. Add tomato sauce, cottage cheese, mozzarella, Parmesan, cheddar, thyme, basil, salt, and pepper. Cover with the lid and cook for 4 hours on Low. When done, remove the lid and serve warm.

Cajun Meatballs with Cheese

Serves: 6 | Total Time: 6 hours 15 minutes

2 cups shredded processed cheese
2 lb ground pork
1 shallot, chopped
2 tbsp beef stock
1 egg

¼ cup breadcrumbs
1 tsp Cajun seasoning
½ tsp dried basil
Salt and pepper to taste

In a bowl, Combine the ground pork, shallot, beef stock, egg, breadcrumbs, cajun seasoning, basil, salt, and pepper. Make small balls out of the mixture and place them into your Slow Cooker. Scatter with shredded cheese. Cover with the lid and cook for 6 hours on Low. When done, remove the lid and serve warm.

Chicken Wings with Teriyaki Sauce

Serves: 6 | Total Time: 6 hours 15 minutes

3 lb chicken wings
2 tbsp canola oil
2 tbsp brown sugar
1 tbsp molasses

½ tsp garlic powder
½ tsp ground ginger
½ cup soy sauce
½ cup pineapple juice

Stir brown sugar, molasses, garlic powder, ginger, soy sauce, pineapple juice, ¼ cup of water, canola oil, and chicken wings in your Slow Cooker. Cover with the lid and cook for 6 hours on Low. Serve warm.

Mushrooms Filled with Goat Cheese

Serves: 6 | Total Time: 4 hours 15 minutes

6 oz goat cheese
12 medium mushrooms
1 egg

½ cup breadcrumbs
1 poblano pepper, chopped
1 tsp dried oregano

In a bowl, combine goat cheese, egg, breadcrumbs, poblano pepper, and oregano. Fill each mushroom with this mixture and place them into your Slow Cooker. Cover with the lid and cook for 4 hours on Low. Serve.

Basil Pepperoni Sauce

Serves: 6 | Total Time: 3 hours 15 minutes

2 shallots, chopped
1 cup shredded mozzarella
1 ½ cups pizza sauce
4 pepperoni, sliced

2 red bell peppers, diced
9 pitted black olives, chopped
1 cup cream cheese
½ tsp dried basil

Mix pizza sauce, pepperoni, shallots, bell peppers, black olives, cream cheese, mozzarella, and basil in your Slow Cooker. Cover with the lid and cook for 3 hours on Low. Serve warm with breadsticks if desired.

Chicken Meatballs Stuffed with Mozzarella

Serves: 6 | Total Time: 6 hours 30 minutes

½ cup breadcrumbs
2 lb ground chicken
1 tsp dried basil
½ tsp dried oregano
1 egg

Mozzarella balls as needed
½ cup chicken stock
Salt and pepper to taste

In a bowl, Combine the ground chicken, basil, oregano, egg, breadcrumbs, salt, and pepper. Make small balls out of the mixture, flatten them a little, and put a mozzarella ball in the center. Cover the mozzarella with the meat, making sure to cover the cheese. Place the balls in your Slow Cooker. Pour in chicken stock and seal the lid. Select Low and cook for 6 hours. Serve warm.

Texas Meatballs

Serves: 6 | Total Time: 7 hours 30 minutes

1 lb ground beef
1 lb ground pork
1 carrot, grated
2 shallots, chopped
1 egg
½ cup breadcrumbs

½ tsp cumin powder
1 cup dark beer
1 cup BBQ sauce
½ tsp chili powder
1 tsp apple cider vinegar
Salt and pepper to taste

Mix dark beer, BBQ sauce, chili powder, and apple vinegar in your Slow Cooker. In a bowl, Combine the ground pork, ground beef, carrot, shallots, egg, breadcrumbs, cumin, salt, and pepper. Make small balls out of the mixture and place them into the pot. Cover with the lid and cook for 7 hours on Low. Serve warm.

Authentic Baba Ganoush

Serves: 4 | Total Time: 4 hours 15 minutes

2 garlic cloves, minced
1 large eggplant, halved
2 tbsp olive oil
1 tbsp tahini paste

1 tbsp lemon juice
1 tbsp chopped parsley
Salt and pepper to taste

Rub each eggplant half with a garlic clove and sprinkle with salt, pepper, and olive oil. Place the eggplant halves in your Slow Cooker. Cover with the lid and cook for 4 hours on Low. When done, remove the lid and remove the eggplant flesh to a bowl. Using a fork, mash it. Mix in tahini paste, lemon juice, and parsley. Serve chilled.

Two-Cheese Beer Fondue

Serves: 6 | Total Time: 2 hours 15 minutes

2 cups grated cheddar
1 cup grated Gruyere cheese
1 shallot, chopped
1 garlic clove, minced
1 tbsp cornstarch

1 tsp Dijon mustard
½ tsp cumin seeds
1 cup beer
Salt and pepper to taste

Stir shallot, garlic, Gruyere, cheddar, cornstarch, mustard, cumin seeds, and beer in your Slow Cooker. Sprinkle with salt and pepper to taste. Cover with the lid and cook for 2 hours on High. Serve warm.

Italian Zucchini Frittata

Serves: 6 | Total Time: 6 hours 15 minutes

½ cup grated Parmesan
6 eggs
2 zucchinis, finely sliced
2 garlic cloves, minced
1 tsp dried mint

1 tsp dried oregano
2 tbsp plain yogurt
1 tbsp chopped parsley
Salt and pepper to taste

Place the zucchinis, garlic, mint, oregano, salt, and pepper in your Slow Cooker. In a bowl, Combine the eggs, yogurt, parsley, and Parmesan. Pour it over the zucchinis and seal the lid. Select Low and cook for 6 hours. When done, remove the lid and serve warm.

Tex-Mex Nacho Dip

Serves: 6 | Total Time: 6 hours 15 minutes

2 cups grated Cheddar	1 can black beans, drained
1 lb ground pork	1 cup diced tomatoes
1 cup apple juice	2 jalapeno peppers, minced
4 garlic cloves, chopped	2 tbsp chopped cilantro
2 cups BBQ sauce	1 lime, juiced
2 tbsp brown sugar	Salt and pepper to taste
1 ½ cups sweet corn	Nachos for serving

Place a skillet over medium heat. Add the ground pork, and cook for 2 minutes, stirring often. Place the cooked meat, apple juice, garlic, BBQ sauce, brown sugar, salt, and pepper in your Slow Cooker. Cover with the lid and cook for 2 hours on High. When done, remove the lid and stir in corn, black beans, tomatoes, jalapeño peppers, cilantro, cheddar, and lime juice. Cover with the lid and cook for 4 hours on Low. Serve with nachos.

Grandma's Onion Dip

Serves: 4 | Total Time: 4 hours 15 minutes

4 large onions, chopped	1 ½ cups sour cream
2 tbsp olive oil	1 pinch nutmeg
1 tbsp butter	Salt and pepper to taste

Mix olive oil, onions, butter, salt, pepper, and nutmeg in your Slow Cooker. Cover with the lid and cook for 4 hours on High. When done, let cool completely and mix in sour cream. Adjust the seasoning. Serve right away.

Turkey Meatballs in Marinara Sauce

Serves: 6 | Total Time: 6 hours 30 minutes

1 potato, grated	4 basil leaves, chopped
2 lb ground turkey	½ tsp dried mint
1 carrot, grated	1 egg
1 shallot, chopped	2 cups marinara sauce
1 tbsp chopped parsley	¼ cup breadcrumbs
1 tbsp chopped cilantro	Salt and pepper to taste

Pour marinara sauce into your Slow Cooker. In a bowl, combine ground turkey, carrot, potato, shallot, parsley, cilantro, basil, mint, egg, breadcrumbs, salt, and pepper. Make small balls out of the mixture and place them into the pot. Cover with the lid and cook for 6 hours on Low. When done, remove the lid and serve warm or chilled.

Chili Turkey Loaf

Serves: 6 | Total Time: 6 hours 15 minutes

1 carrot, grated	¼ cup breadcrumbs
1 sweet potato, grated	¼ tsp chili powder
1 ½ lb ground turkey	Salt and pepper to taste
1 egg	1 cup shredded mozzarella

In a bowl, Combine the ground turkey, carrot, sweet potato, egg, breadcrumbs, chili powder, mozzarella, salt, and pepper. Transfer it into your Slow Cooker and toss to combine. Cover with the lid and cook for 6 hours on Low. When done, remove the lid and serve warm.

Crispy Parmesan Bread

Serves: 6 | Total Time: 1 hour 15 minutes

½ cup grated Parmesan	2 tbsp olive oil
2 cups buttermilk	1 tsp baking soda
4 cups all-purpose flour	½ tsp salt

In a bowl, Combine the flour, salt, Parmesan, and baking soda. Using a fork, whisk in buttermilk and olive oil. Shape the dough into a loaf and place it in your Slow Cooker. Cover with the lid and cook for 1 hour on High. When done, remove the lid and serve warm or chilled.

Special Slow Cook Bread

Serves: 6 | Total Time: 1 hour 30 minutes

½ cup yogurt	1 tsp sugar
1 egg	1 cup warm water
2 tbsp olive oil	3 cups all-purpose flour
2 tsp active dry yeast	½ tsp salt

In a bowl, Combine the dry yeast, water, yogurt, sugar, egg, and olive oil. Mix in flour and salt and knead for 5-10 minutes until it gets a non-sticky dough. Place it into your Slow Cooker. Cover with the lid and cook for 1 ¼ hours on High. Serve warm.

Spicy Turkey Bites

Serves: 6 | Total Time: 7 hours 15 minutes

1 carrot, sliced	1 tsp hot sauce
2 lb turkey breast, cubed	1 cup tomato sauce
½ tsp garlic powder	Salt and pepper to taste
1 tbsp Ranch dressing	

Stir turkey breasts, carrot, garlic powder, Ranch dressing, hot sauce, and tomato sauce in your Slow Cooker. Sprinkle salt and pepper to taste and toss until everything is coat. Cover with the lid and cook for 7 hours on Low. When done, remove the lid and serve warm or chilled.

Special Meatballs with Orange Marmalade

Serves: 6 | Total Time: 7 hours 30 minutes

1 cup orange marmalade	1 bay leaf
2 lb ground pork	1 egg
1 shallot, chopped	2 cups BBQ sauce
4 garlic cloves, minced	1 tsp Worcestershire sauce
1 carrot, grated	Salt and pepper to taste

Stir orange marmalade, BBQ sauce, bay leaf, Worcestershire sauce, salt, and pepper in your Slow Cooker. In a bowl, Combine the ground pork, shallot, garlic, carrot, egg, salt, and pepper. Make small balls out of the mixture and place them into the pot. Cover with the lid and cook for 7 hours on Low. Serve warm.

CHICKEN RECIPES

Chipotle Chicken

Serves: 4 | Total Time: 6 hours 15 minutes

3 chipotle peppers in adobo sauce, minced
1 tbsp adobo sauce from chipotle peppers
1 (10.75-oz) can cream of condensed chicken soup

4 chicken breast halves   ¼ cup melted butter
1 cup cream cheese   Salt and pepper to taste
½ cup chicken broth   2 tbsp chives, chopped
2 cloves garlic, minced

Butter the chicken breasts evenly and season them with salt, pepper, and garlic. Stir the chicken in your Slow Cooker with remaining ingredients to combine. Cover and cook on Low for 6 hours. Serve the dish warm with the liquid from cooking drizzled over the top of it. Garnish with fresh chopped chives and enjoy!

Mediterranean Chicken

Serves: 4 | Total Time: 6 hours 20 minutes

1 (3.5-lb) whole chicken, cut up, skin removed
½ cup dried apricots, chopped
4 carrots, sliced   ½ cup raisins, soaked
2 tbsp lemon juice   1 tsp ground cinnamon
2 large onions, sliced   2 cups chicken broth
2 garlic cloves, minced   2 tbsp whole-wheat flour
1 ½ tsp ground cumin   2 cups couscous, cooked
¼ cup tomato paste   2 tbsp chopped parsley
Salt and pepper to taste   2 tbsp olive oil

Grease the inside of your Slow Cooker lightly with olive oil. Place the carrots and onions into your Slow Cooker. Season the chicken with salt and pepper and add it to the Slow Cooker. Top with apricots and raisins. In a small mixing bowl, whisk broth, tomato paste, lemon juice, flour, cumin, cinnamon, and garlic until well combined. Pour the mixture over the chicken. Cover and cook for 6 hours on Low. Serve dish hot on top of couscous sprinkled with fresh parsley and enjoy!

BBQ Chicken

Serves: 4 | Total Time: 6 hours 10 minutes

4 chicken breast halves   ¼ tsp garlic powder
2 dashes hot pepper sauce   2 tsp lemon juice
1/8 tsp cayenne pepper   2 tbsp mustard
½ tsp chili powder   1 cup ketchup
2 tbsp Worcestershire sauce   2 tbsp cooked brown rice
½ cup maple syrup   2 tbsp chopped chives

Layer the chicken in your Slow Cooker. Combine the remaining ingredients in a bowl and mix well to combine. Add the sauce mixture to the Slow Cooker and coat the chicken with it. Cover and cook on Low heat for 6 hours. With two forks, shred the chicken, then cook for an additional 30 minutes. Stir dish well before serving on top of cooked brown rice. Garnish top of dish with fresh chopped chives and enjoy!

Thai Chicken

Serves: 6 | Total Time: 8 hours 20 minutes

3 chicken breasts, cut into strips
½ cup roasted peanuts, chopped
1 red bell pepper, cut into strips
3 green onions, chopped   3 cloves garlic, minced
¼ cup lime juice   1 tbsp ground cumin
2/3 cup peanut butter   ½ cup chicken broth
2 tbsp cornstarch   1 large onion, chopped
Salt and pepper to taste   ¼ cup cilantro, chopped
½ tsp red pepper flakes   3 cups cooked rice noodles

Carefully add all the ingredients to your Slow Cooker, except for peanut butter, lime juice, and cornstarch. Cover with lid and cook on Low for 8 hours.

In a mixing bowl, add peanut butter, lime juice and cornstarch and 1 cup of cooking liquid. When the sauce becomes thick, add it to the slow cooker and mix in. Cover and cook for an additional 30 minutes on High. Garnish with cilantro, peanutsp and green onions. Enjoy!

Sticky Sweet Chicken Wings

Serves: 4 | Total Time: 4 hours 10 minutes

5 tbsp fig balsamic vinegar   1/3 cup raw honey
2 lb chicken wings   1/3 cup soy sauce
Salt and pepper to taste   1 ½ tsp Sriracha sauce
3 garlic cloves, minced   1 tsp ground coriander
1 tbsp fresh lime juice   3 tbsp potato starch
¼ cup chicken broth   2 tbsp cilantro, chopped

Season the chicken wings with salt and pepper, and place them in your Slow Cooker. In a small mixing bowl, combine the honey, broth, vinegar, soy sauce, garlic, lime juice, ground coriander, and sriracha sauce and mix well. Pour mixture over the chicken wings and toss to coat. Close the lid and cook on High for 4 hours.

Whisk the potato starch with ¼ cup cold water until smooth. Add to the cooker and stir gently. Cook for an additional 15 minutes on High. Serve topped with cilantro.

Honey-Garlic Chicken

Serves: 6 | Total Time: 4 hours 20 minutes

6 chicken thighs, boneless, skinless
1 (20 oz) can pineapple tidbits, drained with juice reserved
3 tbsp vegetable oil   2 cloves garlic, minced
¼ cup water   3 tbsp ketchup
2 tbsp cornstarch   1 tbsp honey
1 tbsp ginger root, minced   2 tbsp chopped cilantro

Warm the vegetable oil in a pan over medium heat. Cook the chicken until no pink meat remains, about 10 minutes. Mix the honey, ginger, ketchup, garlic, and pineapple juice in a bowl. Add along with chicken to your Slow Cooker. Close the lid and cook on High for 4 hours.

In a mixing bowl, mix cornstarch and water. Add this mixture into the slow cooker to thicken the sauce. Drizzle the sauce over chicken and serve topped with cilantro.

Awesome Chicken Tikka Masala

Serves: 4 | Total Time: 2 hours 30 minutes

4 chicken thighs
2 shallots, chopped
4 garlic cloves, minced
2 cups cooked rice
1 cup diced tomatoes
1 lime, juiced
1 cup coconut milk
½ cup chicken stock
2 tbsp canola oil
2 tbsp tomato paste
2 tbsp chopped cilantro
1 tbsp garam masala
Salt and pepper to taste

Warm canola oil in a pan over medium heat, place chicken and cook for 2-3 minutes until golden on all sides. Add it to your Slow Cooker. Put in shallots, garlic, tomato paste, garam masala, tomatoes, lime juice, coconut milk, chicken stock, salt, and pepper. Cover with the lid and cook for 2 hours on High. Serve over cooked rice, and top with chopped cilantro.

Orange & Red Pepper Infused Chicken

Serves: 4 | Total Time: 8 hours 10 minutes

2 tsp red pepper flakes
1 cup orange juice
4 chicken breast halves
1/3 cup honey
Salt and pepper to taste
2 tbsp chopped cilantro

Place the chicken breasts into your greased Slow Cooker. In a mixing bowl, mix together the remaining ingredients until well combined. Then pour mixture over chicken breasts in the cooker. Cover with lid and cook on Low for 8 hours. Serve hot sprinkled with cilantro and enjoy!

Orange Chicken with Sweet Potatoes

Serves: 4 | Total Time: 8 hours 10 minutes

4 pieces chicken thighs with skin removed
1 cup orange marmalade
½ cup chicken broth
4 sweet potatoes, chopped
Salt and pepper to taste

Add the sweet potatoes into your Slow Cooker. Season them with salt and pepper. Place the chicken thighs on top, adding more salt and pepper. In a small mixing bowl, add chicken broth and orange marmalade and mix well. Pour the mixture over the chicken and sweet potatoes. Cover with lid cook on Low for 8 hours. Serve warm.

Cheesy Italian Chicken

Serves: 4 | Total Time: 4 hours 15 minutes

1 sweet onion, chopped
4 garlic cloves, minced
4 chicken breasts
2 tbsp butter
1 tsp dried Italian herbs
1 can cream of chicken soup
1 cup cream cheese
½ cup chicken stock
Salt and pepper to taste

Sprinkle chicken breasts with Italian herbs, salt, and pepper. Melt butter in a pan over medium heat, place chicken and cook until golden brown on all sides. Add it to your Slow Cooker. Add in onion, garlic, chicken soup, cream cheese, and chicken stock and season with salt and pepper to taste. Cover with the lid and cook for 4 hours on Low. Serve warm.

Chicken Chole Bhature

Serves: 6 | Total Time: 3 hours 15 minutes

½ head cauliflower, cut into florets
2 chicken breasts, cubed
1 can (15-oz) garbanzo beans
1 sweet onion, chopped
1 celery stalk, sliced
1 carrot, sliced
1 cup vegetable stock
½ cup coconut milk
2 tbsp olive oil
1 tsp curry powder
¼ tsp chili powder
Salt and pepper to taste

Warm olive oil in a pan over medium heat, place chicken and cook for 2-3 minutes until golden brown on all sides. Add it to your Slow Cooker. Add in onion, celery, carrot, cauliflower, garbanzo, vegetable stock, coconut milk, curry powder, chili powder, salt, and pepper. Cover with the lid and cook for 3 hours on High. When done, remove the lid and serve quickly.

Barley Salad with Chicken & Squash

Serves: 6 | Total Time: 6 hours 15 minutes

2 cups butternut squash cubes
1 lb ground chicken
1 sweet onion, chopped
2 garlic cloves, chopped
1 cup pearl barley
1 cup green peas
2 cups vegetable stock
2 tbsp olive oil
2 tbsp chopped parsley
Salt and pepper to taste
Lemon juice for serving

Warm olive oil in a pan over medium heat, place chicken and cook for 2-3 minutes until golden on all sides. Add it to your Slow Cooker. Put in onion, garlic, barley, green peas, butternut squash, vegetable stock, salt, and pepper. Cover with the lid and cook for 6 hours on Low. When done, remove the lid, sprinkle with lemon juice, and top with parsley to serve.

Cauliflower & Chicken Gratin

Serves: 6 | Total Time: 6 hours 15 minutes

1 can condensed cream of chicken soup
1 head cauliflower, cut into florets
2 chicken breasts, cubed
½ tsp garlic powder
1 tsp cayenne pepper
Salt and pepper to taste
1 ½ cups grated cheddar

Stir cauliflower, chicken, garlic powder, cayenne pepper, chicken soup, salt, and pepper in your Slow Cooker and scatter with cheddar cheese on top. Cover with the lid and cook for 6 hours on Low. Serve immediately.

BBQ Pulled Chicken

Serves: 6 | Total Time: 8 hours 15 minutes

2 sweet onions, sliced
4 chicken breasts
1 cup apple cider
1 cup BBQ sauce
1 tsp grated ginger
Salt and pepper to taste

Mix the chicken, onion, ginger, apple cider, BBQ sauce, salt, and pepper in your Slow Cooker. Cover with the lid and cook for 8 hours on Low. When done, remove the lid, using two forks, shred the chicken finely and serve.

Chicken & Vegetable Casserole

Serves: 6 | Total Time: 7 hours 30 minutes

2 peeled potatoes, cubed	2 cups vegetable stock
1 lb chicken breasts, cubed	1 thyme sprig
2 carrots, sliced	1 rosemary sprig
2 celery stalks, sliced	Salt and pepper to taste
1 parsnip, sliced	

Add chicken, carrots, celery, parsnip, potatoes, vegetable stock, thyme, rosemary, salt, and pepper in your Slow Cooker and toss to combine. Cover with the lid and cook for 7 hours on Low. Serve warm.

Chili Parmesan Chicken

Serves: 4 | Total Time: 6 hours 15 minutes

½ cup chicken stock	¼ tsp chili powder
1 ½ cups grated Parmesan	1 tsp dried thyme
4 chicken breasts	Salt and pepper to taste
½ tsp cumin powder	

Rub chicken breasts with cumin, chili powder, salt, and pepper. Put them into your Slow Cooker, add in thyme and chicken stock, and scatter with Parmesan cheese on top. Cover and cook for 6 hours on Low. Serve warm.

Chicken Pilaf with Edamame

Serves: 6 | Total Time: 6 hours 30 minutes

1 cup frozen edamame	2 garlic cloves, chopped
1 cup green peas	2 cups vegetable stock
1 peeled sweet potato, cubed	½ tsp dried sage
2 chicken breasts, cubed	½ tsp dried oregano
½ cup wild rice	Salt and pepper to taste
½ cup pearl barley	1 tbsp chopped parsley
1 leek, sliced	

Stir chicken, rice, barley, leek, garlic, edamame, green peas, sweet potato, vegetable stock, sage, oregano, salt, and pepper in your Slow Cooker. Cover with the lid and cook for 6 hours on Low. When done, remove the lid, mix in parsley and serve warm.

Creamy Chicken with Green Peas

Serves: 6 | Total Time: 6 hours 30 minutes

2 garlic cloves, chopped	1 ½ cups green peas
2 chicken breasts, cubed	1 tbsp cornstarch
½ lb baby carrots	1 cup vegetables tock
1 shallot, chopped	¼ cup white wine
1 leek, sliced	

FOR TOPPING

½ cup cold butter, cubed	½ cup buttermilk, chilled
1 cup all-purpose flour	Salt and pepper to taste

In your Slow Cooker, Combine the shallot, leek, garlic, chicken, green peas, carrots, cornstarch, vegetable stock, wine, salt, and pepper. In a blender, add flour, butter, buttermilk, salt, and pepper and pulse until crumbly. Pour it over the veggies. Cover with the lid and cook for 6 hours on Low. Serve right away.

Chicken Jambalaya with Shrimp

Serves: 6 | Total Time: 8 hours 15 minutes

1 lb fresh shrimps, peeled and cleaned	
1 ½ lb chicken breasts, cubed	1 ½ cups chicken stock
2 large onions, chopped	2 tbsp olive oil
2 red bell peppers, diced	½ tsp dried oregano
1 celery stalk, sliced	Salt and pepper to taste
2 garlic cloves, chopped	1 cup cooked white rice
1 cup diced tomato	

Warm olive oil in a pan over medium heat, place chicken and cook for 5 minutes until golden on all sides. Add it to your Slow Cooker. Add in onions, bell peppers, celery, garlic, oregano, tomato, chicken stock, salt, and pepper. Cover with the lid and cook for 6 hours on Low. Add in shrimps and cook for another 2 hours. Serve.

Traditional Chicken Stroganoff

Serves: 6 | Total Time: 6 hours 15 minutes

3 chicken breasts, cubed	1 cup vegetable stock
2 celery stalks, sliced	2 tbsp butter
2 shallots, chopped	1 tsp dried Italian herbs
2 garlic cloves, chopped	Salt and pepper to taste
1 cup cream cheese	16 oz cooked macaroni
2 cups sliced mushrooms	

Melt butter in a pan over medium heat, place chicken and cook until golden brown on all sides. Add it to your Slow Cooker. Put in celery, shallots, garlic, Italian herbs, cream cheese, mushrooms, vegetable stock, salt, and pepper. Cover with the lid and cook for 6 hours on Low. Serve over cooked macaroni and enjoy!

Sweet BBQ Chicken

Serves: 6 | Total Time: 8 hours 15 minutes

1 cup BBQ sauce	2 tbsp maple syrup
3 chicken breasts, boneless and skinless, halved	½ tsp chili powder
	1 tsp Worcestershire sauce
1 tsp mustard seeds	½ cup vegetable stock
2 tbsp lemon juice	Salt and pepper to taste
½ tsp garlic powder	

In your Slow Cooker, add chicken, BBQ sauce, mustard seeds, lemon juice, garlic powder, maple syrup, chili powder, Worcestershire sauce, stock, salt, and pepper, and stir. Cover and cook for 8 hours on Low. Serve.

Paprika Chicken with Bok Choy

Serves: 4 | Total Time: 6 hours 30 minutes

1 sweet onion, chopped	2 tbsp soy sauce
4 chicken breasts	1 tbsp brown sugar
1 head bok choy, shredded	1 tsp paprika
4 garlic cloves, minced	1 cup chicken stock

Toss chicken, garlic, onion, soy sauce, sugar, paprika, and chicken stock in your Slow Cooker. Cover with the lid and cook for 4 hours on Low. Add in bok choy and cook for another 2 hours. Serve immediately.

Chicken with Swiss Cheese Sauce

Serves: 4 | Total Time: 3 hours 15 minutes

1 can cream of mushrooms soup
1 shallot, sliced
4 boneless chicken breasts
1 celery stalk, sliced
½ cup chicken stock
1 cup grated Swiss cheese
Salt and pepper to taste

Sprinkle the chicken with salt and pepper. Put it into your Slow Cooker among celery, shallot, mushroom soup, chicken stock, and Swiss cheese. Cover with the lid and cook for 3 hours on High. Serve warm.

Buttered Garlic Chicken

Serves: 6 | Total Time: 8 hours 15 minutes

1 whole chicken
6 garlic cloves, minced
¼ cup butter, softened
½ cup chicken stock
2 tbsp chopped parsley
1 tsp dried sage
Salt and pepper to taste

In a bowl, combine butter, garlic, parsley, sage, salt, and pepper. Put the chicken on a cutting board and slang the breast and thighs´ skin, filling with the herb mixture. Put the chicken into your Slow Cooker and pour in chicken stock. Cover and cook for 8 hours on Low. Serve warm.

Balsamic Chicken Thighs

Serves: 4 | Total Time: 6 hours 15 minutes

½ cup chicken stock
4 chicken thighs
2 tbsp brown sugar
1 tsp cumin powder
½ tsp chili powder
½ tsp garlic powder
2 tbsp balsamic vinegar
1 tbsp soy sauce

In a bowl, whisk sugar, cumin, chili powder, garlic powder, balsamic vinegar, and soy sauce. Rub chicken thighs with the mixture, spreading into the skin, and place them into your Slow Cooker. Pour in chicken stock, cover with the lid, and cook for 6 hours on Low. Serve immediately.

Chicken Casserole with Mushrooms

Serves: 6 | Total Time: 6 hours 15 minutes

4 cups sliced cremini mushrooms
2 chicken breasts, cubed
4 carrots, sliced
1 large onion, chopped
1 cup frozen peas
1 cup vegetable stock
½ tsp dried thyme
1 sheet puff pastry
Salt and pepper to taste

Mix the mushrooms, carrots, chicken, onion, peas, thyme, vegetable stock, salt, and pepper in your Slow Cooker and top with puff pastry. Cover with the lid and cook for 6 hours on Low. Serve immediately.

Citrus Chicken Bake

Serves: 4 | Total Time: 6 hours 15 minutes

2 carrots, sliced
2 oranges, juiced
4 chicken breasts
1 fennel bulb, sliced
1 sweet onion, sliced
1 bay leaf
1 ½ cups chicken stock
Salt and pepper to taste

Mix the chicken, fennel, onion, carrots, orange juice, bay leaf, chicken stock, salt, and pepper in your Slow Cooker. Cover with the lid and cook for 6 hours on Low. When done, remove the lid and serve warm.

Indian-Style Chicken Thighs

Serves: 6 | Total Time: 8 hours 15 minutes

1 cup chicken stock
6 chicken thighs
½ cup plain yogurt
1 tbsp grated ginger
1 tsp curry powder
1 tsp garlic powder
½ tsp onion powder
½ tsp cumin powder
¼ tsp chili powder
Salt and pepper to taste
2 cups cooked white rice

Sprinkle chicken thighs with ginger, curry powder, garlic powder, onion powder, cumin, and chili powder. Place them into your Slow Cooker and pour in yogurt, chicken stock, salt, and pepper. Cover with the lid and cook for 8 hours on Low. Serve over cooked rice.

Oriental Chicken Thighs

Serves: 6 | Total Time: 3 hours 15 minutes

2 shallots, sliced
6 chicken thighs
2 garlic cloves, chopped
¼ cup apple cider
¼ cup soy sauce
1 bay leaf
1 tbsp brown sugar
½ tsp cayenne pepper
Salt and pepper to taste
2 cups cooked rice

Stir chicken, shallots, garlic, apple cider, soy sauce, bay leaf, sugar, cayenne pepper, salt, and pepper in your Slow Cooker. Cover with the lid and cook for 3 hours on High. When done, remove the lid and serve over cooked rice.

Hoisin Chicken with Sesame Seeds

Serves: 6 | Total Time: 3 hours 15 minutes

6 chicken thighs
2 tbsp soy sauce
1 tbsp brown sugar
2 tbsp fresh orange juice
2 tbsp hoisin sauce
1 tbsp sesame oil
1 tsp grated ginger
1 tbsp cornstarch
2 tbsp water
1 tbsp sesame seeds

In your Slow Cooker, put sesame oil, chicken, soy sauce, sugar, orange juice, hoisin sauce, ginger, cornstarch, and water and stir. Cover with the lid and cook for 3 hours on High. When done, remove the lid, scatter with sesame seeds, and serve with your desired side dish.

Garlic & Lemon Chicken

Serves: 6 | Total Time: 6 hours 15 minutes

6 chicken thighs
1 lemon, sliced
6 garlic cloves, chopped
½ cup chicken stock
2 tbsp butter
1 thyme sprig
1 rosemary sprig
Salt and pepper to taste

Sprinkle chicken thighs with salt and pepper and place them into your Slow Cooker. Add lemon slices, garlic, butter, thyme, and rosemary on top and pour in chicken stock. Cover and cook for 6 hours on Low. Serve warm.

Cheddar Chicken

Serves: 2 | Total Time: 2 hours 15 minutes

1 cup grated cheddar
2 chicken breasts
1 cup cream of chicken soup
¼ tsp garlic powder
Salt and pepper to taste

Stir chicken, chicken soup, cheddar, garlic powder, salt, and pepper in your Slow Cooker. Cover with the lid and cook for 2 hours on High. Serve topped with cheese sauce.

Gingery Chicken Drumsticks

Serves: 4 | Total Time: 5 hours 15 minutes

2 green onions, chopped
2 lb chicken drumsticks
¼ cup chicken stock
1 tsp grated ginger
1 cup pineapple juice
2 tbsp soy sauce
2 tbsp brown sugar
¼ tsp chili powder
2 cups cooked white rice

Toss chicken, ginger, pineapple juice, soy sauce, sugar, chili powder, green onions, and chicken stock in your Slow Cooker. Cover and cook for 5 hours on Low. When done, remove the lid and serve over cooked rice.

Hot Creole Chicken Breasts

Serves: 6 | Total Time: 8 hours 15 minutes

4 chicken breasts, cubed
1 can fire-roasted tomatoes
1 celery stalk, sliced
2 large onions, chopped
4 garlic cloves, chopped
1 jalapeno pepper, chopped
½ cup chicken stock
2 tbsp creole seasoning
Salt and pepper to taste

In your Slow Cooker, combine chicken, creole seasoning, tomatoes, celery, onions, garlic, jalapeño peppers, chicken stock, salt, and pepper. Cover with the lid and cook for 8 hours on Low. Serve with your desired side dish.

Spiced Coconut Chicken

Serves: 6 | Total Time: 6 hours 45 minutes

6 chicken thighs
1 large onion, chopped
4 garlic cloves, chopped
2 tbsp butter
1 tsp curry powder
1 tsp garam masala
½ tsp cumin powder
¼ tsp chili powder
1 ½ cups coconut milk
Salt and pepper to taste
½ cup plain yogurt

Melt butter in a pan over medium heat, place chicken and cook until golden brown on all sides. Add it to your Slow Cooker. Add in onion, garlic, curry powder, garam masala, cumin, chili powder, coconut milk, salt, and pepper. Cover with the lid and cook for 6 hours on Low. Serve topped with plain yogurt.

Chicken a la Cordon Bleu

Serves: 4 | Total Time: 6 hours 15 minutes

4 slices Cheddar cheese
4 chicken breasts
4 thick ham slices
1 tsp dried thyme
½ cup vegetable stock
Salt and pepper to taste

Sprinkle chicken breasts with thyme, salt, and pepper and place them into your Slow Cooker. Add ham and cheddar cheese slices on top and pour in vegetable stock. Cover with the lid and cook for 6 hours on Low. Serve.

Chicken Chili with Bacon

Serves: 8 | Total Time: 8 hours 15 minutes

4 bacon slices, chopped
2 lb chicken breasts, cubed
1 can (15 oz) black beans
1 can (15 oz) kidney beans
1 can (15 oz) sweet corn
2 celery stalks, sliced
2 large red onions, chopped
1 cup tomato sauce
2 cups red salsa
2 tbsp canola oil
1 tsp chili powder
1tsp cumin powder
1 tsp garlic powder
1 ½ cups chicken stock
Salt and pepper to taste
2 tbsp grated cheddar

Warm canola oil in a pan over medium heat, place bacon and cook until crispy. Add in chicken and cook for 2-3 minutes until golden brown on all sides. Add it to your Slow Cooker. Put in red salsa, beans, corn, celery, onions, tomato sauce, chili powder, cumin, garlic powder, chicken stock, salt, and pepper. Cover and cook for 8 hours on Low. Top with cheddar cheese to serve.

Chicken Chilli

Serves: 6 | Total Time: 6 hours 15 minutes

2 ripe tomatoes, diced
1 can (15-oz) cannellini beans
2 yellow bell peppers, sliced
6 chicken thighs
1 large fennel bulb, sliced
1 large onion, sliced
2 garlic cloves, chopped
1 cup chicken stock
1 rosemary sprig
Salt and pepper to taste

In your Slow Cooker, combine chicken, fennel, onion, garlic, tomatoes, beans, bell peppers, rosemary, stock, salt, and pepper. Cover and cook for 6 hours on Low. Serve.

Divine Buffalo Chicken

Serves: 6 | Total Time: 7 hours 15 minutes

2 cups hot BBQ sauce
3 lb chicken drumsticks
2 tbsp tomato sauce
1 tbsp cider vinegar
1 tsp Worcestershire sauce
1 cup cream cheese
Salt and pepper to taste

Toss chicken, BBQ sauce, tomato sauce, cider vinegar, Worcestershire sauce, cream cheese, salt, and pepper in your Slow Cooker. Cover with the lid and cook for 7 hours on Low. Serve right away.

Oregano Chicken with Blue Cheese

Serves: 4 | Total Time: 2 hours 15 minutes

½ cup crumbled blue cheese
4 chicken breasts
1 tsp dried oregano
½ cup chicken stock
Salt and pepper to taste

Sprinkle chicken breasts with oregano, salt, and pepper. Put blue cheese, chicken stock, and seasoned chicken in your Slow Cooker. Cover with the lid and cook for 2 hours on High. Serve warm.

Caribbean Chicken Dish

Serves: 6 | Total Time: 2 hours 45 minutes

2 chicken breasts, cut into thin strips
1 large sweet onion, sliced
4 garlic cloves, chopped
1 mango, peeled and cubed
1 chipotle pepper, chopped
1 can fire-roasted tomatoes

1 cup chicken stock
2 tbsp canola oil
½ tsp cumin powder
¼ tsp grated ginger
Salt and pepper to taste

Warm the canola oil in a pan over medium heat. Place the chicken and cook for 2-3 minutes until golden brown on all sides. Add it to your Slow Cooker. Add in onion, garlic, mango, chipotle pepper, cumin, ginger, tomatoes, chicken stock, salt, and pepper. Cover with the lid and cook for 2 ½ hours on High. Serve warm.

Chicken & White Bean Cassoulet

Serves: 6 | Total Time: 6 hours 15 minutes

3 chicken breasts, cubed
2 cans (15-oz) white beans
2 celery stalks, sliced
2 carrots, sliced
1 large onion, chopped

2 garlic cloves, chopped
2 tbsp canola oil
¼ cup dry white wine
1 cup chicken stock
Salt and pepper to taste

Warm canola oil in a pan over medium heat, place chicken and cook for 2-3 minutes until golden brown on all sides. Add it to your Slow Cooker. Put in beans, celery, carrots, onion, garlic, wine, chicken stock, salt, and pepper. Cover with the lid and cook for 6 hours on Low. When done, remove the lid and serve warm.

Sticky Chicken Wings

Serves: 4 | Total Time: 3 hours 15 minutes

1 ½ tsp smoked paprika
2 lb chicken wings
½ tsp sweet paprika

1 tbsp honey
½ cup chicken stock
Salt and pepper to taste

In your Slow Cooker, mix chicken wings, paprika, honey, salt, and pepper until well combined and pour in chicken stock. Cover and cook for 3 hours on High. Serve warm.

Hot Tomato Chicken Thighs

Serves: 6 | Total Time: 8 hours 15 minutes

6 chicken thighs
¼ cup hot sauce
½ cup tomato sauce
½ cup vegetable stock

2 tbsp butter
½ tsp garlic powder
½ tsp cumin powder
Salt and pepper to taste

Put chicken, hot sauce, butter, garlic powder, tomato sauce, vegetable stock, cumin, salt, and pepper in your Slow Cooker and toss to combine. Cover with the lid and cook for 8 hours on Low. Serve right away.

Peanut Chicken Breasts

Serves: 4 | Total Time: 2 hours 15 minutes

¼ cup smooth peanut butter
2 chicken breasts, cut into thin strips

2 tbsp soy sauce
1 tbsp hot sauce

1 tbsp lime juice
1 tsp honey

Mix the chicken, soy sauce, hot sauce, peanut butter, lime juice, and honey in your Slow Cooker. Cover with the lid and cook for 2 hours on High. Serve warm.

Lemony Thyme Chicken Drumsticks

Serves: 6 | Total Time: 3 hours 15 minutes

2 lb chicken drumsticks
2 garlic cloves, chopped
1 lemon, juiced
2 tbsp butter

1 thyme sprig
1 cup vegetable stock
Salt and pepper to taste

In your Slow Cooker, combine chicken, butter, lemon juice, garlic, thyme, vegetable stock, salt, and pepper. Cover with the lid and cook for 3 hours on High. When done, remove the lid and serve warm.

Smoked Chicken Thighs with Snap Peas

Serves: 6 | Total Time: 6 hours 15 minutes

1 lb snap peas
6 chicken thighs
¼ cup vegetable stock
3 tbsp honey

½ tsp cumin powder
½ tsp smoked paprika
½ tsp fennel seeds
2 tbsp soy sauce

In a bowl, whisk chicken, honey, cumin, paprika, fennel seeds, and soy sauce until well coated. Put snap peas and vegetable stock in your Slow Cooker, stir, and top with chicken mixture. Cover with the lid and cook for 6 hours on Low. When done, remove the lid and serve warm.

Chicken Chili with Corn

Serves: 6 | Total Time: 8 hours 15 minutes

1 can (15 oz) black beans
1 can (10 oz) sweet corn
3 chicken breasts, cubed
1 can (15 oz) diced tomatoes
1 cup red salsa

1 tsp taco seasoning
½ tsp chili powder
1 cup chicken stock
½ cup cream cheese
Salt and pepper to taste

Mix the chicken, tomatoes, red salsa, beans, corn, taco seasoning, chili powder, chicken stock, cream cheese, salt, and pepper in your Slow Cooker. Cover with the lid and cook for 8 hours on Low. Serve immediately.

Basil Chicken Orzo with Kalamata Olives

Serves: 6 | Total Time: 6 hours 30 minutes

2 ripe tomatoes, diced
1 cup orzo, rinsed
2 chicken breasts, cubed
1 celery stalk, diced
¼ cup pitted Kalamata olives
2 cups chicken stock

1 tsp dried oregano
½ tsp dried basil
½ tsp dried parsley
Salt and pepper to taste
Feta cheese for serving

Toss orzo, chicken, celery, tomatoes, oregano, basil, parsley, olives, chicken stock, salt, and pepper in your Slow Cooker. Cover with the lid and cook for 6 hours on Low. Scatter with feta cheese to serve.

Chicken Fajitas

Serves: 6 | Total Time: 6 hours 15 minutes

3 chicken breasts, halved	½ tsp celery seeds
1 cup chicken stock	½ tsp cumin powder
1 tbsp taco seasoning	¼ tsp chili powder

Stir chicken, taco seasoning, chicken stock, celery seeds, cumin, and chili powder in your Slow Cooker. Cover with the lid and cook for 6 hours on Low. When done, using two forks, shred it finely and serve in taco shells.

Mole con Pollo

Serves: 6 | Total Time: 5 hours 15 minutes

2 lb chicken drumsticks	2 tbsp smooth peanut butter
4 garlic cloves, chopped	1 can fire-roasted tomatoes
1 chipotle pepper, chopped	1 tsp honey
1 onion, finely chopped	Salt and pepper to taste
½ cup golden raisins	

Toss onion, raisins, garlic, chipotle pepper, peanut butter, tomatoes, honey, chicken, salt, and pepper in your Slow Cooker. Cover with the lid and cook for 5 hours on Low. When done, remove the lid and serve warm.

Chicken Thighs with Hot Orange Glaze

Serves: 4 | Total Time: 2 hours 45 minutes

1 orange, cut into segments	1 tbsp honey
4 chicken thighs	1 tsp hot sauce
½ cup chicken stock	½ tsp sesame seeds
2 tbsp soy sauce	2 cups cooked white rice

Toss chicken, orange wedges, chicken stock, soy sauce, honey, hot sauce, and sesame seeds in your Slow Cooker. Cover with the lid and cook for 2½ hours on High. When done, remove the lid and serve over cooked rice.

Spanish Arroz con Pollo

Serves: 6 | Total Time: 6 hours 15 minutes

3 chicken breasts, halved	2 ripe tomatoes, diced
1 cup wild rice	1 cup sliced mushrooms
1 cup green peas	2 cups vegetable stock
2 celery stalks, sliced	1 thyme sprig
1 onion, chopped	1 rosemary sprig
1 red chili, chopped	Salt and pepper to taste

Add rice, green peas, celery, onion, red chili, tomatoes, mushrooms, vegetable stock, chicken, thyme, rosemary, salt, and pepper in your Slow Cooker and stir. Cover with the lid and cook for 6 hours on Low. Serve immediately.

Sesame Chicken

Serves: 6 | Total Time: 2 hours 30 minutes

3 chicken breasts, sliced	¼ cup chicken stock
2 carrots, sliced	1 tsp sesame oil
2 garlic cloves, minced	2 tbsp sesame seeds
2 green onions, chopped	1 tbsp soy sauce
¼ cup hoisin sauce	

Mix the chicken, hoisin sauce, chicken stock, sesame oil, sesame seeds, soy sauce, carrots, and garlic in your Slow Cooker. Cover with the lid and cook for 2¼ hours on High. Sprinkle with green onions and serve.

Broccoli & Cashew Chicken

Serves: 6 | Total Time: 4 hours 15 minutes

1 head broccoli, cut into florets	
3 chicken breasts, cut into strips	
1 cup cashew nuts, soaked	½ tsp ginger powder
1 shallot, sliced	1 cup chicken stock
1 celery stalk, sliced	Salt and pepper to taste

Mix the chicken, shallot, celery, and broccoli in your Slow Cooker. In a food processor, blitz cashew nuts, ginger powder, and chicken stock until smooth. Pour it over the chicken and sprinkle with salt and pepper. Cover with the lid and cook for 4 hours on Low. Serve immediately.

Creamy Chicken & Rice

Serves: 6 | Total Time: 6 hours 30 minutes

1 cup green peas	1 garlic clove, chopped
2 carrots, sliced	2 cups vegetable stock
3 chicken breasts, cubed	2 tbsp butter
1 cup white rice	½ cup cream cheese
½ lb button mushrooms	1 thyme sprig
1 shallot, chopped	Salt and pepper to taste

Melt the butter in a pan over medium heat. Place the chicken and cook until golden brown on all sides. Add it to your Slow Cooker. Add in rice, mushrooms, shallot, garlic, green peas, carrots, vegetable stock, cream cheese, thyme, salt, and pepper. Cover with the lid and cook for 6 hours on Low. Serve right away.

Cheddar Chicken in Salsa Roja

Serves: 6 | Total Time: 8 hours 15 minutes

1 cup grated cheddar cheese	½ cup chicken stock
6 chicken thighs	Salt and pepper to taste
2 cups red salsa	

Stir chicken, red salsa, chicken stock, cheddar cheese, salt, and pepper in your Slow Cooker. Cover with the lid and cook for 8 hours on Low. Serve warm.

Indonesian Chicken Thighs

Serves: 6 | Total Time: 7 hours 15 minutes

3 lb skinless chicken thighs	1 ½ cups chicken stock
2 red bell peppers, diced	1 tbsp soy sauce
1 large onion, chopped	1 lime, juiced
2 large carrots, sliced	1 tsp grated ginger
3 tbsp smooth peanut butter	Salt and pepper to taste

Toss onion, carrots, bell peppers, chicken, peanut butter, chicken stock, soy sauce, lime juice, ginger, salt, and pepper in your Slow Cooker. Cover with the lid and cook for 7 hours on Low. When done, remove the lid and serve with your desired side dish.

Easy Teriyaki Chicken

Serves: 6 | Total Time: 5 hours 30 minutes

2 lb chicken pieces (drumsticks, wings, thighs)
2 garlic cloves, minced	1 tsp sesame oil
¼ cup soy sauce	1 tsp grated ginger
¼ cup dry sherry	1 tsp rice vinegar
¼ cup chicken stock	2 tbsp sesame seeds

Stir sesame oil, chicken, soy sauce, sherry, chicken stock, ginger, rice vinegar, garlic, and sesame seeds in your Slow Cooker. Cover with the lid and cook for 5 hours on Low. When done, remove the lid and serve right away.

Jalapeño Jerk Chicken

Serves: 4 | Total Time: 7 hours 30 minutes

4 chicken breasts	2 tbsp olive oil
1 jalapeno pepper, chopped	2 tbsp jerk seasoning
½ cup chicken stock	Salt and pepper to taste
¼ cup brewed coffee	

Sprinkle chicken with jerk seasoning, salt, and pepper. Put olive oil, chicken stock, seasoned chicken, coffee, jalapeño pepper, salt, and pepper and stir. Cover with the lid and cook for 7 hours on Low. Serve warm.

Rosemary Chicken Dish with Artichoke

Serves: 6 | Total Time: 6 hours 30 minutes

2 garlic cloves, chopped	1 can fire-roasted tomatoes
2 red bell peppers, sliced	1 tsp dried rosemary
2 chicken breasts, cubed	½ cup chicken stock
1 jar artichoke hearts, diced	2 tbsp lemon juice
1 shallot, chopped	Salt and pepper to taste

Mix the chicken, artichoke hearts, shallot, garlic, bell peppers, tomatoes, rosemary, chicken stock, lemon juice, salt, and pepper in your Slow Cooker. Cover with the lid and cook for 6 hours on Low. Serve immediately.

Parmesan Chicken with Alfredo Sauce

Serves: 6 | Total Time: 6 hours 15 minutes

1 can fire-roasted tomatoes	½ tsp cumin powder
1 cup Alfredo pasta sauce	½ cup chicken stock
2 lb chicken drumsticks	Salt and pepper to taste
2 cups sliced mushrooms	Grated Parmesan cheese
2 tbsp dry sherry	for serving

Stir chicken, mushrooms, tomatoes, Alfredo sauce, sherry, cumin, chicken stock, salt, and pepper in your Slow Cooker. Cover with the lid and cook for 6 hours on Low. When done, remove the lid and scatter with Parmesan cheese to serve.

Pesto Chicken

Serves: 4 | Total Time: 6 hours 15 minutes

½ cup grated Parmesan	1 bunch cilantro
4 chicken breasts	1 lime, zested and juiced
½ cup chicken stock	1 tbsp Italian pesto

In a food processor, blitz cilantro, lime zest, lime juice, chicken stock, and Italian pesto until smooth. Transfer to your Slow Cooker. Stir in chicken until well coated, and scatter Parmesan cheese on top. Cover with the lid and cook for 6 hours on Low. Serve immediately.

Tomato Chicken with Mushrooms

Serves: 6 | Total Time: 5 hours 30 minutes

4 cups sliced Champignon mushrooms
1 cup chopped wild mushrooms
2 carrots, sliced	2 tbsp olive oil
2 tomatoes, diced	2 tbsp tomato paste
6 chicken drumsticks	1 thyme sprig
1 red onion, sliced	1 bay leaf
2 red bell peppers, sliced	1 tsp dried sage
1 ½ cups chicken stock	1 rosemary sprig

In your Slow Cooker, add chicken, mushrooms, olive oil, onion, bell peppers, carrots, tomatoes, chicken stock, tomato paste, thyme, bay leaf, sage, and rosemary and toss to combine. Cover with the lid and cook for 5 hours on Low. When done, remove the lid and serve warm.

Festive Coq au Vin

Serves: 6 | Total Time: 8 hours 30 minutes

1 whole chicken, cut into smaller pieces
1 cup miniature onions	2 bay leaves
4 carrots, sliced	2 tbsp canola oil
1 lb button mushrooms	1 thyme sprig
½ cup red wine	1 rosemary sprig
1 cup tomato sauce	Salt and pepper to taste
2 ripe tomatoes, diced	

Warm the canola oil in a pan over medium heat. Place the chicken and cook for 5 minutes until golden brown on all sides. Add it to your Slow Cooker. Put in onions, carrots, mushrooms, wine, tomato sauce, tomatoes, bay leaves, thyme, rosemary, salt, and pepper. Cover with the lid and cook for 8 hours on Low. Serve right away.

Homedade Chicken Cacciatore

Serves: 6 | Total Time: 7 hours 15 minutes

1 red bell pepper, sliced	2 tbsp canola oil
1 yellow bell pepper, sliced	2 tbsp tomato paste
2 lb chicken drumsticks	1 cup chicken stock
2 celery stalks, sliced	1 tbsp cornstarch
2 cups sliced mushrooms	½ tsp dried oregano
2 carrots, sliced	1 tsp dried basil
1 large onion, sliced	1 bay leaf
2 garlic cloves, minced	Salt and pepper to taste
¼ cup dry white wine	

Warm canola oil in a pan over medium heat, place chicken and cook for 5 minutes until golden brown on all sides. Add it to your Slow Cooker. Add in celery, mushrooms, carrots, onion, garlic, bell peppers, wine, tomato paste, stock, cornstarch, oregano, basil, bay leaf, salt, and pepper. Cover and cook for 7 hours on Low.

Juicy Chicken Thighs with Pears

Serves: 6 | Total Time: 8 hours 15 minutes

2 pears, cored and sliced	1 cup apple cider
1 fennel bulb, sliced	1 bay leaf
2 shallots, sliced	1 thyme sprig
6 chicken thighs	Salt and pepper to taste

Mix the chicken, pears, fennel, shallots, apple cider, bay leaf, thyme, salt, and pepper in your Slow Cooker. Cover with the lid and cook for 8 hours on Low. Serve warm.

Mama Chicken Ragout

Serves: 6 | Total Time: 8 hours 15 minutes

1 lb new potatoes, washed	4 artichoke hearts, chopped
1 lb baby carrots	1 lemon, juiced
1 zucchini, cubed	1 tsp dried oregano
3 chicken breasts, halved	1 ½ cups chicken stock
4 garlic cloves, chopped	Salt and pepper to taste
1 sweet onion, sliced	

Stir chicken, potatoes, carrots, zucchini, garlic, onion, artichoke hearts, lemon juice, oregano, chicken stock, salt, and pepper in your Slow Cooker. Cover with the lid and cook for 8 hours on Low. Serve immediately.

Tomato Stout Chicken with Mushrooms

Serves: 6 | Total Time: 8 hours 15 minutes

6 chicken thighs	2 tbsp canola oil
4 bacon slices, chopped	2 tbsp tomato paste
4 garlic cloves, chopped	1 ½ cups stout beer
1 large onion, chopped	1 tbsp lemon juice
1 lb baby carrots	2 bay leaves
½ lb button mushrooms	1 rosemary sprig
1 cup tomato sauce	Salt and pepper to taste

Warm the canola oil in a pan over medium heat. Place the bacon and cook until crispy. Add in chicken and cook until golden brown on all sides. Add it to your Slow Cooker. Put in garlic, onion, carrots, mushrooms, tomato sauce, tomato paste, beer, lemon juice, bay leaves, rosemary, salt, and pepper. Cover with the lid and cook for 8 hours on Low. Serve immediately.

Pasta with Chicken & Asparagus

Serves: 6 | Total Time: 4 hours 15 minutes

2 chicken breasts, cubed	2 cups chicken stock
1 lb asparagus, chopped	½ cup heavy cream
1 cup green peas	2 tbsp canola oil
1 shallot, chopped	½ tsp dried basil
2 garlic cloves, chopped	½ tsp dried oregano
6 oz short pasta	Salt and pepper to taste

Warm canola oil in a pan over medium heat, place chicken and cook until golden on all sides. Add it to your Slow Cooker. Add in asparagus, green peas, shallot, garlic, pasta, chicken stock, heavy cream, basil, oregano, salt, and pepper. Cover with the lid and cook for 4 hours on Low. Serve warm or chilled.

Thai Chicken Drumsticks

Serves: 6 | Total Time: 7 hours 15 minutes

3 chicken breasts, halved	1 can baby corn, drained
4 garlic cloves, chopped	1 cup green peas
1 lb new potatoes	½ cup green beans, chopped
1 bay leaf	2 tbsp butter
1 shallot, chopped	2 tsp grated ginger
1 ½ cups coconut milk	Salt and pepper to taste
½ cup chicken stock	1 lemongrass stalk, crushed

Melt butter in a pan over medium heat, place chicken and cook for 2-3 minutes until golden brown on all sides. Add it to your Slow Cooker. Put in ginger, garlic, shallot, coconut milk, chicken stock, corn, green peas, green beans, potatoes, bay leaf, lemongrass, salt, and pepper. Cover and cook for 7 hours on Low. Serve warm.

Tasty Chicken Curry with Bananas

Serves: 6 | Total Time: 7 hours 15 minutes

1 jalapeno pepper, chopped	1 tsp curry powder
1 banana, sliced	¼ cup dry white wine
1 ½ cups diced tomatoes	1 bay leaf
2 lb chicken drumsticks	1 lemongrass stalk, crushed
1 large onion, chopped	1 cup coconut milk
4 garlic cloves, chopped	Salt and pepper to taste
1 tsp cumin powder	

Mix the chicken, jalapeño pepper, banana, tomatoes, onion, garlic, cumin, curry powder, wine, bay leaf, lemongrass, coconut milk, salt, and pepper in your Slow Cooker. Cover and cook for 7 hours on Low. Serve warm.

South African Chicken Lentils

Serves: 6 | Total Time: 5 hours 15 minutes

2 lb skinless chicken drumsticks	
2 large red onions, chopped	1 tsp coriander powder
4 garlic cloves, minced	¼ tsp all-spice powder
1 ½ cups red lentils	¼ tsp ground cloves
1 tbsp butter	1 cup coconut milk
1 tsp grated ginger	1 cup vegetable stock
½ tsp chili powder	

Mix the butter, lentils, chicken, onions, garlic, ginger, chili powder, coriander, all-spice powder, cloves, coconut milk, and vegetable stock. Cover with the lid and cook for 5 hours on Low. Serve warm.

Cheddar Chicken Fussili

Serves: 6 | Total Time: 6 hours 15 minutes

2 chicken breasts, diced	1 cup cream cheese
2 cups chicken stock	1 cup grated Cheddar
2 cups fusilli pasta	½ cup grated Parmesan
2 celery stalks, sliced	Salt and pepper to taste

Stir fusilli, chicken, chicken stock, celery, cream cheese, cheddar cheese, Parmesan cheese, salt, and pepper in your Slow Cooker. Cover with the lid and cook for 6 hours on Low. Serve right away.

Tangy Roasted Chicken

Serves: 8 | Total Time: 8 hours 15 minutes

½ cup chicken stock
1 large whole chicken
1 tsp cumin powder
1 tsp chili powder
1 tsp smoked paprika
1 tsp dried thyme
1 tsp dried basil
¼ tsp cayenne pepper
Salt and pepper to taste

In a bowl, combine cumin, chili powder, paprika, cayenne pepper, thyme, basil, salt, and pepper. Rub whole chicken with the spice mixture until well coated. Transfer it into your Slow Cooker and pour in chicken stock. Cover with the lid and cook for 8 hours on Low. Serve immediately.

Rich Chicken Breasts

Serves: 4 | Total Time: 6 hours 15 minutes

4 chicken breasts
4 garlic cloves, minced
1 cup tomato sauce
½ cup hot sauce
2 tbsp butter
Salt and pepper to taste

Toss chicken, tomato sauce, hot sauce, butter, garlic, salt, and pepper in your Slow Cooker. Cover with the lid and cook for 6 hours on Low. Serve warm.

Citrus Honeyed Chicken Drumsticks

Serves: 6 | Total Time: 6 hours 15 minutes

2 garlic cloves, minced
2 lb chicken drumsticks
¼ cup fresh orange juice
1 tbsp grated orange zest
2 tbsp soy sauce
1 tsp rice vinegar
¼ tsp chili powder
¼ cup chicken stock
2 tbsp sesame seeds

Mix the chicken, orange zest, garlic, soy sauce, orange juice, rice vinegar, chili powder, chicken stock, and sesame seeds in your Slow Cooker. Cover with the lid and cook for 6 hours on Low. Serve immediately.

Effortless Chicken Ravioli with Tomato Sauce

Serves: 6 | Total Time: 2 hours 45 minutes

2 cups spinach, torn
16 oz chicken ravioli
1 shallot, chopped
4 garlic cloves, minced
1 can fire-roasted tomatoes
1 cup vegetables stock
¼ tsp coriander powder
1 pinch cumin powder
Salt and pepper to taste

Stir chicken ravioli, shallot, garlic, tomatoes, vegetable stock, coriander, cumin, spinach, salt, and pepper in your Slow Cooker. Cover with the lid and cook for 2 ½ hours on High. When done, remove the lid and serve warm.

Roasted Shredded Chicken

Serves: 6 | Total Time: 8 hours 15 minutes

1 red onion, sliced
2 chipotle peppers, chopped
2 red bell peppers, sliced
3 chicken breasts
1 can fire-roasted tomatoes
1 can (10 oz) sweet corn
1 tsp taco seasoning
1 cup chicken stock
Salt and pepper to taste

Toss chicken, tomatoes, onion, chipotle peppers, bell peppers, corn, taco seasoning, chicken stock, salt, and pepper in your Slow Cooker. Cover with the lid and cook for 8 hours on Low. When done, remove the lid, using two forks, shred it finely, and serve warm or chilled.

Savory Bourbon Chicken with Mushrooms

Serves: 6 | Total Time: 8 hours 15 minutes

2 cups sliced cremini mushrooms
4 red onions, sliced
1 large whole chicken
½ cup Bourbon
1 cup chicken stock
1 tbsp dried thyme
Salt and pepper to taste

In your Slow Cooker, stir onions, thyme, mushrooms, Bourbon, chicken stock, salt, pepper, and top with chicken. Cover with the lid and cook for 8 hours on Low, keeping juicy. Serve immediately.

Grated Chicken Burrito Bowls

Serves: 6 | Total Time: 6 hours 15 minutes

1 ½ lb ground chicken
1 can (15 oz) diced tomatoes
1 can (15 oz) black beans,
1 can (10 oz) sweet corn,
2 cups chicken stock
1 tsp chili powder
1 cup brown rice
2 tbsp canola oil
1 ½ cups grated Cheddar
Salt and pepper to taste

Warm the canola oil in a pan over medium heat. Place the chicken and cook for 2-3 minutes until golden, stirring often. Add it to your Slow Cooker. Add in tomatoes, chicken stock, chili powder, rice, beans, corn, salt, and pepper, and scatter with cheddar cheese on top. Cover with the lid and cook for 6 hours on Low. Serve warm.

Herb & Garlic Whole Chicken

Serves: 6 | Total Time: 8 hours 15 minutes

6 garlic cloves, crushed
1 large whole chicken
1 lemon, sliced
1 rosemary sprig
1 thyme sprig
½ cup vegetable stock
Salt and pepper to taste

Layer half of lemon slices and garlic in your Slow Cooker. Sprinkle chicken with salt and pepper and place it over the slices. Add the remaining lemon slices, rosemary, and thyme on top and pour it vegetable stock. Cover with the lid and cook for 8 hours on Low. Serve warm.

French Chicken Drumsticks

Serves: 6 | Total Time: 6 hours 15 minutes

4 garlic cloves, minced
3 lb chicken drumsticks
½ cup chicken stock
1 tsp dried tarragon
½ cup heavy cream
2 tbsp Dijon mustard
1 tbsp cornstarch
1 tsp lemon zest
Salt and pepper to taste
2 tbsp chopped parsley

Stir chicken, Dijon mustard, chicken stock, garlic, tarragon, heavy cream, cornstarch, lemon zest, salt, and pepper in your Slow Cooker. Cover with the lid and cook for 6 hours on Low. Serve topped with parsley.

Balsamic Chicken with Anchovies

Serves: 6 | Total Time: 8 hours 15 minutes

6 chicken thighs	1 tsp red pepper flakes
1 can (15 oz) diced tomatoes	¼ cup balsamic vinegar
1 large onion, sliced	2 bay leaves
4 garlic cloves, chopped	1 cup chicken stock
1 tsp dried thyme	Salt and pepper to taste
2 anchovy fillets	1 bunch of Swiss chard, torn
2 tbsp olive oil	

Warm olive oil in a pan over medium heat, place onion and garlic and cook for 2 minutes until softened. Add them to your Slow Cooker. Add in thyme, anchovy fillets, red pepper flakes, balsamic vinegar, tomatoes, bay leaves, chicken, Swiss chard, chicken stock, salt, and pepper. Cover with the lid and cook for 8 hours on Low. Serve.

Mouth-Watering Chicken Thighs

Serves: 6 | Total Time: 7 hours 15 minutes

½ cup ketchup	1 tbsp cornstarch
6 chicken thighs	¼ tsp chili powder
1 cup lemonade	Salt and pepper to taste

Toss chicken, lemonade, ketchup, cornstarch, chili powder, salt, and pepper in your Slow Cooker. Cover with the lid and cook for 7 hours on Low. Serve warm.

Mixed Bean Chicken Chili

Serves: 6 | Total Time: 8 hours 15 minutes

1 sweet onion, chopped	2 tbsp canola oil
4 garlic cloves, minced	1 tsp chili powder
3 chicken breasts, cubed	1 tsp dried oregano
2 red bell peppers, diced	1 tsp dried thyme
1 yellow bell pepper, diced	1 tsp Cajun seasoning
1 celery stalk, sliced	Salt and pepper to taste
1 can (15 oz) red beans	1 can fire-roasted tomatoes
1 can (15-oz) cannellini beans	1 cup chicken stock
1 cup frozen sweet corn	

Warm canola oil in a pan over medium heat, place chicken and cook until golden on all sides. Add it to your Slow Cooker. Add in bell peppers, onion, garlic, celery, beans, corn, chili powder, oregano, thyme, cajun seasoning, tomatoes, chicken stock, salt, and pepper. Cover and cook for 8 hours on Low. Serve immediately.

Sweet & Spicy Chicken Breasts

Serves: 4 | Total Time: 6 hours 15 minutes

4 chicken breasts	½ tsp red pepper flakes
2 garlic cloves, minced	1 tsp sesame oil
¼ cup ketchup	1 tsp grated ginger
¼ cup chicken stock	2 tbsp soy sauce
3 tbsp honey	2 tbsp sesame seeds

Mix the chicken, honey, red pepper flakes, garlic, ginger, soy sauce, ketchup, chicken stock, sesame oil, and sesame seeds in your Slow Cooker. Cover with the lid and cook for 6 hours on Low. Serve immediately.

Vegetable & Chicken Meatloaf

Serves: 6 | Total Time: 6 hours 15 minutes

1 cup cauliflower florets, chopped	
4 garlic cloves, chopped	2 eggs
2 lb ground chicken	1 tsp dried oregano
1 shallot, chopped	1 tsp dried basil
1 carrot, grated	½ tsp cumin powder
1 zucchini, grated	¼ tsp cayenne pepper
½ cup almond flour	Salt and pepper to taste
¼ cup chopped cilantro	

In a bowl, mix chicken, cauliflower, garlic, shallot, cilantro, carrot, zucchini, oregano, basil, cumin, cayenne pepper, eggs, and flour until well combined. Place chicken mixture in your Slow Cooker and season with salt and pepper to taste. Cook for 6 hours on Low. Serve.

Pollo en Salsa Verde

Serves: 6 | Total Time: 4 hours 15 minutes

1 jar salsa verde	¼ cup chicken stock
1 cup cream cheese	Salt and pepper to taste
2 lb chicken breast, cubed	1 ripe avocado for serving
2 tbsp chopped cilantro	1 lime for serving

Toss chicken, salsa verde, cream cheese, cilantro, chicken stock, salt, and pepper in your Slow Cooker. Cover with the lid and cook for 4 hours on Low. When done, remove the lid and top with avocado and lime juice to serve.

Asian Chicken Breasts

Serves: 4 | Total Time: 3 hours 15 minutes

1 green onion, chopped	¼ cup soy sauce
6 garlic cloves, minced	½ cup chicken stock
4 boneless and skinless chicken breasts	1 tsp chili paste
	1 tsp grated ginger
2 tbsp brown sugar	1 tbsp rice vinegar

Mix the chicken, sugar, soy sauce, chicken stock, chili paste, ginger, rice vinegar, garlic, and green onions in your Slow Cooker. Cover and cook for 3 hours on High.

Peppers Stuffed with Rice & Chicken

Serves: 6 | Total Time: 8 hours 30 minutes

1 carrot, grated	1 can fire-roasted tomatoes
6 red bell peppers, cored	1 bay leaf
¼ cup white rice	1 thyme sprig
1 lb ground pork	1 lemon, juiced
½ lb ground beef	2 tbsp chopped parsley
2 shallots, chopped	1 tsp dried thyme
2 cups beef stock	¼ tsp cumin powder
4 cups water	Salt and pepper to taste

In a bowl, combine ground pork, ground beef, shallots, carrot, rice, parsley, dried thyme, cumin, salt, and pepper. Fill each bell pepper with meat mixture and place them in your Slow Cooker. Add in beef stock, water, tomatoes, bay leaf, thyme sprig, and lemon juice. Cover with the lid and cook for 8 hours on Low. Serve and enjoy!

Italian Chicken

Serves: 6 | Total Time: 8 hours 10 minutes

12 chicken tenders	½ cup red cider vinegar
6 turkey sausage links	1 (14-oz) can tomatoes, diced
½ tsp thyme	1 green bell pepper, sliced
½ tsp rosemary	2 tbsp olive oil
½ tsp oregano, dried	1 leek, chopped
½ tsp basil	1 carrot, chopped
1 tsp onion powder	4 garlic cloves, minced
Salt and pepper to taste	2 tbsp chopped cilantro
1 cup turkey broth	

Lightly coat the inside of your Slow Cooker with olive oil. Add in the chicken tenders. In a small bowl, combine all of your spices and mix well. Sprinkle the mix over the chicken tenders in the slow cooker. Lay the sausage links on top of the chicken. Add the garlic, carrot, leek, and pepper strips on top of the sausages. Pour in the diced tomatoes, broth, and vinegar. Season with more salt and pepper to taste. Close the lid and cook on Low for 8 hours. Serve hot topped with cilantro and enjoy!

Hot Chicken Wings

Serves: 6 | Total Time: 7 hours 15 minutes

4 lb chicken wings	1 tsp grated ginger
2/3 cup hoisin sauce	1 tbsp molasses
4 garlic cloves, minced	1 tsp hot sauce
1 tsp sesame oil	Salt and pepper to taste

Combine hoisin sauce, garlic, ginger, sesame oil, molasses, hot sauce, salt, and pepper in your Slow Cooker, add chicken wings, and toss until everything is coat. Cover and cook for 7 hours on Low. Serve and enjoy!

Chicken Marrakesh

Serves: 4 | Total Time: 4 hours 25 minutes

2 lb chicken breasts, cut into 2-inch pieces	
2 large sweet potatoes, peeled and diced	
Salt and pepper to taste	2 carrots, peeled and diced
1 onion, sliced	2 cloves garlic, minced
¼ tsp ground cinnamon	1 tsp parsley, dried
½ tsp ground turmeric	1 (14 oz) can diced tomatoes
½ tsp ground cumin	2 tbsp chopped chives
1 (14-oz) can garbanzo beans	1 cup water

Mix the chicken, cumin, cinnamon, black pepper, parsley, turmeric, and salt in a mixing bowl and stir well to coat. Transfer the ingredients into your Slow Cooker and add the remaining ingredients; mix well. Cover with the lid, set the cooker on High, and cook for 4 hours. Serve hot topped with chives and enjoy!

Delicious Chicken Noodles

Serves: 6 | Total Time: 8 hours 15 minutes

1 lb chicken breasts, cubed	1 onion, chopped
2 cups dried egg noodles	2 cups chicken stock
2 large carrots, sliced	1 thyme sprig
2 celery stalks, sliced	Salt and pepper to taste

Stir chicken breasts, carrots, celery, onion, chicken stock, 4 cups of water, thyme, noodles, salt, and pepper in your Slow Cooker. Cover with the lid and cook for 8 hours on Low. When done, remove the lid and serve immediately.

Prosciutto-Wrapped Chicken & Asparagus

Serves: 4 | Total Time: 4 hours 10 minutes

8 slices Prosciutto	Salt and pepper to taste
4 chicken breast halves	1 lb asparagus, trimmed
2 garlic cloves, minced	2 tbsp parsley, chopped

Cut the chicken into small pieces. Use a mallet to flatten the chicken pieces. Season with salt and pepper. Take 3-4 pieces of asparagus along with some minced garlic and roll the chicken around it. Now roll the Prosciutto around the chicken and use toothpicks to secure in place. Repeat the process with the rest of the pieces. Place the pieces in your Slow Cooker and close the lid. Cook on High for 4 hours. Serve garnished with parsley and enjoy!

Chicken Sliders with Bacon

Serves: 6 | Total Time: 4 hours 30 minutes

6 bacon slices	½ cup breadcrumbs
2 lb ground chicken	1 shallot, chopped
1 egg	Salt and pepper to taste

In a bowl, combine ground chicken, egg, breadcrumbs, shallot, salt, and pepper. Make small sliders out of the mixture and wrap each slider with a bacon slice. Place the sliders in your Slow Cooker and seal the lid. Select High and cook for 4 hours, stirring once. Serve warm.

Cheesy Chicken Dip

Serves: 6 | Total Time: 3 hours 15 minutes

2 cups shredded Monterey Jack cheese	
1 ½ cups cooked and diced chicken breasts	
2 garlic cloves, chopped	1 lime, juiced
1 cup cream cheese	¼ tsp cumin powder
¼ cup white wine	Salt and pepper to taste

Mix the cream cheese, chicken, Monterey Jack, white wine, lime juice, cumin, and garlic in your Slow Cooker. Sprinkle with salt and pepper to taste. Cover with the lid and cook for 3 hours on Low. Serve and enjoy!

Wild Rice with Chicken & Mushrooms

Serves: 6 | Total Time: 7 hours 15 minutes

1 cup wild rice	2 cups vegetable stock
6 chicken thighs	1 tsp cumin powder
2 celery stalks, diced	½ tsp chili powder
1 carrot, diced	Salt and pepper to taste
2 cups sliced mushrooms	

Sprinkle chicken thighs with cumin, chili powder, salt, and pepper. In your Slow Cooker, combine rice, celery, carrot, mushrooms, and vegetable stock. Season with salt and pepper to taste and top with chicken thighs. Cover with the lid and cook for 7 hours on Low. Serve warm.

BEEF RECIPES

Beef Meatloaf

Serves: 6 | Total Time: 8 hours 10 minutes

2 lb ground beef	1 tsp thyme, minced
1 potato, shredded	½ cup ketchup
1 onion, chopped	2 eggs
2 garlic cloves, minced	Salt and pepper to taste
2 tbsp parsley, minced	1 tsp olive oil

In a bowl, place the ground beef, potato, onion, garlic, parsley, thyme, ketchup, egg, salt, and pepper and mix thoroughly with your hands. Grease your Slow Cooker with the olive oil. Add the meat mixture to the cooker and form it into a loaf-like shape. Cover and cook for 8 hours on Low. Allow the meatloaf to rest for 10 minutes before slicing and serving. Enjoy!

Pot Roast with Vegetables

Serves: 4 | Total Time: 8 hours 10 minutes

2 lb chuck roast, trimmed of visible fat	
Salt and pepper to taste	2 red potatoes, quartered
1 onion, cut into 8 wedges	1 tsp minced rosemary
1 parsnip, sliced	1 cup beef broth
2 carrots, sliced	

Rub the chuck roast salt and pepper. Place it into your Slow Cooker. Arrange the onion, parsnip, carrots, and potatoes around the sides and on top of the meat. Sprinkle with rosemary and pour in the broth. Cover and cook for 8 hours on Low until the meat is meltingly tender. Serve and enjoy!

French Beef Ragoût

Serves: 4 | Total Time: 8 hours 10 minutes

4 (8-oz) pieces beef brisket	2 plum tomatoes, diced
1 yellow onion, chopped	2 cups beef broth
1 tsp minced fresh thyme	1 cup dry red wine
1 garlic clove, minced	1 tbsp red wine vinegar
1 small carrot, diced	1 tsp tomato paste
1 bay leaf	Salt to taste

Toss all the ingredients in your Slow Cooker. Cover and cook for 8 hours on Low until the meat is very tender. When ready, remove the brisket to a cutting board and shred it with a fork. Place it back to the pot and stir it into the liquid to soak in even more flavor. Delicious served with mashed potatoes.

Twisted Bolognese Sauce

Serves: 6 | Total Time: 8 hours 15 minutes

6 garlic cloves, minced	1 tsp chili powder
2 sweet onions, chopped	2 tbsp tomato paste
2 lb ground beef	1 tsp dried basil
½ lb mushrooms, chopped	1 tsp dried oregano
1 can fire-roasted tomatoes	1 tbsp balsamic vinegar
3 tbsp canola oil	Salt and pepper to taste

Warm the canola oil in a pan over medium heat. Place the beef and cook for 2-3 minutes until golden on all sides. Add it to your Slow Cooker. Put in garlic, onions, mushrooms, tomatoes, chili powder, tomato paste, basil, oregano, balsamic vinegar, salt, and pepper. Cover with the lid and cook for 8 hours on Low. Serve right away.

Saucy Beef Casserole

Serves: 6 | Total Time: 7 hours 30 minutes

2 carrots, diced	1 leek, sliced
2 red bell peppers, diced	1 ½ cups red salsa
2 lb beef roast, cubed	1 bay leaf
2 red onions, chopped	2 tbsp canola oil
2 garlic cloves, chopped	1 tsp cumin seeds
2 cups dried black bean	1 tsp chili powder
4 cups chicken stock	Salt and pepper to taste

Warm the canola oil in a pan over medium heat. Place the beef and cook for 2-3 minutes until golden on all sides. Add it to your Slow Cooker. Put in onions, garlic, carrots, bell peppers, leek, red salsa, bay leaf, cumin seeds, chili powder, beans, chicken stock, salt, and pepper. Cover and cook for 7 hours on Low. Serve warm.

Beef Roast with Caramelized Onions

Serves: 6 | Total Time: 8 hours 30 minutes

1 celery root, cubed	2 carrots, sliced
2 potatoes, cubed	1 cup beef stock
4 lb beef roast	3 tbsp canola oil
1 onion, sliced	½ cup water
4 garlic cloves, chopped	Salt and pepper to taste

Warm the canola oil in a pan over medium heat. Place the onion and cook for 10 minutes until caramelized. Add it to your Slow Cooker. Add in beef, garlic, carrots, celery, potatoes, beef stock, water, salt, and pepper. Cover and cook for 8 hours on Low. Serve.

Beef & Onion Sandwiches

Serves: 6 | Total Time: 9 hours 15 minutes

3 bacon slices, chopped	½ cup white wine
2 lb beef roast	1 thyme sprig
1 onion, sliced	Salt and pepper to taste
1 tsp garlic powder	

Mix the beef roast, onion, bacon, garlic powder, wine, thyme, salt, and pepper in your Slow Cooker. Cover with the lid and cook for 9 hours on Low. When done, remove the lid, using two forks, shred it finely and serve warm.

Mom´s Beef Brisket

Serves: 6 | Total Time: 6 hours 15 minutes

¼ cup apple cider vinegar	1 tsp smoked paprika
½ cup beef stock	1 tsp chili powder
1 cup ketchup	1 tsp celery seeds
2 lb beef brisket	1 tsp salt
2 tbsp brown sugar	1 tbsp Worcestershire sauce
1 tsp cumin powder	2 tbsp soy sauce

In a bowl, combine sugar, cumin, paprika, chili powder, celery seeds, and salt. Rub beef brisket with the spice mixture and massage until well coated. Mix the apple cider vinegar, beef stock, ketchup, Worcestershire sauce, and soy sauce in your Slow Cooker. Add in beef brisket. Cover with the lid and cook for 6 hours on Low. When done, remove the lid and cut it into slices before serving.

Beef Enchiladas

Serves: 6 | Total Time: 6 hours 15 minutes

1 shallot, chopped	2 cups enchilada sauce
4 garlic cloves, chopped	6 flour tortillas, shredded
1 lb ground beef	2 tbsp canola oil
1 leek, sliced	2 cups grated cheddar
2 cups sliced mushrooms	

Warm the canola oil in a pan over medium heat. Place the ground beef and cook for 2-3 minutes. Add in leek, shallot, and garlic. Transfer everything to your Slow Cooker. Add in mushrooms, enchilada sauce, and tortillas, and scatter with cheddar cheese on top. Cover with the lid and cook for 6 hours on Low. Serve warm.

Bell Peppers Stuffed with Dilly Beef

Serves: 6 | Total Time: 6 hours 30 minutes

2 onions, finely chopped	1 egg
2 garlic cloves, minced	1 cup white rice
6 red bell peppers	2 tbsp chopped parsley
1 lb ground beef	1 tbsp chopped dill
1 ½ cups beef stock	Salt and pepper to taste
1 lemon, juiced	

In a bowl, combine ground beef, onions, garlic, egg, rice, parsley, dill, salt, and pepper. Slice the top of bell peppers and fill them with the beef mixture. Transfer them into your Slow Cooker and pour in beef stock and lemon juice. Cover with the lid and cook for 6 hours on Low. When done, remove the lid and serve warm.

Herbed Beef Roast

Serves: 6 | Total Time: 7 hours 15 minutes

1 ½ lb potatoes, halved	½ cup white wine
1 ½ lb beef chuck	1 thyme sprig
2 large onions, sliced	1 rosemary sprig
6 shallots, peeled	Salt and pepper to taste
1 cup beef stock	

Stir beef, onions, shallots, potatoes, beef stock, wine, thyme, rosemary, salt, and pepper in your Slow Cooker. Cover and cook for 7 hours on Low. Serve warm.

Country Beef Sirloin

Serves: 6 | Total Time: 6 hours 15 minutes

6 bacon slices, chopped	1 cup BBQ sauce
2 onions, sliced	1 tsp chili powder
4 garlic cloves, chopped	Salt and pepper to taste
2 lb beef sirloin roast	Coleslaw for serving
1 can (15 oz) red beans	

Combine sirloin, bacon, onions, garlic, beans, BBQ sauce, chili powder, salt, and pepper in your Slow Cooker. Cover with the lid and cook for 6 hours on Low. When done, remove the lid and serve topped with coleslaw.

Paprika Beef & Zucchini Casserole

Serves: 6 | Total Time: 2 hours 45 minutes

2 garlic cloves, minced	2 bay leaves
3 zucchinis, sliced	2 tbsp canola oil
1 lb ground beef	¼ tsp paprika
1 leek, sliced	¼ tsp cumin seeds
1 can fire-roasted tomatoes	Salt and pepper to taste
½ cup beef stock	

Warm the canola oil in a pan over medium heat. Place ground beef and cook for 2-3 minutes, stirring often. Add it to your Slow Cooker. Add in leek, garlic, zucchinis, tomatoes, beef stock, bay leaves, paprika, cumin seeds, salt, and pepper. Cover with the lid and cook for 21/2 hours on High. Serve immediately.

Beef Goulash

Serves: 6 | Total Time: 7 hours 15 minutes

2 lb potatoes, cubed	1 cup tomato sauce
2 lb beef steak, cubed	1 cup beef stock
2 red bell peppers, diced	2 tbsp tomato paste
1 carrot, sliced	2 tbsp canola oil
2 garlic cloves, chopped	1 tsp smoked paprika
1 red onion, chopped	1 tsp cumin seeds
1 can fire-roasted tomatoes	Salt and pepper to taste
2 bay leaves	Sour cream for serving

Warm the canola oil in a pan over medium heat. Place the beef and cook for 2-3 minutes. Add it to your Slow Cooker. Put in bell peppers, carrot, garlic, onion, tomatoes, tomato paste, potatoes, paprika, cumin seeds, bay leaves, tomato sauce, beef stock, salt, and pepper. Cover and cook for 7 hours on Low. When done, remove the lid and drizzle with sour cream to serve.

Shepherd's Pie with Sweet Potatoes

Serves: 6 | Total Time: 6 hours 45 minutes

2 lb sweet potatoes, cubed	1 cup diced tomatoes
1 lb ground beef	½ cup grated Parmesan
1 onion, finely chopped	2 tbsp canola oil
2 carrots, grated	½ tsp chili powder
2 celery stalks, chopped	Salt and pepper to taste
4 garlic cloves, chopped	

Place sweet potatoes in a steamer and cook for 15 minutes until softened. Transfer it into a bowl and mash them. Season with salt and pepper to taste. Set aside. Warm the canola oil in a pan over medium heat. Place the ground beef and cook for 2-3 minutes, stirring often. Add it to your Slow Cooker. Add in onion, carrots, celery, garlic, tomatoes, chili powder, salt, and pepper, top with mashed potatoes, and scatter with Parmesan cheese on top. Cover and cook for 6 hours on Low. Serve warm.

Cabbage Rolls Stuffed with Rice & Beef

Serves: 6 | Total Time: 6 hours 30 minutes

2 onions, finely chopped	2 lemons, juiced
2 garlic cloves, minced	2 tbsp chopped parsley
16 green cabbage leaves	1 egg
1 ½ lb ground beef	1 tbsp all-purpose flour
½ cup white rice	Salt and pepper to taste
1 ½ cups beef stock	

Place cabbage leaves in a pot with boiling water and cook for 2 minutes until slightly softened. Strain and let cool aside. In a bowl, combine ground beef, rice, onions, garlic, parsley, egg, flour, salt, and pepper. Lay cabbage leaves on a flat surface, spoon the beef mixture on each, and wrap them, pulling the ends inside. Add cabbage rolls, beef stock, and lemon juice to your Slow Cooker. Cover with the lid and cook for 6 hours on Low. Serve.

Hot BBQ Short Ribs

Serves: 6 | Total Time: 9 hours 15 minutes

1 cup BBQ sauce	1 tbsp apricot preserves
1 red onion, sliced	1 tbsp Worcestershire sauce
2 lb beef short ribs	1 tsp Dijon mustard
2 tsp balsamic vinegar	1 tsp garlic powder
1 tbsp brown sugar	1 tsp cumin powder
1 tbsp hot sauce	Salt and pepper to taste

Mix the BBQ sauce, onions, balsamic vinegar, sugar, hot sauce, apricot preserves, Worcestershire sauce, mustard, garlic powder, cumin, salt, and pepper in your Slow Cooker, add in short ribs, and toss until well coated. Cover with the lid and cook for 9 hours on Low. When done, remove the lid and serve warm.

Korean Beef Roast

Serves: 6 | Total Time: 7 hours 15 minutes

½ lb shiitake mushrooms	1 tbsp rice vinegar
½ lb baby carrots	1 ½ cups beef stock
2 lb beef roast	1 thyme sprig
¼ cup soy sauce	Salt and pepper to taste

Toss beef roast, mushrooms, carrots, soy sauce, rice vinegar, beef stock, thyme, salt, and pepper in your Slow Cooker. Cover with the lid and cook for 7 hours on Low. When done, remove the lid and serve warm or chilled.

Palermo Shredded Beef

Serves: 6 | Total Time: 8 hours 15 minutes

½ cup tomato juice	1 rosemary sprig
2 lb beef sirloin roast	1 tbsp honey
1 lemon, juiced	1 tsp Italian seasoning
¼ cup white wine	Salt and pepper to taste

Mix the sirloin, lemon juice, wine, honey, Italian seasoning, tomato juice, rosemary, salt, and pepper in your Slow Cooker. Cover with the lid and cook for 8 hours on Low. When done, remove the lid, using two forks, shred it finely, and serve immediately.

Sirloin in Salsa Roja

Serves: 6 | Total Time: 8 hours 15 minutes

8 potatoes, halved	1 cup beef stock
2 lb beef sirloin roast	Salt and pepper to taste
½ lb baby carrots	1 thyme sprig
1 cup red salsa	

Toss sirloin, potatoes, carrots, red salsa, beef stock, thyme, salt, and pepper in your Slow Cooker. Cover with the lid and cook for 8 hours on Low. Serve warm.

Original Sloopy Joes

Serves: 6 | Total Time: 7 hours 15 minutes

1 onion, finely chopped	½ cup beef stock
2 lb ground beef	1 tbsp Worcestershire sauce
¼ cup hot ketchup	Salt and pepper to taste
½ cup tomato juice	Bread buns for serving

Mix the ground beef, onion, Worcestershire sauce, ketchup, tomato juice, beef stock, salt, and pepper in your Slow Cooker. Cover with the lid and cook for 7 hours on Low. Serve with bread buns.

Mushroom & Snap Pea Beef Roast

Serves: 6 | Total Time: 6 hours 30 minutes

4 potatoes, halved	1 celery root, cubed
2 carrots, sliced	1 cup beef stock
1 onion, quartered	¼ cup horseradish sauce
2 lb beef roast	1 cup water
2 cups sliced mushrooms	Salt and pepper to taste
2 cups snap peas	

Toss beef roast, potatoes, carrots, onion, mushrooms, snap peas, celery, beef stock, water, salt, and pepper in your Slow Cooker. Cover with the lid and cook for 6 hours on Low. Serve with the prepared horseradish.

German-Style Beef Roast

Serves: 6 | Total Time: 10 hours 15 minutes

1 cup apple juice	2 tbsp mustard seeds
½ cup beef stock	1 tsp prepared horseradish
2 lb beef roast	Salt and pepper to taste
2 tbsp all-purpose flour	

Sprinkle beef roast with salt, pepper, and flour. Place seasoned beef, mustard seeds, horseradish, apple juice, beef stock, salt, and pepper in your Slow Cooker, and stir. Cover with the lid and cook for 10 hours on Low. When done, remove the lid and serve immediately.

Chipotle Beef Roast with Corn

Serves: 6 | Total Time: 8 hours 15 minutes

1 can fire-roasted tomatoes	½ tsp cayenne pepper
1 cup frozen corn	½ tsp cumin powder
2 lb beef roast	½ tsp garlic powder
2 chipotle peppers, chopped	1 cup beef stock
1 tsp chili powder	Salt and pepper to taste

Combine beef roast, chipotle peppers, chili powder, cayenne pepper, cumin, tomatoes, corn, garlic powder, beef stock, salt, and pepper in your Slow Cooker. Cover with the lid and cook for 8 hours on Low. When done, remove the lid and serve immediately.

Homemade Beef Stroganoff

Serves: 6 | Total Time: 6 hours 15 minutes

1 large onion, chopped	1 tbsp Worcestershire sauce
4 garlic cloves, minced	½ cup water
2 lb beef stew meat, cubed	Salt and pepper to taste
1 cup cream cheese	Cooked pasta for serving

Toss beef stew, onion, garlic, Worcestershire sauce, water, cream cheese, salt, and pepper in your Slow Cooker. Cover with the lid and cook for 6 hours on Low. When done, remove the lid and serve with your desired cooked pasta.

Beef & Pepperoncini Casserole

Serves: 8 | Total Time: 7 hours 15 minutes

4 red bell peppers, sliced	2 tbsp canola oil
2 lb beef roast, cubed	1 jar pepperoncini
6 garlic cloves, minced	1 can fire-roasted tomatoes
1 onion, finely chopped	1 bay leaf
1 celery stalk, diced	Salt and pepper to taste

Warm the canola oil in a pan over medium heat. Place beef and cook for 2-3 minutes until golden brown on all sides. Add it to your Slow Cooker. Put in garlic, onion, celery, bell peppers, pepperoncini, tomatoes, bay leaf, salt, and pepper. Cover with the lid and cook for 7 hours on Low. When done, remove the lid and serve warm.

Classic Corned Beef with Sauerkraut

Serves: 6 | Total Time: 8 hours 15 minutes

1 lb sauerkraut, shredded	½ tsp cumin seeds
3 lb corned beef brisket	1 cup beef stock
4 large carrot, sliced	Salt and pepper to taste
1 onion, sliced	

Mix the beef, carrot, onion, cumin seeds, beef stock, salt, and pepper in your Slow Cooker. Cover with the lid and cook for 8 hours on Low. Serve with sauerkraut.

Beef Roast & Heirloom Tomatoes

Serves: 6 | Total Time: 5 hours 15 minutes

1 shallot, sliced	2 tbsp canola oil
4 garlic cloves, minced	½ tsp cumin powder
4 heirloom tomatoes, cubed	½ tsp dried oregano
2 lb beef roast, cubed	Salt and pepper to taste
1 cup beef stock	

Warm the canola oil in a pan over medium heat. Place the beef and cook for 5 minutes until golden on all sides. Add it to your Slow Cooker. Add in shallot, garlic, tomatoes, beef stock, cumin, oregano, salt, and pepper. Cover and cook for 5 hours on Low. Serve and enjoy!

Saucy Sirloin with Bell Peppers

Serves: 4 | Total Time: 6 hours 15 minutes

2 lb beef sirloin, cut into thin strips	
4 garlic cloves, chopped	1 tbsp brown sugar
2 shallots, sliced	1 tbsp apple cider vinegar
2 red bell peppers, sliced	1 tbsp soy sauce
2 yellow bell peppers, sliced	Salt and pepper to taste

Toss sirloin, garlic, shallots, bell peppers, sugar, apple cider vinegar, soy sauce, salt, and pepper in your Slow Cooker. Cover with the lid and cook for 6 hours on Low. When done, remove the lid and serve right away.

Beef & Mushroom Casserole

Serves: 6 | Total Time: 6 hours 30 minutes

2 carrots, diced	1 red chili, chopped
2 lb beef roast, cubed	1 cup beef stock
1 celery root, diced	1 tbsp all-purpose flour
1 can fire-roasted tomatoes	2 tbsp canola oil
1 lb button mushrooms	Salt and pepper to taste
2 bay leaves	

Sprinkle beef roast with salt, pepper, and flour. Warm the canola oil in a pan over medium heat. Place the beef and cook for 2-3 minutes until golden on all sides. Add it to your Slow Cooker. Add in carrots, celery, tomatoes, mushrooms, beef stock, bay leaves, red chili, salt, and pepper. Cover with the lid and cook for 6 hours on Low. When done, remove the lid and serve warm.

Favorite Chili con Carne

Serves: 6 | Total Time: 7 hours 15 minutes

4 garlic cloves, chopped	2 tbsp canola oil
2 cans (15-oz) kidney beans	1 tsp chili powder
2 lb ground beef	1 tsp cumin powder
1 onion, chopped	¼ cup red wine
1 can fire-roasted tomatoes	1 cup beef stock
2 celery stalks, sliced	Salt and pepper to taste
2 carrots, sliced	Sour cream for serving

Warm the canola oil in a pan over medium heat. Place the ground beef and cook for 2-3 minutes, stirring often. Add it to your Slow Cooker. Put in onion, garlic, beans, tomatoes, celery, carrots, chili powder, cumin, red wine, beef stock, salt, and pepper. Cover with the lid and cook for 7 hours on Low. Top with sour cream to serve.

Country-Style Sirloin

Serves: 6 | Total Time: 8 hours 15 minutes

2 potatoes, cubed	4 garlic cloves, chopped
1 celery stalk, sliced	1 thyme sprig
2 lb beef sirloin	1 cup dark beer
½ lb baby carrots	¼ cup beef stock
1 sweet onion, chopped	Salt and pepper to taste

Toss sirloin, carrots, potatoes, celery, onion, garlic, thyme, beer, beef stock, salt, and pepper in your Slow Cooker. Cover and cook for 8 hours on Low. Serve immediately.

Jalapeño Beef Curry

Serves: 6 | Total Time: 7 hours 15 minutes

1 cup diced tomatoes	2 tbsp canola oil
1 cup green peas	1 tsp grated ginger
2 lb beef roast, cubed	1 tbsp curry powder
2 garlic cloves, chopped	1 bay leaf
1 sweet onion, chopped	1 lemongrass stalk, crushed
1 jalapeno pepper, chopped	Salt and pepper to taste
1 cup beef stock	2 tbsp chopped cilantro

Warm the canola oil in a pan over medium heat. Place the beef and cook for 5 minutes until golden on all sides. Add it to your Slow Cooker. Put in garlic, ginger, onion, jalapeño pepper, curry powder, beef stock, tomatoes, green peas, bay leaf, lemongrass, salt, and pepper. Cover and cook for 7 hours on Low. Top with cilantro to serve.

Mixed Bean Beef Chili with Bacon & Cheese

Serves: 6 | Total Time: 6 hours 15 minutes

2 carrots, diced	1 ½ cups grated cheddar
1 celery stalk, diced	2 tbsp canola oil
4 garlic cloves, chopped	1 tbsp molasses
1 lb ground beef	¼ tsp cayenne pepper
4 bacon slices, chopped	1 cup beef stock
1 can (15 oz) black beans	¼ cup tomato paste
1 can (15 oz) red beans	Salt and pepper to taste
1 can (15 oz) kidney beans	

Warm the canola oil in a pan over medium heat. Place the ground beef and bacon and cook for 5 minutes, stirring often. Transfer everything to your Slow Cooker. Put in beans, carrots, celery, garlic, molasses, cayenne pepper, beef stock, tomato paste, salt, pepper, and scatter with cheddar. Cover and cook for 6 hours on Low. Serve.

Mustardy Rump Roast

Serves: 6 | Total Time: 10 hours 15 minutes

1 tsp smoked paprika	1 tsp mustard seeds
1 tsp chili powder	1 cup water
2 lb rump roast	Salt and pepper to taste
1 tsp garlic powder	

In a bowl, combine black pepper, paprika, chili powder, garlic powder, mustard seeds, and salt. Rub rump roast with the spice mixture and massage until well coated. Add seasoned meat and water to your Slow Cooker. Cover and cook for 10 hours on Low. Serve sliced.

Flank Steaks a la Marinara

Serves: 4 | Total Time: 5 hours 15 minutes

2 cups marinara sauce	1 tbsp balsamic vinegar
4 flank steaks	1 tsp dried Italian herbs
1 cup shredded mozzarella	Salt and pepper to taste

Put flank steaks, marinara sauce, balsamic vinegar, Italian herbs, salt, and pepper in your Slow Cooker, and scatter with mozzarella cheese on top. Cover with the lid and cook for 5 hours on Low. Serve warm.

Beef & Onion Glazed with Red Wine

Serves: 6 | Total Time: 7 hours 15 minutes

2 red onions, sliced	1 tsp ground coriander
2 lb beef chuck roast	1 tsp cumin powder
1 cup red wine	Salt and pepper to taste
1 thyme sprig	

Sprinkle chuck roast with coriander, cumin, salt, and pepper. Place seasoned meat, red wine, onions, and thyme in your Slow Cooker. Cover with the lid and cook for 7 hours on Low. Cut it into slices before serving.

Brewed Sirloin

Serves: 6 | Total Time: 4 hours 15 minutes

4 garlic cloves, minced	½ cup beef stock
2 lb beef sirloin	2 tbsp olive oil
1 cup strong brewed coffee	Salt and pepper to taste

Toss sirloin, olive oil, garlic, coffee, beef stock, salt, and pepper in your Slow Cooker. Cover with the lid and cook for 4 hours on High. Serve and enjoy!

Beef & Winter Vegetable Casserole

Serves: 6 | Total Time: 8 hours 30 minutes

2 carrots, sliced	1 turnip, peeled and cubed
2 parsnips, sliced	1 bay leaf
1 celery root, cubed	1 lemon, juiced
2 lb beef sirloin roast, cubed	1 tsp Worcestershire sauce
3 garlic cloves, chopped	1 cup beef stock
4 potatoes, cubed	Salt and pepper to taste

Mix the sirloin, carrots, parsnips, celery, garlic, potatoes, turnip, bay leaf, lemon juice, Worcestershire sauce, beef stock, salt, and pepper in your Slow Cooker. Cover with the lid and cook for 8 hours on Low. Serve warm.

Bolognese Pasta Sauce

Serves: 6 | Total Time: 6 hours 15 minutes

1 can (15 oz) diced tomatoes	½ tsp dried oregano
2 lb ground beef	½ tsp dried basil
1 carrot, grated	¼ cup red wine
1 celery stalk, chopped	½ cup beef stock
4 garlic cloves, minced	Salt and pepper to taste
2 tbsp canola oil	2 tbsp grated Parmesan
2 tbsp tomato paste	16 oz cooked pasta

Warm the canola oil in a pan over medium heat. Place the ground beef and cook for 2-3 minutes, stirring often. Add it to your Slow Cooker. Add in carrot, celery, garlic, tomatoes, tomato paste, oregano, basil, wine, stock, salt, and pepper. Cover and cook for 6 hours on Low. Serve over cooked pasta topped with Parmesan cheese.

Cheeseburger Casserole

Serves: 6 | Total Time: 7 hours 30 minutes

1 ½ lb beef sirloin, cut into thin strips
1 cup processed meat, shredded

1 can condensed cream of mushroom soup
2 potatoes, sliced
1 celery stalk, sliced
2 onions, sliced

1 cup green peas
1 cup grated cheddar cheese
Salt and pepper to taste

Combine sirloin, potatoes, celery, onions, green peas, mushroom soup, salt, and pepper in your Slow Cooker, and scatter with processed meat and cheddar cheese. Cover with the lid and cook for 7 hours on Low. Serve.

Cowboy Sirloin

Serves: 6 | Total Time: 8 hours 15 minutes

1 chipotle pepper, chopped
1 green chile pepper, chopped
2 lb beef sirloin roast
1 shallot, chopped
1 cup BBQ sauce

1 tbsp brown sugar
½ tsp garlic powder
½ tsp chili powder
Salt and pepper to taste

Stir chipotle pepper, green chile, shallot, BBQ sauce, sugar, garlic powder, chili powder, salt, and pepper in your Slow Cooker. Put in sirloin and toss until well coated. Cover and cook for 8 hours on Low. Serve.

Italian Pork & Sausages Pasta Sauce

Serves: 6 | Total Time: 8 hours 15 minutes

1 lb pork sausages, casings removed
1 can (29 oz) diced tomatoes
1 cup tomato juice
1 lb ground beef
2 large onions, chopped
8 garlic cloves, minced
½ cup red wine

2 tbsp olive oil
1 tsp Italian herbs
½ tsp dried marjoram
¼ tsp cayenne pepper
1 tbsp brown sugar
Salt and pepper to taste

Mix the beef, sausages, onions, garlic, olive oil, Italian herbs, marjoram, tomatoes, tomato juice, red wine, cayenne pepper, sugar, salt, and pepper in your Slow Cooker. Cover and cook for 8 hours on Low. Serve.

Tomato Beef Steaks

Serves: 4 | Total Time: 8 hours 15 minutes

2 red bell peppers, sliced
1 shallot, sliced
1 can (15 oz) diced tomatoes
4 beef steaks

2 tbsp canola oil
2 tbsp all-purpose flour
Salt and pepper to taste

Sprinkle the beef steaks with salt, pepper, and flour. Warm the canola oil in a pan over medium heat. Place the beef and cook for 5 minutes until golden on all sides. Add it to your Slow Cooker. Put in bell peppers, shallot, and tomatoes. Cover and cook for 8 hours on Low. Serve.

Beef Fajitas

Serves: 6 | Total Time: 6 hours 30 minutes

2 shallots, chopped
3 garlic cloves, minced
4 potatoes, cubed
2 lb beef chuck roast, cubed
2 red bell peppers, diced

¼ tsp chili powder
½ tsp cumin powder
1 ½ cups beef stock
1 cup tomato sauce
Salt and pepper to taste

Stir chuck roast, bell peppers, shallots, garlic, potatoes, chili powder, cumin, beef stock, tomato sauce, salt, and pepper in your Slow Cooker. Cover with the lid and cook for 6 hours on Low. Serve with tortillas or in burritos.

Beef & Rice Casserole with Cole Slaw

Serves: 6 | Total Time: 6 hours 30 minutes

1 lb beef roast, cut into thin strips
1 head green cabbage, shredded
2 ripe tomatoes, diced
1 cup white rice
1 onion, chopped
1 carrot, grated
1 cup beef stock

2 tbsp canola oil
2 tbsp tomato paste
½ tsp cumin seeds
½ tsp chili powder
Salt and pepper to taste

Warm the canola oil in a pan over medium heat. Place the beef and cook for 2-3 minutes until golden on all sides. Add it to your Slow Cooker. Put in cabbage, onion, carrot, tomatoes, rice, beef stock, ¼ cup of water, tomato paste, cumin seeds, chili powder, salt, and pepper. Cover with the lid and cook for 6 hours on Low. Serve warm.

Sweet BBQ Ground Beef

Serves: 6 | Total Time: 7 hours 15 minutes

1 large onion, chopped
4 garlic cloves, chopped
2 celery stalks, chopped
2 lb ground beef
1 ½ cups BBQ sauce

½ cup beef sauce
1 tbsp apple cider vinegar
1 tsp Dijon mustard
1 tbsp brown sugar
Salt and pepper to taste

Mix the ground beef, onion, garlic, celery, apple cider vinegar, mustard, sugar, BBQ sauce, beef sauce, salt, and pepper in your Slow Cooker. Cover with the lid and cook for 7 hours on Low. Serve warm.

Tomato Beef & Okra Casserole

Serves: 6 | Total Time: 6 hours 15 minutes

1 ½ lb beef roast, cut into thin strips
2 large potatoes, cubed
1 can (15 oz) diced tomatoes
1 large onion, chopped
4 garlic cloves, minced
12 oz frozen okra, chopped

1 cup beef stock
1 thyme sprig
Salt and pepper to taste
2 tbsp chopped parsley

Stir beef, onion, garlic, tomatoes, okra, potatoes, beef stock, thyme, salt, and pepper in your Slow Cooker. Cover with the lid and cook for 6 hours on Low. Serve.

Simple Beef Barbacoa

Serves: 6 | Total Time: 6 hours 30 minutes

2 red onions, sliced
6 garlic cloves, chopped
2 lb beef chuck roast
3 tbsp white wine vinegar

1 ½ cups tomato sauce
1 ½ tsp chili powder
Salt and pepper to taste

Toss chuck roast, onions, garlic, vinegar, tomato sauce, chili powder, salt, and pepper in your Slow Cooker. Cover and cook for 6 hours on Low. Serve immediately.

Spiced Chuck Roast

Serves: 6 | Total Time: 8 hours 15 minutes

2 lb boneless beef chuck roast
4 garlic cloves, chopped
2 large onions, sliced
1 celery stalk, sliced
2 tbsp brown sugar
1 ½ cups tomato sauce

1 tbsp cocoa powder
1 tsp chili powder
½ tsp cumin powder
½ tsp dried oregano
Salt and pepper to taste

Combine chuck roast, garlic, onions, celery, sugar, tomato sauce, cocoa powder, chili powder, cumin, oregano, salt, and pepper in your Slow Cooker. Cover with the lid and cook for 8 hours on Low. Serve warm.

Flank Steaks Filled with Cheese

Serves: 2 | Total Time: 6 hours 30 minutes

1 red bell pepper, diced
2 thick flank steaks
½ cup beef stock

½ cup grated Cheddar
¼ cup cream cheese
Salt and pepper to taste

In a bowl, combine cheddar cheese, cream cheese, bell pepper, salt, and pepper. Poke each steak into a small pocket and stuff with the cheese mixture. Using toothpicks, secure the sides. Add steak pockets and beef stock in your Slow Cooker. Cover with the lid and cook for 6 hours on Low. When done, remove the lid and serve with your desired side dish.

Beef & Hominy Chili with Cheddar Cheese

Serves: 6 | Total Time: 3 hours 15 minutes

2 red bell peppers, diced
1 can (15 oz) hominy
1 can fire-roasted tomatoes
1 lb ground beef
1 large onion, chopped
4 garlic cloves, chopped
2 carrots, diced

2 jalapeno peppers, chopped
2 cups frozen corn
1 bay leaf
½ tsp cumin powder
1 tsp chili powder
Salt and pepper to taste
Grated Cheddar for serving

In your Slow Cooker, combine ground beef, onion, garlic, carrots, bell peppers, hominy, tomatoes, jalapeño peppers, cumin, chili powder, corn, salt, and pepper, and top with bay leaf. Cover with the lid and cook for 3 hours on High. Scatter with cheddar cheese to serve.

Bell Peppers Stuffed with Chipotle Beef

Serves: 6 | Total Time: 6 hours 30 minutes

2 chipotle peppers, chopped
6 green bell peppers
1 lb ground beef
½ cup white rice
1 cup frozen corn
1 cup tomato sauce
1 cup beef stock

1 lime, juiced
1 tbsp chopped parsley
½ tsp cumin powder
¼ tsp chili powder
Salt and pepper to taste
Sour cream for serving

Slice the bell peppers on top and discard the seeds. Combine ground beef, rice, corn, parsley, chipotle pepper, cumin, chili powder, salt, and pepper in a bowl. Spoon the beef mixture into each pepper.

Place them into your Slow Cooker. Add in tomato sauce, chipotle pepper, stock, and lime juice. Cover and cook for 6 hours on Low. Drizzle with sour cream to serve.

Parmesan Macaroni with Ground Beef

Serves: 6 | Total Time: 5 hours 15 minutes

8 oz macaroni pasta, cooked
in a large pot of water
1 lb ground beef
1 shallot, chopped
2 garlic cloves, minced
1 can (28 oz) diced tomatoes

1 cup beef stock
½ cup grated Parmesan
1 tbsp canola oil
1 cup shredded mozzarella
Salt and pepper to taste

Warm the canola oil in a pan over medium heat. Place the ground beef and cook for 2 minutes. Add in shallot, garlic, and tomatoes and cook for 5 minutes. Transfer everything to your Slow Cooker. Add in beef stock, macaroni, Parmesan, mozzarella, salt, and pepper. Cover with the lid and cook for 6 hours on Low. Serve warm.

Red Cabbage & Apple Corned Beef

Serves: 6 | Total Time: 6 hours 30 minutes

1 ½ lb beef chuck roast, cubed
1 red cabbage, shredded
2 red apples, cored and diced
1 bay leaf
½ tsp cumin seeds
1 cinnamon stick

1 star anise
½ cup red wine
1 tbsp red wine vinegar
½ cup beef stock
Salt and pepper to taste

Toss chuck roast, cabbage, cumin seeds, cinnamon stick, star anise, red wine, vinegar, beef stock, apples, bay leaf, salt, and pepper in your Slow Cooker. Cover with the lid and cook for 6 hours on Low. Serve immediately.

Beef & Mushroom Pasta Sauce

Serves: 6 | Total Time: 6 hours 30 minutes

2 lb beef sirloin, cut into thin strips
1 can (28 oz) diced tomatoes
2 cups sliced mushrooms
1 carrot, diced
1 celery stalk, diced
2 garlic cloves, chopped

¼ cup red wine
1 cup tomato sauce
1 bay leaf
Salt and pepper to taste

Mix the sirloin, carrot, celery, garlic, tomatoes, mushrooms, red wine, tomato sauce, bay leaf, salt, and pepper in your Slow Cooker. Cover with the lid and cook for 6 hours on Low. Serve with cooked pasta.

Spiced Beef Pot Roast

Serves: 4 | Total Time: 6 hours 15 minutes

2 garlic cloves, minced
1 ½ lb beef roast
1 cup freshly brewed coffee
1 tsp Worcestershire sauce

1 tbsp Sriracha sauce
½ cup beef stock
Salt and pepper to taste

Mix the beef roast, coffee, Worcestershire sauce, Sriracha sauce, garlic, beef stock, salt, and pepper in your Slow Cooker. Cover and cook for 6 hours on Low. Serve.

Chipotle Corned Beef

Serves: 6 | Total Time: 6 hours 15 minutes

2 chipotle peppers, chopped	2 tbsp balsamic vinegar
2 lb corned beef	1 tbsp Dijon mustard
1 cup beef stock	Salt and pepper to taste

Stir corned beef, beef stock, balsamic vinegar, mustard, chipotle peppers, salt, and pepper in your Slow Cooker. Cover and cook for 6 hours on Low. Serve immediately.

Greek-Style Beef Brisket

Serves: 6 | Total Time: 7 hours 15 minutes

½ cup pitted Kalamata olives, sliced

4 garlic cloves, chopped	1 rosemary sprig
2 lb beef brisket	1 thyme sprig
1 can (15 oz) diced tomatoes	Salt and pepper to taste
½ cup dry red wine	

Toss beef brisket, tomatoes, wine, olives, garlic, rosemary, thyme, salt, and pepper in your Slow Cooker. Cover with the lid and cook for 7 hours on Low. Serve warm.

Hot Corned Beef

Serves: 6 | Total Time: 5 hours 15 minutes

4 garlic cloves, chopped	1 tsp sesame oil
2 lb corned beef	½ tsp onion powder
2 shallots, sliced	1 tbsp Sriracha
½ cup beef stock	1 tbsp rice vinegar
¼ cup soy sauce	Salt and pepper to taste
2 tbsp brown sugar	

Combine soy sauce, sugar, garlic, onion powder, Sriracha sesame oil, rice vinegar, shallots, beef stock, salt, and pepper in your Slow Cooker. Put in corned beef and toss until well coated. Cover with the lid and cook for 5 hours on Low. Cut it into slices before serving.

Creamy Beef Sirloin with Mushrooms

Serves: 6 | Total Time: 8 hours 15 minutes

2 carrots, sliced	1 celery stalk, sliced
4 large onions, sliced	1 cup beef stock
3 garlic cloves, chopped	1 thyme sprig
2 lb beef sirloin	1 rosemary sprig
1 cup dry white wine	Salt and pepper to taste
½ lb button mushrooms	

Sprinkle sirloin with salt and pepper. Mix the wine, onions, garlic, mushrooms, carrots, celery, stock, thyme, and rosemary in your Slow Cooker and top with seasoned sirloin. Cover and cook for 8 hours on Low. Serve warm.

Restaurant-Style Veal Osso Buco

Serves: 4 | Total Time: 7 hours 15 minutes

2 red onions, chopped	¼ cup red wine
1 can (15 oz) diced tomatoes	1 tsp dried thyme
4 veal shanks	¼ tsp cayenne pepper
2 tbsp butter	½ tsp garlic powder
2 tbsp all-purpose flour	Salt and pepper to taste

Sprinkle veal shanks with salt, pepper, and flour. Melt butter in a pan over medium heat. Place veal shanks and cook until golden on all sides. Transfer them to your Slow Cooker. Add in onions, tomatoes, red wine, thyme, cayenne pepper, garlic powder, salt, and pepper. Cover and cook for 7 hours on Low. Serve right away.

Gourmet Veal Paprikash

Serves: 6 | Total Time: 5 hours 15 minutes

2 carrots, diced	1 tsp sweet paprika
1 celery stalk, diced	1 tsp smoked paprika
2 lb veal roast, cubed	2 tbsp red pepper paste
2 garlic cloves, sliced	1 can fire-roasted tomatoes
2 bay leaves	½ cup beef stock
2 tbsp all-purpose flour	Salt and pepper to taste
2 tbsp butter	Sour cream for serving

Sprinkle veal roast with salt, pepper, and flour. Melt the butter in a pan over medium heat. Put the veal and cook for 2-3 minutes until golden on all sides. Add it to your Slow Cooker. Put in carrots, celery, garlic, paprika, red pepper paste, tomatoes, beef stock, salt, pepper, and bay leaves. Cover with the lid and cook for 5 hours on Low. Serve topped with sour cream.

Strong Mushroom & Beef Casserole

Serves: 6 | Total Time: 8 hours 15 minutes

6 bacon slices, chopped	1 ½ cups brown stout
4 garlic cloves, minced	2 tbsp canola oil
2 lb beef roast, cubed	2 tbsp tomato paste
1 celery stalk, chopped	1 tsp dried thyme
2 shallots, finely chopped	½ tsp chili powder
1 cup chopped mushrooms	Salt and pepper to taste

Warm the canola oil in a pan over medium heat. Place the beef and bacon and cook for 2-3 minutes until golden on all sides. Transfer everything to your Slow Cooker. Put in garlic, celery, shallots, mushrooms, stout, tomato paste, thyme, chili powder, salt, and pepper. Cover with the lid and cook for 8 hours on Low. Serve and enjoy!

Effortless Beef Tagine

Serves: 6 | Total Time: 7 hours 15 minutes

2 ripe tomatoes, diced	½ tsp saffron threads
2 lb beef sirloin, cubed	2 tbsp sliced almonds
1 large onion, chopped	½ cup couscous
4 garlic clove, chopped	1 ½ cups vegetable stock
1 celery stalk, sliced	Salt and pepper to taste
1 cup dried plums, chopped	2 tbsp chopped parsley
1 orange, sliced	Lime juice for serving
2 tbsp olive oil	

Warm the olive oil in a pan over medium heat. Place the beef and cook for 2-3 minutes until golden on all sides. Add it to your Slow Cooker. Add in onion, garlic, celery, tomatoes, plums, saffron, couscous, stock, orange slices, almonds, salt, and pepper. Cover and cook for 7 hours on Low. Top with lime juice and parsley and serve.

Beef Short Ribs in Curried Tomato

Serves: 6 | Total Time: 8 hours 15 minutes

2 shallots, chopped
3 lb beef short ribs
1 cup tomato sauce
3 tbsp red curry paste
1 tsp curry powder
½ tsp garlic powder
1 tsp grated ginger
1 lime, juiced
Salt and pepper to taste

Toss curry paste, tomato sauce, curry powder, garlic powder, shallots, ginger, lime juice, salt, and pepper in your Slow Cooker. Put in short ribs and toss until well coated. Cover and cook for 8 hours on Low. Serve warm.

Barley & Beef Chili

Serves: 6 | Total Time: 6 hours 30 minutes

2 garlic cloves, chopped
1 carrot, diced
1 lb beef chuck roast strips
1 shallot, chopped
1 celery stalk, diced
1 cup pearl barley
2 tbsp canola oil
¼ cup dried currants
¼ cup pine nuts
2 cups beef stock
Salt and pepper to taste

Warm the canola oil in a pan over medium heat. Place the beef and cook for 2-3 minutes until golden on all sides. Add it to your Slow Cooker. Add in shallot, garlic, carrot, celery, barley, currants, pine nuts, beef stock, salt, and pepper. Cover and cook for 6 hours on Low. Serve.

Turnip & Parsnip Beef Roast

Serves: 6 | Total Time: 7 hours 15 minutes

1 shallot, chopped
1 garlic clove, chopped
1 ½ lb beef roast, cubed
2 parsnips, chopped
½ cup red wine
2 tbsp all-purpose flour
2 tbsp canola oil
2 tbsp tomato paste
1 cup beef stock
1 turnip, shredded
Salt and pepper to taste

Sprinkle beef roast with salt, pepper, and flour. Warm the canola oil in a pan over medium heat. Place the beef and cook for 2-3 minutes until golden on all sides. Add it to your Slow Cooker. Put in parsnips, shallot, garlic, red wine, tomato paste, beef stock, turnip, salt, and pepper. Cover and cook for 7 hours on Low. Serve immediately.

Nachos con Carne

Serves: 6 | Total Time: 6 hours 30 minutes

12 oz nachos
1 lb ground beef
1 can (10 oz) corn, drained
2 cups grated cheddar
2 garlic cloves, minced
1 shallot, chopped
1 chipotle pepper, chopped
2 tbsp canola oil
½ cup tomato sauce
Salt and pepper to taste

Warm the canola oil in a pan over medium heat. Place the beef and cook for 5 minutes. Add in garlic, shallot, chipotle pepper, tomato sauce, salt, and pepper and cook for 5 more minutes. Put nachos in your Slow Cooker, add in beef mixture and corn, and scatter with cheddar cheese on top. Cover and cook for 6 hours on Low.

Beef Roast in Curried Yogurt Sauce

Serves: 6 | Total Time: 8 hours 15 minutes

1 ½ cups plain yogurt
2 lb beef roast, cubed
½ cup beef stock
1 ½ tsp curry powder
2 tbsp olive oil
½ tsp cumin powder
1 tsp chili powder
1 tsp smoked paprika
1 tsp dried mint
Salt and pepper to taste
3 cups cooked basmati rice

Place beef roast, yogurt, curry powder, cumin, chili powder, paprika, mint, olive oil, salt, and pepper in a resealable bag and let marinate in the fridge for 2 hours. Place the beef roast, marinade, and beef stock in your Slow Cooker, cover with the lid, and cook for 6 hours on Low. Serve over cooked basmati rice.

Squash & Beef Red Curry

Serves: 6 | Total Time: 7 hours 30 minutes

1 lb butternut squash, cubes
2 tomatoes, diced
1 ½ lb beef roast, cubed
1 shallot, chopped
4 garlic cloves, minced
1 sweet potato, cubed
1 star anise
1 cinnamon stick
1 bay leaf
3 red curry paste
2 tbsp coconut oil
½ tsp chili powder
1 ½ cups coconut milk
Salt and pepper to taste

Melt the coconut oil in a pan over medium heat. Place the beef and cook until golden on all sides. Transfer it to your Slow Cooker. Mix in shallot, garlic, butternut squash, tomatoes, sweet potato, star anise, cinnamon stick, bay leaf, curry paste, chili powder, coconut milk, salt, and pepper. Cover and cook for 7 hours on Low. Serve.

Cheesy Flank Steaks

Serves: 4 | Total Time: 3 hours 15 minutes

1 cup crumbled Gruyere cheese
½ cup cream cheese
4 flank steaks
½ cup white wine
1 tsp Worcestershire sauce
1 tsp Dijon mustard
Salt and pepper to taste

Sprinkle flank steaks with salt and pepper. Transfer them to your Slow Cooker. In a bowl, combine gruyere cheese, wine, Worcestershire sauce, cream cheese, and mustard and pour it over the meat. Cover with the lid and cook for 3 hours on High. Serve and enjoy!

Beef & Collard Green Sauté

Serves: 6 | Total Time: 3 hours 15 minutes

1 ½ lb beef roast, cut into thin strips
4 cups collard greens, torn
¼ cup beef stock
1 tbsp all-purpose flour
2 tbsp canola oil
½ tsp cumin powder
Salt and pepper to taste

Sprinkle beef roast with cumin, salt, pepper, and flour. Warm the canola oil in a pan over medium heat. Place the beef and cook for 2-3 minutes until golden on all sides. Add it to your Slow Cooker. Add in collard greens and stock. Cook for 3 hours on High. Serve and enjoy!

African Short Ribs

Serves: 6 | Total Time: 8 hours 15 minutes

1 can (15 oz) diced tomatoes   1 tsp cinnamon powder
3 lb beef short ribs   1 tsp chili powder
2 tbsp olive oil   1 tsp cumin powder
1 tbsp dried thyme   1 lime, juiced
1 tsp ground ginger   Salt and pepper to taste

In a bowl, combine olive oil, thyme, ginger, cinnamon powder, chili powder, cumin, salt, and pepper. Brush short ribs with the spice mixture and massage until well coated. Place seasoned ribs, tomatoes, and lime juice in your Slow Cooker. Cover and cook for 8 hours on Low. Serve.

Garlicky Beef Roast

Serves: 8 | Total Time: 9 hours 15 minutes

2 shallots, sliced   1 cup beef stock
4 lb beef roast   Salt and pepper to taste
4 whole garlic heads, peeled   1 thyme sprig
2 tbsp olive oil

Preheat the oven to 350°F. In an oven pot, whisk garlic, olive oil, salt, and pepper. Add in beef roast and toss until well combined. Cover with aluminum foil and roast for 1 hour. Place cooked meat, shallots, thyme and beef stock in your Slow Cooker. Cover with the lid and cook for 8 hours on Low. Cut it into slices before serving.

Roasted Jalapeño Flank Steaks

Serves: 4 | Total Time: 6 hours 15 minutes

red bell peppers, and sliced   ½ tsp cumin seeds
4 flank steaks   ½ tsp mustard seeds
4 jalapeno peppers, minced   Salt and pepper to taste
1 can fire-roasted tomatoes

Toss steaks, jalapeño peppers, bell peppers, tomatoes, cumin seeds, mustard seeds, salt, and pepper in your Slow Cooker. Cover with the lid and cook for 6 hours on Low. When done, remove the lid and serve warm.

Peppercorn Rump Roast

Serves: 6 | Total Time: 6 hours 15 minutes

4 black peppercorns   1 star anise
2 whole cloves   1 cinnamon stick
2 lb rump roast   1 ½ cups beef stock
1 lemon, sliced   Salt and pepper to taste
1 tsp grated ginger

Toss rump roast, lemon slices, ginger, peppercorns, cloves, star anise, cinnamon stick, beef stock, salt, and pepper in your Slow Cooker. Cover with the lid and cook for 6 hours on Low. Serve immediately.

Thyme Beef Tenderloin Wrapped in Bacon

Serves: 6 | Total Time: 8 hours 15 minutes

8 slices bacon   1 tsp cumin powder
2 lb beef tenderloin   1 tsp smoked paprika
1 tsp dried thyme   1 cup beef stock
2 tbsp olive oil   Salt and pepper to taste

Sprinkle beef tenderloin with cumin, paprika, thyme, salt, and pepper. Drizzle with olive oil and massage until well coated. Place bacon slices on a flat surface, add in beef, and wrap them. Put wrapped beef and beef stock in your Slow Cooker. Cover with the lid and cook for 8 hours on Low. Cut it into slices before serving.

Spicy Beef Noodles

Serves: 6 | Total Time: 5 hours 15 minutes

2 lb beef roast, cut into thin strips
1 shallot, sliced   ½ tsp chili powder
2 red bell peppers, sliced   2 tbsp soy sauce
½ cup tomato sauce   1 tsp Worcestershire sauce
2 tbsp peanut oil   1 tsp orange zest
¼ cup fresh orange juice   Salt and pepper to taste
½ tsp grated ginger   3 cups cooked egg noodles

Warm the peanut oil in a pan over medium heat. Put the beef and cook for 5 minutes until golden on all sides. Add it to your Slow Cooker. Put in shallot, bell peppers, ginger, chili powder, soy sauce, tomato sauce, Worcestershire sauce, orange zest, orange juice, salt, and pepper. Cook for 5 hours on Low. Serve over cooked noodles.

Sirloin Curry

Serves: 6 | Total Time: 7 hours 30 minutes

2 carrots, sliced   2 tbsp tomato paste
3 cups cauliflower florets   2 cardamom pods, crushed
1 lb beef sirloin, cubed   2 kaffir lime leaves
4 garlic cloves, chopped   1 lemongrass stalk, crushed
1 shallot, chopped   1 cup coconut milk
2 red bell peppers, diced   1 cup beef stock
4 potatoes, cut into wedges   1 tbsp brown sugar
2 tbsp coconut oil   1 tbsp lime juice
3 tbsp red curry paste   Salt and pepper to taste

Melt the coconut oil in a pan over medium heat. Cook the beef for 5 minutes until golden. Add it to your Slow Cooker. Add in garlic, shallot, carrots, cauliflower, bell peppers, potatoes, curry paste, tomato paste, cardamom pods, lime leaves, lemongrass, coconut milk, stock, sugar, lime juice, salt, and pepper. Cook for 7 hours on Low.

Sticky Pomegranate Short Ribs

Serves: 6 | Total Time: 6 hours 15 minutes

2 carrots, sliced   2 tbsp brown sugar
3 lb beef short ribs   2 tbsp olive oil
1 large onion, sliced   1 tsp Worcestershire sauce
1 cup pomegranate juice   1 tsp dried thyme
½ cup pomegranate kernels   1 rosemary sprig
¼ cup soy sauce

Stir short ribs, olive oil, onion, carrots, sugar, pomegranate juice, pomegranate kernels, soy sauce, Worcestershire sauce, thyme, and rosemary in your Slow Cooker. Cover with the lid and cook for 6 hours on Low. Serve warm.

Roasted Beef Ragu

Serves: 6 | Total Time: 6 hours 15 minutes

1 cup green peas	1 tbsp canola oil
1 can fire-roasted tomatoes	1 tbsp red wine vinegar
1 ½ lb ground beef	1 tsp smoked paprika
1 shallot, chopped	2 tbsp tomato paste
4 garlic cloves, chopped	Salt and pepper to taste
2 red bell peppers, chopped	2 tbsp grated Parmesan
1 cup chopped mushrooms	Cooked spaghetti or your
1 bay leaf	favorite pasta for serving

Warm the canola oil in a pan over medium heat. Place the ground beef and cook for 2-3 minutes until golden on all sides. Add it to your Slow Cooker. Put in shallot, garlic, paprika, tomato paste, bell peppers, mushrooms, green peas, tomatoes, bay leaf, vinegar, salt, and pepper. Cover with the lid and cook for 6 hours on Low. When done, remove the lid and serve with your desired pasta, and scatter with Parmesan cheese on top.

Sirloin & Mushroom Roast

Serves: 6 | Total Time: 6 hours 30 minutes

6 oz button mushrooms	1 thyme sprig
½ lb baby carrots	1 ½ cups hard cider
6 small shallots, peeled	1 bay leaf
2 lb beef sirloin roast	Salt and pepper to taste
1 lb small new potatoes	

Toss shallots, sirloin, mushrooms, potatoes, carrots, thyme, cider, bay leaf, salt, and pepper in your Slow Cooker. Cover and cook for 6 hours on Low. Serve.

Oriental Short Ribs

Serves: 6 | Total Time: 7 hours 15 minutes

1 large onion, sliced	1 cup beef stock
1 carrot, sliced	2 tbsp brown sugar
3 lb beef short ribs	1 star anise
4 garlic cloves, chopped	2 tbsp rice vinegar
½ cup light soy sauce	

In your Slow Cooker, combine onion, carrot, soy sauce, sugar, garlic, star anise, rice vinegar, and beef stock. Add in short ribs and toss until well coated. Cover and cook for 7 hours on Low. Serve topped with green onions.

Beef & White Bean Chili with Kale

Serves: 6 | Total Time: 5 hours 15 minutes

2 shallots, chopped	1 tsp dried oregano
4 garlic cloves, chopped	½ tsp dried sage
2 lb beef roast, cubed	1 bunch kale, shredded
2 cans (15-oz) white beans	Salt and pepper to taste
2 tbsp canola oil	

Warm the canola oil in a pan over medium heat. Place the beef and cook for 2-3 minutes until golden on all sides. Add it to your Slow Cooker. Put in beans, shallots, garlic, oregano, sage, kale, salt, and pepper. Cover with the lid and cook for 5 hours on Low. Serve right away.

Californian Short Ribs

Serves: 6 | Total Time: 7 hours 15 minutes

¼ cup brown sugar	1 ½ cups ginger ale drink
3 lb beef short ribs	1 rosemary sprig
1 tsp grated ginger	Salt and pepper to taste
1 tsp cumin powder	

In a bowl, combine ginger, sugar, cumin, rosemary, salt, and pepper. Rub short ribs with the spice mixture and massage until well coated. Place the ribs and ginger ale in your Slow Cooker, cover with the lid, and cook for 7 hours on Low. Serve warm.

Spiced Short Ribs with Green Onions

Serves: 6 | Total Time: 8 hours 15 minutes

8 green onions, chopped	1 tbsp five-spice powder
½ cup beef stock	1 tsp garlic powder
3 lb beef short ribs	1 tsp chili powder
¼ cup molasses	2 tbsp soy sauce
2 tbsp peanut oil	1 tsp fish sauce

In a bowl, combine molasses, five-spice powder, garlic powder, chili powder, peanut oil, soy sauce, and fish sauce. Rub short ribs with the spice mixture and massage until well coated. Place the seasoned ribs, green onions, and beef stock in your Slow Cooker. Cover with the lid and cook for 8 hours on Low. Serve immediately.

Veal Shanks with Fruit Sauce

Serves: 4 | Total Time: 3 hours 15 minutes

½ cup dried apricots, chopped	
2 sweet potatoes, cubed	1 cup diced tomatoes
4 veal shanks	1 rosemary sprig
1 orange, zested and juiced	1 thyme sprig
¼ cup dried cranberries	Salt and pepper to taste
1 cup beef stock	

Sprinkle veal shanks with salt and pepper. Stir orange juice, orange zest, apricots, cranberries, beef stock, tomatoes, rosemary, and thyme in your Slow Cooker. Add in seasoned shanks, sweet potatoes, salt, and pepper. Cover with the lid and cook for 3 hours on High. Serve.

Smoky Beef Tenderloin

Serves: 6 | Total Time: 7 hours 15 minutes

4 lb beef tenderloin	2 tbsp honey
2 tbsp olive oil	½ tsp ground cloves
1 tbsp cumin powder	¼ tsp nutmeg
1 tsp chili powder	1 tsp ground coriander
1 tsp smoked paprika	1 cup beef stock
1 tsp ground ginger	Salt to taste

In a bowl, combine cumin, chili powder, paprika, ginger, honey, olive oil, cloves, nutmeg, coriander, and salt. Rub beef tenderloin with the spice mixture and massage until well coated. Add the seasoned beef and beef stock in your Slow Cooker. Cover with the lid and cook for 7 hours on Low. Serve warm.

Lentils with Beef & Goat Cheese

Serves: 6 | Total Time: 5 hours 15 minutes

2 lb beef roast, cut into thin strips
1 onion, chopped
2 garlic cloves, minced
2 tbsp canola oil
1 cup brown lentils
¼ cup red lentils
½ tsp chili powder
½ tsp fennel seeds
1 cup diced tomatoes
1 cups beef stock
1 bay leaf
1 thyme sprig
Salt and pepper to taste
2 tbsp crumbled goat cheese

Warm the canola oil in a pan over medium heat. Place the beef and cook for 2-3 minutes until golden on all sides. Add it to your Slow Cooker. Put in onion, garlic, lentils, chili powder, fennel seeds, tomatoes, beef stock, bay leaf, thyme, salt, and pepper. Cover with the lid and cook for 5 hours on Low. Serve and enjoy!

Juicy Oxtails

Serves: 4 | Total Time: 6 hours 15 minutes

1 large onion, sliced
4 garlic cloves, chopped
1 carrot, sliced
2 lb oxtails, sliced
2 tbsp olive oil
1 parsnip, sliced
20 cherry tomatoes, halved
1 orange, juiced
1 bay leaf
1 rosemary sprig
Salt and pepper to taste

Warm the olive oil in a pan over medium heat. Place the beef and cook for 5 minutes until golden on all sides. Add it to your Slow Cooker. Put in onion, garlic, carrot, parsnip, tomatoes, orange juice, bay leaf, rosemary, salt, and pepper. Cover and cook for 6 hours on Low. Serve.

Nona Osso Bucco

Serves: 4 | Total Time: 6 hours 15 minutes

2 garlic cloves, sliced
1 fennel bulb, sliced
4 veal osso bucco pieces
1 orange, zested and juiced
1 tbsp olive oil
2 tbsp tomato paste
½ cup tomato sauce
¼ cup beef stock
1 bay leaf
Salt and pepper to taste

Mix the Osso Bucco, olive oil, garlic, fennel, orange zest, orange juice, tomato paste, tomato sauce, beef stock, bay leaf, salt, and pepper. Cover with the lid and cook for 6 hours on Low. Serve right away.

Rosemary Beef with Apples & Parsnips

Serves: 4 | Total Time: 7 hours 15 minutes

4 red apples, peeled, cored and sliced
2 large parsnips, diced
2 large carrots, sliced
2 shallots, sliced
4 flank steaks
¼ cup white wine
1 cup beef stock
1 rosemary sprig
Salt and pepper to taste

Toss steaks, apples, parsnips, carrots, shallots, wine, beef stock, rosemary, salt, and pepper in your Slow Cooker. Cover with the lid and cook for 7 hours on Low. Serve.

Sesame Broccoli & Beef Sauté

Serves: 4 | Total Time: 2 hours 15 minutes

2 flank steaks, cut into thin strips
1 lb broccoli florets
¼ cup peanuts, chopped
1 tbsp peanut oil
½ tsp sesame oil
1 tbsp tomato paste
2 tbsp soy sauce
¼ cup beef stock
1 tsp hot sauce
1 tbsp sesame seeds
Salt and pepper to taste

Stir the steaks, peanut oil, broccoli, peanuts, tomato paste, soy sauce, beef stock, hot sauce, sesame oil, sesame seeds, salt, and pepper in your Slow Cooker. Cover and cook for 2 hours on High. Serve immediately.

Chipotle Chili con Carne

Serves: 6 | Total Time: 8 hours 15 minutes

1 can (15 oz) diced tomatoes
1 can (15 oz) black beans
1 lb ground beef
2 red bell peppers, diced
1 sweet onion, chopped
2 tbsp canola oil
2 cups beef stock
½ cup red salsa
1 chipotle pepper, chopped
Salt and pepper to taste

Warm the canola oil in a skillet over medium heat. Place ground beef and cook for 5 minutes, stirring often. Add it to your Slow Cooker. Add in bell peppers, onion, beef stock, tomatoes, beans, 4 cups of water, red salsa, chipotle, salt, and pepper. Cover with the lid and cook for 8 hours on Low. Serve warm or chilled

Hot Beef Steaks with Mushrooms

Serves: 4 | Total Time: 6 hours 15 minutes

2 large onions, sliced
4 beef steaks
2 red bell peppers, diced
2 cups sliced mushrooms
½ cup beef stock
2 tbsp soy sauce
1 tbsp hot sauce
1 tsp dried basil
Salt and pepper to taste

In a bowl, combine bell peppers, mushrooms, soy sauce, hot sauce, onions, basil, salt, and pepper. Sprinkle beef steaks with salt and pepper. Place them into your Slow Cooker and pour in mushroom mixture and beef stock. Cover and cook for 6 hours on Low. Serve right away.

Basil Beef Tenderloin

Serves: 6 | Total Time: 6 hours 30 minutes

¼ cup white wine
2 lb beef tenderloin
2 tbsp olive oil
1 tbsp dried rosemary
1 tbsp dried basil
1 tbsp dried oregano
2 tbsp chopped parsley
1 tbsp Dijon mustard
Salt and pepper to taste

Rub beef with olive oil, mustard, salt, and pepper. Place rosemary, basil, oregano, and parsley on a flat surface in a single layer. Add in seasoned beef and roll it until well coated. Place herbed beef and wine in your Slow Cooker. Cover and cook for 6 hours on Low. Serve warm.

PORK RECIPES

Pork Chops with Apples & Onions

Serves: 4 | Total Time: 8 hours 10 minutes

1 apple, cored, peeled, and cut into 8 wedges
1 tbsp olive oil   ¼ cup apple cider
1 sweet onion, cut into rings   4 pork chops
1 tsp fresh thyme   Salt and pepper to taste
¼ tsp ground cinnamon

Grease your Slow Cooker with olive oil. Add the apple, onion, thyme, and cinnamon and stir to combine. Pour in the apple cider. Sprinkle the pork with salt and pepper.

Arrange the chops on the top of the apple and onion mixture. Cover and cook for 8 hours on Low until the apples and onion are soft and the pork is cooked through. Serve and enjoy!

Cuban-Inspired Pork Street Tacos

Serves: 4 | Total Time: 8 hours 20 minutes

1 tbsp olive oil   1 tsp ground coriander
1 lb pork tenderloin   Salt and pepper to taste
1 orange, zested and juiced   1 yellow onion, thinly sliced
1 lime, zested and juiced   1 red bell pepper, sliced
2 garlic cloves, minced   1 green bell pepper, sliced
½ tsp chili powder   8 corn tortillas, warm
1 tsp ground cumin   2 tbsp cilantro, chopped

Grease your Slow Cooker with olive oil. Add the pork tenderloin. In a small bowl, whisk together the orange zest, orange juice, lime zest, lime juice, garlic, chili powder, cumin, coriander, salt, and pepper.

Pour the mixture over the pork. Place the onion and bell peppers around and on top of the pork. Cover and cook for 8 hours on Low until the meat is cooked through.

When ready, remove the pork to a plate and let it rest for 10 minutes. Shred-it with a fork. Add the shredded meat back to the slow cooker and toss it with the vegetables and juices. Divide the meat mixture among the tortillas and top with cilantro. Serve and enjoy!

Balsamic-Glazed Pork with Potatoes

Serves: 4 | Total Time: 8 hours 10 minutes

1 tbsp olive oil   1 lb pork tenderloin
1 red onion, sliced   Salt and pepper to taste
4 potatoes, sliced   ½ cup balsamic vinegar
2 garlic cloves, minced   1 cup chicken broth

Grease your Slow Cooker with olive oil. Add the onion, potatoes, and garlic and stir to combine. Season the pork tenderloin with salt and pepper. Place the tenderloin on top of the vegetables.

Pour the vinegar and broth over the meat. Cover and cook for 8 hours on Low until the vegetables are tender and the meat is cooked through. Serve and enjoy!

Pork Chops with Parmentier Potatoes

Serves: 4 | Total Time: 8 hours 10 minutes

4 potatoes, diced   1 cup chicken broth
1 tbsp chopped rosemary   4 pork chops
2 garlic cloves, minced   Salt and pepper to taste

Place the potatoes, garlic, and broth in your Slow Cooker and gently stir together. Season the pork chops with salt and pepper and arrange them on top of the potatoes. Cover and cook for 8 hours on Low until the potatoes are completely soft and the pork is cooked through. Sprinkle with rosemary. Serve and enjoy!

Tenderloin in Salsa Roja

Serves: 6 | Total Time: 8 hours 15 minutes

2 red onions, sliced   1 tsp garlic powder
2 lb pork tenderloin   2 tbsp brown sugar
1 tsp cumin powder   2 cups red salsa
1 tsp ground coriander   ¼ cup red wine
1 tsp smoked paprika   Salt and pepper to taste

In a bowl, combine the cumin, coriander seeds, paprika, sugar, garlic powder, salt, and pepper. Rub pork tenderloin with the spice mixture until well coated. Stir red salsa, onions, and wine in your Slow Cooker and top with seasoned pork. Cover with the lid and cook for 8 hours on Low. When done, remove the lid and serve with your desired side dish.

Chipotle Pulled Pork

Serves: 6 | Total Time: 9 hours 15 minutes

2 chipotle peppers, chopped   1 tbsp cumin powder
6 garlic cloves, minced   1 tsp chili powder
2 lb pork shoulder   1 tsp dry mustard
1 cup pineapple juice   ¼ tsp ground cloves
1 cup chicken stock   Salt to taste
¼ cup brown sugar

In a bowl, combine the cumin, chili powder, sugar, mustard, chipotle peppers, garlic, cloves, and salt. Rub the pork with the spice mixture until well coated. Transfer it into your Slow Cooker and pour in pineapple juice and chicken stock. Cover with the lid and cook for 9 hours on Low. When done, remove the lid, using two forks, shred it finely, and serve right away.

Short Ribs with BBQ Sauce

Serves: 8 | Total Time: 11 hours 15 minutes

1 large onion, sliced   1 tbsp Dijon mustard
1 celery stalk, sliced   1 tsp chili powder
4 garlic cloves, minced   1 tbsp brown sugar
5 lb pork short ribs   ¼ cup chicken stock
2 cups BBQ sauce   Salt and pepper to taste

Toss short ribs, BBQ sauce, onion, celery, mustard, chili powder, sugar, garlic, chicken stock, salt, and pepper in your Slow Cooker. Cover with the lid and cook for 11 hours on Low. When done, remove the lid and serve.

Syrupy BBQ Pork Ribs

Serves: 8 | Total Time: 8 hours 15 minutes

5 lb pork short ribs	1 tbsp molasses
1 cup BBQ sauce	1 tsp chili powder
1 cup red wine	1 tsp cumin powder
2 tbsp olive oil	1 tsp dried thyme
4 tbsp brown sugar	Salt to taste

In a bowl, combine the sugar, molasses, olive oil, chili powder, cumin, thyme, and salt. Run short ribs with the spice mixture until well coated. Transfer them to to your Slow Cooker. Pour in BBQ sauce and red wine. Cover and cook for 8 hours on Low. Serve immediately.

Pork Tenderloin with Caramelized Onions

Serves: 6 | Total Time: 8 hours 15 minutes

3 large sweet onions, sliced	½ cup white wine
2 lb pork tenderloin	½ cup chicken stock
6 bacon slices	2 tbsp canola oil
1 thyme sprig	Salt and pepper to taste

Warm the canola oil in a pan over medium heat. Place onions and cook for 10 minutes until softened and caramelized. Transfer them to your Slow Cooker. Add the pork, bacon, thyme, wine, chicken stock, salt, and pepper. Cover and cook for 8 hours on Low. Serve warm.

Orange Glazed Pork Ham

Serves: 8 | Total Time: 6 hours 15 minutes

2 fennel bulbs, sliced	1 cup chicken stock
1 orange, zested and juiced	2 bay leaves
1 (4-lb) piece of pork ham	1 thyme sprig
½ cup white wine	Salt and pepper to taste

Toss the fennel, orange zest, orange juice, wine, chicken stock, bay leaves, thyme, salt, and pepper in your Slow Cooker and top with ham. Cover with the lid and cook for 6 hours on Low. Serve right away.

Kentucky Pork Ribs

Serves: 4 | Total Time: 6 hours 15 minutes

1 cup pineapple juice	1 tsp garlic powder
3 lb short pork ribs	1 tbsp brown sugar
1 tsp salt	1 tsp dried thyme

Sprinkle the pork ribs with salt, garlic powder, sugar, and thyme. Transfer them to your Slow Cooker and pour in pineapple juice. Cover with the lid and cook for 6 hours on Low. When done, remove the lid and serve warm.

Bourbon Pork Chops with Apples

Serves: 6 | Total Time: 8 hours 15 minutes

4 red apples, cored and sliced	
6 pork chops	1 thyme sprig
½ cup applesauce	1 rosemary sprig
¼ cup bourbon	Salt and pepper to taste
½ cup chicken stock	

Sprinkle the pork chops with salt and pepper. Stir the apples, applesauce, bourbon, stock, thyme, and rosemary in your Slow Cooker and top with seasoned pork. Cover with the lid and cook for 8 hours on Low. When done, remove the lid and drizzle with the sauce to serve.

Pork in Salsa Verde

Serves: 8 | Total Time: 7 hours 15 minutes

2 lb tomatillos, chopped	1 tsp dried oregano
2 lb pork shoulder, cubed	1 tsp cumin powder
1 large onion, chopped	½ tsp smoked paprika
4 garlic cloves, chopped	¼ tsp chili powder
2 green chilis, chopped	1 bunch cilantro, chopped
1 ½ cups chicken stock	Salt and pepper to taste
2 tbsp canola oil	

Warm the canola oil in a pan over medium heat. Place pork and cook for 2-3 minutes until golden on all sides. Add it into your Slow Cooker. Add in tomatillos, onion, garlic, oregano, cumin, paprika, chili powder, cilantro, green chilis, chicken stock, salt, and pepper. Cover with the lid and cook for 7 hours on Low. Serve warm.

Vegetable & Pork Roast

Serves: 6 | Total Time: 8 hours 15 minutes

1 can fire-roasted tomatoes	1 tsp smoked paprika
2 carrots, sliced	½ tsp cumin powder
2 lb pork shoulder, cubed	1 bay leaf
2 celery stalks, sliced	1 cup chicken stock
1 large onion, chopped	Salt and pepper to taste

Mix the pork, tomatoes, carrots, celery, onion, paprika, cumin, bay leaf, chicken stock, salt, and pepper in your Slow Cooker. Cover with the lid and cook for 8 hours on Low. When done, remove the lid and serve immediately.

Five-Spice Pork Roast

Serves: 8 | Total Time: 6 hours 15 minutes

¼ cup balsamic vinegar	1 tsp garlic powder
4 lb pork shoulder, cubed	2 tbsp honey
2 tbsp brown sugar	1 tsp hot sauce
1 tsp five-spice powder	Salt and pepper to taste

In a bowl, combine the sugar, five-spice powder, garlic powder, honey, and hot sauce. Brush pork with the marinade until well coated. Transfer them to your Slow Cooker and pour in balsamic vinegar, salt, and pepper. Cover with the lid and cook for 6 hours on Low. Serve.

Pulled Pork with Red Sauce

Serves: 6 | Total Time: 7 hours 15 minutes

1 large onion, chopped	2 red chilis, chopped
2 lb pork roast	1 cup red salsa
1 cup tomato sauce	Salt and pepper to taste

Stir pork roast, tomato sauce, red chilis, onion, red salsa, salt, and pepper in your Slow Cooker. Cover with the lid and cook for 7 hours on Low. Serve warm.

Tropical Pork Ham

Serves: 6 | Total Time: 7 hours 15 minutes

1 cup cranberry sauce
1 cup pineapple juice
2 lb smoked ham
½ tsp chili powder
½ tsp cumin powder

1 cinnamon stick
1-star anise
1 bay leaf
Salt and pepper to taste

Toss the cranberry sauce, pineapple juice, chili powder, cumin, cinnamon stick, star anise, bay leaf, salt, and pepper in your Slow Cooker and add ham on top. Cover with the lid and cook for 7 hours on Low. Serve warm.

Pork Shoulder in Herbed Tomato Sauce

Serves: 6 | Total Time: 7 hours 15 minutes

1 large onion, sliced
4 garlic cloves, chopped
2 lb pork shoulder
2 celery stalks, sliced
2 ripe tomatoes, diced

¼ cup white wine
1 tsp dried thyme
1 tsp dried basil
1 thyme sprig
Salt and pepper to taste

In your Slow Cooker, combine the pork, onion, garlic, celery, tomatoes, wine, thyme, basil, sprig, salt, and pepper. Cover with the lid and cook for 7 hours on Low. When done, remove the lid and serve warm.

Cowboy Short Ribs

Serves: 6 | Total Time: 8 hours 15 minutes

½ cup BBQ sauce
1 cup vegetable stock
1 cup apple butter
2 lb pork short ribs
2 tbsp brown sugar

1 tsp garlic powder
1 tsp onion powder
½ tsp chili powder
Salt and pepper to taste

Stir the apple butter, sugar, sugar, garlic powder, onion powder, chili powder, BBQ sauce, and vegetable stock in your Slow Cooker. Put in short ribs and sprinkle with salt and pepper. Cover with the lid and cook for 8 hours on Low. When done, remove the lid and serve warm.

Southern Short Ribs

Serves: 6 | Total Time: 6 hours 45 minutes

1 cup ginger beer
½ cup ketchup
2-3 lb pork short ribs
1 tbsp Worcestershire sauce

1 tbsp Dijon mustard
½ tsp smoked paprika
1 tbsp brown sugar
Salt and pepper to taste

Mix the short ribs, beer, ketchup, Worcestershire sauce, mustard, paprika, sugar, salt, and pepper in your Slow Cooker. Cover with the lid and cook for 6 ½ hours on Low. When done, remove the lid and serve warm.

Lemony Pork Tenderloin

Serves: 6 | Total Time: 7 hours 15 minutes

1 cup vegetable stock
2 lb pork tenderloin
1 lemon, sliced

1 cup canola oil
1 tsp black pepper kernels
Salt and pepper to taste

Mix the pork, lemon slices, black pepper kernels, canola oil, vegetable stock, salt, and pepper in your Slow Cooker. Cover and cook for 7 hours on Low. Serve sliced.

Pork Tenderloin with Cinnamon-Maple Glaze

Serves: 6 | Total Time: 4 hours 15 minutes

1 can condensed cream of chicken soup
2 lb pork tenderloin
2 tbsp maple syrup
1 tbsp soy sauce
1 tsp hot sauce

1 tsp garlic powder
½ tsp cinnamon powder
¼ tsp allspice powder
½ tsp ground ginger
1 tsp salt

In a bowl, combine maple syrup, soy sauce, hot sauce, garlic powder, cinnamon powder, allspice powder, ginger, and salt. Brush pork tenderloin with the spice mixture and massage until well coated. Place marinated pork and chicken soup in your Slow Cooker. Cover with the lid and cook for 4 hours on High. Serve right away.

Peanut Teriyaki Tenderloin

Serves: 6 | Total Time: 7 hours 15 minutes

4 garlic cloves, minced
1 onion, chopped
2 lb pork tenderloin
¼ cup soy sauce
¼ cup ketchup

1 tbsp smooth peanut butter
1 tbsp brown sugar
1 tbsp hot sauce
¼ cup chicken stock

Stir the pork, soy sauce, ketchup, onion, peanut butter, sugar, hot sauce, garlic, and chicken stock in your Slow Cooker. Cover and cook for 7 hours on Low. Serve.

German Pork with Sauerkraut

Serves: 6 | Total Time: 6 hours 15 minutes

1 large onion, chopped
2 carrots, grated
1 ½ lb sauerkraut, shredded
1 ½ lb pork shoulder, cubed
1 ½ tsp cumin seeds

¼ tsp red pepper flakes
1 cup chicken stock
1 bay leaf
Salt and pepper to taste

Toss the pork, sauerkraut, onion, carrots, cumin seeds, red pepper flakes, chicken stock, bay leaf, salt, and pepper in your Slow Cooker. Cover with the lid and cook for 6 hours on Low. Serve warm.

Parmesan Cilantro Pork

Serves: 6 | Total Time: 6 hours 15 minutes

¼ cup pine nuts
½ cup chicken stock
½ cup grated Parmesan
1 lemon, juiced
2 lb pork tenderloin

1 cup chopped parsley
½ cup chopped cilantro
4 basil leaves
Salt and pepper to taste

In a food processor, blitz parsley, cilantro, basil, pine nuts, chicken stock, lemon juice, salt, pepper, and Parmesan cheese until smooth. Place pork tenderloin and herb mixture in your Slow Cooker and toss until well coated. Cover with the lid and cook for 6 hours on Low. Serve.

BBQ Short Ribs

Serves: 6 | Total Time: 8 hours 30 minutes

2 cups BBQ sauce	1 tsp Worcestershire sauce
3 lb pork short ribs	1 ½ tsp chili powder
2 tbsp brown sugar	1 tsp cumin powder
2 tbsp red wine vinegar	Salt and pepper to taste

In your Slow Cooker, combine BBQ sauce, chili powder, cumin, sugar, vinegar, Worcestershire sauce, salt, and pepper. Place in short ribs and toss until well coated. Cover with the lid and cook for 8 ¼ hours on Low. When done, remove the lid and serve immediately.

Creamy Parsley Pork Chops

Serves: 6 | Total Time: 6 hours 15 minutes

2 green onions, chopped	½ cup chicken stock
6 pork chops, bone-in	2 tbsp chopped parsley
1 cup sour cream	Salt and pepper to taste

Stir the pork chops, sour cream, stock, green onions, parsley, salt, and pepper in your Slow Cooker. Cover and cook for 6 hours on Low. Drizzle with sauce to serve.

Fruity Pork Roast

Serves: 6 | Total Time: 8 hours 15 minutes

1 mango, peeled and cubed	2 tbsp red wine vinegar
1 cup pineapple juice	1 bay leaf
1 cup frozen cranberries	1 rosemary sprig
2 lb pork roast	Salt and pepper to taste

Toss the pork roast, mango, pineapple juice, cranberries, vinegar, bay leaf, rosemary, salt, and pepper in your Slow Cooker. Cover with the lid and cook for 8 hours on Low. When done, remove the lid and serve right away.

Tomato Pork Chili

Serves: 6 | Total Time: 9 hours 15 minutes

2 red onions, chopped	2 chipotle peppers, chopped
4 garlic cloves, chopped	1 tsp dried oregano
1 lb dried black beans	1 tsp dried basil
1 can fire-roasted tomatoes	1 tsp cumin powder
2 lb pork roast, cubed	1 tsp chili powder
2 cups chicken stock	Salt and pepper to taste

In your Slow Cooker, add onions, garlic, beans, tomatoes, chicken stock, chipotle peppers, oregano, basil, cumin, chili powder, pork roast, salt, and pepper, and stir. Cover with the lid and cook for 9 hours on Low. Serve warm.

Pork Chops in Saucy Plum Glaze

Serves: 6 | Total Time: 7 hours 15 minutes

6 pitted plums, chopped	1-star anise
6 pork chops	1 cinnamon stick
½ cup apple cider	1 bay leaf
½ cup chicken stock	2 whole cloves
1 tbsp balsamic vinegar	Salt and pepper to taste
2 tbsp brown sugar	

Toss the plums, apple cider, chicken stock, balsamic vinegar, sugar, star anise, cinnamon stick, bay leaf, and cloves in your Slow Cooker. Add the pork chops, salt, and pepper. Cover with the lid and cook for 7 hours on Low. Serve topped with the sauce and enjoy!

Sweet BBQ Pork Ribs

Serves: 6 | Total Time: 8 hours 15 minutes

¼ cup BBQ sauce	1 tbsp maple syrup
1 cup chicken stock	1-star anise
4 lb pork ribs	1 tsp salt
2 tbsp honey mustard	½ tsp cayenne pepper
2 tbsp honey	

Mix the mustard, honey, maple syrup, star anise, BBQ sauce, chicken stock, salt, and cayenne pepper in your Slow Cooker. Put in pork ribs and toss until well coated. Cover and cook for 8 hours on Low. Serve warm.

Caribbean Pulled Pork

Serves: 6 | Total Time: 7 hours 15 minutes

2 lb pork roast, cut into large pieces

1 ripe mango, diced	1 cup chicken stock
1 chipotle pepper, chopped	1 tbsp balsamic vinegar
1 cup BBQ sauce	Salt and pepper to taste
¼ cup bourbon	

Stir pork roast, mango, bourbon, chicken stock, chipotle pepper, balsamic vinegar, BBQ sauce, salt, and pepper in your Slow Cooker. Cover with the lid and cook for 7 hours on Low. When done, remove the lid, using two forks, shred it finely, and serve warm or chilled.

Pork with Sweet Potatoes & Apples

Serves: 6 | Total Time: 6 hours 15 minutes

3 sweet potatoes, cubed	1 tsp Dijon mustard
2 shallots, chopped	2 tbsp tomato paste
2 lb pork tenderloin, cubed	2 cups chicken stock
2 peeled red apples, cubed	Salt and pepper to taste
1 pinch nutmeg	

Mix the pork, sweet potatoes, shallots, apples, nutmeg, mustard, tomato paste, chicken stock, salt, and pepper in your Slow Cooker. Cover with the lid and cook for 6 hours on Low. Serve warm.

Pork Tenderloin with Blackberry Sauce

Serves: 6 | Total Time: 7 hours 15 minutes

2 cups fresh blackberries	2 tbsp honey
2 red onions, sliced	1 tbsp balsamic vinegar
2 lb pork tenderloin	½ cup chicken stock
½ tsp dried sage	Salt and pepper to taste
½ tsp dried oregano	

Toss pork, blackberries, onions, sage, oregano, honey, balsamic vinegar, chicken stock, salt, and pepper in your Slow Cooker. Cover with the lid and cook for 7 hours on Low. Cut it into slices and drizzle with the sauce to serve.

Cuban Pork Roast

Serves: 6 | Total Time: 6 hours 15 minutes

1 onion, sliced
1 celery stalk, sliced
4 garlic cloves, chopped
2 lb pork roast
½ cup fresh orange juice
1 lemon, zested and juiced
1 tsp cumin powder
¼ tsp chili powder
1 bay leaf
Salt and pepper to taste

In your Slow Cooker, combine pork roast, onion, celery, garlic, orange juice, lemon zest, lemon juice, cumin, chili powder, bay leaf, salt, and pepper. Cover with the lid and cook for 6 hours on Low. Serve immediately.

Dijon Pork Shoulder

Serves: 6 | Total Time: 7 hours 15 minutes

4 garlic cloves, chopped
1 large onion, chopped
4 lb pork tenderloin
2 cups sliced mushrooms
2 tbsp canola oil
2 tbsp Dijon mustard
1 can condensed cream of mushroom soup
Salt and pepper to taste

Sprinkle pork roast with salt and pepper. Warm canola oil in a pan over medium heat. Cook the pork until golden brown and crusty on all sides. Add it to your Slow Cooker. Add in garlic, onion, mushrooms, mustard, mushroom soup, salt, and pepper. Cover with the lid and cook for 7 hours on Low. Drizzle with the sauce to serve.

Marsala Pork Chops with Mushrooms

Serves: 6 | Total Time: 6 hours 15 minutes

1 onion, sliced
4 garlic cloves, chopped
2 cups sliced mushrooms
½ cup Marsala wine
6 pork chops
2 tbsp all-purpose flour
1 tsp garlic powder
1 can condensed cream of mushroom soup
Salt and pepper to taste

Sprinkle the pork chops with garlic powder, salt, and pepper. Add seasoned pork, flour, onion, garlic, mushrooms, wine, mushroom soup, salt, and pepper in your Slow Cooker. Cover with the lid and cook for 6 hours on Low. Drizzle with the sauce to serve.

Authentic Ragú with Pork Sausages

Serves: 6 | Total Time: 6 hours 15 minutes

1 lb fresh pork sausages, casings removed
4 garlic cloves, minced
1 can fire-roasted tomatoes
1 cup chicken stock
2 celery stalks, chopped
2 carrots, diced
½ tsp dried oregano
1 bay leaf
2 tbsp olive oil
½ tsp red pepper flakes
¼ cup dry red wine
Salt and pepper to taste

Warm the olive oil in a pan over medium heat. Put the sausages and cook for 2-3 minutes, stirring often. Transfer them to your Slow Cooker. Add in celery, carrots, oregano, garlic, tomatoes, chicken stock, bay leaf, red pepper flakes, wine, salt, and pepper. Cover with the lid and cook for 6 hours on Low. Serve warm.

Favorite Chipotle Pork Chili

Serves: 6 | Total Time: 8 hours 30 minutes

2 cans (15-oz) black beans
1 can fire-roasted tomatoes
2 lb pork shoulder, cubed
2 shallots, chopped
4 garlic cloves, chopped
3 chipotle peppers, chopped
1 cup tomato sauce
1 cup chicken stock
2 tbsp canola oil
1 tsp cumin powder
½ tsp ground coriander
2 tbsp tomato paste
2 bay leaves
Salt and pepper to taste
1 lime, juiced

Warm the canola oil in a pan over medium heat. Put the pork and cook until golden on all sides. Add it to your Slow Cooker. Put in shallots, garlic, chipotle peppers, beans, tomatoes, cumin, coriander, tomato sauce, chicken stock, tomato paste, bay leaves, salt, and pepper. Cover and cook for 8 hours on Low. Sprinkle with lime juice.

Pork Tenderloin in Savory Tomato Sauce

Serves: 8 | Total Time: 8 hours 15 minutes

2 cups tomato sauce
4 lb pork tenderloin
2 bay leaves
2 tbsp tomato paste
1 tsp cumin seeds
1 tsp fennel seeds
1 tsp celery seeds
1 tsp garlic powder
Salt and pepper to taste

Mix the pork, tomato sauce, cumin seeds, fennel seeds, celery seeds, tomato paste, garlic powder, bay leaves, salt, and pepper in your Slow Cooker. Cover with the lid and cook for 8 hours on Low. Serve sliced.

Honeyed Balsamic Pork Chops

Serves: 6 | Total Time: 3 hours 15 minutes

1 large onion, sliced
2 garlic cloves, chopped
1 celery stalk, sliced
6 pork chops
2 tbsp balsamic vinegar
2 tbsp honey
1 cup apple cider
1 bay leaf
¼ tsp cumin seeds
Salt and pepper to taste

Stir onion, garlic, celery, balsamic vinegar, honey, apple cider, bay leaf, and cumin seeds in your Slow Cooker. Sprinkle pork chops with salt and pepper and place them into the pot. Cover with the lid and cook for 3 hours on High. When done, remove the lid and serve right away.

Pork & Bean Chili with Chorizo & Bacon

Serves: 6 | Total Time: 3 hours 15 minutes

1 ½ lb pork roast, cubed
1 chorizo link, sliced
4 bacon slices, chopped
½ lb dried red beans, rinsed
4 garlic cloves, chopped
1 red onion, chopped
1 tsp hot sauce
1 can fire-roasted tomatoes
2 cups vegetable stock
Salt and pepper to taste
1 bay leaf

Mix the beans, pork roast, chorizo, bacon, garlic, onion, and hot sauce in your Slow Cooker. Put in tomatoes, vegetable stock, bay leaf, salt, and pepper. Cover with the lid and cook for 3 hours on High. Serve and enjoy!

Easy Pork Roast in Tomato Sauce

Serves: 4 | Total Time: 3 hours 15 minutes

2 tbsp tomato paste
2 lb pork roast, cubed
½ cup tomato sauce
½ cup chicken stock
2 tbsp canola oil
¼ tsp cayenne pepper
Salt and pepper to taste

Toss the canola oil, pork roast, tomato sauce, chicken stock, tomato paste, cayenne pepper, salt, and pepper in your Slow Cooker. Cover with the lid and cook for 3 hours on High. Serve and enjoy!

Chinese Pork Shoulder

Serves: 6 | Total Time: 7 hours 15 minutes

6 garlic cloves, minced
2 lb pork shoulder
3 tbsp canola oil
1 tbsp grated ginger
2 tbsp miso paste
1 cup vegetable stock
1 lemongrass stalk, crushed

In your Slow Cooker, combine pork, garlic, ginger, canola oil, miso paste, vegetable stock, and lemongrass. Cover with the lid and cook for 7 hours on Low. Serve.

Farmer's Ham & Lima Bean Chili

Serves: 6 | Total Time: 6 hours 15 minutes

1 lb dried lima beans
2 cups diced smoked ham
1 cup chicken stock
1 cup diced tomatoes
2 cups water
1 tsp Cajun seasoning
¼ tsp garlic powder
¼ tsp onion powder
¼ tsp cayenne pepper
Salt and pepper to taste

Stir the ham, lima beans, water, chicken stock, tomatoes, cajun seasoning, garlic powder, onion powder, cayenne pepper, salt, and pepper in your Slow Cooker. Cover with the lid and cook for 6 hours on Low. Serve warm.

Pork Roast with Green Sauce

Serves: 6 | Total Time: 8 hours 15 minutes

2 chipotle peppers, chopped
2 lb pork roast
2 cups green enchilada sauce
½ cup chopped cilantro
½ cup vegetable stock
Salt and pepper to taste

In your Slow Cooker, add the enchilada sauce, cilantro, chipotle peppers, and vegetable stock and stir. Top with the pork roast, salt, and pepper. Cover with the lid and cook for 8 hours on Low. Serve and enjoy!

Rosemary Roast with Celery & Potatoes

Serves: 6 | Total Time: 6 hours 30 minutes

1 ½ lb potatoes, cubed
2 lb pork roast, cubed
3 large carrots, sliced
1 celery root, cubed
1 cup chicken stock
2 rosemary sprigs
Salt and pepper to taste

Stir pork roast, carrots, celery, potatoes, rosemary, chicken stock, salt, and pepper in your Slow Cooker. Cover and cook for 6 hours on Low. Serve immediately.

Savory Pork Chili with Bacon

Serves: 8 | Total Time: 6 hours 15 minutes

6 bacon slices, chopped
1 lb ground pork
2 onions, chopped
4 garlic cloves, chopped
1 lb dried black beans
2½ cups vegetable stock
1 cup diced tomatoes
2 bay leaves
2 tbsp tomato paste
1 cup dark beer
1 tbsp canola oil
1 ½ tsp smoked paprika
1 tsp cumin powder
1 thyme sprig
Salt and pepper to taste

Warm the canola oil in a pan over medium heat. Place the bacon and cook until crispy. Add in ground pork and cook for 2-3 minutes until golden, stirring often. Transfer everything to your Slow Cooker. Put the onions, garlic, tomato paste, beer, paprika, cumin, beans, stock, tomatoes, bay leaves, thyme, salt, and pepper. Cover with the lid and cook for 6 hours on Low. Serve warm.

Pork Roast Casserole

Serves: 6 | Total Time: 8 hours 15 minutes

2 lb pork roast, cut into quarters
2 potatoes, cubed
½ lb baby carrots
1 large onion, sliced
2 cups snap peas
2 parsnips, sliced
1 cup vegetable stock
1 tbsp molasses
¼ cup red wine vinegar
2 tbsp soy sauce
2 tbsp ketchup
1 tsp garlic powder
¼ tsp cayenne pepper
Salt and pepper to taste
1 lemon, sliced

Toss the pork roast, onion, carrots, snap peas, parsnips, potatoes, vegetable stock, molasses, vinegar, soy sauce, ketchup, garlic powder, cayenne pepper, salt, and pepper in your Slow Cooker and put lemon slices on top. Cover and cook for 8 hours on Low. Serve right away.

Spicy BBQ Pork Belly

Serves: 4 | Total Time: 7 hours 15 minutes

1 onion, sliced
2 lb pork belly, trimmed
1 cup BBQ sauce
1 habanero pepper, chopped
2 garlic cloves, chopped
Salt to taste
1 thyme sprig

Mix the pork belly, BBQ sauce, habanero pepper, onion, garlic, thyme, and salt in your Slow Cooker. Cover with the lid and cook for 7 hours on Low. When done, remove the lid and serve with your desired side dish.

Texas-Style Pork Roast

Serves: 6 | Total Time: 8 hours 15 minutes

2 onions, sliced
2 ½ lb pork shoulder
1 cup BBQ sauce
1 cup cola drink
1 thyme sprig
1 red chili, chopped
1 rosemary sprig
Salt and pepper to taste

In your Slow Cooker, add pork, BBQ sauce, cola, thyme, red chili, rosemary, onions, salt, and pepper, and stir. Cover and cook for 8 hours on Low. Serve immediately.

Smoked Ham with Potato Gratin

Serves: 6 | Total Time: 6 hours 30 minutes

1 lb smoked ham, sliced
1 large onion, sliced
2 lb potatoes, finely sliced
2 cups whole milk

1 tbsp all-purpose flour
1 cup heavy cream
Salt and pepper to taste
2 cups grated cheddar

In a bowl, combine the milk, flour, heavy cream, salt, and pepper. In your Slow Cooker, place potatoes, ham, and onion on layers. Pour cream mixture over the potatoes, sprinkle with cheddar cheese on top and cover with the lid, and cook for 6 hours on Low. Serve right away.

Gingery Pork Roast

Serves: 6 | Total Time: 7 hours 15 minutes

1 tbsp soy sauce
1 tbsp honey
2 lb pork shoulder

2 tsp grated ginger
1 ½ cups vegetable stock
Salt and pepper to taste

Rub pork shoulder with ginger, soy sauce, honey, salt, and pepper and massage until well coated. Add marinated pork and vegetable stock in your Slow Cooker. Cover with the lid and cook for 7 hours on Low. Serve warm.

Herbed Pork Chili

Serves: 6 | Total Time: 3 hours 45 minutes

1 ½ cups cannellini beans, soaked
2 red bell peppers, diced
1 lb pork tenderloin, cubed
2 celery stalks, sliced
2 carrots, sliced
2 tbsp canola oil

½ tsp dried basil
½ tsp dried oregano
3 cups chicken stock
1 rosemary sprig
Salt and pepper to taste

Warm the canola oil in a pan over medium heat. Cook the pork until golden on all sides. Add it to your Slow Cooker. Add in celery, carrots, basil, oregano, bell peppers, beans, chicken stock, rosemary, salt, and pepper. Cover with the lid and cook for 31/2 hours on High. Serve warm.

Minty Pork Roast

Serves: 6 | Total Time: 6 hours 15 minutes

4 garlic cloves, minced
1 cup coconut milk
2 lb pork roast
1 ½ tsp curry powder

½ tsp chili powder
1 tsp dried mint
1 tsp dried basil
Salt and pepper to taste

Rub the pork roast with curry powder, chili powder, garlic, mint, basil, salt, and pepper, and massage until well coated. Place seasoned pork and coconut milk in your Slow Cooker. Cover with the lid and cook for 6 hours on Low. When done, remove the lid and serve warm.

Pork Chops with French Onions

Serves: 6 | Total Time: 6 hours 15 minutes

1 (10.75-oz) can condensed onion soup
6 pork chops
¼ cup white wine

1 tsp garlic powder
Salt and pepper to taste

Stir pork chops, wine, onion soup, garlic powder, salt, and pepper in your Slow Cooker. Cover with the lid and cook for 6 hours on Low. Serve and enjoy!

Korean Pork Roast

Serves: 6 | Total Time: 6 hours 15 minutes

2 lb boneless chuck roast, trimmed and halved
1 lb baby carrots
4 potatoes, halved
¼ cup soy sauce
4 garlic cloves, minced
2 shallots, sliced

1 cup chicken stock
2 tbsp tomato paste
1 tbsp hot sauce
½ lemongrass stalk, crushed
Salt and pepper to taste

Mix the chuck roast, soy sauce, garlic, shallots, chicken stock, tomato paste, hot sauce, carrots, potatoes, lemongrass, salt, and pepper in your Slow Cooker. Cover with the lid and cook for 6 hours on Low. Serve.

Havana Pork Chops

Serves: 6 | Total Time: 6 hours 15 minutes

4 garlic cloves, chopped
2 large onions, sliced
6 pork chops
1 tsp grated ginger
1 tsp cumin seeds

1 tsp chili powder
1 lemon, juiced
1 bay leaf
1 cup chicken stock
Salt and pepper to taste

Toss pork chops, onions, ginger, cumin seeds, garlic, chili powder, lemon juice, bay leaf, chicken stock, salt, and pepper in your Slow Cooker. Cover with the lid and cook for 6 hours on Low. Serve warm.

Western Gammon

Serves: 8 | Total Time: 6 hours 15 minutes

1 (3-lb) piece of gammon joint
½ cup apricot preserve
1 tsp cumin powder
¼ tsp chili powder

1 cup vegetable stock
Salt and pepper to taste

In a bowl, combine apricot preserve, cumin, chili powder, salt, and pepper. Brush gammon with the apricot mixture and massage until well coated. Place marinated gammon and vegetable stock in your Slow Cooker. Cover with the lid and cook for 6 hours on Low. Serve warm.

Pork Tenderloin in Fruit Sauce

Serves: 6 | Total Time: 8 hours 15 minutes

½ cup chopped dried apricots
1 cup apple juice
1 onion, chopped
2 lb pork tenderloin
½ lb pitted plums, sliced
½ cup frozen cranberries

½ cup golden raisins
½ tsp garlic powder
1 cinnamon stick
1-star anise
Salt and pepper to taste

Mix the plums, apricots, cranberries, raisins, apple juice, onion, garlic powder, cinnamon stick, star anise, salt, and pepper in your Slow Cooker. Place the pork on top. Cover with the lid and cook for 8 hours on Low. Drizzle with the sauce and fruits to serve.

Green Pea & Roast Casserole

Serves: 6 | Total Time: 2 hours 45 minutes

1 lb green peas	¼ tsp grated ginger
1 lb pork roast, cubed	2 tbsp canola oil
1 onion, finely chopped	1 tsp dried mint
4 garlic cloves, chopped	½ tsp dried oregano
1 bay leaf	1 ½ cups chicken stock
1 tbsp cornstarch	Salt and pepper to taste

Warm the canola oil in a pan over medium heat. Place the pork roast and cook until golden brown on all sides. Add it to your Slow Cooker. Add the onion, garlic, ginger, green peas, mint, oregano, stock, bay leaf, cornstarch, salt, and pepper. Cover with the lid and cook for 2 ½ hours on High. Serve warm.

Roasted Pork & Chickpea Pot

Serves: 6 | Total Time: 2 hours 15 minutes

1 lb pork roast, cubed	1 cup chicken stock
1 can fire-roasted tomatoes	2 tbsp canola oil
1 can (15 oz) chickpeas	1 bay leaf
2 celery stalks, sliced	1 thyme sprig
2 carrots, sliced	Salt and pepper to taste
2 red bell peppers, diced	

Warm canola oil in a pan over medium heat, place pork and cook until golden brown on all sides. Add it to your Slow Cooker. Add in celery, carrots, bell peppers, tomatoes, chickpeas, chicken stock, bay leaf, thyme, salt, and pepper. Cover with the lid and cook for 2 hours on High. When done, remove the lid and serve warm.

Saucy Pork Belly

Serves: 6 | Total Time: 7 hours 15 minutes

2 garlic cloves, minced	1 tsp chili powder
3 lb piece of pork belly	1 tsp grated ginger
½ cup white wine	1 tbsp molasses
1 tbsp cumin powder	1 tbsp soy sauce
1 tbsp brown sugar	

In a bowl, whisk cumin, sugar, chili powder, ginger, molasses, garlic, and soy sauce. Brush pork belly with the spice mixture and massage until well coated. Add marinated belly and wine to your Slow Cooker. Cover with the lid and cook for 7 hours on Low. Serve warm.

Cauliflower & Pork Casserole

Serves: 6 | Total Time: 7 hours 15 minutes

2 carrots, sliced	4 garlic cloves
1 shallot	1 cup cauliflower florets
2 lb pork tenderloin	1 cup chicken stock
2 heirloom tomatoes, peeled	Salt and pepper to taste

In a food processor, blitz tomatoes, carrots, shallot, garlic, cauliflower, chicken stock, salt, and pepper until smooth. Pour it into your Slow Cooker and top with pork tenderloin. Cover with the lid and cook for 7 hours on Low. When done, remove the lid and serve warm.

Pork Belly with Peanut Butter Sauce

Serves: 6 | Total Time: 6 hours 15 minutes

4 garlic cloves	½ cup vegetable stock
2 lb pork belly	1 tsp grated ginger
¼ cup smooth peanut butter	1 tbsp honey
2 tbsp soy sauce	1 chipotle pepper, chopped
1 tbsp hot sauce	

Stir peanut butter, soy sauce, hot sauce, vegetable stock, garlic, ginger, honey, and chipotle pepper in your Slow Cooker. Add in pork belly and toss until well coated. Cover and cook for 6 hours on Low. Serve immediately.

Ground Pork Tacos

Serves: 6 | Total Time: 6 hours 30 minutes

1 lb tomatillos, chopped	1 cup pineapple juice
1 cup frozen corn	2 tbsp canola oil
2 lb ground pork	½ cup chopped cilantro
2 shallots, chopped	Salt and pepper to taste
4 garlic cloves, chopped	1 lime, juiced
2 chipotle peppers, chopped	Flour tortillas for serving
1 cup ginger beer	

Warm the canola oil in a pan over medium heat. Stir-fry the ground pork for 2-3 minutes. Add it to your Slow Cooker. Add in shallots, garlic, chipotle peppers, beer, pineapple juice, cilantro, tomatillos, corn, salt, and pepper. Cover with the lid and cook for 6 hours on Low. When done, remove the lid, divide between tortillas, and wrap them. Sprinkle with lime juice to serve.

Bacon & Apple Butter Pork Chops

Serves: 4 | Total Time: 4 hours 15 minutes

4 pork chops	1 cup apple butter
6 bacon slices, chopped	½ cup tomato sauce
1 tbsp butter	1 bay leaf
1 tsp smoked paprika	Salt and pepper to taste

Place a pan over medium heat. Add the bacon and cook until crispy, 5 minutes. Add the butter and pork chops and cook for 2 minutes until golden brown on all sides. Transfer everything to your Slow Cooker. Put in paprika, apple butter, tomato sauce, bay leaf, salt, and pepper. Cover and cook for 4 hours on Low. Serve warm.

Diavolo Pork Ribs

Serves: 4 | Total Time: 7 hours 15 minutes

2 onions, sliced	1 tsp hot sauce
2 garlic cloves, chopped	1 tsp Worcestershire sauce
3 lb pork ribs	½ tsp allspice powder
1 can crushed pineapple	¼ tsp chili powder
2 tbsp honey	Salt and pepper to taste

Stir pineapple, honey, hot sauce, Worcestershire sauce, allspice powder, chili powder, onions, garlic, salt, and pepper in your Slow Cooker. Add in pork ribs and toss until well coated. Cover with the lid and cook for 7 hours on Low. Serve warm.

Granny Pork Belly with Sauerkraut

Serves: 6 | Total Time: 8 hours 30 minutes

4 bacon slices, chopped	1 tsp cumin seeds
4 lb pork belly	½ tsp dried thyme
1 lb sauerkraut, chopped	1 cup chicken stock
1 tsp smoked paprika	Salt and pepper to taste

Sprinkle pork belly with salt and pepper. Toss sauerkraut, bacon, paprika, cumin seeds, thyme, and chicken stock in your Slow Cooker, and add seasoned pork belly on top. Cover with the lid and cook for 8 hours on Low. Serve.

Harvest Pork Shoulder

Serves: 6 | Total Time: 7 hours 15 minutes

1 hot red pepper, chopped	¼ cup brown sugar
2 lb pork shoulder	1 tsp grated ginger
6 garlic cloves, minced	2 tbsp white wine vinegar
½ cup soy sauce	½ cup vegetable stock

Mix the pork, ginger, garlic, soy sauce, sugar, vinegar, red pepper, and vegetable stock in your Slow Cooker. Cover with the lid and cook for 7 hours on Low. Using two forks, shred it finely and serve right away.

Cheesy Pork & Mushroom Casserole

Serves: 6 | Total Time: 5 hours 15 minutes

1 lb button mushrooms	1 tbsp cornstarch
1 lb pork roast, cubed	1 cup cream cheese
1 ½ cups chicken stock	1 thyme sprig
2 tbsp canola oil	Salt and pepper to taste

Warm the canola oil in a pan over medium heat. Place the pork and cook until golden on all sides. Add it to your Slow Cooker. Put in mushrooms, chicken stock, cornstarch, cream cheese, thyme, salt, and pepper. Cover with the lid and cook for 5 hours on Low. Serve warm.

Pork Chops Glazed with Bubbly Maple

Serves: 6 | Total Time: 4 hours 15 minutes

4 shallots, sliced	3 tbsp maple syrup
4 garlic cloves, chopped	¼ cup white wine
6 pork chops	½ tsp chili powder
2 tbsp canola oil	Salt and pepper to taste

Warm the canola oil in a pan over medium heat. Cook the pork for 2-3 minutes until golden brown on all sides. Transfer it to your Slow Cooker. Add in shallots, garlic, maple syrup, wine, chili powder, salt, and pepper. Cover with the lid and cook for 4 hours on Low. Serve warm.

Hearty Pork Roast with Vegetables

Serves: 6 | Total Time: 6 hours 30 minutes

2 sweet potatoes, cubed	2 thyme sprigs
1 lb pork shoulder, cubed	1 bay leaf
1 lb pork sausages, sliced	1-star anise
1 lb butternut squash cubes	1 whole clove
2 cups chicken stock	Salt and pepper to taste

Mix the pork, sausages, butternut squash, sweet potatoes, chicken stock, thyme, bay leaf, star anise, clove, salt, and pepper in your Slow Cooker. Cover with the lid and cook for 6 hours on Low. Serve right away.

French Pork Chops with Dijon Sauce

Serves: 4 | Total Time: 5 hours 15 minutes

2 onions, finely chopped	1 tbsp apple cider vinegar
4 garlic cloves, minced	½ cup white wine
4 pork chops, bone-in	2 tbsp Dijon mustard
1 tsp dried mustard	½ cup heavy cream
¼ tsp cayenne pepper	Salt and pepper to taste

Toss the pork chops, onions, garlic, mustard, cayenne pepper, apple cider vinegar, wine, mustard, heavy cream, salt, and pepper in your Slow Cooker. Cover with the lid and cook for 5 hours on Low. Serve warm.

Chinese-Style Pork Roast

Serves: 8 | Total Time: 8 hours 15 minutes

1 cup water chestnuts, chopped	
2 shallots, sliced	1 tbsp rice vinegar
4 lb pork shoulder, trimmed	2 tbsp red bean paste
1 can (8 oz) bamboo shoots	1 tsp garlic powder
1 tsp sesame oil	1 tsp hot sauce
1 tbsp Worcestershire sauce	1 cup chicken stock
¼ cup soy sauce	

Stir the pork, bamboo shoots, water chestnuts, shallots, Worcestershire sauce, soy sauce, rice vinegar, red bean paste, sesame oil, garlic powder, hot sauce, and chicken stock in your Slow Cooker. Cover with the lid and cook for 8 hours on Low. Drizzle with the sauce to serve.

Rich Chipotle Pork Roast

Serves: 6 | Total Time: 7 hours 15 minutes

1 chipotle pepper, chopped	1 cup water
6 garlic cloves, chopped	2 bay leaves
2 lb pork roast	1 tbsp red wine vinegar
¼ cup soy sauce	½ tsp chili powder

Mix the pork roast, vinegar, soy sauce, water, bay leaves, chipotle pepper, garlic, and chili powder in your Slow Cooker. Cover with the lid and cook for 7 hours on Low. When done, remove the lid and serve right away.

Garlicky Pork Belly

Serves: 6 | Total Time: 8 hours 15 minutes

2 garlic cloves	1 tsp garlic powder
2 lb pork belly	1 tsp cayenne pepper
1 cup dry white wine	Salt and pepper to taste
1 tsp cumin powder	

Poke some holes in the pork belly and fill them with garlic cloves. Rub the meat with cumin, garlic powder, cayenne pepper, salt, and pepper. Add them to your Slow Cooker and pour in the wine. Cover with the lid and cook for 8 hours on Low. Serve warm.

Hawaiian Pork Ribs

Serves: 6 | Total Time: 8 hours 15 minutes

1 cup crushed pineapple in juice
2 shallots, chopped
3 lb short pork ribs
½ cup hot ketchup
¼ cup hoisin sauce
2 tbsp maple syrup

1 tsp onion powder
1 tsp garlic powder
1 tsp grated ginger
2 tbsp soy sauce

Toss the pork ribs, ketchup, hoisin sauce, maple syrup, onion powder, garlic powder, pineapple, shallots, ginger, and soy sauce in your Slow Cooker. Cover with the lid and cook for 8 hours on Low. Serve warm.

Coffee Pulled Pork

Serves: 6 | Total Time: 8 hours 15 minutes

¼ cup brewed coffee
½ cup chicken stock
2 lb pork shoulder
¼ cup Kahlua liqueur

2 bay leaves
1 chipotle pepper, chopped
½ tsp cumin seeds
Salt and pepper to taste

Toss the pork, Kahlua liqueur, coffee, chicken stock, bay leaves, chipotle peppers, cumin seeds, salt, and pepper in your Slow Cooker. Cover with the lid and cook for 8 hours on Low. Using two forks, shred it, and serve.

Jamaican Pork Roast

Serves: 6 | Total Time: 6 hours 15 minutes

2 tbsp Jamaican jerk seasoning
1 large onion, sliced
4 garlic cloves, chopped
1 cup BBQ sauce
2 lb pork roast

1 tsp dried thyme
1 tsp dried mint
½ cup water
Salt and pepper to taste

Sprinkle pork roast with jerk seasoning, thyme, salt, and pepper. In your Slow Cooker, stir mint, onion, garlic, BBQ sauce, and water. Place seasoned pork on top. Cover and cook for 6 hours on Low. Serve right away.

Pork Chop Pizza with Mozarella & Olives

Serves: 6 | Total Time: 6 hours 30 minutes

2 red bell peppers, sliced
1 ½ cups tomato sauce
6 pork chops
1 tsp dried oregano

12 pitted black olives, sliced
2 cups shredded mozzarella
Salt and pepper to taste

Layer pork chops in your Slow Cooker and add tomato sauce, bell peppers, oregano, olives, salt, and pepper. Scatter with mozzarella cheese on top. Cover with the lid and cook for 6 hours on Low. Serve immediately.

Sweet Mustard Pork Chops

Serves: 4 | Total Time: 5 hours 15 minutes

1 shallot, finely chopped
4 garlic cloves, minced
4 pork chops
2 tbsp Dijon mustard

2 tbsp olive oil
1 tbsp honey
1 cup chicken stock
Salt and pepper to taste

Sprinkle the pork chops with salt and pepper. Place seasoned pork, mustard, honey, olive oil, shallot, garlic, chicken stock, salt, and pepper in your Slow Cooker.

Cover and cook for 5 hours on Low. When done, remove the lid and drizzle with the sauce before serving.

Pork Chops with Apple-Cherry Gravy

Serves: 6 | Total Time: 3 hours 15 minutes

1 onion, chopped
1 garlic clove, minced
6 pork chops
4 apples, cored and sliced
1 cup frozen sour cherries

½ cup apple cider vinegar
½ cup tomato sauce
1 bay leaf
Salt and pepper to taste

Toss the pork chops, apples, cherries, apple cider vinegar, tomato sauce, onion, garlic, bay leaf, salt, and pepper in your Slow Cooker. Cover with the lid and cook for 3 hours on High. Serve warm.

Dijon Tenderloin with Roasted Peppers

Serves: 8 | Total Time: 8 hours 15 minutes

1 cup chicken stock
3 lb pork tenderloin
2 tbsp Dijon mustard

¼ cup three pepper mix
Salt and pepper to taste

Sprinkle the pork tenderloin with salt and pepper. Rub it with mustard and dust with pepper mix until well coated on all sides. Place seasoned pork and chicken stock in your Slow Cooker. Cover with the lid and cook for 8 hours on Low. When done, remove the lid and cut it into slices before serving with your desired side dish.

Pork Chops with Mango Chutney

Serves: 4 | Total Time: 5 hours 15 minutes

1 jar mango chutney
4 pork chops
3/4 cup chicken stock

1 bay leaf
Salt and pepper to taste

Mix the pork chops, mango chutney, chicken stock, bay leaf, salt, and pepper in your Slow Cooker. Cover with the lid and cook for 5 hours on Low. Serve right away.

Varadero-Style Pork Roast with Beans

Serves: 6 | Total Time: 6 hours 15 minutes

1 large onion, sliced
4 garlic cloves, minced
2 lb pork roast, cubed
½ cup fresh orange juice
½ cup chicken stock
1 lime, juiced

½ tsp cumin powder
½ tsp chili powder
1 tsp smoked paprika
Salt and pepper to taste
2 cups canned black beans

Mix the pork, orange juice, chicken stock, lime juice, onion, garlic, cumin, chili powder, paprika, salt, and pepper in your Slow Cooker. Cover with the lid.

Cook for 6 hours on Low. When done, remove the lid and serve over black beans and drizzle with the sauce.

MEATLESS RECIPES

Mushroom & Cauliflower Bolognese

Serves: 4 | Total Time: 8 hours 10 minutes

1 lb cremini mushrooms, finely chopped
1 head cauliflower, cut into florets
1 shallot, chopped
2 (14-oz) cans diced tomatoes
¼ cup vegetable stock
1 tsp garlic powder
1 tsp dried oregano
1 tsp sea salt
1 tsp red pepper flakes
2 tbsp chopped cilantro

Place the the mushrooms, cauliflower, shallot, tomatoes, stock, garlic powder, oregano, salt, and red pepper flakes in your Slow Cooker and mix to combine. Cover and cook for 8 hours on Low. When done, remove the lid and using a potato masher, lightly mash the sauce to break up the cauliflower. Sprinkle with cilantro and serve.

Soy Chorizo Stuffed Bell Peppers

Serves: 4 | Total Time: 6 hours 10 minutes

8 oz soy chorizo, crumbled
1 tsp butter, melted
1 cup corn kernels
¼ cup minced onions
1 tsp minced garlic
1 tsp ground cumin
1 tsp smoked paprika
2 tbsp pepper Jack cheese
Sea salt to taste
4 red bell peppers

Brush the inside of your Slow Cooker with the butter. In a medium bowl, combine the soy chorizo, corn, onions, garlic, cumin, paprika, cheese, and salt. Slice the tops of the peppers and discard the seeds. Reserve the lids. Spoon the soy chorizo mixture into the peppers and put the lids on top. Arrange the peppers onto your Slow Cooker.Cover and cook for 6 hours on Low until the peppers are tender. Serve and enjoy!

Baked Spicy Rice

Serves: 4 | Total Time: 6 hours 10 minutes

2 tbsp roasted peanuts, chopped
4 collard leaves, cut into thin ribbons
1 cup brown rice
6 cups vegetable broth
1 tbsp soy sauce
1 sweet onion, chopped
1 tbsp minced ginger
2 tbsp tomato paste
½ cup peanut butter
1 tsp Sriracha
2 tbsp chopped cilantro
1 lime, cut into wedges

Spritz the inside of your Slow Cooker with cooking spray. Add the rice, 4 cups of broth, soy sauce, collard greens, and onion and stir. In a medium bowl, whisk together the remaining broth, ginger, tomato paste, peanut butter, and Sriracha.Pour the mixture into the slow cooker. Cover and cook for 6 hours on Low. Serve garnished with cilantro, lime wedges, and peanuts.

Crustless Veggie Quiche

Serves: 4 | Total Time: 8 hours 10 minutes

4 whole-grain bread slices, crusts removed, cubed
1 cup diced button mushrooms
8 eggs, beaten
1 tsp fresh thyme
Salt and pepper to taste
2 green onions, chopped
2 cups shredded spinach
1 cup grated cheddar cheese

In a bowl, combine together the eggs, thyme, salt, and pepper. Put the bread, mushrooms, green onions, spinach, and cheese in your greased Slow Cooker. Top with the egg mixture and stir gently to combine. Cover and cook for 8 hours on Low. Cut into wedges and serve.

Spinach & Bean Enchiladas with Corn

Serves: 6 | Total Time: 3 hours 15 minutes

2 cups spinach, shredded
2 shallots, chopped
2 garlic cloves, chopped
1 can (15 oz) white beans
1 can sweet corn, drained
1 cup vegetable stock
½ tsp cumin powder
1 cup red salsa
2 tbsp olive oil
Salt and pepper to taste
6 flour tortillas
3 tbsp grated cheddar

Warm the olive oil in a pan over medium heat. Place the shallot and cook for 2 minutes, stirring frequently. Add it into your Slow Cooker. Put in garlic, white beans, corn, spinach, vegetable stock, cumin, red salsa, salt, and pepper. Cover with the lid and cook for 3 hours on High. When done, remove the lid, divide between tortillas, and top with grated cheese. Serve immediately.

Ricotta & Spinach Lasagna

Serves: 6 | Total Time: 6 hours 30 minutes

6 lasagna noodles
16 oz spinach, torn
2 cups shredded mozzarella
1 cup ricotta cheese
½ tsp dried marjoram
½ tsp dried basil
2 garlic cloves, chopped
½ cup grated Parmesan
2 ½ cups tomato sauce
Salt and pepper to taste

In a bowl, combine spinach, ricotta, marjoram, basil, garlic, Parmesan, salt, and pepper. In your Slow Cooker, put a layer of lasagna noodles, then a layer of spinach filling, and finally a layer of tomato sauce. Repeat the process until any ingredients left. Scatter with mozzarella cheese on top. Cover with the lid and cook for 6 hours on Low. When done, remove the lid and serve right away.

Spicy Sweet Potato Curry

Serves: 6 | Total Time: 2 hours 30 minutes

1 lb sweet potatoes, cubed
1 shallot, chopped
2 garlic cloves, chopped
2 red bell peppers, diced
1 carrot, diced
½ tsp cumin powder
½ tsp curry powder
½ tsp chili powder
2 tbsp tomato paste
1 cup vegetable stock
2 tbsp olive oil
½ cup coconut milk
1 bay leaf
Salt and pepper to taste

Warm the olive oil in a pan over medium heat. Place the shallot and garlic and cook for 2 minutes until softened. Transfer everything to your Slow Cooker. Add in bell peppers, carrot, cumin, curry powder, chili powder, tomato paste, sweet potatoes, stock, coconut milk, bay leaf, salt, and pepper. Cook for 2 hours on High. Serve.

Chickpea & Summer Squash Lasagna

Serves: 6 | Total Time: 6 hours 30 minutes

2 summer squashes, cut into thin strips
4 ripe tomatoes, pureed
1 ½ cups shredded
4 tbsp Italian pesto
1 can chickpeas, drained
½ cup red lentils
1 shallot, chopped
½ cup chopped parsley
1 lemon, juiced
½ tsp dried thyme
½ tsp chili flakes
Salt and pepper to taste

In a bowl, combine chickpeas, lentils, parsley, lemon juice, thyme, chili flakes, salt, and pepper. In your Slow Cooker, first put a layer of squash slices, brush them with Italian pesto, and finally top with chickpea mixture. Spoon some tomato puree and repeat the process until no ingredients left. Scatter with mozzarella cheese on top. Cover and cook for 6 hours on Low. Serve immediately.

Minestra di Ceci

Serves: 6 | Total Time: 6 hours 30 minutes

2 ripe tomatoes, peeled and diced
1 red bell pepper, diced
1 potato, peeled and diced
2 /3 cup chickpeas, rinsed
2 cups vegetable stock
4 cups water
1 celery stalk, sliced
1 carrot, diced
1 shallot, chopped
1 tbsp lemon juice
Salt and pepper to taste

Mix the chickpeas, stock, water, celery, carrot, shallot, tomatoes, bell pepper, potato, lemon juice, salt, and pepper in your Slow Cooker. Cook for 6 hours on Low.

Vegetable Couscous

Serves: 6 | Total Time: 2 hours 30 minutes

½ head broccoli, cut into florets
2 red bell peppers, diced
2 carrots, diced
1 cup couscous
2 cups vegetable stock
1 lemon, juiced
½ cup chopped parsley
2 tbsp chopped cilantro
Salt and pepper to taste

Mix the couscous, vegetable stock, bell peppers, carrots, broccoli, salt, and pepper in your Slow Cooker. Cover with the lid and cook for 2 hours on High. Stir in lemon juice, parsley, and cilantro and serve. Enjoy!

Caribbean Black Beans

Serves: 6 | Total Time: 8 hours 15 minutes

1 cup chopped onion
2 red bell peppers, diced
1 green bell pepper, diced
1 cup black beans, soaked
2 cups vegetable stock
1 tsp fennel seeds
½ tsp cumin seeds
½ tsp ground coriander
1 tsp sherry wine vinegar
1 can fire-roasted tomatoes
1 green chile, chopped
Salt and pepper to taste

Mix the beans, vegetable stock, 2 cups of water, onion, bell peppers, fennel seeds, cumin seeds, coriander, sherry vinegar, roasted tomatoes, green chile, salt, and pepper in your Slow Cooker. Cover with the lid and cook for 8 hours on Low. Serve with tortillas if desired.

Zucchini Chili

Serves: 6 | Total Time: 2 hours 15 minutes

1 can diced tomatoes
2 garlic cloves, chopped
1 can (15 oz) white beans
1 red bell pepper, diced
1 bay leaf
1 zucchini, cubed
1 cup vegetable stock
1 celery stalk, diced
1 tsp dried Italian herbs
Salt and pepper to taste

Stir white beans, bell pepper, zucchini, celery, tomatoes, garlic, Italian herbs, salt, pepper, vegetable stock, and bay leaf in your Slow Cooker. Cover with the lid and cook for 2 hours on High. Serve right away.

Mixed-Bean & Vegetable Stew

Serves: 6 | Total Time: 8 hours 30 minutes

½ cup cannellini beans, soaked
½ cup white beans, soaked
½ cup kidney beans, soaked
2 carrots, diced
1 celery stalk, diced
1 onion, chopped
2 garlic cloves, chopped
2 tbsp tomato paste
½ cup diced tomatoes
1 bay leaf
½ red chili, sliced
½ tsp cumin powder
2 cups vegetable stock
1 cup water
Salt and pepper to taste

Mix the beans, carrots, celery, onion, garlic, tomato paste, tomatoes, bay leaf, red chili, cumin, vegetable stock, water, salt, and pepper in your Slow Cooker. Cover with the lid and cook for 8 hours on Low. Serve immediately.

Black Bean & Wild Rice Casserole

Serves: 6 | Total Time: 6 hours 15 minutes

1 celery stalk, diced
2 tomatoes, diced
½ cup wild rice
1 can black beans, drained
½ lemon, juiced
2 tbsp pine nuts
2 tbsp chopped parsley
2 cups vegetable stock
Salt and pepper to taste

Stir the rice, beans, celery, tomatoes, pine nuts, vegetable stock, salt, and pepper in your Slow Cooker. Cover with the lid and cook for 6 hours on Low. Mix in lemon juice and sprinkle with parsley. Serve warm.

Roasted Vegetable Casserole

Serves: 6 | Total Time: 2 hours 30 minutes

3 roasted red bell peppers, chopped
1 large onion, chopped
3 garlic cloves, minced
1 carrot, grated
1 parsnip, grated
2 tbsp tomato paste
1 cup tomato sauce
2 tbsp olive oil
½ cup vegetable stock
¼ tsp cumin powder
¼ tsp dried oregano
1 thyme sprig
Salt and pepper to taste

Warm the olive oil in a pan over medium heat. Place the onion, garlic, and carrot and cook for 5 minutes until softened. Transfer everything to your Slow Cooker. Add in parsnip, bell pepper, tomato paste, tomato sauce, vegetable stock, cumin, oregano, thyme, salt, and pepper. Cover and cook for 2 hours on High. Serve right away.

Homemade Marinara Sauce

Serves: 6 | Total Time: 6 hours 30 minutes

2 lb fresh tomatoes, pureed
2 large onions, chopped
2 carrots, grated
1 celery stalk, diced
4 garlic cloves, minced
½ tsp dried oregano
¼ tsp red pepper flakes

2 tbsp tomato paste
3 tbsp olive oil
1 tsp honey
1 tsp red wine vinegar
1 bay leaf
½ cup vegetable stock
Salt and pepper to taste

Warm the olive oil in a pan over medium heat. Place the onions and garlic and cook for 5 minutes until softened. Transfer everything to your Slow Cooker. Add in carrots, celery, oregano, red pepper flakes, tomato paste, tomatoes, salt, pepper, honey, vinegar, bay leaf, and vegetable stock. Cover with the lid and cook for 6 hours on Low. Serve immediately.

Chickpea Curry with Tofu

Serves: 6 | Total Time: 6 hours 30 minutes

12 oz firm tofu, cubed
1 can (15 oz) chickpeas
1 cup diced tomatoes
1 large onion, chopped
2 garlic cloves, chopped
2 cups cauliflower florets
1 sweet potato, cubed

1 tsp curry powder
1 cup coconut milk
1 cup vegetable stock
2 tbsp olive oil
1 kaffir lime leaf
1 tsp grated ginger
Salt and pepper to taste

Warm the olive oil in a pan over medium heat. Place the tofu and cook until golden and crusty on all sides. Add in curry powder and cook for another minute. Add it to your Slow Cooker. Put in onion, garlic, cauliflower, sweet potato, chickpeas, tomatoes, coconut milk, vegetable stock, kaffir leaf, ginger, salt, and pepper. Cover with the lid and cook for 6 hours on Low. Serve immediately.

Coconut Chickpea Curry

Serves: 6 | Total Time: 2 hours 15 minutes

2 shallots, chopped
2 garlic cloves, chopped
2 cans (15 oz) can chickpeas
1 can diced tomatoes
1 cup coconut milk

½ cup vegetable stock
2 tbsp chopped cilantro
1 tsp curry powder
Salt and pepper to taste

Stir chickpeas, shallots, garlic, tomatoes, coconut milk, vegetable stock, curry powder, salt, and pepper in your Slow Cooker. Cover with the lid and cook for 2 hours on High. Mix in cilantro before serving. Enjoy!

Artichoke Ragout with Cannellini Beans

Serves: 6 | Total Time: 6 hours 15 minutes

2 cans (15-oz) cannellini beans, drained
6 canned artichoke hearts, drained and chopped
1 carrot, sliced
4 garlic cloves, chopped
2 potatoes, cubed
1 small fennel bulb, sliced
2 tbsp olive oil

2 leeks, sliced
½ tsp dried basil
1 cup vegetable stock
Salt and pepper to taste

Warm the olive oil in a pan over medium heat. Place the leeks and cook for 5 minutes until softened. Add them to your Slow Cooker. Put in carrot, garlic, beans, potatoes, artichoke hearts, fennel, basil, vegetable stock, salt, and pepper. Cover and cook for 6 hours on Low. Serve warm.

Creamy Grits with Chili

Serves: 6 | Total Time: 6 hours 45 minutes

2 cups white beans, soaked
2 cups vegetable stock
2 garlic cloves, chopped
1 carrot, diced
1 onion, chopped
1 celery stalk, diced
1 red chili, chopped
½ tsp cumin powder

1 cup fire-roasted tomatoes
1 bay leaf
2 cups spinach, shredded
1 cup grits
2 cups water
2 cups whole milk
1 cup grated Cheddar
Salt and pepper to taste

Mix the beans, vegetable stock, water, onion, garlic, carrot, celery, red chili, cumin, roasted tomatoes, bay leaf, salt, and pepper in your Slow Cooker. Sprinkle with shredded spinach on top. Cook for 6 ½ hours on Low.

Meanwhile, for the topping, pour milk in a pot and bring it to a boil. Add in grits and cook on Low heat until creamy. Turn the heat off and scatter with grated cheese. Divide between bowls. When beans are ready, remove the lid and share them into the bowl and serve. Enjoy!

Chickpea Curry with Vegetables

Serves: 6 | Total Time: 6 hours 15 minutes

2 potatoes, diced
1 red bell pepper, diced
1 poblano pepper, chopped
1 cup chickpeas, rinsed
1 large onion, soaked
1 carrot, sliced
1 tsp curry

1 tsp grated ginger
2 garlic cloves, chopped
1 cup fire-roasted tomatoes
2 cups vegetable stock
1 bay leaf
Salt and pepper to taste
2 tbsp chopped cilantro

Mix the chickpeas, onion, carrot, curry, ginger, garlic, potatoes, bell pepper, poblano pepper, roasted tomatoes, vegetable stock, salt, pepper, and bay leaf in your Slow Cooker. Cover with the lid and cook for 6 hours on Low. Serve topped with cilantro. Enjoy!

Vegetables & White Bean Cassoulet

Serves: 6 | Total Time: 6 hours 30 minutes

2 garlic cloves, chopped
2 cans white beans, drained
1 large onion, chopped
2 carrots, diced
2 tbsp olive oil
1 parsnip, diced

1 cup vegetable stock
1 thyme sprig
1 ½ cups diced tomatoes
1 bay leaf
Salt and pepper to taste

Warm the olive oil in a pan over medium heat. Place the onion, carrot, and garlic, and cook for 5 minutes until softened. Transfer everything to your Slow Cooker. Add in parsnip, beans, vegetable stock, thyme, tomatoes, bay leaf, salt, and pepper. Cover with the lid and cook for 6 hours on Low. Serve right away.

Smoked Bean Chilli with Corn Chips

Serves: 6 | Total Time: 2 hours 45 minutes

2 garlic cloves, chopped	½ tsp cumin powder
1 carrot, sliced	1 cup vegetable stock
1 red bell pepper, diced	1 bay leaf
2 (15-oz) cans kidney beans	2 cups corn chips
1 red onion, chopped	2 tbsp olive oil
½ red chili, chopped	1 tsp smoked paprika
1 cup diced tomatoes	Salt and pepper to taste

Mix the beans, onion, red chili, garlic carrot, bell pepper, tomatoes, cumin, vegetable stock, bay leaf, salt, and pepper in your Slow Cooker. Cover with the lid and cook for 2 ½ hours on High. Meanwhile, for the topping, preheat the oven to 400°F. Lay corn chips in a baking tray, sprinkle with olive oil and paprika and bake for 10 minutes until golden. Serve topped with corn chips.

Kidney Bean & Veggies Gumbo

Serves: 6 | Total Time: 8 hours 30 minutes

1 cup diced tomatoes	2 cups vegetable stock
1 can (15 oz) kidney beans	2 cups sliced mushrooms
1 sweet onion, chopped	1 summer squash, cubed
1 celery stalk, sliced	1 cup chopped okra
2 garlic cloves, chopped	1 tsp Cajun seasoning
1 red bell pepper, diced	½ cup coconut milk
2 tbsp olive oil	Salt and pepper to taste
2 tbsp all-purpose flour	

Warm the olive oil in a pan over medium heat. Place the onion, celery, garlic, and bell pepper and cook for 5 minutes until softened. Add in flour and cook for another minute. Transfer everything to your Slow Cooker. Put in vegetable stock, tomatoes, beans, mushrooms, squash, okra, cajun seasoning, coconut milk, salt, and pepper. Cover and cook for 8 hours on Low. Serve immediately.

Tomato Butternut Squash Curry

Serves: 6 | Total Time: 6 hours 30 minutes

1 can (15 oz) chickpeas	1 cup vegetable stock
1 cup diced tomatoes	2 cups fresh spinach
2 shallots, chopped	2 tbsp chopped parsley
4 garlic cloves, chopped	2 tbsp red curry paste
4 cups butternut squash	Salt and pepper to taste
1 cup coconut milk	

Stir shallots, garlic, butternut squash, chickpeas, tomatoes, coconut milk, vegetable stock, curry paste, spinach, parsley, salt, and pepper in your Slow Cooker. Cover and cook for 6 hours on Low. Serve warm.

Vegetarian Stroganoff

Serves: 6 | Total Time: 6 hours 15 minutes

1 ½ lb mushrooms, sliced	2 tbsp olive oil
2 tbsp all-purpose flour	1 cup half and half
1 onion, chopped	½ cup vegetable stock
4 garlic cloves, chopped	Salt and pepper to taste
½ tsp smoked paprika	

Warm the olive oil in a pan over medium heat. Place the onion and garlic and cook for 2 minutes. Transfer everything to your Slow Cooker. Add in mushrooms, flour, paprika, half and half, vegetable stock, salt, and pepper. Cover and cook for 6 hours on Low. Serve warm.

Chickpea & Vegetable Curry

Serves: 6 | Total Time: 3 hours 15 minutes

½ head green cabbage, shredded	
1 green apple, peeled and diced	
4 garlic cloves, chopped	1 cup tomato sauce
2 carrots, sliced	1 cup vegetable stock
2 shallots, chopped	½ tsp chili powder
1 parsnip, diced	½ tsp cumin powder
1 red bell pepper, diced	1 tsp curry powder
2 celery stalks, sliced	1 tbsp brown sugar
1 cup canned chickpeas	½ cup coconut milk
2 cups cauliflower florets	Salt and pepper to taste
2 tbsp olive oil	

Warm olive oil in your Slow Cooker, place shallots, garlic, carrots, bell pepper, and celery, and cook for 5 minutes until softened. Add in parsnip, cabbage, apple, chickpeas, cauliflower, tomato sauce, vegetable stock, chili powder, cumin, curry powder, brown sugar, coconut milk, salt, and pepper. Cover with the lid and cook for 3 hours on High. When done, remove the lid and serve warm.

Veggie Lover's Chili

Serves: 6 | Total Time: 7 hours 30 minutes

1 can (15 oz) cannellini beans	1 potato, peeled and cubed
4 cups spinach, shredded	2 tbsp tomato paste
1 red bell pepper, diced	½ cup diced tomatoes
1 green bell pepper, diced	½ cup butter
1 yellow bell pepper, diced	1 cup vegetable stock
1 zucchini, cubed	½ tsp chili powder
1 carrot, sliced	1 thyme sprig
1 shallot, chopped	Salt and pepper to taste
4 garlic cloves, chopped	

Melt the butter in a pan over medium heat, place shallot, garlic, and bell peppers and cook for 5 minutes until softened. Transfer everything to your Slow Cooker. Add in zucchini, carrot, potato, tomato paste, tomatoes, beans, spinach, vegetable stock, chili powder, thyme, salt, and pepper. Cover and cook for 7 hours on Low. Serve.

Coconut Potato & Green Pea Curry

Serves: 6 | Total Time: 7 hours 30 minutes

2 red bell peppers, diced	½ tsp chili powder
1 ½ lb potatoes, cubed	½ tsp red pepper flakes
2 carrots, sliced	1 ½ cups coconut milk
1 cup green peas	½ cup vegetable stock
1 tsp curry powder	Salt and pepper to taste

Stir potatoes, carrots, green peas, curry powder, chili powder, red pepper flakes, bell peppers, coconut milk, vegetable stock, salt, and pepper in your Slow Cooker. Cover and cook for 7 hours on Low. Serve immediately.

Meatless Fajitas

Serves: 6 | Total Time: 6 hours 15 minutes

1 can (15 oz) kidney beans	¼ tsp chili powder
4 heirloom tomatoes, diced	½ tsp dried oregano
4 oz green chilies, chopped	½ cup vegetable stock
2 red bell peppers, diced	Salt and pepper to taste
1 small onion, chopped	Flour tortillas for serving
1 tsp cumin powder	

Mix the tomatoes, green chilies, bell peppers, onion, cumin, chili powder, oregano, vegetable stock, beans, salt, and pepper in your Slow Cooker. Cover with the lid and cook for 6 hours on Low. Divide the mixture between flour tortillas, and wrap them before serving.

Bell Peppers Stuffed with Rice & Lentils

Serves: 6 | Total Time: 6 hours 30 minutes

2 carrots, grated	½ tsp dried oregano
1 large onion, chopped	½ tsp dried basil
6 red bell peppers, cored	1 pinch nutmeg
3 cups cooked red lentils	1 cup tomato sauce
½ cup red rice	2 cups vegetable stock
2 tbsp tomato paste	Salt and pepper to taste
1 celery stalk, diced	

In a bowl, mix lentils, rice, carrots, onion, tomato paste, celery, oregano, basil, nutmeg, salt, and pepper. Spoon the mixture into the bell peppers and place them in your Slow Cooker. Pour in tomato sauce and vegetable stock. Cover and cook for 6 hours on Low. Serve immediately.

Sweet Pinto Bean Curry

Serves: 6 | Total Time: 6 hours 30 minutes

2 garlic cloves, chopped	1 tsp curry powder
2 cans pinto beans, drained	1 cup coconut milk
1 shallot, chopped	1 cup vegetable stock
1 tbsp olive oil	2 tbsp tomato paste
1 tsp grated ginger	1 bay leaf
½ tsp chili powder	1 tsp brown sugar
½ tsp cumin powder	Salt and pepper to taste

Stir beans, olive oil, shallot, garlic, ginger, chili powder, cumin, curry powder, coconut milk, vegetable stock, tomato paste, bay leaf, sugar, salt, and pepper in your Slow Cooker. Cover and cook for 6 hours on Low. Serve.

Seedy Okra Stew

Serves: 6 | Total Time: 2 hours 15 minutes

1 lb fresh okra, trimmed	½ tsp mustard seeds
1 cup fire-roasted tomatoes	¼ tsp smoked paprika
1 shallot, chopped	½ cup vegetable stock
2 garlic cloves, chopped	Salt and pepper to taste
½ tsp cumin seeds	

Stir shallot, garlic, cumin seeds, mustard seeds, paprika, okra, roasted tomatoes, vegetable stock, salt, and pepper in your Slow Cooker. Cover with the lid and cook for 2 hours on High. Serve immediately.

Easy BBQ Tofu

Serves: 4 | Total Time: 2 hours 15 minutes

1 cup BBQ sauce	2 garlic cloves, minced
1 tsp Worcestershire sauce	¼ tsp cumin powder
4 thick slices firm tofu	1 pinch cayenne pepper
1 shallot, sliced	1 thyme sprig

Stir shallot, garlic, BBQ sauce, Worcestershire sauce, cumin, cayenne pepper, and thyme in your Slow Cooker. Put in tofu and toss to combine. Cover with the lid and cook for 2 hours on High. Serve warm.

Oriental Braised Tofu

Serves: 4 | Total Time: 2 hours 15 minutes

2 garlic cloves, minced	1 tbsp soy sauce
4 slices firm tofu	1 tsp grated ginger
½ cup hoisin sauce	1 tsp rice vinegar
½ tsp sesame oil	1 tsp molasses

Combine hoisin sauce, soy sauce, ginger, rice vinegar, sesame oil, garlic, and molasses in your Slow Cooker. Put in tofu and toss to combine. Cover with the lid and cook for 2 hours on High. Serve warm.

Porcini & Mushroom Wild Rice

Serves: 6 | Total Time: 6 hours 30 minutes

2 carrots, diced	3 cups vegetable stock
2 celery stalks, diced	1 oz dried porcini, crushed
1 shallot, chopped	1 cup sliced mushrooms
1 cup wild rice	Salt and pepper to taste

Stir rice, vegetable stock, carrots, celery, shallot, porcini, mushrooms, salt, and pepper in your Slow Cooker Cover and cook for 6 hours on Low. Serve right away.

Potato & Cauliflower Mash

Serves: 4 | Total Time: 4 hours 30 minutes

1 lb potatoes, cubed	¼ cup vegetable stock
2 cups cauliflower florets	¼ cup coconut milk
2 tbsp coconut oil	Salt and pepper to taste

Mix the potatoes, cauliflower, vegetable stock, coconut oil, coconut milk, salt, and pepper in your Slow Cooker. Cover with the lid and cook for 4 hours on Low. Using a potato masher, mash it until smooth and serve. Enjoy!

Twisted Potato Purée

Serves: 4 | Total Time: 2 hours 30 minutes

1 green onion, chopped	1 cup water
1 garlic clove, minced	¼ cup coconut milk
1 ½ lb potatoes, cubed	Salt and pepper to taste

Mix the potatoes, water, salt, and pepper in your Slow Cooker. Cover with the lid and cook for 2 hours on High. When done, remove the lid and, using a potato masher, mash it until puree. Mix in coconut milk, green onion, and garlic, and serve right away.

Spinach & Pumpkin Casserole

Serves: 8 | Total Time: 6 hours 30 minutes

2 cups fresh spinach	½ tsp cumin seeds
2 sweet onions, chopped	1 pinch cayenne pepper
4 garlic cloves, chopped	2 tbsp olive oil
1 small pumpkin, cubed	1 cup vegetable stock
1 cup diced tomatoes	Salt and pepper to taste
1 tbsp tomato paste	

Warm the olive oil in a pan over medium heat. Place the onions and garlic and cook for 2 minutes until softened. Transfer everything to your Slow Cooker. Put in pumpkin, tomatoes, tomato paste, cumin seeds, cayenne pepper, vegetable stock, spinach, salt, and pepper. Cover and cook for 6 hours on Low. Serve right away.

Rosemary Artichokes

Serves: 4 | Total Time: 6 hours 30 minutes

2 garlic cloves, minced	3/4 cup vegetable stock
4 large artichokes	1 rosemary sprig
1 lemon, juiced	Salt and pepper to taste

Place the artichokes on a flat surface and peel them well. Rinse under water and place them in your Slow Cooker. Add in lemon juice, garlic, vegetable stock, rosemary, salt, and pepper. Cover with the lid and cook for 6 hours on Low. When done, remove the lid and serve warm.

Vegan Zucchini Boats

Serves: 4 | Total Time: 2 hours 30 minutes

1 small eggplant, peeled and diced	
2 garlic cloves, chopped	2 tbsp tomato paste
1 carrot, grated	1 cup tomato sauce
2 zucchinis	1 thyme sprig
1 shallot, chopped	Salt and pepper to taste

Add tomato sauce and thyme in your Slow Cooker. Place the zucchinis on a flat surface, cut them in half, and scoop out the flesh, leaving ½-inch thick intact. Cut the flesh and place it in a bowl. Stir in shallot, garlic, carrot, eggplant, tomato paste, salt, and pepper. Stuff each zucchini half with eggplant mixture and place them in the cooker. Cover and cook for 2 hours on High. Serve.

Cheesy Mushrooms

Serves: 6 | Total Time: 6 hours 15 minutes

1 lb cremini mushrooms, sliced	
4 garlic cloves, chopped	2 tbsp olive oil
2 tbsp all-purpose flour	1 cup whole milk
2 shallots, chopped	½ cup cream cheese
¼ cup vegetable stock	Salt and pepper to taste

Dust mushrooms with flour. Warm the olive oil in a pan over medium heat. Place the mushrooms and cook for a few minutes until golden on each side. Remove them to your Slow Cooker. Add in shallots, vegetable stock, garlic, milk, cream cheese, salt, and pepper. Cover with the lid and cook for 6 hours on Low. Serve immediately.

Miso Seaman Jambalaya

Serves: 6 | Total Time: 6 hours 30 minutes

1 red bell pepper, diced	1 tbsp olive oil
1 celery stalk, sliced	1 tsp miso paste
2 shallots, chopped	1 tsp Cajun seasoning
2 garlic cloves, chopped	1 cup white rice
8 oz seaman, cubed	½ tsp turmeric powder
2 cups vegetable stock	Salt and pepper to taste

Warm the olive oil in a pan over medium heat. Place the shallots and garlic and cook for 2 minutes until softened. Transfer everything to your Slow Cooker. Add in seaman, bell pepper, celery, vegetable stock, miso paste, cajun seasoning, rice, turmeric, salt, and pepper. Cover with the lid and cook for 6 hours on Low. Serve warm.

Traditional Lentil Dal

Serves: 10 | Total Time: 6 hours 15 minutes

2 cups red lentils, rinsed	4 cups water
1 sweet onion, chopped	½ tsp cumin powder
2 garlic cloves, chopped	½ tsp fenugreek seeds
1 can diced tomatoes	½ tsp mustard seeds
1 tsp grated ginger	1 tsp fennel seeds
1 tsp turmeric powder	Salt and pepper to taste
¼ tsp ground cardamom	1 lemon, juiced for serving
1 bay leaf	Cooked rice for serving

Stir fenugreek seeds, mustard seeds, and fennel seeds in a pan over medium heat and cook for 1 minute until the flavor release. Mix the lentils, water, tomatoes, onion, garlic, ginger, turmeric, cardamom, bay leaf, cumin, salt, and pepper in your Slow Cooker. Add in toasted seeds on top. Cover with the lid and cook for 6 hours on Low. Serve over cooked rice and sprinkle with lemon juice.

Spicy-Soy Glazed Mushrooms

Serves: 6 | Total Time: 8 hours 15 minutes

½ cup butter	1 cup soy sauce
18 oz mushrooms, sliced	¼ tsp chili powder
1 cup water	1 tsp rice vinegar

Mix the mushrooms, butter, water, soy sauce, chili powder, and rice vinegar in your Slow Cooker. Cover with the lid and cook for 8 hours on Low. Serve warm.

Bean, Corn & Rice Casserole

Serves: 6 | Total Time: 6 hours 30 minutes

2 garlic cloves, chopped	¼ tsp chili powder
1 can (10 oz) sweet corn	½ tsp cumin powder
1 can diced tomatoes	½ cup wild rice
1 cup black eyed peas, soaked	4 cups vegetable stock
1 red bell pepper, diced	Salt and pepper to taste
1 shallot, chopped	

Mix the black-eyed peas, bell pepper, shallot, garlic, corn, tomatoes, chili powder, cumin, rice, vegetable stock, salt, and pepper in your Slow Cooker. Cover with the lid and cook for 6 hours on Low. Serve warm.

Herbed Eggplant with Pasta

Serves: 6 | Total Time: 5 hours 30 minutes

2 large eggplants, peeled and cubed
1 sweet onion, chopped
2 garlic cloves, chopped
½ tsp dried thyme
½ tsp dried oregano
2 tbsp olive oil

1 cup fire-roasted tomatoes
1 ½ cups vegetable stock
½ cup cavatappi pasta
Salt and pepper to taste

Mix the eggplants, onion, garlic, thyme, oregano, olive oil, tomatoes, vegetable stock, cavatappi pasta, salt, and pepper in your Slow Cooker. Cover with the lid and cook for 5 hours on Low. Serve right away.

Home-Style Ratatouille

Serves: 6 | Total Time: 6 hours 30 minutes

1 large eggplant, peeled and cubed
2 cups sliced mushrooms
3 ripe tomatoes, diced
2 red bell peppers, diced
1 tbsp olive oil
1 large onion, chopped

4 garlic cloves, chopped
1 large zucchini, cubed
½ cup vegetable stock
1 thyme sprig
Salt and pepper to taste

Stir onion, olive oil, garlic, zucchini, eggplant, mushrooms, tomatoes, bell peppers, vegetable stock, thyme, salt, and pepper in your Slow Cooker. Cover with the lid and cook for 6 hours on Low. Serve warm or chilled.

Red Chickpea Curry

Serves: 6 | Total Time: 4 hours 15 minutes

1 sweet onion, chopped
2 garlic cloves, chopped
4 cups cooked chickpeas
1 can diced tomatoes
½ tsp grated ginger
½ tsp cumin powder
¼ tsp ground coriander

½ tsp turmeric powder
¼ tsp curry powder
½ cup vegetable stock
½ cup coconut milk
2 tbsp coconut oil
Salt and pepper to taste

Melt coconut oil in a pan over medium heat, place onion and garlic, and cook for 2 minutes until softened. Add in ginger, cumin, coriander, turmeric, and curry powder and cook for 30 seconds until the flavor release. Transfer everything to your Slow Cooker. Add in chickpeas, tomatoes, vegetable stock, coconut milk, salt, and pepper. Cover and cook for 4 hours on Low. Serve immediately.

Lentil & Sweet Potato Mash

Serves: 6 | Total Time: 6 hours 15 minutes

1 garlic clove, chopped
1 lb sweet potatoes, cubed
1 shallot, chopped
2/3 cup red lentils, rinsed

2 cups vegetable stock
Salt and pepper to taste
¼ tsp cumin seeds
1 pinch chili powder

In your Slow Cooker, add sweet potatoes, lentils, shallot, garlic, vegetable stock, cumin seeds, chili powder, salt, and pepper and stir. Cover with the lid and cook for 6 hours on Low. When done, remove the lid, using a potato masher, mash it until puree, and serve warm.

Cheddar Potato Meal

Serves: 6 | Total Time: 6 hours 30 minutes

2 tomatoes, sliced
4 garlic cloves, minced
2 ½ lb potatoes, sliced
2 large onions, sliced
1 ½ cups tomato sauce

½ tsp dried oregano
½ tsp dried thyme
½ cup vegetable stock
Salt and pepper to taste
1 ½ cups grated Cheddar

Spread the potatoes and onions in your Slow Cooker and top with a single layer of tomatoes. In a bowl, combine garlic, tomato sauce, oregano, thyme, vegetable stock, salt, and pepper and pour it over the vegetables. Scatter with grated cheddar on top. Cover with the lid and cook for 6 hours on Low. Serve immediately.

Bean & Corn Tacos

Serves: 10 | Total Time: 6 hours 15 minutes

10-14 taco shells
1 red onion, chopped
1 cup frozen corn
1 can (15 oz) black beans,
1 cup fire-roasted tomatoes
1 cup pearl barley

2 cups vegetable stock
½ tsp cumin powder
½ tsp chili powder
½ cup chopped cilantro
2 limes for serving
Salt and pepper to taste

Stir onion, corn, beans, tomatoes, pearl barley, vegetable stock, cumin, chili powder, salt, and pepper in your Slow Cooker. Cover with the lid and cook for 6 hours on Low. When done, remove the lid, divide between taco shells, and top with cilantro. Sprinkle with lime juice to serve.

Bell Peppers Stuffed with Bean & Wild Rice

Serves: 6 | Total Time: 6 hours 30 minutes

1 can (15 oz) black beans
1 shallot, chopped
1 carrot, grated
6 red bell peppers, cored
½ cup tomato sauce

2 cups cooked wild rice
1 ½ cups vegetable stock
1 thyme sprig
Salt and pepper to taste

In a bowl, combine tomato sauce, beans, rice, shallot, carrot, salt, and pepper. Spoon the mixture into the bell peppers and place them in your Slow Cooker. Pour in vegetable stock and thyme. Cover with the lid and cook for 6 hours on Low. Serve warm.

Cauliflower & Lentil Curry

Serves: 6 | Total Time: 6 hours 15 minutes

2 cups fresh spinach
1 cup diced tomatoes
1 shallot, chopped
3 garlic cloves, chopped
1 cup red lentils, rinsed
2 cups cauliflower florets
2 carrots, sliced

1 tsp grated ginger
½ tsp cumin powder
1 tsp curry powder
1 tbsp tomato paste
2 cups vegetable stock
1 tsp brown sugar
Salt and pepper to taste

Mix the shallot, garlic, lentils, cauliflower, carrots, ginger, cumin, curry powder, tomatoes, tomato paste, vegetable stock, sugar, spinach, salt, and pepper in your Slow Cooker. Cover and cook for 6 hours on Low. Serve.

Useful Tomato Pasta Sauce

Serves: 10 | Total Time: 8 hours 15 minutes

2 onions, chopped	1 cup tomato sauce
4 garlic cloves, chopped	1 cup vegetable stock
1 large fennel bulb, chopped	1 bay leaf
1 can (28 oz) diced tomatoes	1 thyme sprig
2 tbsp tomato paste	Salt and pepper to taste
2 tbsp olive oil	

Warm the olive oil in a pan over medium heat. Place the onions and garlic and cook for 5 minutes until softened and caramelized. Transfer everything to your Slow Cooker. Put in fennel, tomatoes, tomato paste, tomato sauce, vegetable stock, bay leaf, thyme, salt, and pepper. Cover and cook for 8 hours on Low. Serve warm.

Sweet Potato & Cauliflower Mash

Serves: 6 | Total Time: 6 hours 15 minutes

1 head cauliflower, cut into florets	
1 shallot, chopped	1 cup vegetable stock
2 garlic cloves, chopped	Salt and pepper to taste
1 lb sweet potatoes, cubed	

Mix the cauliflower, sweet potatoes, shallot, garlic, vegetable stock, salt, and pepper in your Slow Cooker. Cover and cook for 6 hours on Low. When done, remove the lid, using a potato masher, mash it, and serve warm.

Effortless Tomato Chili

Serves: 6 | Total Time: 8 hours

1 lb heirloom tomatoes, halved	
2 cans (15-oz) black beans	1 tsp chili powder
2 red onions, sliced	½ tsp cumin powder
2 red bell peppers, sliced	½ tsp ground coriander
1 tsp dried thyme	1 cup vegetable stock
2 tbsp olive oil	Salt and pepper to taste

Preheat the oven to 400°F. Combine tomatoes, onions, bell peppers, olive oil, and thyme on a baking sheet. Sprinkle with salt and pepper and roast for 30 minutes. When done, transfer everything to your Slow Cooker. Put in beans, chili powder, cumin, coriander, vegetable stock, salt, and pepper. Cover and cook for 7 hours on Low. When done, remove the lid and serve immediately.

Barbecued Lentils

Serves: 6 | Total Time: 2 hours 15 minutes

1 cup red lentils	1 red bell pepper, diced
¼ cup brown lentils	3 garlic cloves, chopped
1 cup BBQ sauce	1 tbsp apple cider vinegar
1 ½ cups vegetable stock	½ tsp mustard seeds
2 shallots, chopped	½ tsp cumin seeds
1 carrot, diced	Salt and pepper to taste

Stir shallots, carrot, bell pepper, garlic, vinegar, mustard seeds, cumin seeds, lentils, BBQ sauce, vegetable stock, salt, and pepper in your Slow Cooker. Cover with the lid and cook for 2 hours on High. Serve right away.

Curried Bell Pepper & Potato Stew

Serves: 6 | Total Time: 4 hours 30 minutes

2 red bell peppers, diced	½ celery stalk, diced
2 lb potatoes, cubed	1 tbsp red curry paste
1 shallot, chopped	1 tbsp tomato paste
2 garlic cloves, chopped	½ lemongrass stalk, crushed
1 cup diced tomatoes	Salt and pepper to taste
1 cup vegetable stock	2 tbsp chopped cilantro

Stir potatoes, shallot, garlic, bell peppers, celery, curry paste, tomato paste, tomatoes, vegetable stock, lemongrass, salt, and pepper in your Slow Cooker. Cover with the lid and cook for 4 hours on Low. When done, remove the lid and top with cilantro to serve.

Mumbai Lentils

Serves: 6 | Total Time: 6 hours 15 minutes

2 garlic cloves, chopped	½ tsp cumin powder
1 sweet onion, chopped	¼ tsp chili powder
1 cup red lentils, rinsed	½ tsp turmeric powder
1 sweet potato, cubed	½ tsp garam masala
1 cup tomato sauce	½ tsp grated ginger
2 cups vegetable stock	Salt and pepper to taste
2 tbsp olive oil	

Mix the garlic, onion, olive oil, lentils, sweet potato, cumin, chili powder, turmeric, garam masala, tomato sauce, vegetable stock, ginger, salt, and pepper in your Slow Cooker. Cover with the lid and cook for 6 hours on Low. When done, remove the lid and serve warm.

BBQ Bourbon Black Beans

Serves: 6 | Total Time: 10 hours 15 minutes

1 cup BBQ sauce	1 tsp mustard seeds
2 cups vegetable stock	1 tbsp molasses
1 lb black beans, soaked	1 tbsp apple cider vinegar
1 tbsp bourbon	1 tsp Worcestershire sauce
¼ cup maple syrup	Salt and pepper to taste
½ cup ketchup	

In your Slow Cooker, combine beans, bourbon, maple syrup, BBQ sauce, vegetable stock, ketchup, mustard seeds, molasses, vinegar, Worcestershire sauce, salt, and pepper. Cover with the lid and cook for 10 hours on Low. When done, remove the lid and serve warm.

Tomato Chickpeas

Serves: 6 | Total Time: 2 hours 15 minutes

1 cup diced tomatoes	½ celery stalk, diced
1 cup tomato sauce	3 garlic cloves, minced
2 cans chickpeas, drained	1 tbsp lemon juice
2 shallots, chopped	1 tbsp chopped parsley
1 red bell pepper, diced	Salt and pepper to taste

Mix the chickpeas, shallots, bell pepper, celery, garlic, tomatoes, tomato sauce, lemon juice, parsley, salt, and pepper in your Slow Cooker. Cover with the lid and cook for 2 hours on High. Serve warm.

Pizza a la Puttanesca

Serves: 6 | Total Time: 2 hours 30 minutes

DOUGH:

2 cups all-purpose flour	1 cup warm water
1 tsp active dry yeast	¼ tsp salt
2 tbsp olive oil	

TOPPING:

½ cup crushed fire-roasted tomatoes	
12 Kalamata olives, sliced	½ tsp dried basil
¼ cup green olives, sliced	½ tsp dried oregano
1 tbsp capers, chopped	

In a bowl, whisk olive oil, flour, yeast, water, and salt for 2-3 minutes until well combined. Flatten the dough into a round sheet. Spread tomatoes, olives, and capers and sprinkle with basil and oregano. Put the pizza in your Slow Cooker, cover with it the lid and cook for 1 ½ hours on High. Serve right away.

Pesto Quinoa with Tofu & Vegetables

Serves: 6 | Total Time: 6 hours 15 minutes

1 cup cauliflower florets	1 carrot, diced
1 cup broccoli florets	½ cup green peas
6 oz firm tofu, cubed	1 tbsp Pesto sauce
½ cup quinoa, rinsed	2 tbsp green lentils
1 celery stalk, sliced	1 cup vegetable stock
1 parsnip, diced	Salt and pepper to taste

Stir tofu, quinoa, celery, parsnip, carrot, green peas, cauliflower, broccoli, pesto sauce, lentils, vegetable stock, salt, and pepper in your Slow Cooker. Cover with the lid and cook for 6 hours on Low. Serve immediately.

Tasty Potato & Spinach Casserole

Serves: 6 | Total Time: 4 hours 15 minutes

2 lb potatoes, cubed	¼ tsp coriander powder
4 cups spinach	¼ tsp fennel seeds
1 shallot, chopped	2 tbsp olive oil
2 garlic cloves, chopped	1 cup vegetable stock
¼ tsp cumin powder	Salt and pepper to taste

Warm the olive oil in a pan over medium heat. Place the shallot and garlic and cook for 2 minutes until softened. Sprinkle with cumin, coriander, and fennel seeds and toast for 30 seconds to release flavors. Transfer everything to your Slow Cooker. Add in potatoes, spinach, vegetable stock, salt, and pepper. Cover with the lid and cook for 4 hours on Low. Serve warm. Enjoy!

Southern Pie in a Pot

Serves: 6 | Total Time: 6 hours 30 minutes

1 red bell pepper, diced	1 tbsp all-purpose flour
1 onion, chopped	1 cup green peas
1 celery stalk, diced	1 cup chopped green beans
1 carrot, diced	1 cup vegetable stock
6 oz biscuit dough	Salt and pepper to taste
½ tsp dried oregano	

In a bowl, mix celery, carrot, bell pepper, onion, oregano, and flour until well combined. Pour it into your Slow Cooker. Add in green peas, green beans, vegetable stock, salt, and pepper and put the biscuit dough on top. Cover with the lid and cook for 6 hours on Low. Serve warm.

The Ultimate Teriyaki Tofu

Serves: 6 | Total Time: 2 hours 15 minutes

1 ½ lb firm tofu, cubed	2 tbsp brown sugar
1 cup pineapple juice	1 tsp grated ginger
½ cup vegetable stock	½ tsp garlic powder
1 tbsp tamarind paste	2 tbsp soy sauce
1 tbsp mirin	3 cups cooked rice
1 tsp sesame oil	

Add the tofu, pineapple juice, vegetable stock, tamarind paste, mirin, sugar, sesame oil, ginger, garlic powder, and soy sauce in your Slow Cooker and stir. Cover and cook for 2 hours on High. Serve over cooked rice.

Mushroom Risotto

Serves: 6 | Total Time: 4 hours 15 minutes

2 cups sliced mushrooms	2 tbsp olive oil
1 shallot, chopped	¼ cup white wine
1 garlic clove, chopped	1 ½ cups vegetable stock
3/4 cup risotto rice	Salt and pepper to taste

Mix the olive oil, mushrooms, shallot, garlic, risotto rice, wine, vegetable stock, salt, and pepper in your Slow Cooker. Cover with the lid and cook for 4 hours on Low. When done, remove the lid and serve warm.

Parmesan Barley Risotto

Serves: 6 | Total Time: 6 hours 15 minutes

1 carrot, diced	2 cups vegetable stock
1 cup pearl barley	¼ cup grated Parmesan
1 shallot, chopped	2 tbsp olive oil
1 celery stalk, diced	Salt and pepper to taste
1 garlic clove, minced	1 thyme sprig

Warm the olive oil in a pan over medium heat. Place the shallot, celery, garlic, and carrot and cook for 2 minutes until softened. Transfer everything to your Slow Cooker. Put in barley, vegetable stock, thyme, salt, and pepper. Cover with the lid and cook for 6 hours on Low. Stir in Parmesan cheese and serve immediately. Enjoy!

Roasted Quinoa & Tomato Chili

Serves: 6 | Total Time: 6 hours 15 minutes

1 can (15 oz) black beans	1 ½ cups vegetable stock
1 can fire-roasted tomatoes	¼ tsp chili powder
1 sweet onion, chopped	¼ tsp cumin powder
2 garlic cloves, chopped	Salt and pepper to taste
½ cup quinoa, rinsed	

Mix the quinoa, beans, tomatoes, onion, garlic, vegetable stock, chili powder, cumin, salt, and pepper in your Slow Cooker. Cover and cook for 6 hours on Low. Serve.

Cheddar Sweet Corn

Serves: 6 | Total Time: 3 hours 15 minutes

1 cup grated cheddar cheese	1 cup cream cheese
½ cup heavy cream	Salt and pepper to taste
2 cans (15 oz) sweet corn	1 pinch nutmeg

Put corn, cream cheese, cheddar cheese, heavy cream, nutmeg, salt, and pepper in your Slow Cooker and stir. Cover and cook for 3 hours on Low. Serve right away.

Asparagus & Green Pea Farro

Serves: 6 | Total Time: 5 hours 15 minutes

1 bunch asparagus, trimmed and chopped	
1 cup green peas	2 cups vegetable stock
1 small onion, chopped	2 tbsp olive oil
1 celery stalk, sliced	½ lemon, juiced
1 cup farro	Salt and pepper to taste

Mix the olive oil, onion, celery, farro, vegetable stock, asparagus, green peas, salt, and pepper in your Slow Cooker. Cover and cook for 5 hours on Low. Serve.

Tomato Cauliflower

Serves: 4 | Total Time: 6 hours 15 minutes

1 cup tomato sauce	½ tsp dried thyme
1 head cauliflower	¼ tsp salt
¼ tsp garlic powder	1 pinch cayenne pepper
¼ tsp onion powder	½ cup vegetable stock

Add cauliflower to your Slow Cooker. In a bowl, whisk tomato sauce, garlic powder, onion powder, thyme, salt, cayenne pepper, and vegetable stock and pour it into the pot. Cover and cook for 6 hours on Low. Serve warm.

Orzo & Bean Tacos

Serves: 6 | Total Time: 8 hours 15 minutes

1 can (15 oz) black beans	2 cups vegetable stock
1 large onion, chopped	2 tbsp tomato paste
2 carrots, diced	2 tbsp olive oil
1 celery stalk, diced	2 tbsp chopped cilantro
1 cup orzo	Salt and pepper to taste
1 cup diced tomatoes	Flour tortillas for serving

Warm the olive oil in a pan over medium heat. Place the onion, carrots, and celery and cook for 5 minutes until softened. Transfer everything to your Slow Cooker. Put in orzo, tomatoes, vegetable stock, tomato paste, beans, salt, and pepper. Cover and cook for 8 hours on Low. Divide between tortillas and top with cilantro to serve.

Hearty Lasagna

Serves: 6 | Total Time: 6 hours 30 minutes

1 ½ cups grated mozzarella	1 celery stalk, diced
1 large zucchini	½ tsp dried oregano
1 large eggplant	2 tbsp chopped parsley
1 can diced tomatoes	2 cups vegetable stock
1 cup white rice	Salt and pepper to taste

Using a vegetable peeler, make eggplant and zucchini ribbons. Set aside. In a bowl, combine tomatoes, rice, celery, oregano, parsley, salt, and pepper. In your Slow Cooker, put a layer of veggie ribbons, then a layer of rice mixture, and finally a layer of veggie ribbons. Repeat the process until any ingredients are left. Pour in the stock and top with mozzarella. Cook for 6 hours on Low.

Cauliflower & Chickpea Casserole

Serves: 8 | Total Time: 8 hours 30 minutes

1 head cauliflower, cut into florets	
1 can diced tomatoes	½ tsp ground ginger
2 large onions, chopped	2 tbsp olive oil
4 garlic cloves, chopped	1 pinch cinnamon powder
1 celery stalk, sliced	2 cups chickpeas, soaked
1 carrot, diced	3 cups vegetable stock
¼ tsp cumin seeds	1 thyme sprig
½ tsp fennel seeds	Salt and pepper to taste

Warm the olive oil in a pan over medium heat. Place the onions, garlic, celery, and carrots, and cook for 5 minutes until softened. Transfer everything to your Slow Cooker. Add in cumin seeds, fennel seeds, ginger, cinnamon powder, chickpeas, cauliflower, tomatoes, vegetable stock, thyme, salt, and pepper. Cover with the lid and cook for 8 hours on Low. Serve immediately.

Curry Lentils with Tofu

Serves: 6 | Total Time: 6 hours 15 minutes

1 head cauliflower, cut into florets	
2 tbsp canola oil	2 tbsp red curry paste
8 oz firm tofu, cubed	1 bay leaf
1 cup red lentils	½ lemongrass stalk, crushed
2 cups vegetable stock	½ tsp grated ginger
2 tbsp tomato paste	Salt and pepper to taste

Warm the canola oil in a pan over medium heat. Place the tofu and cook until golden brown and crispy on all sides. Add it to your Slow Cooker. Add in curry paste, lentils, vegetable stock, cauliflower, tomato paste, bay leaf, lemongrass, ginger, salt, and pepper. Cover with the lid and cook for 6 hours on Low. Serve warm.

Saucy Zucchini Rolls

Serves: 8 | Total Time: 7 hours

1 large eggplant, cut into sticks	
2 carrots, cut into match sticks	
2 parsnips, cut into matchsticks	
1 cup tomato sauce	1 tsp dried thyme
2 large zucchinis	½ tsp dried oregano
1 cup vegetable stock	Salt and pepper to taste

Make zucchini ribbons with a vegetable peeler and place them onto a cutting board. Top with some parsnip, carrot, and eggplant sticks and wrap them. Place the rolls in your Slow Cooker and add in tomato sauce, vegetable stock, thyme, oregano, salt, and pepper. Cover with the lid and cook for 6 hours on Low. Serve warm.

Rice with Tofu & Broccoli

Serves: 6 | Total Time: 4 hours 15 minutes

1 large head broccoli, cut into small florets	
8 oz firm tofu, cubed	1 tbsp lemon juice
1 cup white rice	¼ tsp garlic powder
¼ cup white wine	¼ tsp onion powder
2 cups vegetable stock	½ tsp dried oregano
2 tbsp olive oil	Salt and pepper to taste

Warm the olive oil in a pan over medium heat. Place the tofu and cook until golden on all sides. Add it to your Slow Cooker. Add in broccoli, rice, wine, vegetable stock, lemon juice, garlic powder, onion powder, oregano, salt, and pepper. Cover with the lid and cook for 6 hours on Low. When done, remove the lid and serve right away.

Special Tofu Kurma

Serves: 6 | Total Time: 8 hours 15 minutes

2 cups cauliflower florets	½ tsp grated ginger
1 cup diced tomatoes	½ tsp turmeric powder
8 oz firm tofu, cubed	¼ tsp chili powder
2 red bell peppers, diced	½ tsp curry powder
1 carrot, diced	1 cup vegetable stock
½ celery stalk, diced	½ cup coconut milk
2 tbsp olive oil	Salt and pepper to taste

Warm the olive oil in a pan over medium heat. Place the tofu and cook until golden and crispy on all sides. Add it to your Slow Cooker. Put in bell peppers, carrot, celery, cauliflower, tomatoes, ginger, turmeric, chili powder, curry powder, vegetable stock, coconut milk, salt, and pepper. Cover and cook for 8 hours on Low. Serve warm.

Tofu Bolognese Sauce

Serves: 6 | Total Time: 8 hours 15 minutes

1 can (15 oz) diced tomatoes	1 parsnip, grated
12 oz firm tofu, crumbled	1 tsp dried basil
2 large onions, chopped	1 tsp dried oregano
6 garlic cloves, minced	2 tbsp tomato paste
2 celery stalks, diced	1 cup vegetable stock
2 carrots, grated	2 tbsp lemon juice
2 tbsp olive oil	Salt and pepper to taste

Warm the olive oil in a pan over medium heat. Place the tofu and cook for 2-3 minutes until golden and crispy on all sides. Add it to your Slow Cooker. Add in onions, garlic, celery, carrots, parsnip, basil, oregano, tomato paste, tomatoes, vegetable stock, lemon juice, salt, and pepper. Cover and cook for 8 hours on Low. Serve.

Artichoke & Eggplant Tapenade

Serves: 6 | Total Time: 4 hours 15 minutes

1 large eggplant, peeled and diced	
1 cup green olives, sliced	1 tbsp olive oil
½ cup black olives, sliced	¼ tsp dried basil
1 can fire-roasted tomatoes	¼ tsp dried oregano
2 artichoke hearts, diced	Salt and pepper to taste
1 cup vegetable stock	

Stir eggplant, olive oil, olives, tomatoes, artichoke hearts, vegetable stock, basil, oregano, salt, and pepper in your Slow Cooker. Cover with the lid and cook for 2 hours on Low, then cook for 2 hours on High. Serve warm.

Hoisin Eggplant Casserole

Serves: 4 | Total Time: 2 hours 15 minutes

1 large eggplant, peeled and cubed	
¼ cup hoisin sauce	1 tbsp soy sauce
½ cup coconut milk	1 tsp rice vinegar
3 tbsp coconut oil	1 tsp cayenne pepper

Melt the coconut oil in a pan over medium heat. Place the eggplant and cook until golden brown on all sides. Add it to your Slow Cooker. Add in hoisin sauce, soy sauce, coconut milk, vinegar, and cayenne pepper. Cover and cook for 4 hours on High. Serve.

Roasted Tomato & Chickpea Meal

Serves: 6 | Total Time: 8 hours 15 minutes

1 can fire-roasted tomatoes	2 cups vegetable stock
1 ½ cups chickpeas, soaked	1 bay leaf
2 shallots, chopped	½ tsp garlic powder
1 celery stalk, diced	¼ tsp chili powder
1 tsp dried oregano	Salt and pepper to taste

Stir chickpeas, shallots, celery, tomatoes, oregano, vegetable stock, bay leaf, garlic powder, chili powder, salt, and pepper in your Slow Cooker. Cover with the lid and cook for 7 hours on Low. Serve immediately.

Tofu & Noodle Stroganoff

Serves: 6 | Total Time: 6 hours 30 minutes

1 can condensed cream of mushroom soup	
2 Portobello mushrooms, sliced	
1 oz dried wild mushrooms, chopped	
1 cup tofu cream	1 ½ cup vegetable stock
1 tsp Worcestershire sauce	½ cup farfalle pasta
1 large onion, chopped	Salt and pepper to taste

Stir mushrooms, Worcestershire sauce, onion, mushroom soup, tofu cream, vegetable stock, salt, pepper, and farfalle pasta in your Slow Cooker. Cover with the lid and cook for 6 hours on Low. Serve warm.

Sweet Holiday Vegetable Stew

Serves: 6 | Total Time: 6 hours 30 minutes

2 red apples, peeled and cubed	
4 cups pumpkin cubes	¼ cup red wine
½ cinnamon stick	2 tbsp olive oil
2 shallots, chopped	1 cup vegetable stock
2 garlic cloves, chopped	1 thyme sprig
2 ripe tomatoes, diced	Salt and pepper to taste

Mix the pumpkin, apples, cinnamon stick, olive oil, shallots, garlic, tomatoes, wine, vegetable stock, thyme, salt, and pepper in your Slow Cooker. Cover with the lid and cook for 6 hours on Low. Serve warm.

Original Chole

Serves: 6 | Total Time: 8 hours 15 minutes

2 cups vegetable stock	2 tbsp tomato paste
½ cup tomato sauce	½ tsp cumin powder
1 cup coconut milk	½ tsp dried oregano
1 ½ cups dried chickpeas	1 stalk lemongrass, crushed
1 lb butternut squash cubes	2 kaffir lime leaves
½ tsp chili powder	1 lime, juiced
1 tsp curry powder	2 tbsp chopped cilantro
½ tsp garam masala	Salt and pepper to taste

In your Slow Cooker, combine chickpeas, butternut squash, chili powder, curry powder, garam masala, tomato paste, tomato sauce, cumin, oregano, vegetable stock, coconut milk, lemongrass, kaffir leaves, salt, and pepper. Cover with the lid and cook for 8 hours on Low. Sprinkle with lime juice and cilantro to serve.

Sweet Potato & Red Lentil Casserole

Serves: 6 | Total Time: 7 hours 15 minutes

1 sweet potato, diced	2 cups vegetable stock
1 carrot, diced	½ tsp cumin seeds
1 cup red lentils	½ red chili, chopped
2 ripe tomatoes, diced	Salt and pepper to taste

In your Slow Cooker, stir lentils, sweet potato, carrot, tomatoes, vegetable stock, cumin seeds, red chili, salt, and pepper. Cover and cook for 7 hours on Low. Serve.

Tomato Vegetarian Stew

Serves: 6 | Total Time: 2 hours 15 minutes

1 lb frozen green peas	1 red bell pepper, diced
1 cup diced tomatoes	1 carrot, diced
2 shallots, chopped	2 tbsp olive oil
2 garlic cloves, chopped	1 bay leaf
1 celery stalk, sliced	Salt and pepper to taste

Warm the olive oil in a pan over medium heat. Place the shallots and garlic and cook for 2 minutes until softened. Transfer everything to your Slow Cooker. Put in celery, bell pepper, carrot, green peas, tomatoes, bay leaf, salt, and pepper. Cover and cook for 2 hours on High. Serve.

Quinoa & Squash Bites

Serves: 6 | Total Time: 2 hours 30 minutes

1 can diced tomatoes	1 shallot, chopped
1 cup vegetable stock	½ tsp dried cumin powder
1 small butternut squash	½ tsp dried oregano
1 cup cooked quinoa	Salt and pepper to taste
1 garlic clove, chopped	

Pour tomatoes and vegetable stock in your Slow Cooker and stir. Clean and peel the butternut squash, and using a fine grater, shred it. Add in quinoa, garlic, shallot, cumin, oregano, salt, and pepper, and toss until well combined. Make small balls out of the mixture and place them into the pot. Cover with the lid and cook for 2 hours on High. Serve warm with cooked rice or potato purée if desired.

Exotic Tofu Curry

Serves: 6 | Total Time: 3 hours 15 minutes

1 ripe mango, cubed	¼ tsp cumin powder
8 oz firm tofu, cubed	1 bay leaf
2 shallots, chopped	1 cup coconut milk
2 garlic cloves, minced	2 tbsp olive oil
¼ tsp cayenne pepper	2 tbsp tomato paste
¼ tsp garam masala	1 cup vegetable stock
¼ tsp ground ginger	Salt and pepper to taste

Warm the olive oil in a pan over medium heat. Place the tofu and cook until golden and crispy on all sides. Add it to your Slow Cooker. Add in shallots, garlic, cayenne pepper, garam masala, ginger, cumin, bay leaf, coconut milk, mango, tomato paste, vegetable stock, salt, and pepper. Cover and cook for 3 hours on High. Serve.

Brown Rice & Mung Bean Casserole

Serves: 6 | Total Time: 6 hours 15 minutes

1 carrot, diced	½ tsp dried oregano
2 ripe tomatoes, diced	½ tsp dried basil
1 cup mung beans, rinsed	¼ tsp cumin seeds
½ cup brown rice	¼ tsp smoked paprika
3 cups vegetable stock	Salt and pepper to taste
1 celery stalk, sliced	

In your Slow Cooker, add beans, rice, vegetable stock, celery, carrot, tomatoes, oregano, basil, cumin seeds, paprika, salt, and pepper and stir. Cover with the lid and cook for 6 hours on Low. Serve warm.

No-Meat Shepherd's Pie

Serves: 6 | Total Time: 7 hours 30 minutes

1 ½ lb potatoes, cubed	1 ½ cups vegetable stock
1 cup frozen green peas	½ tsp dried oregano
1 cup frozen corn	1 tbsp cornstarch
2 large carrots, diced	Salt and pepper to taste
2 cups sliced mushrooms	

Put potatoes in a pot with salted boiling water and cook until tender. Using a potato masher, mash them until smooth, adding some cooking liquid. In a bowl, mix green peas, corn, carrots, mushrooms, cornstarch, oregano, salt, and pepper. Transfer everything to your Slow Cooker. Pour in vegetable stock and top with potato purée. Cover and cook for 7 hours on Low. Serve warm.

Cottage & Spinach Side Dish

Serves: 6 | Total Time: 6 hours 15 minutes

1 cup green peas	4 eggs
2 cups cottage cheese	¼ cup all-purpose flour
16 oz frozen spinach	½ tsp baking powder
2 tbsp butter	Salt and pepper to taste

In a bowl, mix spinach, green peas, cottage cheese, butter, eggs, flour, baking powder, salt, and pepper. Transfer everything to your Slow Cooker. Cover with the lid and cook for 6 hours on Low. Serve immediately.

Barley, Corn & Mushroom Casserole

Serves: 6 | Total Time: 6 hours 30 minutes

2 garlic cloves, chopped	½ tsp dried oregano
3 cups cooked barley	½ tsp dried sage
2 cups sliced mushrooms	½ cup tomato sauce
½ cup sweet corn	2 tbsp pine nuts
1 small onion, chopped	Salt and pepper to taste
2 tbsp olive oil	

Warm the olive oil in a pan over medium heat. Place the onion and garlic and cook for 2 minutes until softened. Transfer everything to your Slow Cooker. Add in barley, oregano, sage, tomato sauce, mushrooms, corn, pine nuts, salt, and pepper. Cook for 6 hours on Low. Serve.

New Chickpea Tikka Masala

Serves: 6 | Total Time: 6 hours 30 minutes

2 cans (15-oz) chickpeas	1 tsp garam masala
1 can diced tomatoes	2 tbsp olive oil
1 cup coconut milk	½ tsp turmeric powder
1 large onion, chopped	½ tsp red chili, sliced
4 garlic cloves, chopped	Salt and pepper to taste
1 tsp grated ginger	2 tbsp chopped cilantro

Warm the olive oil in a pan over medium heat. Place the onion and garlic and cook for 2 minutes until softened. Transfer everything to your Slow Cooker. Add in ginger, garam masala, turmeric, red chili, chickpeas, tomatoes, coconut milk, salt, and pepper. Cover with the lid and cook for 6 hours on Low. Serve topped with cilantro.

Cauliflower & Tofu Casserole

Serves: 6 | Total Time: 2 hours 15 minutes

1 head cauliflower, cut into florets	
8 oz firm tofu, cubed	½ tsp turmeric powder
1 ½ cups coconut milk	2 tbsp olive oil
1 tsp cumin powder	1 bay leaf
½ tsp chili powder	½ lemongrass stalk, crushed
¼ tsp ground coriander	Salt and pepper to taste

Sprinkle the tofu with cumin, chili powder, coriander, and turmeric. Warm the olive oil in a pan over medium heat. Cook the tofu until golden on all sides. Add it to your Slow Cooker. Add in coconut milk, cauliflower, bay leaf, lemongrass, salt, and pepper. Cover with the lid and cook for 2 hours on High. Serve warm.

Parmesan Asparagus & Barley Casserole

Serves: 6 | Total Time: 6 hours 15 minutes

½ cup grated Parmesan	½ tsp fennel seeds
1 lb asparagus, chopped	1 cup pearl barley
1 shallot, chopped	2 cups vegetable stock
1 garlic clove, chopped	Salt and pepper to taste

Mix the asparagus, shallot, garlic, fennel seeds, barley, vegetable stock, salt, and pepper in your Slow Cooker. Cover with the lid and cook for 6 hours on Low. Sprinkle with Parmesan cheese. Serve and enjoy!

Butternut Squash Quinoa with Beans

Serves: 6 | Total Time: 6 hours 15 minutes

2 cups bread cubes	1 shallot, chopped
1 can (15 oz) black beans	2 garlic cloves, chopped
1 ½ cups cooked quinoa	4 eggs, beaten
1 lb butternut squash cubes	Salt and pepper to taste

Mix the quinoa, butternut squash, shallot, garlic, bread cubes, beans, eggs, salt, and pepper in your Slow Cooker. Cover and cook for 6 hours on Low. Serve right away.

Parsnip & Sweet Potato Risotto

Serves: 6 | Total Time: 6 hours 15 minutes

1 cup white rice	1 ¾ cups vegetable stock
1 parsnip, diced	2 tbsp grated Parmesan
1 carrot, diced	½ tsp dried sage
1 parsley root, diced	2 tbsp olive oil
1 sweet potato, diced	Salt and pepper to taste
¼ cup white wine	

In your Slow Cooker, combine rice, olive oil, parsnip, carrot, parsley, sweet potato, sage, wine, vegetable stock, salt, and pepper. Cover with the lid and cook for 6 hours on Low. Mix in Parmesan cheese and serve.

Tempeh & Figs in Red Wine Glaze

Serves: 6 | Total Time: 8 hours 15 minutes

16 oz tempeh, cubed	1 cup tomato sauce
2 red onions, sliced	2 tbsp olive oil
¼ cup dried figs, chopped	1 bay leaf
1 cup red wine	Salt and pepper to taste

Mix the tempeh, onions, figs, olive oil, wine, tomato sauce, bay leaf, salt, and pepper in your Slow Cooker. Cover and cook for 8 hours on Low. Serve warm.

Fresh Ratatouille with Tofu

Serves: 6 | Total Time: 3 hours 30 minutes

1 small eggplant, peeled and cubed	
2 ripe tomatoes, diced	1 red onion, chopped
1 carrot, diced	2 tbsp olive oil
2 red bell peppers, diced	1 zucchini, cubed
10 oz firm tofu, cubed	½ tsp dried oregano
1 tsp cumin powder	Salt and pepper to taste

Sprinkle the tofu with cumin, salt, and pepper. Warm the olive oil in a pan over medium heat. Put the tofu and cook until golden on all sides. Add it to your Slow Cooker. Put in eggplant, onion, tomatoes, carrot, bell peppers, zucchini, and oregano. Cover with the lid and cook for 3 hours on High. Serve immediately.

Oregano Rice Pilaf with Broccoli

Serves: 4 | Total Time: 2 hours 15 minutes

1 shallot, chopped	1 cup vegetable stock
2/3 cup white rice	½ tsp dried oregano
10 oz broccoli florets	Salt and pepper to taste

In your Slow Cooker, put broccoli, shallot, wine, vegetable stock, 1 cup of water, oregano, salt, and pepper and stir. Cover and cook for 2 hours on High. Serve right away.

Jalapeño Quinoa with Black Beans

Serves: 6 | Total Time: 6 hours 15 minutes

2 ripe tomatoes, diced	1 shallot, chopped
1 can (15 oz) black beans	2 garlic cloves, chopped
½ cup red quinoa, rinsed	½ cup frozen sweet corn
2 red bell peppers, diced	1 ½ cups vegetable stock
2 jalapenos, chopped	Salt and pepper to taste

Stir quinoa, bell peppers, jalapeños, tomatoes, shallot, garlic, tomatoes, beans, corn, vegetable stock, salt, and pepper in your Slow Cooker. Cover with the lid and cook for 6 hours on Low. Serve warm.

Simple White Rice with Peas

Serves: 6 | Total Time: 4 hours

1 bay leaf	1 cup green peas
2 cups white rice	Salt and pepper to taste

Mix the rice, green peas, 4 cups of water, bay leaf, salt, and pepper in your Slow Cooker. Cover with the lid and cook for 4 hours on Low. Serve warm.

Original Jambalaya

Serves: 6 | Total Time: 6 hours 30 minutes

½ head cauliflower, cut into florets

2 ripe tomatoes, diced	½ tsp Cajun seasoning
1 sweet potato, cubed	2 tbsp olive oil
8 oz firm tofu, cubed	1 tbsp tomato paste
1 large onion, chopped	1¼ cups vegetable stock
2 red bell peppers, diced	Salt and pepper to taste
2 garlic cloves, chopped	

Warm the olive oil in a pan over medium heat. Place the tofu and cook until golden on all sides. Add it to your Slow Cooker. Put in onion, bell peppers, garlic, cajun seasoning, tomatoes, cauliflower, sweet potato, tomato paste, vegetable stock, salt, and pepper. Cover with the lid and cook for 6 hours on Low. Serve right away.

Herbed Tomato Dish with Croutons

Serves: 6 | Total Time: 6 hours 15 minutes

4 ripe heirloom tomatoes, peeled and cubed

2 sweet onions, chopped	4 cups bread croutons
2 garlic cloves, chopped	2 tbsp olive oil
2 red bell peppers, diced	½ tsp dried thyme
2 tbsp tomato paste	½ tsp dried oregano
1 ½ cups vegetable stock	Salt and pepper to taste

Warm the olive oil in a pan over medium heat. Place the onions and garlic and cook for 2 minutes until softened. Transfer everything to your Slow Cooker. Add in tomatoes, bell peppers, tomato paste, vegetable stock, croutons, thyme, oregano, salt, and pepper. Cover with the lid and cook for 6 hours on Low. Serve right away.

Homestyle Chinese Hot Pot

Serves: 6 | Total Time: 2 hours 15 minutes

4 oz shiitake mushrooms, chopped

10 oz firm tofu, cubed	1 cup chopped chestnuts
2 red bell peppers, sliced	1 cup vegetable stock
2 garlic cloves, chopped	1 tbsp canola oil
1 tsp grated ginger	½ tsp sesame oil
1 shallot, chopped	¼ tsp chili flakes
1 carrot, cut into sticks	1 tsp tamarind paste
1 celery stalk, cut into sticks	2 tbsp soy sauce

Warm the canola oil in a pan over medium heat. Place garlic, ginger, shallot, and carrot and cook for 2 minutes until softened. Transfer everything to your Slow Cooker. Add in celery, chestnuts, vegetable stock, tofu, mushrooms, bell peppers, chili flakes, tamarind paste, soy sauce, and sesame oil. Cook for 2 hours on High. Serve.

Sticky Baked Beans

Serves: 6 | Total Time: 6 hours 15 minutes

1 large onion, chopped	2 tbsp brown sugar
1 lb dried kidney beans	½ tsp celery seeds
2 cups vegetable stock	½ tsp cumin seeds
2 tbsp molasses	1 cup water
1 tsp mustard seeds	1 bay leaf
1 tsp Worcestershire sauce	Salt and pepper to taste

In your Slow Cooker, combine beans, molasses, mustard seeds, Worcestershire sauce, sugar, onion, vegetable stock, celery seeds, cumin seeds, water, bay leaf, salt, and pepper. Cover and cook for 6 hours on Low. Serve warm.

Shallot & Fennel Risotto

Serves: 6 | Total Time: 4 hours 15 minutes

1 shallot, chopped	¼ cup white wine
1 small fennel bulb, sliced	2 cups vegetable stock
2 garlic cloves, chopped	2 tbsp olive oil
1 cup white rice	Salt and pepper to taste

Warm the olive oil in a pan over medium heat. Place the garlic and shallot and cook for 2 minutes until softened. Add in fennel and cook for 2 more minutes. Transfer everything to your Slow Cooker. Put in rice, wine, vegetable stock, salt, and pepper. Cover with the lid and cook for 4 hours on Low. Serve and enjoy!

Cheesy Summer Squash & Rice Meal

Serves: 6 | Total Time: 4 hours 15 minutes

3 summer squashes, sliced	2 cups cooked rice
2 green bell peppers, diced	4 eggs, beaten
1 lb cherry tomatoes, halved	2 tbsp olive oil
2 garlic cloves, minced	Salt and pepper to taste
1 sweet onion, chopped	1 cup shredded mozzarella

Mix the squashes, olive oil, garlic, onion, bell peppers, tomatoes, rice, eggs, salt, and pepper in your Slow Cooker. Cover with the lid and cook for 4 hours on Low. Stir in mozzarella cheese and serve immediately.

South Korean Eggplants & Mushrooms

Serves: 6 | Total Time: 2 hours 15 minutes

1 oz dried porcini mushrooms, rehydrated and chopped
2 eggplants, peeled and cubed

2 garlic cloves, chopped	2 tbsp olive oil
1 large onion, sliced	½ tsp dried oregano
½ tsp cumin seeds	¼ cup soy sauce
¼ tsp chili powder	1 tsp hot sauce

Mix the olive oil, eggplants, garlic, onion, cumin seeds, chili powder, mushrooms, oregano, soy sauce, and hot sauce in your Slow Cooker. Cover with the lid and cook for 2 hours on High. Serve chilled.

Vegetarian Sloppy Joes

Serves: 6 | Total Time: 8 hours 15 minutes

1 small head green cabbage, shredded

2 carrots, sliced	2 cups water
1 shallot, chopped	2 tbsp olive oil
4 garlic cloves, minced	1 tbsp balsamic vinegar
1 cup diced tomatoes	2 tbsp tomato paste
1 cup dried pinto beans	½ tsp chili powder
2 red bell peppers, diced	½ tsp mustard seeds
1 cup frozen corn	Salt and pepper to taste

Warm the olive oil in a pan over medium heat. Place the carrots, shallot, and garlic and cook for 5 minutes until softened. Transfer everything to your Slow Cooker. Put in chili powder, beans, bell peppers, balsamic vinegar, tomato paste, tomatoes, water, cabbage, corn, mustard seeds, salt, and pepper. Cover with the lid and cook for 8 hours on Low. Serve warm and enjoy!

Zucchini & Bell Pepper Casserole

Serves: 6 | Total Time: 2 hours 15 minutes

1 yellow bell pepper, diced	1 zucchini, cubed
6 sun-dried tomatoes, diced	2 tbsp olive oil
1 shallot, chopped	1 tbsp lemon juice
2 garlic cloves, minced	1 cup vegetable stock
1 fennel bulb, sliced	Salt and pepper to taste

Warm the olive oil in a pan over medium heat. Place the shallot, garlic, and fennel and cook for 5 minutes until softened. Transfer everything to your Slow Cooker. Add in zucchini, bell pepper, tomatoes, lemon juice, vegetable stock, salt, and pepper. Cook for 2 hours on High. Serve.

Spicy Thre Bean Cornbread in a Pot

Serves: 6 | Total Time: 6 hours 30 minutes

1 can (15 oz) red beans	½ cup yellow cornmeal
1 can (15 oz) white beans	½ cup all-purpose flour
1 can (15 oz) black beans	2 tbsp tomato sauce
1 cup fire-roasted tomatoes	1 tsp baking powder
2 red bell peppers, diced	½ cup buttermilk
1 cup frozen corn	½ cup whole milk
1 jalapeno pepper, chopped	¼ tsp cumin seeds
1 cup vegetable stock	Salt and pepper to taste
½ tsp dried thyme	

Mix the beans, tomatoes, bell peppers, tomato sauce, corn, jalapeño pepper, vegetable stock, thyme, cumin seeds, salt, and pepper in your Slow Cooker. Whisk cornmeal, flour, baking powder, buttermilk, and milk in a bowl until well combined and pour it into the pot. Cover and cook for 6 hours on Low. Serve right away.

Hong-Kong Hot Pot

Serves: 6 | Total Time: 6 hours 15 minutes

4 oz shiitake mushrooms, chopped

12 oz firm tofu, cubed	4 garlic cloves, chopped
2 carrots, sliced	1 star anise
1 lb chopped green beans	½ cinnamon stick
1 large onion, chopped	1 tbsp balsamic vinegar
2 cups baby carrots	2 tbsp soy sauce
1 turnip, cubed	1 tbsp brown sugar
1 parsnip, diced	Salt and pepper to taste

Mix the onion, carrots, turnip, parsnip, baby carrots, green beans, garlic, star anise, cinnamon stick, mushrooms, balsamic vinegar, tofu, soy sauce, sugar, salt, and pepper in your Slow Cooker. Cover with the lid and cook for 6 hours on Low. When done, remove the lid and serve right away or store it in a container in the freezer.

Syrupy Teriyaki Tofu with Chipotle

Serves: 6 | Total Time: 6 hours 15 minutes

18 oz firm tofu, cubed	1 tbsp date syrup
1 chipotle pepper, chopped	½ tsp sesame oil
1 can crushed pineapple	2 tbsp soy sauce
1 shallot, chopped	2 tbsp tomato paste
4 garlic cloves, minced	1 lime, juiced
1 tsp grated ginger	Salt and pepper to taste

In your Slow Cooker, add tofu, pineapple, shallot, garlic, ginger, date syrup, chipotle pepper, soy sauce, tomato paste, lime juice, sesame oil, salt, and pepper, and stir. Cover and cook for 6 hours on Low. Serve warm.

Refried White Beans

Serves: 6 | Total Time: 2 hours 30 minutes

1 chipotle pepper, diced	½ tsp cumin powder
1 can fire-roasted tomatoes	2 tbsp tomato paste
2 cans (15-oz) white beans	1 cup vegetable stock
1 tsp chili powder	Salt and pepper to taste

Stir the beans, bell peppers, tomatoes, chili powder, cumin, tomato paste, vegetable stock, chipotle pepper, salt, and pepper in your Slow Cooker. Cover with the lid and cook for 2 hours on High. Serve warm.

Creamy Corn Grits with Tomato Beans

Serves: 6 | Total Time: 2 hours 30 minutes

8 sun-dried tomatoes, diced	1 ½ cups whole milk
1 can fire-roasted tomatoes	2/3 cup corn grits
2 cans (15-oz) white beans	1 tbsp butter
1 thyme sprig	½ cup grated cheddar
1 bay leaf	Salt and pepper to taste

Mix the beans, sun-dried tomatoes, roasted tomatoes, thyme, bay leaf, salt, and pepper in your Slow Cooker. Cover with the lid and cook for 2 hours on High. Meanwhile, pour the milk in a pot over high heat and bring it to a boil. Low the heat put in corn grits and butter, and cook until the liquid is absorbed. Stir in cheddar cheese. Serve over cooked grits.

Hot Squash & Tempeh Dish

Serves: 6 | Total Time: 6 hours 15 minutes

10 oz tempeh, cubed	½ tsp mustard seeds
1 lb butternut squash cubes	¼ tsp all-spice powder
1 can fire-roasted tomatoes	1 dried ancho chile, minced
2 shallots, chopped	1 bay leaf
3 garlic cloves, chopped	1 thyme sprig
2 tbsp olive oil	Salt and pepper to taste
½ tsp cumin seeds	

Warm the olive oil in a pan over medium heat. Place the tempeh and cook until golden on all sides. Add it to your Slow Cooker. Add in shallots, garlic, cumin seeds, mustard seeds, all-spice powder, chile ancho, butternut squash, tomatoes, bay leaf, thyme, salt, and pepper. Cover with the lid and cook for 6 hours on Low. Serve warm.

Vegetable Rotini Pasta

Serves: 6 | Total Time: 6 hours 15 minutes

½ head cauliflower, cut into florets	
1 cup diced tomatoes	½ tsp dried oregano
1 cup green peas	½ tsp dried basil
1 lb chopped green beans	1 cup rotini pasta
1 large onion, chopped	2 cups vegetable stock
1 celery stalk, sliced	Salt and pepper to taste
2 garlic cloves, chopped	

Mix the onion, celery, garlic, cauliflower, tomatoes, green peas, green beans, oregano, basil, vegetable stock, rotini pasta, salt, and pepper in your Slow Cooker. Cover with the lid and cook for 6 hours on Low. Serve right away.

Basil Quinoa with Tempeh

Serves: 6 | Total Time: 6 hours 15 minutes

2 red bell peppers, diced	3/4 cup red quinoa, rinsed
1 cup diced tomatoes	2 cups vegetable stock
8 oz tempeh, crumbled	½ tsp dried oregano
1 celery stalk, sliced	½ tsp dried basil
1 carrot, diced	Salt and pepper to taste
1 garlic clove, minced	

Stir the tempeh, celery, carrot, garlic, bell peppers, tomatoes, quinoa, basil, oregano, vegetable stock, salt, and pepper in your Slow Cooker. Cover with the lid and cook for 6 hours on Low. Serve immediately.

Jalapeño & Corn Quinoa

Serves: 6 | Total Time: 3 hours 15 minutes

2 cups frozen corn	1 large shallot, chopped
½ cup quinoa, rinsed	2 garlic cloves, minced

1 jalapeno pepper, chopped	¼ tsp cumin powder
1 celery stalk, diced	¼ tsp fennel seeds
1 ½ cups vegetable stock	¼ tsp chili powder
1 tbsp olive oil	Salt and pepper to taste

In your Slow Cooker, combine corn, quinoa, olive oil, shallot, garlic, jalapeño pepper, celery, cumin, fennel seeds, chili powder, vegetable stock, salt, and pepper. Cover with the lid and cook for 2 hours on High, then cook for 1 hour on Low. Serve warm.

Root Veggie Curry

Serves: 6 | Total Time: 8 hours 15 minutes

1 head cauliflower, cut into florets	
4 potatoes, cubed	¼ tsp chili powder
1 cup green peas	½ tsp cumin powder
1 cup snap peas	1 tsp curry powder
2 sweet potatoes, cubed	½ tsp turmeric powder
1 zucchini, cubed	2 tbsp tomato paste
2 heirloom tomatoes, diced	3 cups vegetable stock
2 tbsp canola oil	Salt and pepper to taste

Stir the canola oil, cauliflower, potatoes, green peas, snap peas, sweet potatoes, zucchini, tomatoes, chili powder, cumin, curry powder, turmeric, tomato paste, vegetable stock, salt, and pepper in your Slow Cooker. Cover with the lid and cook for 8 hours on Low. Serve immediately.

Seitan & Bell Pepper Fajitas

Serves: 6 | Total Time: 6 hours 15 minutes

12 oz seitan, crumbled	2 tbsp olive oil
½ cup vegetable stock	¼ tsp chili powder
½ cup tomato sauce	¼ tsp cumin powder
2 red bell peppers, sliced	1 tbsp soy sauce
1 yellow bell pepper, sliced	Salt and pepper to taste
1 shallot, sliced	Flour tortillas for serving
4 garlic cloves, chopped	

Warm the olive oil in a pan over medium heat. Place the seitan and fry until golden on all sides. Add it to your Slow Cooker. Add in bell peppers, shallot, garlic, chili powder, cumin, soy sauce, vegetable stock, tomato sauce, salt, and pepper. Cover with the lid and cook for 6 hours on Low. Divide between tortillas and wrap them to serve.

Mushroom & Bok Choy Cassoulet

Serves: 6 | Total Time: 2 hours 15 minutes

1 cup chopped shiitake mushrooms	
1 lb sliced button mushrooms	
2 green onions, chopped	2 cups bok choy, torn
2 garlic cloves, minced	2 tbsp canola oil
1 tsp grated ginger	1 tsp sesame oil
1 sweet onion, sliced	¼ tsp chili powder

Warm the canola oil in a pan over medium heat. Place the garlic, ginger, and onion and cook for 5 minutes until fragrant. Transfer everything to your Slow Cooker. Add in mushrooms, bok choy, green onions, sesame oil, and chili powder. Cover and cook for 2 hours on High. Serve.

Quinoa & Bean Loaf

Serves: 6 | Total Time: 6 hours 15 minutes

2 cups cooked quinoa	1 tsp dried oregano
1 can (15-oz) cannellini beans	2 tbsp chopped cilantro
1 large onion, chopped	¼ cup chopped parsley
4 garlic cloves, minced	2 eggs
2 tbsp olive oil	¼ cup breadcrumbs
1 tsp dried thyme	Salt and pepper to taste

Add the olive oil, onion, garlic, thyme, oregano, quinoa, beans, cilantro, parsley, eggs, breadcrumbs, salt, and pepper to your Slow Cooker and toss to combine. Cover with the lid and cook for 6 hours on Low. Serve.

Hawaiian Black Bean Bake

Serves: 6 | Total Time: 2 hours 15 minutes

1 cup crushed pineapple	½ cup BBQ sauce
1 shallot, chopped	1 tbsp maple syrup
2 garlic cloves, chopped	½ tsp cumin powder
1 can (15 oz) black beans	½ tsp ground ginger
1 can fire-roasted tomatoes	Salt and pepper to taste

Stir beans, tomatoes, pineapple, shallot, garlic, BBQ sauce, maple syrup, cumin, ginger, salt, and pepper in your Slow Cooker. Cover with the lid and cook for 2 hours on High. Serve warm and enjoy!

Cauliflower & Lime Bean Casserole

Serves: 6 | Total Time: 6 hours 15 minutes

1 head cauliflower, cut into florets	
2 carrots, sliced	2 cups dried lime beans
2 celery stalks, sliced	2 cups vegetable stock
1 tsp grated ginger	1 bay leaf
1 cup diced tomatoes	1 thyme sprig
1 cup tomato sauce	Salt and pepper to taste

Mix the lime beans, carrots, celery, cauliflower, ginger, tomatoes, tomato sauce, vegetable stock, bay leaf, thyme, salt, and pepper in your Slow Cooker. Cover with the lid and cook for 6 hours on Low. Serve right away.

Cheesy Potatoes

Serves: 8 | Total Time: 5 hours 30 minutes

2 lb Yukon gold potatoes, peeled and finely sliced	
2 garlic cloves, minced	1 cup whole milk
1 tsp dried oregano	1 pinch nutmeg
1 cup cream cheese	Salt and pepper to taste

Sprinkle potatoes with salt and pepper and place them in your Slow Cooker. In a bowl, combine garlic, oregano, cream cheese, milk, and nutmeg and pour it into the pot. Cover and cook for 5 hours on Low. Serve warm.

Refried Chipotle Black Beans

Serves: 6 | Total Time: 6 hours 15 minutes

1 tbsp adobo sauce from chipotle	
1 chipotle pepper, chopped	4 garlic cloves, minced

2 cans (15-oz) black beans	2 tbsp tomato paste
1 cup vegetable stock	Salt and pepper to taste

Mix the beans, vegetable stock, tomato paste, chipotle pepper, garlic, adobo sauce, salt, and pepper in your Slow Cooker. Cover with the lid and cook for 6 hours on Low. When done, remove the lid and serve warm or chilled.

Creamy Sweet Potatoes

Serves: 6 | Total Time: 6 hours 30 minutes

2 sweet potatoes, sliced	½ cup cream cheese
2 onions, finely sliced	2 eggs, beaten
1 pinch nutmeg	½ tsp garlic powder
2 cups whole milk	Salt and pepper to taste

Lay sweet potatoes and onion in the bottom of a greased Slow Cooker. In a bowl, whisk nutmeg, milk, cream cheese, eggs, and garlic powder and pour it over the veggies. Adjust seasoning to taste. Cover with the lid and cook for 6 hours on Low. Serve immediately.

Herbed Spinach & Cottage Cheese Meal

Serves: 6 | Total Time: 6 hours 15 minutes

4 eggs, beaten	½ tsp dried oregano
2 lb spinach, torn	½ tsp dried basil
1 ½ cups cottage cheese	Salt and pepper to taste
2 tbsp all-purpose flour	

In a bowl, whisk the spinach, cottage cheese, flour, oregano, basil, and eggs until combined. Sprinkle with salt and pepper to taste and pour it into your Slow Cooker. Cover and cook for 6 hours on Low. Serve warm.

Classic Parmigiana with Eggplants

Serves: 6 | Total Time: 8 hours 15 minutes

4 medium eggplants, peeled and finely sliced	
¼ cup all-purpose flour	1 cup grated Parmesan
4 cups marinara sauce	Salt and pepper to taste

Sprinkle the eggplants with salt, pepper, and flour. Place layers of eggplant slices and marinara sauce in your Slow Cooker and scatter with Parmesan cheese on top. Cover with the lid and cook for 8 hours on Low. When done, remove the lid and serve warm or chilled.

Basil Tempeh

Serves: 6 | Total Time: 6 hours 30 minutes

1 lb tempeh, cut into thin strips	
4 garlic cloves, minced	2 tbsp canola oil
1 onion, finely chopped	1 cup vegetable stock
½ tsp dried oregano	Salt and pepper to taste
½ tsp dried basil	

Warm the canola oil in a pan over medium heat. Put the tempeh and cook until golden on all sides. Add it to your Slow Cooker. Add in garlic, onion, oregano, basil, vegetable stock, salt, and pepper. Cover with the lid and cook for 6 hours on Low. Serve warm.

Easy Chow Mein with Seitan

Serves: 6 | Total Time: 2 hours 15 minutes

1 cup water chestnuts, chopped
2 carrots, sliced
2 green onions, chopped
½ lb seitan, diced
2 celery stalks, sliced
2 tbsp soy sauce

½ cup vegetable stock
1 pinch chili flakes
1 cup green peas
1 tbsp cornstarch
¼ cup cold water

Mix the seitan, celery, carrots, green onions, soy sauce, vegetable stock, chili flakes, green peas, and chestnuts in your Slow Cooker. Cover with the lid and cook for 1 hour on High. Pour in cornstarch and water and cook for 1 hour on High. Serve immediately.

Spinach & Green Bean Casserole

Serves: 6 | Total Time: 6 hours 15 minutes

1 shallot, chopped
1 cup whole milk
1 lb green beans, chopped
½ lb fresh spinach, torn

½ cup cream cheese
4 eggs, beaten
½ cup breadcrumbs
Salt and pepper to taste

In your Slow Cooker, stir green beans, spinach, cream cheese, shallot, milk, eggs, breadcrumbs, salt, and pepper. Cover and cook for 6 hours on Low. Serve warm.

Gourmet Tofu Kung Pao

Serves: 6 | Total Time: 6 hours 15 minutes

1 onion, sliced
¼ tsp red pepper flakes
2 red bell peppers, sliced
2 cups sliced mushrooms
1 small bok choy, shredded
1 lb firm tofu, cubed
½ cup peanuts, chopped

1 tbsp canola oil
1 tbsp lime juice
1 tbsp soy sauce
1 tbsp tahini paste
1 tsp grated ginger
Salt and pepper to taste

In a bowl, add tofu, lime juice, soy sauce, and tahini paste and toss to coat. Warm the canola oil in a pan over medium heat. Place the marinated tofu and cook for 2-3 minutes until golden. Add it to your Slow Cooker. Stir in ginger, onion, red pepper flakes, bell peppers, mushrooms, bok choy, salt, and pepper. Cover and cook for 6 hours on Low. Serve topped with peanuts.

Cheddar Hominy Casserole with Olives

Serves: 6 | Total Time: 2 hours 15 minutes

1 (10.75-oz) can condensed cream of onion soup
½ cup pitted black olives
16 oz canned hominy
1 ½ cups grated cheddar
½ cup breadcrumbs
1 can fire-roasted tomatoes

1 can green chilies, chopped
1 onion, chopped
¼ tsp cayenne pepper
¼ tsp cumin powder
Salt and pepper to taste

Add the hominy, onion soup, breadcrumbs, tomatoes, green chilies, onion, olives, cayenne pepper, cumin, salt, and pepper to your Slow Cooker and toss to combine. Scatter with the cheddar cheese on top, cover with the lid, and cook for 2 hours on High. Serve right away.

Healthy Hungarian Goulash

Serves: 8 | Total Time: 8 hours 30 minutes

4 roasted red bell peppers, chopped
1 can (15 oz) white beans
1 can fire-roasted tomatoes
2 onions, finely chopped
4 garlic cloves, chopped
2 carrots, diced
1 celery stalk, diced
1 tsp smoked paprika

2 tbsp olive oil
2 tbsp tomato paste
2 lb potatoes, cubed
2 bay leaves
2 cups vegetable stock
Salt and pepper to taste

Warm the olive oil in a pan over medium heat. Stir-fry the onions and garlic for 5 minutes until softened. Add them to your Slow Cooker. Add in carrots, celery, beans, bell peppers, tomatoes, paprika, tomato paste, potatoes, bay leaves, vegetable stock, salt, and pepper. Cover with the lid and cook for 8 hours on Low. Serve right away.

Spinach Ravioli with Cannellini Beans

Serves: 6 | Total Time: 6 hours 15 minutes

10 oz spinach ravioli
1 can (15 oz) cannellini beans
1 shallot, chopped
1 celery stalk, sliced
2 carrots, sliced
2 garlic cloves, chopped

½ tsp dried basil
1 cup diced tomatoes
1 cup vegetable stock
Salt and pepper to taste
2 tbsp grated Parmesan

In your Slow Cooker, combine the celery, carrots, garlic, beans, shallot, basil, tomatoes, spinach ravioli, vegetable stock, salt, and pepper. Cover with the lid and cook for 6 hours on Low. Top with Parmesan cheese and serve.

Butternut Squash Stuffed with Lentils

Serves: 6 | Total Time: 6 hours 30 minutes

1 shallot, chopped
2 garlic cloves, minced
1 butternut squash, halved
2 cups cooked lentils

½ cup vegetable stock
½ tsp cumin powder
¼ tsp chili powder
Salt and pepper to taste

Put the butternut squash in your Slow Cooker. In a bowl, combine lentils, shallot, garlic, cumin, chili powder, salt, and pepper and pour it over the squash. Pour in vegetable stock, cover and cook for 6 hours on Low. Serve warm.

Parmesan Pumpkin Farro

Serves: 6 | Total Time: 6 hours 15 minutes

1 shallot, chopped
1 cup farro, rinsed
2 cups pumpkin cubes
1 garlic clove, minced
½ cup grated Parmesan
2 tbsp butter

¼ tsp cumin seeds
¼ tsp fennel seeds
¼ cup white wine
2½ cups vegetable stock
Salt and pepper to taste

Toss the butter, farro, pumpkin, shallot, garlic, cumin seeds, fennel seeds, wine, vegetable stock, salt, and pepper in your Slow Cooker. Cover with the lid and cook for 6 hours on Low. When done, remove the lid and serve warm or chilled topped with Parmesan cheese.

Veggie & Chickpea Curry

Serves: 6 | Total Time: 3 hours 15 minutes

1 small head cauliflower, cut into florets
1 lb potatoes, cubed
1 can (15-oz) chickpeas
2 shallots, chopped
4 garlic cloves, chopped
1 cup diced tomatoes
2 red bell peppers, diced
2 tbsp red curry paste

1 cup vegetable stock
½ cup coconut cream
1 lemongrass stalk, crushed
1 lime, juiced
Salt and pepper to taste
2 cups cooked jasmine rice

Add the shallots, garlic, cauliflower, bell peppers, potatoes, chickpeas, curry paste, tomatoes, vegetable stock, coconut cream, lemongrass, lime juice, salt, and pepper to your Slow Cooker and toss to combine. Cover with the lid and cook for 3 hours on High. When done, remove the lid and serve over cooked jasmine rice.

Simple Five-Spice Tofu

Serves: 6 | Total Time: 8 hours 15 minutes

2 garlic cloves, minced
18 oz firm tofu, cubed
1 cup vegetable stock
¼ cup soy sauce

1 tsp sesame oil
1 tsp grated ginger
1 tsp five spices powder

In your Slow Cooker, combine the tofu, soy sauce, sesame oil, garlic, ginger, five-spice powder, and vegetable stock. Cover and cook for 8 hours on Low. Serve warm.

Green Pea & Seitan Rice Pilaf

Serves: 6 | Total Time: 8 hours 15 minutes

1 cup white rice
1 lb seitan, cubed
1 large onion, chopped
1 celery stalk, diced

1 large carrot, diced
½ cup green peas
2 cups vegetable stock
Salt and pepper to taste

Mix the seitan, onion, celery, carrot, green peas, rice, vegetable stock, salt, and pepper in your Slow Cooker. Cover and cook for 8 hours on Low. Serve warm.

Delicious Apple & Sweet Potato Dish

Serves: 6 | Total Time: 6 hours 15 minutes

4 red apples, peeled, cored and diced
2 shallots, chopped
1 ½ lb sweet potatoes, cubed
2 garlic cloves, minced
1 tbsp brown sugar

1 pinch nutmeg
1 cup vegetable stock
Salt and pepper to taste

In your Slow Cooker, stir sweet potatoes, apples, shallots, garlic, sugar, nutmeg, vegetable stock, salt, and pepper. Cover and cook for 6 hours on Low. Serve warm.

Hot Tofu

Serves: 6 | Total Time: 2 hours 15 minutes

½ cup vegetable stock
12 oz firm tofu, cubed
1 tbsp hot sauce

1 tsp grated ginger
2 tbsp soy sauce

In a bowl, mix the tofu with hot sauce, ginger, and soy sauce until well coated. Add them to your Slow Cooker and pour in vegetable stock. Cover with the lid and cook for 2 hours on High. Serve and enjoy!

Basic Artichoke Tagine with Black Olives

Serves: 6 | Total Time: 4 hours 15 minutes

12 oz canned artichoke hearts, chopped
1 can (15 oz) chickpeas
2 garlic cloves, chopped
1 shallot, chopped
1 cup diced tomatoes
½ tsp smoked paprika
½ tsp cumin powder

1 tsp turmeric powder
1 lime, juiced
½ cup pitted black olives
½ tsp dried oregano
Salt and pepper to taste

Mix the artichoke hearts, shallot, chickpeas, garlic, paprika, cumin, turmeric, lime juice, olives, oregano, tomatoes, salt, and pepper in your Slow Cooker. Cover and cook for 4 hours on Low. Serve warm.

Special Bourginon with Kidney Beans

Serves: 6 | Total Time: 8 hours 15 minutes

2 carrots, sliced
2 large onions, chopped
2 leeks, sliced
4 garlic cloves, chopped
2 cups kidney beans, rinsed
2 cups sliced mushrooms

½ cup dry red wine
4 cups vegetable stock
2 tbsp olive oil
1 tsp dried thyme
2 bay leaves
Salt and pepper to taste

Warm the olive oil in a pan over medium heat. Place the onions, leeks, and garlic and cook for 5 minutes until softened. Transfer everything to your Slow Cooker. Put in thyme, beans, mushrooms, carrots, wine, vegetable stock, bay leaves, salt, and pepper. Cover with the lid and cook for 8 hours on Low. Serve warm.

Creamy Asparagus & Egg Casserole

Serves: 6 | Total Time: 6 hours 30 minutes

1 can condensed cream of mushroom soup
1 lb asparagus, chopped
2 hard-boiled eggs, cubed
1 cup grated cheddar

2 cups bread croutons
Salt and pepper to taste

Place asparagus, mushroom soup, eggs, cheddar cheese, croutons, salt, and pepper in your Slow Cooker and toss to combine. Cover and cook for 6 hours on Low. Serve.

Tomato Lentil & Rice

Serves: 6 | Total Time: 6 hours 15 minutes

1 cup diced tomatoes
1 shallot, chopped
1 cup white rice
½ cup red lentils

3 cups vegetable stock
2 tbsp tomato paste
¼ tsp garlic powder
Salt and pepper to taste

Add the rice, lentils, tomatoes, tomato paste, vegetable stock, garlic powder, shallot, salt, and pepper in your Slow Cooker and stir. Cover with the lid and cook for 6 hours on Low. Serve immediately.

Saucy Cheddar & Corn Tortilla Casserole

Serves: 6 | Total Time: 2 hours 30 minutes

6 oz tortilla chips	½ tsp cumin powder
1 ½ cups grated cheddar	½ tsp chili powder
1 ½ cups frozen corn	2 potatoes, cubed
1 can fire-roasted tomatoes	1 cup water
1 cup red salsa	Salt and pepper to taste

In your Slow Cooker, add corn, tomatoes, red salsa, cumin, chili powder, potatoes, water, salt, and pepper, and toss to combine. Scatter with tortilla chips and cheddar cheese, cover with the lid, and cook for 2 hours on High. When done, remove the lid and serve warm.

Spinach & Ricotta Zucchini Lasagna

Serves: 6 | Total Time: 6 hours 30 minutes

10 oz chopped cauliflower florets	
10 oz spinach, torn	2 cups tomato sauce
2 zucchinis, finely sliced	2 cups grated mozzarellas
2 cups ricotta cheese	

In a bowl, combine ricotta cheese, spinach, and cauliflower. Make a layer of zucchini slices in your Slow Cooker. Top with ricotta filling and spread the tomato sauce all over. Repeat the process until any ingredients are left. Scatter with mozzarella cheese on top, cover with the lid, and cook for 6 hours on Low. Serve immediately.

Black Bean, Corn & Spinach Sauce

Serves: 6 | Total Time: 6 hours 15 minutes

1 cup tomato sauce	½ tsp chili powder
1 can (15 oz) black beans	1 can fire-roasted tomatoes
10 oz spinach, torn	½ lime, juiced
1 cup frozen corn	Salt and pepper to taste
½ tsp cumin powder	

Stir the beans, spinach, corn, cumin, chili powder, tomato sauce, tomatoes, lime juice, salt, and pepper in your Slow Cooker. Cover with the lid and cook for 6 hours on Low.

Winter Biscuit in a Pot

Serves: 8 | Total Time: 7 hours 30 minutes

2 garlic cloves, chopped	2 cups sliced mushrooms
1 onion, finely chopped	1 cup green peas
2 carrots, diced	2 tbsp olive oil
1 parsnip, diced	Salt and pepper to taste
1 turnip, diced	

FOR THE BISCUIT

½ cup buttermilk	1 cup grated Parmesan
½ cup all-purpose flour	¼ cup cold butter, cubed
½ tsp baking powder	

Add the olive oil, garlic, onion, carrots, parsnip, turnip, mushrooms, green peas, salt, and pepper to your Slow Cooker. In a bowl, whisk the flour, baking powder, Parmesan cheese, and butter until crumbly. Stir in buttermilk until slightly smooth and pour it over the veggies. Cover and cook for 7 hours on Low. Serve warm.

Amazing Potato Casserole

Serves: 6 | Total Time: 6 hours 30 minutes

2 lb potatoes, cubed	2 ripe tomatoes, diced
2 carrots, sliced	2 cups vegetable stock
1 large onion, chopped	2 bay leaves
2 garlic cloves, chopped	2 tbsp chopped parsley
2 red bell peppers, diced	Salt and pepper to taste
1 celery root, cubed	

Mix the onion, garlic, bell peppers, carrots, celery, potatoes, tomatoes, vegetable stock, bay leaves, salt, and pepper in your Slow Cooker. Cover with the lid and cook for 6 hours on Low. Sprinkle with parsley to serve.

Saucy Bell Pepper Rice Pilaf with Corn

Serves: 6 | Total Time: 6 hours 15 minutes

1 green bell pepper, diced	1 cup frozen corn
1 red bell pepper, diced	1 cup green peas
1 cup white rice	2 cups vegetable stock
1 onion, chopped	¼ tsp chili powder
1 cup red salsa	Salt and pepper to taste

Mix the rice, onion, bell pepper, red salsa, corn, green peas, vegetable stock, chili powder, salt, and pepper in your Slow Cooker. Cover with the lid and cook for 6 hours on Low. Serve right away.

Cauliflower & Tomato Pasta Sauce

Serves: 6 | Total Time: 4 hours 15 minutes

1 head cauliflower, cut into florets	
2 carrots, sliced	4 garlic cloves, minced
2 celery stalks, sliced	1 cup vegetable stock
1 cup tomato puree	2 tbsp olive oil
2 ripe tomatoes, diced	1 bay leaf
1 onion, finely chopped	Salt and pepper to taste

Warm the olive oil in a pan over medium heat. Place the garlic and onion and cook for 2 minutes until softened. In a food processor, blend the cauliflower, carrots, and celery until crumbly. Add in onion mixture and toss to combine. Pour the mixture into your Slow Cooker among tomato puree, tomatoes, vegetable stock, bay leaf, salt, and pepper. Cover with the lid and cook for 4 hours on Low. Serve immediately or store it in the freezer.

Tofu Chili

Serves: 6 | Total Time: 8 hours 15 minutes

4 garlic cloves, chopped	1 yellow bell pepper, diced
2 sweet onions, chopped	½ tsp chili powder
2 cups dried kidney beans	½ tsp cumin powder
10 oz firm tofu, cubed	¼ tsp chili flakes
1 can fire-roasted tomatoes	Salt and pepper to taste
2 red bell peppers, diced	2 tbsp chopped cilantro

Mix the tofu, tomatoes, bell peppers, garlic, onions, beans, 4 cups of water, chili powder, cumin, chili flakes, salt, and pepper in your Slow Cooker. Cover with the lid and cook for 8 hours on Low. Top with cilantro to serve.

Teriyaki Eggplant & Tofu

Serves: 4 | Total Time: 2 hours 15 minutes

6 oz firm tofu, cubed
4 garlic cloves, minced
1 peeled eggplant, cubed
1 tsp grated ginger
2 shallots, sliced
2 tbsp olive oil

1 tsp Worcestershire sauce
1 tbsp soy sauce
½ tsp cumin seeds
¼ tsp fennel seeds
Salt and pepper to taste

Warm the olive oil in a pan over medium heat. Place the tofu and cook until golden and crusty on all sides. Add it to your Slow Cooker. Add in the eggplant, garlic, ginger, shallots, Worcestershire sauce, soy sauce, cumin seeds, fennel seeds, salt, and pepper. Cover with the lid and cook for 2 hours on High. Serve warm.

Italian Cauliflower Couscous

Serves: 6 | Total Time: 4 hours 15 minutes

1 head cauliflower, cut into florets
2 cups diced tomatoes
½ cup couscous
1 large onion, sliced
2 cups vegetable stock

1 tsp dried Italian herbs
¼ tsp chili powder
Salt and pepper to taste
Lemon juice for serving

In your Slow Cooker, place couscous, onion, and cauliflower. In a bowl, combine the tomatoes, vegetable stock, Italian herbs, chili powder, salt, and pepper and pour it over the veggies. Cover with the lid and cook for 4 hours on Low. Drizzle with lemon juice and serve.

Grandma´s Caponata with Eggplant

Serves: 6 | Total Time: 6 hours 30 minutes

2 eggplants, peeled and cubed
1 sweet onion, chopped
½ cup tomato puree
2 ripe tomatoes, cubed
1 zucchini, cubed
1 celery stalk, sliced
1 cup vegetable stock

2 tbsp olive oil
1 tbsp balsamic vinegar
½ tsp dried oregano
Salt and pepper to taste
2 tbsp chopped parsley

Stir the olive oil, tomatoes, eggplants, zucchini, celery, onion, tomato puree, vegetable stock, balsamic vinegar, oregano, salt, and pepper in your Slow Cooker. Cover and cook for 6 hours on Low. Top with parsley and serve.

Bean & Corn Pasta Sauce

Serves: 6 | Total Time: 8 hours 15 minutes

1 can (15 oz) kidney beans
1 can (15 oz) black beans,
2 cups tomato sauce
1 cup green peas
1 cup fire-roasted tomatoes
1 cup frozen corn

1 celery stalk, sliced
1 tsp cumin powder
1 tsp dried oregano
1 cup vegetable stock
Salt and pepper to taste

Add beans, tomato sauce, tomatoes, corn, green peas, celery, cumin, oregano, vegetable stock, salt, and pepper to your Slow Cooker and stir. Cover and cook for 8 hours on Low. Serve immediately or store it in the freezer.

Dinner Vegetable Stew with Chickpeas

Serves: 6 | Total Time: 6 hours 30 minutes

1 can (15 oz) chickpeas
1 cup frozen pearl onions
3 large carrots, sliced
1 cup frozen corn
1 cup frozen green peas

1 cup vegetable stock
2 zucchinis, cubed
2 ripe tomatoes, cubed
1 tsp herbs de Provence
Salt and pepper to taste

In your Slow Cooker, add onions, carrots, corn, green peas, vegetable stock, zucchinis, tomatoes, herb de Provence, chickpeas, salt, and pepper, and stir. Cover and cook for 6 hours on Low. Serve over cooked rice.

Roasted Tomato Orzo with Black Beans

Serves: 6 | Total Time: 3 hours 15 minutes

1 cup frozen green peas
1 can (15 oz) black beans
1 cup orzo
1 can fire-roasted tomatoes
1 cup tomato sauce

1 cup vegetable stock
1 cup frozen corn
1 thyme sprig
1 cup grated cheddar
Salt and pepper to taste

Mix the orzo, tomatoes, tomato sauce, vegetable stock, corn, green peas, beans, thyme, salt, and pepper in your Slow Cooker. Cover with the lid and cook for 3 hours on High. Serve sprinkled with cheddar cheese.

Carrot & Spinach Chili

Serves: 6 | Total Time: 2 hours 15 minutes

1 ripe heirloom tomato, peeled and diced
1 lb potatoes, cubed
1 can (15 oz) white beans
4 cups spinach, torn
2 large carrots, sliced

¼ tsp cumin seeds
¼ tsp chili powder
½ cup vegetable stock
Salt and pepper to taste

Mix the carrots, beans, spinach, cumin seeds, chili powder, potatoes, tomato, vegetable stock, salt, and pepper in your Slow Cooker. Cover with the lid and cook for 2 hours on High. Serve warm.

Spiced Balsamic Tomato Sauce

Serves: 6 | Total Time: 6 hours 30 minutes

2 red bell peppers, diced
2 cans (15-oz) diced tomatoes
1 large onion, chopped
4 garlic cloves, chopped
10 oz soy crumbles

2 cups vegetable stock
2 tbsp balsamic vinegar
½ tsp dried basil
½ tsp dried oregano
Salt and pepper to taste

Stir the onion, garlic, bell peppers, tomatoes, soy crumbles, stock, balsamic vinegar, basil, oregano, salt, and pepper in your Slow Cooker. Cook for 6 hours on Low. Serve immediately or store in the freezer.

Garlicky Broccoli

Serves: 4 | Total Time: 1 hour 30 minutes

2 heads broccoli, cut into florets
1 shallot, sliced
2 garlic cloves, chopped

4 tbsp butter
Salt and pepper to taste

Toss broccoli, shallot, garlic, butter, salt, and pepper in your Slow Cooker. Cover with the lid and cook for 11/2 hours on High. Serve warm.

Lemony Broccoli & Peanuts

Serves: 6 | Total Time: 2 hours 15 minutes

2 heads broccoli, cut into florets
4 garlic cloves, chopped   2 tbsp olive oil
1 cup raw peanuts, chopped   1 tbsp soy sauce
1 shallot, sliced   Salt and pepper to taste
1 lemon, juiced

Stir the broccoli, peanuts, garlic, shallot, olive oil, lemon juice, soy sauce, salt, and pepper in your Slow Cooker. Cover and cook for 2 hours on High. Serve warm.

Parmesan Tomato Baked Eggplant

Serves: 6 | Total Time: 4 hours 15 minutes

2 large eggplants, peeled and sliced
2 cups tomato sauce   1 tsp dried basil
2 cups grated Parmesan   Salt and pepper to taste
½ tsp chili powder

In a bowl, combine tomato sauce, chili powder, and basil. Place eggplants, then tomato mixture, and top with Parmesan cheese in your Slow Cooker. Season with salt and pepper to taste. Cover with the lid and cook for 4 hours on Low. Serve immediately.

Tofu al Orange

Serves: 4 | Total Time: 4 hours 15 minutes

1 garlic clove, minced   2 tbsp soy sauce
1 orange, zested and juiced   1 tsp Worcestershire sauce
12 oz firm tofu, cubed   ¼ cup vegetable stock
1 tbsp grated ginger

Mix the tofu, ginger, garlic, orange zest, orange juice, soy sauce, Worcestershire sauce, and vegetable stock in your Slow Cooker. Cook for 4 hours on Low. Serve warm.

Crispy Parmesan Artichokes

Serves: 2 | Total Time: 4 hours 15 minutes

¼ cup breadcrumbs   2 large artichokes
½ cup grated Parmesan   ½ cup vegetable stock

In a bowl, combine breadcrumbs and Parmesan cheese. Trim and clean the artichokes, sprinkle with cheese mixture and place them in your Slow Cooker. Pour in vegetable stock, cover with the lid, and cook for 4 hours on Low. When done, remove the lid and serve warm.

Tofu with Hoisin Sauce

Serves: 6 | Total Time: 6 hours 15 minutes

2 garlic cloves   2 tbsp canola oil
12 oz firm tofu, sliced   ¼ tsp chili powder
¼ cup smooth peanut butter ¼ tsp cumin powder
¼ cup soy sauce   ½ cup water

In a food processor, blend canola oil, peanut butter, soy sauce, garlic, chili powder, cumin, and water until smooth. Combine tofu and sauce in your Slow Cooker. Cover and cook for 6 hours on Low. Serve warm.

Cheddar Broccoli Soufflé

Serves: 6 | Total Time: 2 hours 15 minutes

1 cup grated cheddar   2 eggs, beaten
1 ½ lb broccoli   ½ tsp onion powder
1 can cream of celery soup   ½ tsp garlic powder
1 cup mayonnaise   Salt and pepper to taste
1 cup crushed crackers

Place the broccoli in a pot with boiling water and cook for 10 minutes. Strain and transfer it into a food processor. Blend until crumbly and remove it to a bowl. Add in celery soup, mayonnaise, onion powder, garlic powder, eggs, salt, and pepper, and toss to combine. Pour the mixture in your Slow Cooker and scatter with crackers and cheddar cheese. Cover with the lid and cook for 2 hours on High. Serve warm.

Orange Glazed Beets

Serves: 6 | Total Time: 6 hours 15 minutes

4 beets, peeled and sliced   1 tsp orange zest
½ cup fresh orange juice   ½ tsp cumin seeds
2 tbsp olive oil   ¼ tsp fennel seeds
2 tbsp balsamic vinegar   ½ tsp salt
1 tbsp brown sugar

Mix the beets, olive oil, sugar, orange zest, orange juice, cumin seeds, fennel seeds, salt, and balsamic vinegar in your Slow Cooker. Cover with the lid and cook for 6 hours on Low. Serve warm.

Balsamic Root Veggies

Serves: 4 | Total Time: 3 hours 15 minutes

1 turnip, peeled and sliced   2 tbsp olive oil
1 large red onion, sliced   1 tbsp brown sugar
½ lb baby carrots   2 tbsp balsamic vinegar
2 sweet potatoes, cubed   ¼ cup vegetable stock
2 parsnips, sliced   Salt and pepper to taste

Mix the carrots, sweet potatoes, parsnips, turnip, onion, olive oil, sugar, balsamic vinegar, vegetable stock, salt, and pepper in your Slow Cooker. Cover with the lid and cook for 3 hours on High. Serve immediately.

Buttered Spring Veggies

Serves: 6 | Total Time: 4 hours 15 minutes

½ lb green beans, chopped   3 tbsp butter
2 carrots, sliced   1 sweet onion, sliced
2 cups snap peas   1 celery stalk, sliced
1 cup green peas   Salt and pepper to taste

Toss carrots, snap peas, green peas, green beans, onion, celery, butter, salt, and pepper in your Slow Cooker Cover with the lid and cook for 4 hours on Low. Serve.

Antioxidant Sauce

Serves: 6 | Total Time: 6 hours 15 minutes

1 red onion, chopped
1 lb fresh cranberries
½ cup brown sugar
1 cup fresh orange juice
¼ cup red wine

1 tsp grated ginger
½ tsp cumin powder
1 tsp orange zest
Salt and pepper to taste

Mix the cranberries, sugar, orange juice, ginger, cumin, orange zest, wine, onion, salt, and pepper in your Slow Cooker. Cover with the lid and cook for 6 hours on Low. Serve right away or store it in a container in the freezer.

Green Bean Casserole in Alfredo Sauce

Serves: 6 | Total Time: 3 hours 15 minutes

1 cup water chestnuts, chopped
1 shallot, sliced
1 lb green beans, chopped
1 cup Alfredo sauce
2 cups sliced mushrooms

½ cup grated Parmesan
½ cup vegetable stock
Salt and pepper to taste

Stir green beans, Alfredo sauce, water chestnuts, mushrooms, shallot, vegetable stock, salt, and pepper in your Slow Cooker and scatter with Parmesan cheese on top. Cook for 3 hours on High. Serve warm.

Artichokes in Alfredo Sauce

Serves: 6 | Total Time: 6 hours 15 minutes

1 jar artichoke hearts, drained and chopped
2 celery stalks, sliced
4 peppercorns, chopped
1 cup vegetable stock

1 cup Alfredo sauce
1 tbsp lemon juice
Salt and pepper to taste

Toss artichoke hearts, peppercorns, lemon juice, celery, vegetable stock, Alfredo sauce, salt, and pepper in your Slow Cooker. Cover with the lid and cook for 6 hours on Low. Serve warm or store it in a container in the fridge.

Black Beans in Spicy Red Salsa

Serves: 6 | Total Time: 6 hours 15 minutes

2 cups spicy red salsa
1 lb black beans, soaked
½ tsp cumin seeds
¼ tsp fennel seeds

2 tbsp tomato paste
2 cups vegetable stock
Salt and pepper to taste

Add the beans, red salsa, cumin seeds, fennel seeds, tomato paste, vegetable stock, salt, and pepper, and toss to combine to your Slow Cooker. Cover with the lid and cook for 6 hours on Low. Serve warm.

Sweet Coleslaw

Serves: 6 | Total Time: 6 hours 15 minutes

1 large head red cabbage, shredded
1 red onion, sliced
2 apples, cored and diced
½ cup red wine
¼ cup vegetable stock

2 tbsp olive oil
1 tsp cumin seeds
Salt and pepper to taste

Mix the cabbage, onion, apples, olive oil, red wine, vegetable stock, cumin seeds, salt, and pepper in your Slow Cooker. Cover with the lid and cook for 6 hours on Low. When done, remove the lid and serve warm.

Creamy Green Casserole

Serves: 6 | Total Time: 4 hours 15 minutes

1 cup green peas
2 cups fresh spinach
1 lb asparagus, chopped
1 can cream of celery soup

2 celery stalks, sliced
½ cup breadcrumbs
1 cup grated cheddar
Salt and pepper to taste

Mix the asparagus, celery soup, green peas, spinach, celery, salt, and pepper in your Slow Cooker and sprinkle with breadcrumbs and cheddar cheese on top. Cover with the lid and cook for 4 hours on Low. Serve immediately.

Fiery Red Bean Pot

Serves: 6 | Total Time: 8 hours 15 minutes

1 can (15 oz) fire-roasted tomatoes
2 sweet potatoes, peeled and cubed
2 cups baby carrots
1 lb dried red beans, rinsed
4 garlic cloves, chopped
2 red onions, finely chopped
4 cups vegetable stock

½ cup coconut milk
1 tsp curry powder
¼ tsp chili powder
¼ tsp all-spice powder
Salt and pepper to taste

Stir the beans, garlic, onions, tomatoes, curry powder, chili powder, vegetable stock, carrots, sweet potatoes, coconut milk, all-spice, salt, and pepper in your Slow Cooker. Cover and cook for 8 hours on Low. Serve.

Chessy Carrot Pudding

Serves: 6 | Total Time: 6 hours 15 minutes

2 sweet onions, sliced
6 large carrots, finely sliced
1 pinch nutmeg
4 eggs, beaten

1 cup whole milk
Salt and pepper to taste
1 cup grated Cheddar

In your Slow Cooker, lay carrots and onions and sprinkle with salt, pepper, and nutmeg. In a bowl, beat eggs and milk, pour it over the veggies, and top with cheddar cheese. Cover and cook for 6 hours on Low. Serve warm.

Creamy Chickpeas with Asiago Cheese

Serves: 4 | Total Time: 2 hours 15 minutes

2 ripe tomatoes, diced
2 cans (15-oz) chickpeas
1 cup grated Asiago cheese
½ cup vegetable stock

½ cup heavy cream
½ tsp dried oregano
Salt and pepper to taste

In your Slow Cooker, combine chickpeas, tomatoes, vegetable stock, heavy cream, oregano, salt, and pepper, and scatter with Asiago cheese on top. Cover with the lid and cook for 2 hours on High. Serve right away.

FISH & SEAFOOD

Flounder Risotto

Serves: 6 | Total Time: 5 hours 10 minutes

6 flounder fillets	1 tsp dried thyme
1 cup mushrooms, sliced	6 cups vegetable Broth
2 onions, chopped	2 cups baby spinach
3 garlic cloves, minced	2 tbsp butter
2 cups Arborio rice, rinsed	½ cup grated Parmesan

Add the mushrooms, onions, garlic, rice, thyme, and vegetable broth to your Slow Cooker and mix to combine. Cover and cook for 4 hours on Low. Place the fish fillets on top of the rice. Continue to cook for 30-35 minutes until the fish is easily flaked. Gently stir the fish into the risotto. Add the baby spinach, butter, and Parmesan cheese and stir. Cook for 10 minutes. Serve.

Baked Cod Ratatouille

Serves: 4 | Total Time: 8 hours 20 minutes

1 eggplant, peeled and sliced into rounds	
1 cup sliced button mushrooms	
1 zucchini, sliced into rounds	2 garlic cloves, minced
2 tomatoes, chopped	2 tablespoons olive oil
1 onion, sliced	1 tsp herbes de Provence
1 red bell pepper, chopped	1 lb cod fillets

Mix the olive oil, garlic, tomatoes, onion, and herbs de Provence in a bowl. Add the eggplant, mushrooms, bell peppers, and zucchini and toss to coat. Transfer to your Slow Cooker. Cover and cook for 6 7 hours on Low until the vegetables are tender. Arrange the cod fillets on top and cook for 2 more hours on Low. Gently stir the fish into the vegetables. Serve and enjoy!

Fennel-Scented Fish Stew

Serves: 6 | Total Time: 8 hours 20 minutes

2 lb firm cod fillets, cubed	1 cup carrots, chopped
2 cups fish stock	1 cup onion, diced
½ cup dry white wine	¼ cup parsley, chopped
Salt and pepper to taste	3 garlic cloves, minced
1 tbsp orange zest	3 large tomatoes, chopped
1 tsp crushed fennel seeds	

Add fish stock, wine, orange zest, crushed fennel seeds, carrots, onion, tomatoes, and cloves into your Slow Cooker. Stir to mix. Close and cook on Low for 4 hours. Add the fish into the cooker and continue to cook for 4 hours. Adjust the seasoning and top with parsley. Serve.

Citrus Fish

Serves: 4 | Total Time: 4 hours 10 minutes

1 ½ lb fish fillets	½ cup onion, chopped
2 tsp grated orange rind	2 tbsp chopped parsley
1 tbsp olive oil	Orange and lemon slices
Salt and pepper to taste	2 tbsp parsley, chopped
2 tsp grated lemon rind	Cooking spray

Use cooking spray to coat the inside of your Slow Cooker. Season the fish fillets with salt and pepper. Place fillets inside the slow cooker. Add oil, parsley, onion, grated orange rind. Close and cook on Low for 4 hours. Top with orange and lemon slices and enjoy!

Creamy Salmon

Serves: 4 | Total Time: 5 hours 20 minutes

1 can cream of celery soup, condensed	
1 can cream of onion soup, condensed	
2 crushed chicken bouillon cubes	
4 salmon fillets, chopped	1 cup breadcrumbs
6 eggs, well beaten	Salt and pepper to taste
15 oz tomato sauce	½ cup milk
1 tbsp lemon juice	1 tbsp olive oil
1 green bell pepper, diced	

Grease your Slow Cooker with olive oil. Add salmon, beaten eggs, breadcrumbs, cream of onion soup, chicken bouillon, and lemon juice. Close the lid and cook on Low for 5 hours. Heat the milk and cream of celery soup in a pan over medium heat and simmer for 5 minutes, stirring often. Serve salmon with sauce poured over it.

White Beans with Tuna

Serves: 4 | Total Time: 8 hours 10 minutes

2 (5-oz) cans white tuna in water, drained and flaked	
1 cup white beans, soaked	Salt and pepper to taste
2 cups tomatoes, chopped	2 tbsp olive oil
1 clove garlic, crushed	2 tbsp chopped basil

Fry the garlic in oil in a pan over medium heat. When the garlic browns, discard the garlic. Add the beans and 6 cups of water into your Slow Cooker. Cook on High for the first 2 hours. Switch to Low and cook for an additional 5 hours. Add the tuna, garlic-flavored oil, tomatoes, salt, and pepper. Continue to cook for an additional 1 more hour. Serve hot and enjoy!

Salmon Loaf with Cucumber Sauce

Serves: 6 | Total Time: 5 hours 10 minutes

1 (14.75-oz) can salmon, drained	
1 egg, whisked	3 green onions, chopped
1 tbsp dried dill weed	Salt and pepper to taste
1 tbsp capers	1 cup breadcrumbs
1 tbsp lemon juice	¼ cup milk

CUCUMBER SAUCE:

½ cup plain yogurt	½ tsp dill weeds
½ cup cucumber, chopped	Salt and pepper to taste

In a large mixing bowl, add salmon, egg, dill weed, capers, lemon juice, green onions, milk, breadcrumbs, salt, and pepper. Shape into a loaf. Place the loaf in your greased Slow Cooker after you coat the inside of the cooker with cooking spray. Close and cook on Low for 5 hours. Mix all the cucumber sauce ingredients in a bowl. Remove the salmon loaf from the slow cooker. Serve at room temperature topped with cucumber sauce.

Tuna Casserole

Serves: 4 | Total Time: 6 hours 20 minutes

2 (5-oz) cans tuna, flaked and drained	
1 cup celery, diced	Salt and pepper to taste
½ cup mayonnaise	1 cup crushed potato chips
4 chopped hard-boiled eggs	1 cup green peas

Stir the tuna, celery, mayonnaise, eggs, salt, peas, and pepper in your greased Slow Cooker. Put the potato chips on top and cook for 6 hours on Low. Serve.

Poached Salmon with Lemon-Caper Sauce

Serves: 4 | Total Time: 4 hours 15 minutes

4 salmon steaks	Salt and pepper to taste
½ cup dry white wine	1 yellow onion, sliced thin
1 bay leaf	½ cup lemon caper sauce

Add ½ cup of water, onion, wine, and bay leaf in your Slow Cooker. Cook on High for 2 hours. Add the salmon cook on High for an additional 2 hours. Serve at room temperature topped with lemon caper sauce and enjoy!

Greek Fish Kakavia

Serves: 6 | Total Time: 8 hours 15 minutes

1 lb skinless halibut fillets, cubed	
12 oz peeled shrimp, deveined	1 tsp thyme, dried
1 (14-oz) can diced tomatoes	2 carrot, chopped
2 leeks, thinly sliced	1 tbsp garlic, minced
Salt and pepper to taste	1 rib celery, chopped
12 mussels	½ cup dry white wine
12 clams	4 tbsp lemon juice

Add tomatoes, leeks, mussels, clams, thyme, carrot, garlic, celery, and lemon juice to your Slow Cooker. Close cooker lid. Cook on Low for 4 hours. Add the fish, shrimp, salt, and pepper and continue to cook for 4 more hours. Discard the bay leaves and any unopened clams and mussels. Adjust the seasoning and serve warm.

Citrusy Salmon Slow Roasted

Serves: 6 | Total Time: 4 hours 15 minutes

1 lb salmon fillets	¾ cup olive oil
1 Fresno chili, minced	1 fennel bulb, crushed
Salt and pepper to taste	1 seedless orange, sliced
1 tsp dry dill	1 seedless lemon, thin sliced

Mix in your Slow Cooker the chili, lemon, orange slices, crushed fennel, dill sprigs, and olive oil. Stir. Add the fish on top of this mixture and cook for 4 minutes on High.

Salmon Mediterranean Style

Serves: 4 | Total Time: 6 hours 10 minutes

1 tbsp Italian seasoning	Salt and pepper to taste
1 red bell pepper, chopped	1 small zucchini, sliced
1 tbsp olive oil	1 tsp garlic powder
1 tomato, sliced	1 lb salmon fillets
1 tsp onion powder	

Put in Italian seasoning, red bell pepper, onion powder, garlic powder, tomato, zucchini, olive oil, salt, and pepper in your Slow Cooker. Stir to combine. Top with the fish. Close and cook on Low for 6 hours. Serve warm.

Saucy Mango Halibut Fillets

Serves: 4 | Total Time: 4 hours 10 minutes

FOR THE FISH:

1 lb halibut steaks	1 tbsp fresh lime juice
½ tsp chili powder	1 tbsp olive oil
Salt and pepper to taste	

FOR MANGO SAUCE:

3 tbsp lime juice	1 tbsp cilantro, chopped
1 mango, chopped	1 garlic clove, minced
1 Jalapeno pepper, minced	¼ tsp salt

Mix 1 tbsp of olive oil, 1 tbsp lime juice, salt, pepper, and chili powder in a small bowl. Rub the mixture onto the halibut fillets and arrange them on your Slow Cooker.

Blend all the mango sauce ingredients, except the cilantro, in your food processor. Stir in the cilantro. Pour the mango sauce over the fish. Close and cook on High for 4 hours. Serve warm and enjoy!

Eggplant & Tilapia Curry

Serves: 6 | Total Time: 4 hours 10 minutes

1 eggplant, sliced	1 tsp ground turmeric
2 tbsp ginger puree	2 chilies, minced
4 tbsp coconut oil	1 ½ cups fish stock
3 garlic cloves, minced	1 cup coconut milk
1 onion, minced	1 tbsp curry powder
2 tomatoes, diced	1 lb tilapia fillets
1 handful of curry leaves	1 tsp ground coriander
1 tsp ground cumin	

In a large pan over medium heat, heat the coconut oil, and fry the eggplant for 2 minutes on each side; set aside. In the same pan, fry onion and chilies with curry leaves for 3 minutes. Add the fish and fry it for 2 minutes. Add all of the ingredients to your Slow Cooker, and cook on High for 4 hours. Serve the dish hot and enjoy!

Salmon with Pomegranate

Serves: 4 | Total Time: 4 hours 10 minutes

4 salmon fillets	2 cups pomegranate juice
4 lemon, sliced	1 crushed fennel bulb
¼ cup pomegranate seeds	1 tbsp olive oil
1 tbsp white wine vinegar	½ cup purple onions, sliced
2 oranges, sliced	1 tbsp allspice berries
1 tbsp honey	Salt and pepper to taste
2 tbsp fresh mint, chopped	1 cup water

Mix the water, honey, and pomegranate juice in your Slow Cooker. Cook for 4 hours on High. Add the fish and lemon, and cook for an additional 4 hours on High. On a serving platter, cover it with crushed fennel and orange slices. Place the fish on top of the platter. Serve.

Simple Butter Trout

Serves: 4 | Total Time: 4 hours 10 minutes

1 cup fish stock	1 lb trout, skinned
½ cup butter	

Combine all ingredients in your Slow Cooker. Close with the lid. Cook for 4 hours on Low. Serve and enjoy!

Crab, Shrimp & Clam Cassoulet

Serves: 6 | Total Time: 4 hours 15 minutes

12 oz crab meat	2 onions, chopped
16 oz cooked shrimp	1 red bell pepper, sliced
6 oz clams	1 celery rib, chopped
2 tsp Italian seasoning	1 (14-oz) can diced tomatoes
Salt and pepper to taste	12 oz Albacore (tuna)
1 tbsp garlic, minced	¾ tsp red pepper flakes
1 tsp honey	1 tbsp parsley, chopped

Add tomatoes, red pepper flakes, salt, pepper, celery, red bell pepper, onions, honey, garlic, and Italian seasoning to your Slow Cooker. Stir to combine.

Close and cook for 2 hours on Low. Add the seafood to the Slow Cooker and mix. Top with parsley and serve.

Cod Fillets with Cherry Tomatoes

Serves: 4 | Total Time: 4 hours 10 minutes

1 lb cod fillets	2 pints cherry tomatoes
1 tbsp tomato paste	¼ tsp ground allspice
1 tsp honey	1 garlic clove, minced
1 Fresno chili, minced	1 tbsp red wine vinegar
2 tbsp cilantro, chopped	1 tsp paprika
¼ cup olive oil	½ tsp red pepper flakes

Add the tomato paste, Fresno chili, honey, cilantro leaves, olive oil, allspice, garlic, paprika and red pepper flakes in a bowl and mix well.

Place the fish into your Slow Cooker, pour the mixture over the fish. Slice cherry tomatoes in half, then put them over top of fish. Close and cook on High for 4 hours. Serve and enjoy!

Spicy Salmon Curry

Serves: 6 | Total Time: 4 hours 10 minutes

½ cup vegetable stock	2 tsp ginger, minced
2 tsp chopped cilantro	2 carrots, sliced
2 tsp chopped parsley	2 garlic cloves, minced
Salt and pepper to taste	1 celery stalk, chopped
6 salmon fillets	1 (13.5-oz) can coconut milk
1 tsp smoked paprika	1 tbsp tomato paste
1 tsp chili powder	

Add coconut milk, tomato paste, vegetable stock, celery, garlic, carrots, cilantro, ginger, chili powder, smoked paprika, parsley, cilantro, salt, and pepper into your Slow Cooker and stir to mix well. Top with the salmon. Close cooker lid. Cook on High for 4 hours. Serve warm.

Fresh Salmon Chowder with Potatoes

Serves: 4 | Total Time: 4 hours 15 minutes

1 cup whole milk	1 onion, chopped
2 tbsp cornstarch	4 cups fish stock
3 cups potatoes, cubed	½ lb salmon steaks, cubed
½ tsp dried marjoram	Salt and pepper to taste

Add potatoes, marjoram, dry mustard, and onions into your Slow Cooker. Cook on High for 2 hours. Add the mixture into your food processor and blend until smooth. Place mixture back into the slow cooker and add the salmon. Continue cooking on High for an additional 2 hours. Add milk and cornstarch and stir for a few minutes. Season with salt and pepper. Serve warm.

Wild Rice & Salmon Soup

Serves: 6 | Total Time: 8 hours 25 minutes

1 cup fried bacon, crumbled	1 lb skinless salmon, cubed
6 cups fish stock	1 cup milk
1 tsp garlic, minced	½ cup wild rice
½ tsp dry mustard	1 cup mushrooms, sliced
Salt to taste	½ cup celery, sliced
1 tsp cayenne pepper	1 onion, chopped

Add the vegetables, garlic, dry mustard, rosemary, and stock in your Slow Cooker. Close and cook on Low for 4 hours. Add the milk and wild rice and stir. Place the salmon in the cooker, sprinkle with cayenne pepper and salt, and cook for 4 more hours. Top with bacon. Serve.

Chickpea with Infused Salmon

Serves: 4 | Total Time: 4 hours 10 minutes

½ tsp butter, melted	1 tsp honey
1 lb salmon fillets	2 tsp fish seasoning
FOR CHICKPEA:	
15 oz canned chickpeas	1 green onion, chopped
½ tsp lime juice	Salt and pepper to taste

Mix the fish seasoning, honey, and butter in a bowl. Rub the mixture all over the salmon and add it to your Slow Cooker. Cook on Low for 4 hours. In a bowl, mix all of the chickpea ingredients. Add cooked fish to serving plate and top with chickpea mixture. Enjoy!

White Fish & Chicken Jambalaya

Serves: 4 | Total Time: 4 hours 10 minutes

½ lb chicken breasts, cubed	2 tsp honey
½ lb white fish fillets	1 small zucchini, sliced
12 cooked shrimp	1 bay leaf
½ cup carrots, sliced	½ tsp cumin
1 onion, sliced	Salt and pepper to taste
2 red bell peppers, sliced	1 tsp dry mustard
1 stalk celery, diced	2 tbsp olive oil

Add the chicken, mustard, salt, pepper, bay leaf, cumin, zucchini, honey, red bell peppers, onion, olive oil, and carrots to your Slow Cooker. Cook on High for 2 hours. Add the fish and shrimp and cook for 2 hours. Serve.

Prawn & Beef Stock Mix

Serves: 4 | Total Time: 4 hours 15 minutes

1 lb prawns	1 onion, chopped
Salt and pepper to taste	2 cloves garlic, crushed
½ red chili pepper, minced	2 tbsp fresh ginger, minced
1 cup carrots, thinly sliced	2 beef stock cubes
2 tbsp chopped cilantro	1 stick lemongrass

Add the lemongrass, 4 cups of water, stock, ginger, garlic, cilantro, carrots, red chili pepper, salt, and pepper to your Slow Cooker. Cook for 2 hours on High. Add the prawns. Cook for 2 more hours on High. Serve warm.

Avocado Salsa with Salmon

Serves: 4 | Total Time: 4 hours 10 minutes

1 tbsp cilantro, chopped	1 tsp cumin
½ purple onion, diced	1 avocado, sliced
1 tsp olive oil	1 tsp garlic powder
Salt and pepper to taste	2 tsp lime juice
1 tsp paprika	1 lb salmon steaks
1 tsp chili powder	

To make the salsa-mix the avocado, lime juice, cilantro and red onion in a small bowl. Mix together garlic powder, cumin, chili powder, paprika, salt and pepper in a small bowl to make a rub for salmon. Stir well. Add the rub all over the salmon. Place the salmon into your Slow Cooker. Cook on High for 4 hours. Serve hot with avocado salsa.

Orange & Honey Flavored Tilapia

Serves: 4 | Total Time: 4 hours 10 minutes

10 oz orange wedges	Salt and pepper to taste
4 tilapia fillets	1 tbsp honey
2 tbsp Balsamic vinegar	

Place the fish fillets inside some foil, and put into your Slow Cooker. In a small mixing bowl, mix mandarin orange pieces, balsamic vinegar, salt, white pepper, and honey. Stir to combine. Add mixture on top of fish. Seal the foil. Let fish cook on High for 4 hours. Serve warm.

Basic Boiled Pollock

Serves: 4 | Total Time: 4 hours 15 minutes

2 lb pollock	3 cups water
1 tsp salt	

Add pollock, water, and salt to your Slow Cooker and stir. Closes the lid to the cooker. Cook on Low for 4 hours. Strain fish. Serve warm and enjoy!

Sweet & Sour Shrimp

Serves: 4 | Total Time: 4 hours 15 minutes

15 oz pineapple tidbits in juice	
6 oz Chinese pea pods	½ tsp ground ginger
1 cup chicken broth	2 tbsp cider vinegar
2 cups cooked rice	1 tbsp soy sauce
3 tbsp sugar	2 tbsp cornstarch

Drain the pineapple bits. Reserve ½ cup pineapple juice. Add pineapple bits and pea pods in your Slow Cooker. In a small pan, mix sugar and cornstarch, reserved pineapple juice, chicken broth, soy sauce and ginger over medium-high heat. Stir to combine well. Cook for about 1 minute. Add sauce to the slow cooker, then cook for 2 hours on Low. Add the cooked shrimp, and cook for an additional 2 hours on Low. Add the vinegar and stir. Serve the dish hot over a bed of cooked rice, and enjoy!

Bean Hummus & Seafood Stew

Serves: 6 | Total Time: 8 hours 15 minutes

6.5 oz chopped clams with juice, canned and undrained	
1 lb tilapia, cut into 1-inch pieces	
8 oz large shrimps, deveined, peeled, and tail-less	
2 cups kale, chopped	Salt and pepper to taste
¼ cup instant potato flakes?	1 tsp dry thyme
15 oz canned diced tomatoes	1 cup onion, chopped
4 cups vegetable broth	1 tbsp garlic, chopped

Mix the broth and tomatoes in your Slow Cooker. Then add the kale, onion, clams, garlic, salt, pepper, and thyme into the slow cooker and stir. Finally, add the fish and shrimp and mix well. Cook on Low for 8 hours. Stir in the potato flakes. Serve hot and enjoy!

Octopus with Chilies & Beans

Serves: 6 | Total Time: 4 hours 15 minutes

2 lb cleaned octopus, rinsed	3 tbsp olive oil
2 red chilies, minced	2 bay leaves
1 celery rib, chopped	½ cup white beans, soaked
3 garlic cloves, minced	Salt and pepper to taste

Cook the beans for 2 hours in your Slow Cooker on High. Once beans are cooked, remove them from the slow cooker. Add the remaining ingredients to the slow cooker and cook for 2 hours on High. After cooking, remove the octopus and cut it into pieces. Evenly add all ingredients to the slow cooker and mix well. Cook for an additional 10 minutes on High. Serve hot and enjoy!

Shrimp, Chicken & Sausage Gumbo

Serves: 6 | Total Time: 8 hours 15 minutes

1 green bell pepper, diced	½ lb smoked sausage, sliced
1 ½ cups frozen okra	¾ lb boneless chicken thighs
3 tbsp olive oil	½ shrimp, cleaned
1 tbsp flour	4 cups chicken broth
1 (14-oz) can diced tomatoes	¼ tsp black pepper
1 onion, chopped	¼ tsp cayenne pepper
2 cups cooked long-grain rice	3 cloves garlic, minced

Combine flour and oil in a pan over medium heat and cook for 6 minutes. Add the shrimp to the pan. Lower temperature and cook for another 2-3 minutes. Add all of the ingredients into your Slow Cooker and stir, except shrimp and rice. Cook for 4 hours on Low. Add the shrimp into the cooker and cook on Low for another 4 hours. Serve the shrimp on a bed of cooked rice.

Octopus in Olives & Fennel

Serves: 6 | Total Time: 4 hours 15 minutes

2 lb cleaned octopus (tubes and tentacles), rinsed
½ cup Ouzo   3 garlic cloves
¼ cup red wine vinegar   2 cups warm water
12 Kalamata olives   2 cups fennel bulb
1 cup onions, chopped   1 tbsp mustard

Add octopus' pieces into your Slow Cooker along with warm water and cook for 2 hours on Low. Once octopus' is cooked, add fennel bulb, garlic, and onions. Now, cook for an additional 2 hours. Once cooked, add olives, red wine vinegar, and mustard. Serve hot and enjoy!

Rich Shrimps with Cherry Tomatoes

Serves: 4 | Total Time: 4 hours 15 minutes

¼ cup olive oil   1 tbsp chopped parsley
1-pint cherry tomatoes   Salt and pepper to taste
2 green onions, chopped   4 tbsp capers
1 tsp crushed red peppers   2 oz anchovies
1 Jalapeno chili, minced   20 Kalamata olives
5 black olives   1 lb cleaned shrimp, deveined
8 garlic cloves, minced   1 tbsp chopped chives
1 small zucchini, sliced

Sauté the zucchini in a pan with olive oil over medium heat for 3-4 minutes. Carefully add all of the ingredients to your Slow Cooker, including the sautéed zucchini. Close and cook for 4 hours on High. Serve and enjoy!

Garlic Shrimp

Serves: 6 | Total Time: 4 hours 10 minutes

2 lb cleaned shrimp, deveined   1 tbsp parsley
¾ cup olive oil   6 garlic cloves
¼ tsp red pepper flakes   1 tsp paprika
Salt and pepper to taste

Add olive oil, red pepper flakes, salt, pepper, parsley, garlic, and paprika. Mix to combine. Close cooker lid. Set on High and cook for 2 hours. Add the shrimp to your Slow Cooker and cook for an additional 2 hours. Serve.

Crab & Shrimp Boil

Serves: 6 | Total Time: 4 hours 15 minutes

6 oz crab   3 lb shrimp, cleaned
4 cups water   1 tbsp salt

Pour the water into your Slow Cooker. Add salt and stir. Add the crab and shrimp. Close the lid. Cook on Low setting for 4 hours. Serve hot and enjoy!

Grits with Shrimp

Serves: 4 | Total Time: 6 hours 15 minutes

1 cup grits   1 lb cooked, deveined shrimp
1 tbsp chopped chives   2 tsp hot sauce
1 cup cheese, shredded   Salt to taste
¼ cup heavy cream   2 tbsp butter

Add 4 cups water, salt, and grits into your Slow Cooker and toss. Cook on Low for 6 hours. Combine cream, hot sauce, cheese, and butter. Stir and melt the cheese in a pan over medium heat. Top grits with shrimp and pour cheese sauce on top. Serve hot and enjoy!

Sausage & Shrimp Jambalaya

Serves: 4 | Total Time: 8 hours 10 minutes

1 lb shrimp   2 tsp garlic, minced
30 oz stewed tomatoes   2 stalks celery, chopped
½ tsp cayenne pepper   2 bell peppers, chopped
2 sausages, sliced

Carefully add all of the ingredients into your Slow Cooker, then stir to combine. Cook on Low for 8 hours.

Hot Shrimp

Serves: 4 | Total Time: 4 hours 15 minutes

¼ lb shrimp, cleaned   2 garlic cloves, minced
1 tbsp parsley, chopped   1 tbsp avocado oil
14 oz diced tomatoes   Salt and pepper to taste
1 onion, chopped   1 tsp red pepper flakes

Sauté in a small pan over medium heat the garlic, onion, and red pepper flakes for about 3 minutes. Add ingredients into your Slow Cooker, except for the shrimp. Cook on Low for 2 hours. Place the shrimp in the slow cooker, then cook for an additional 2 hours. Serve warm.

Manhattan- Style Clam Chowder

Serves: 4 | Total Time: 8 hours 15 minutes

6 bacon slices, diced   2 large potatoes, diced
3 ribs celery, sliced   1 tsp dried thyme
2 carrots, thinly sliced   1 bay leaf
1 cup onion, chopped   Salt and pepper to taste
8 oz clam juice   30 oz canned tomatoes, diced
20 oz minced clams   1 tbsp parsley, chopped

Add the diced cooked bacon to your Slow Cooker. Add the remaining ingredients and stir. Close and cook on Low for 8 hours. Serve hot and enjoy!

Tasty King Crab Legs

Serves: 4 | Total Time: 4 hours 15 minutes

4 lb king crab legs   4 lemon wedges
½ cup melted butter   ½ tsp salt

Break the crab legs in half and place in your Slow Cooker with salt and 1 cup of water. Close and cook for 4 hours on High. Top with butter and serve with lemon wedges.

DESSERTS

Rum Muffin Cake with Berries

Serves: 6 | Total Time: 6 hours 20 minutes

1 tsp dark rum	2 tsp grated lemon zest
1 tbsp butter, melted	1 ½ tsp baking powder
3 cups flour	1 tsp vanilla extract
½ cup Greek yogurt	½ tsp baking soda
¼ cup sugar	¼ tsp salt
3 large eggs	1 cup fresh berries

In a large bowl, combine the flour, yogurt, sugar, eggs, lemon zest, baking powder, vanilla, baking soda, and salt and whisk with hand mixer until well blended. Carefully fold in the berries. Grease your Slow Cooker with butter.

Pour the batter into the slow cooker. Cover and cook for 6 hours on Low or until a cake tester inserted in center comes out clean and dry. Let it cool to room temperature.

Awesome Peach Cobbler

Serves: 6 | Total Time: 6 hours 30 minutes

2 lb ripe peaches, pitted and sliced
1 tbsp cornstarch 2 tbsp brown sugar

FOR THE COBBLER

¼ cup sugar	2/3 cup buttermilk, chilled
1 ½ cups all-purpose flour	½ tsp baking powder
½ cup cold butter, cubed	½ tsp salt

Toss the peaches, cornstarch, and sugar in your Slow Cooker. In a bowl, whisk flour, baking powder, salt, sugar, and butter until sandy. Pour in buttermilk and mix until slightly crumbly. Top the peaches with the butter mixture. Cover with the lid and cook for 6 hours on Low. When done, remove the lid and serve warm or chilled.

Aromatic Blackberry Crumble

Serves: 6 | Total Time: 2 hours 15 minutes

¼ cup white sugar	1 tsp vanilla extract
1 ½ lb fresh blackberries	1 tsp dried lavender buds
2 tbsp cornstarch	

FOR THE CRUMBLE

1 cup all-purpose flour	1 pinch of salt
½ cup cold butter, cubed	

Combine blackberries, cornstarch, vanilla extract, sugar, and lavender buds in your Slow Cooker. In a bowl, mix the flour, salt, and butter until sandy and pour it over the berry mixture. Cover with the lid and cook for 2 hours on High. When done, remove the lid and serve chilled.

Homemade Apple Butter

Serves: 6 | Total Time: 8 hours 15 minutes

4 lb Granny Smith apples, peeled and cored

2 lb peeled apples, cored	1 tsp cinnamon powder
2 cups white sugar	½ tsp ground ginger
1 cup fresh apple juice	

Mix the Granny Smith apples, tart apples, sugar, apple juice, cinnamon powder, and ginger in your Slow Cooker. Cover with the lid and cook for 8 hours on Low. When done, remove the lid, using a hand mixer, blitz until puree, and share it into sealable jars. Store it in your storage space for up to 2-3 months.

Pineapple & Carrot Cake

Serves: 6 | Total Time: 2 hours 45 minutes

1 cup crushed pineapple, drained

1 cup grated carrots	1 tsp vanilla extract
½ cup pecans, chopped	1 tsp baking powder
½ cup canola oil	½ tsp baking soda
1 ½ cups all-purpose flour	½ tsp ground ginger
3/4 cup white sugar	1 tsp cinnamon powder
¼ cup dark brown sugar	¼ tsp cardamom powder
2 eggs	½ tsp salt

In a bowl, combine canola oil, white sugar, brown sugar, eggs, and vanilla extract until creamy. Add in flour, baking powder, baking soda, ginger, cinnamon powder, cardamom powder, and salt and toss until well combined. Fold in carrots, pineapple, and pecans. Pour the mixture into your Slow Cooker. Cover with the lid and cook for 2 ¼ hours on High. Let cool before slicing to serve.

Apple Cake with White Chocolate

Serves: 6 | Total Time: 6 hours 30 minutes

4 tart apples, peeled, cored and sliced	
½ cup white chocolate chips	1 cup all-purpose flour
5 eggs, separated	1 tsp baking powder
3/4 cup white sugar	¼ tsp salt
½ cup butter, melted	½ tsp cinnamon powder
½ cup whole milk	

In a bowl, beat egg yolks and half of the sugar until it increases the volume. Mix in butter and milk until smooth. Add in flour, baking powder, and salt and toss to combine. In another bowl, whisk egg whites and the remaining sugar until it forms peaks. Pour it into the flour mixture and toss until well combined. Fold in chocolate chips, transfer everything to your Slow Cooker, and top with apple slices and cinnamon powder. Cook for 6 hours on Low. Let cool before serving.

Peanut Butter Fudgy Cake

Serves: 6 | Total Time: 2 hours 15 minutes

¼ cup whole milk	½ cup smooth peanut butter
1 cup all-purpose flour	3/4 cup white sugar
¼ cup cocoa powder	1 tsp vanilla extract
2 eggs	1 tsp baking powder
¼ cup canola oil	¼ tsp salt

In a bowl, combine canola oil, sugar, peanut butter, vanilla extract, and eggs. Put in milk, flour, cocoa powder, baking powder, and salt and toss until well combined. Pour it into your Slow Cooker, cover with the lid, and cook for 2 hours on High. Let cool before serving.

Mocha Cake

Serves: 6 | Total Time: 4 hours 15 minutes

2 eggs	½ cup brewed coffee
1 cup whole milk	1 tsp baking powder
1 ½ cups sugar	1 tsp baking soda
1 ½ cups all-purpose flour	½ tsp salt
½ cup cocoa powder	1 tsp vanilla extract
½ cup canola oil	

Using an electric mixer, beat sugar, flour, cocoa powder, baking powder, baking soda, salt, eggs, milk, canola oil, vanilla extract, and coffee until smooth. Transfer everything to your Slow Cooker. Cover with the lid and cook for 4 hours on Low. Let cool before slicing to serve.

Apples with Oats & Raisins

Serves: 6 | Total Time: 4 hours 15 minutes

6 apples

FOR THE TOPPING

1 cup golden raisins	¼ cup all-purpose flour
¼ cup cold butter, cubed	½ cup apple cider
1 cup rolled oats	2 tbsp brown sugar

In a bowl, combine raisins, sugar, oats, flour, and butter until crumbly. Discard the core of each apple, fill them with the raisin mixture, and place them into your Slow Cooker. Pour in apple cider, cover with the lid, and cook for 4 hours on Low. Serve chilled.

Apple Brioche

Serves: 6 | Total Time: 6 hours 30 minutes

4 apples, peeled and cubed	4 eggs
16 oz brioche bread, cubed	1 tsp cinnamon powder
1 cup evaporated milk	½ tsp ground ginger
1 cup condensed milk	2 tbsp white sugar
1 cup whole milk	1 tsp vanilla extract

Add brioche bread, apples, cinnamon powder, ginger, and sugar in your Slow Cooker. In a bowl, whisk milk, condensed milk, and evaporated milk until well combined. Add in eggs and vanilla extract and beat until smooth. Pour it over the bread, cover with the lid, and cook for 6 hours on Low. Serve and enjoy!

Peanut Butter Cake with Chocolate Chips

Serves: 6 | Total Time: 4 hours 15 minutes

½ cup dark chocolate chips	3 eggs
1 cup all-purpose flour	1 tsp vanilla extract
½ cup butter, softened	1 tsp baking powder
½ cup smooth peanut butter	¼ tsp salt
½ cup light brown sugar	

In a bowl, combine butter, peanut butter, and sugar until creamy. Pour in eggs, one by one, and vanilla extract. Mix in flour, baking powder, and salt until well combined and fold in chocolate chips. Transfer everything to your Slow Cooker. Cover with the lid and cook for 4 hours on Low. Let cool before slicing to serve.

Cocoa Amarena Cherry Cake

Serves: 6 | Total Time: 4 hours 15 minutes

2 cups Amarena cherries, pitted	
½ cup whole milk	¼ cup light brown sugar
1 ½ cups all-purpose flour	1 tsp vanilla extract
¼ cup cocoa powder	¼ tsp salt
½ cup butter, melted	½ tsp baking powder
1 cup cola	½ tsp baking soda

In a bowl, combine cola, sugar, butter, vanilla extract, and milk. Add in flour, cocoa powder, salt, baking powder, and baking soda and toss until well combined. Fold in cherries and pour the mixture into your Slow Cooker. Cover and cook for 4 hours on Low. Serve chilled.

Cardamom Poached Pears

Serves: 6 | Total Time: 6 hours 30 minutes

1-inch ginger, sliced	1-star anise
3/4 cup white sugar	4 whole cloves
6 ripe but firm pears	2 cinnamon stick
2 cups white wine	2 cardamom pods, crushed
1 ½ cups water	

Peel and discard the core from the pears. Add pears, wine, water, sugar, star anise, ginger, cloves, cinnamon stick, and cardamom pods to your Slow Cooker and stir. Cover and cook for 6 hours on Low. Serve chilled.

Ginger Orange Cheesecake

Serves: 6 | Total Time: 7 hours 30 minutes

CRUST:

6 oz graham crackers, crushed	
½ cup butter, melted	1 tbsp grated orange zest

FILLING:

1 cup sour cream	1 tsp grated ginger
4 eggs	1 tsp grated orange zest
20 oz cream cheese	½ cup white sugar
1 tbsp cornstarch	1 pinch of salt

In a bowl, combine crackers, butter, and orange zest until crumbly. Transfer everything to your Slow Cooker and press down. Combine cream cheese, sour cream, eggs, cornstarch, ginger, orange zest, sugar, and salt in a bowl until creamy and pour it over the crust. Cover and cook for 7 hours on Low. Serve chilled.

Light Lemon Cheesecake

Serves: 6 | Total Time: 6 hours 15 minutes

4 eggs	2/3 cup white sugar
24 oz cream cheese	2 tbsp cornstarch
½ cup heavy cream	1 tsp vanilla extract
1 lemon, zested and juiced	

In a bowl, beat cream cheese, heavy cream, eggs, cornstarch, lemon zest, lemon juice, sugar, and vanilla extract. Grease the pot of your Slow Cooker and pour in the batter. Cook for 6 hours on Low. Serve chilled.

Cherry Cobbler

Serves: 6 | Total Time: 4 hours 30 minutes

4 red apples, peeled and sliced
1 lb cherries, pitted
4 tbsp maple syrup

2 tbsp cornstarch
1 tbsp lemon juice

FOR THE TOPPING

½ cup buttermilk, chilled
½ cup cold butter, cubed

1 ¼ cups all-purpose flour
2 tbsp white sugar

Mix the cherries, apples, maple syrup, cornstarch, and lemon juice in your Slow Cooker. In a bowl, combine flour, butter, and sugar until sandy. Pour in buttermilk and stir until well combined. Pour the crumble over the fruits and cook for 4 hours on Low. Serve chilled.

Apfelstrudel

Serves: 4 | Total Time: 4 hours 30 minutes

4 large apples, peeled and cubed
½ cup golden raisins

1 tsp cinnamon powder

FOR THE TOPPING

½ cup pecans, chopped
1 cup ground almonds
2 tbsp melted butter

2 tbsp all-purpose flour
2 tbsp brown sugar
1 pinch of salt

In your Slow Cooker, combine apples, raisins, and cinnamon powder. In a bowl, whisk pecans, almonds, flour, butter, sugar, and salt until crumbly and pour over the fruits. Cook for 4 hours on Low. Serve chilled.

Fudgy Strawberry Brownies

Serves: 6 | Total Time: 2 hours 15 minutes

1 ½ cups strawberries, halved
1 cup dark chocolate chips
2 eggs
½ cup butter, cubed
½ cup white sugar

½ cup applesauce
¼ cup cocoa powder
½ cup all-purpose flour
1 pinch of salt

Put a heatproof bowl over a pot of boiling water. Add the butter and chocolate and stir with a spatula until melted and smooth. Take the bowl off the heat and stir in sugar and applesauce. Let the mixture cool slightly. Add eggs one at a time, mixing gently. Add in the cocoa powder, flour, and salt and mix until well incorporated. Spoon the batter into your Slow Cooker. Put strawberries on top and cook for 2 hours on High. Let cool before slicing into small squares. Serve and enjoy!

Cinnamon Pumpkin Cheesecake

Serves: 6 | Total Time: 6 hours 30 minutes

CRUST:

½ cup butter, melted

8 oz graham crackers, crushed

FILLING:

1 ½ cups pumpkin puree
24 oz cream cheese
3 eggs
2 tbsp cornstarch
½ cup white sugar

1 tsp vanilla extract
½ tsp cinnamon powder
½ tsp ground ginger
1 pinch of salt

In a bowl, combine crackers and butter until well combined. Add the mixture to your Slow Cooker. Add the cream cheese, pumpkin puree, eggs, cornstarch, sugar, vanilla, cinnamon powder, ginger, and salt to a bowl and toss until well combined. Pour it over the crust and cook for 6 hours on Low. Serve.

Black & White Chocolate Bread Pudding

Serves: 6 | Total Time: 4 hours 30 minutes

¼ cup white chocolate chips
1 ½ cups whole milk
8 cups brioche bread cubes
1 cup heavy cream
1 cup dark chocolate chips

4 eggs
2 tsp instant coffee
¼ cup light brown sugar
1 tsp orange zest

Place heavy cream in a pot over high heat and bring it to a boil. Turn the heat off and stir in dark chocolate chips until melted. Transfer it to a bowl, add milk, eggs, coffee, sugar, and orange zest, and toss until well combined. Put brioche cubes and white chocolate chips in your Slow Cooker and cover with the coffee mixture. Cover with the lid and cook for 4 hours on Low. Serve and enjoy!

Apple Crisp with Walnuts

Serves: 6 | Total Time: 4 hours 30 minutes

½ lb Granny Smith apples, peeled, cored and sliced
4 tbsp light brown sugar
1 tsp cinnamon powder
1 tsp ground ginger

1 tbsp lemon juice
1 tbsp cornstarch

FOR THE TOPPING

1 cup ground walnuts
¼ cup butter, melted
½ cup all-purpose flour

2 tbsp white sugar
1 pinch of salt
Caramel sauce for serving

In your Slow Cooker, combine apples, cinnamon powder, ginger, sugar, lemon juice, and cornstarch. In a bowl, beat flour, walnuts, butter, sugar, and salt until crumbly and pour it over the apples. Cover with the lid and cook for 4 hours on Low. When done, remove the lid and serve sprinkled with caramel sauce.

Amaretto Cheesecake

Serves: 6 | Total Time: 6 hours 30 minutes

CRUST:

6 oz Amaretti cookies, crushed
¼ cup butter, melted

FILLING:

4 eggs
24 oz cream cheese
½ cup sour cream

½ cup white sugar
1 tbsp vanilla extract
1 tbsp Amaretto liqueur

In a bowl, combine cookies and butter until crumbly. Transfer it into your Slow Cooker and press down. In a bowl, whisk cream cheese, sour cream, eggs, sugar, vanilla extract, and Amaretto liqueur until smooth and pour it over the crust. Cover with the lid and cook for 6 hours on Low. Serve and enjoy!

Holiday Gingerbread

Serves: 6 | Total Time: 2 hours 30 minutes

½ cup golden raisins	1 tbsp cocoa powder
½ cup buttermilk	1 tsp ground ginger
1¼ cups all-purpose flour	1 tsp cinnamon powder
3/4 cup butter, softened	¼ tsp ground cloves
½ cup white sugar	1 tsp baking powder
½ cup dark brown sugar	¼ tsp baking soda
3 eggs	¼ tsp salt
1 tsp vanilla extract	

In a bowl, beat butter, white sugar, and brown sugar until creamy. Pour in eggs, one by one, and vanilla extract and toss to well combined. Mix in buttermilk, flour, cocoa powder, ginger, cinnamon powder, cloves, baking powder, baking soda, salt, and raisins until well combined. Pour the mixture into your Slow Cooker. Cover and cook for 2 hours on High. Serve chilled.

Divine Crème Brulee

Serves: 4 | Total Time: 6 hours 15 minutes

2 egg yolks	1 tsp vanilla extract
2 whole eggs	2 tbsp maple syrup
2½ cups milk	2 tbsp white sugar
1 ½ cups heavy cream	1 cup sugar for topping

In a bowl, combine milk, heavy cream, egg yolks, vanilla extract, eggs, maple syrup, and sugar. Divide the mixture between 4 ramekins and place them into your Slow Cooker. Pour in enough water to cover 3/4, cover with the lid, and cook for 6 hours on Low. When done, remove the lid, sprinkle with the remaining sugar and using a torch, burn it until caramelized. Serve right away.

Ginger Rice Pudding

Serves: 6 | Total Time: 4 hours 15 minutes

1 cup Arborio rice	1 cinnamon stick
3 cups whole milk	1-star anise
½-inch ginger, sliced	2 whole cloves
½ cup white sugar	½ tsp rose water

Toss rice, sugar, milk, cinnamon stick, star anise, cloves, ginger, and rose water in your Slow Cooker. Cover with the lid and cook for 4 hours on Low. Serve chilled.

Apricot & White Chocolate Bread Pudding

Serves: 6 | Total Time: 5 hours 30 minutes

1 cup dried apricots, diced	4 eggs
1 cup white chocolate chips	1 tsp vanilla extract
8 cups bread cubes	1 tsp orange zest
2 cups milk	½ cup white sugar
1 cup heavy cream	

Toss the bread cubes, apricots, and chocolate chips in your Slow Cooker. In a bowl, whisk milk, heavy cream, eggs, vanilla extract, orange zest, and sugar until well combined and pour it over the bread. Cover with the lid and cook for 5 hours on Low. Serve and enjoy!

Peanut Butter & Caramel Cheesecake

Serves: 6 | Total Time: 6 hours 30 minutes

CRUST:
1 ½ cups crushed graham crackers
½ cup butter, melted

FILLING:

20 oz cream cheese	½ cup caramel sauce
4 eggs	1 tbsp cornstarch
½ cup light brown sugar	1 tsp vanilla extract
½ cup smooth peanut butter	

In a bowl, combine crackers and butter until crumbly, transfer it to your Slow Cooker, and press down on the bottom. In a separate bowl, beat peanut butter, caramel sauce, cream cheese, eggs, cornstarch, vanilla extract, and sugar until smooth and pour it over the crust. Cover with the lid and cook for 6 hours on Low. When done, remove the lid and serve

Walnut Cinnamon Streusel

Serves: 6 | Total Time: 4 hours 30 minutes

CINNAMON STREUSEL:

½ cup all-purpose flour	1 cup chopped walnuts
½ cup light brown sugar	1 tsp cinnamon powder

CAKE:

1 ½ cups all-purpose flour	4 eggs
1 cup sour cream	1 tsp vanilla extract
3/4 cup butter, softened	½ tsp salt
3/4 cup sugar	1 ½ tsp baking powder

In a bowl, combine walnuts, flour, sugar, and cinnamon powder. Set aside. Using an electric mixer, beat butter and sugar until creamy, mix in eggs, one by one, and vanilla extract. Add in the flour, salt, baking powder, and sour cream and pulse for 2 minutes until well combined. Pour half of the batter into your Slow Cooker, add the streusel mixture, and top with the remaining batter. Cover with the lid and cook for 4 hours on Low. Let cool before serving.

Chocolate & Dulce de Leche Pie

Serves: 6 | Total Time: 2 hours 30 minutes

CRUST:

¼ cup chilled milk	1 pinch of salt
½ cup cold butter, cubed	¼ tsp baking powder
1 cup all-purpose flour	2 tbsp sugar

FILLING:
2 cups dark chocolate chips 1 can (14 oz) dulce de leche

In a blender, add butter, flour, salt, baking powder, sugar and pulse until sandy. Pour in milk and pulse for a few seconds until combined. Put the dough on a floured surface, roll it into a round, and place it on the bottom of your Slow Cooker. Pour dulce de leche over the crust and scatter with chocolate chips. Cover and cook for 2 hours on High. Serve and enjoy!

Zesty Berry Cake

Serves: 6 | Total Time: 4 hours 30 minutes

1 cup fresh mixed berries	1 tsp vanilla extract
4 eggs	2 tsp lemon zest
1 cup all-purpose flour	1 tsp baking powder
1 cup butter, softened	¼ tsp salt
1 cup white sugar	

Using an electric mixer, beat butter, sugar, and vanilla extract until creamy. Pour in eggs, one by one, and lemon zest and pulse for 1 minute at high speed. Add in flour, baking powder, and salt and pulse to combine. Transfer everything to your Slow Cooker and top with berries. Cook for 4 hours on Low. Let cool before serving.

Caramel Pear Cake

Serves: 6 | Total Time: 4 hours 30 minutes

4 ripe pears, cored and sliced	½ cup sugar
3/4 cup caramel sauce	¼ tsp salt
2/3 cup all-purpose flour	½ tsp cinnamon powder
1 tsp baking powder	¼ cup whole milk
¼ cup butter, melted	

In a bowl, whisk flour, baking powder, sugar, salt, and cinnamon powder. Pour in milk and butter and toss to combine. Put pears in your Slow Cooker, top with the flour mixture, and sprinkle with caramel sauce. Cover with the lid and cook for 4 hours on Low. Serve chilled.

Rum Chocolate Fondue

Serves: 6 | Total Time: 2 hours 15 minutes

10 strawberries	¼ cup whole milk
1 cup heavy cream	1 ½ cups dark chocolate chips
¼ cup condensed milk	2 tbsp dark rum

Mix the heavy cream, condensed milk, milk, chocolate chips, and rum in your Slow Cooker. Cover with the lid and cook for 2 hours on Low. When done, remove the lid and serve with the dipping strawberries.

Pears Poached with Coconut Milk

Serves: 6 | Total Time: 6 hours 15 minutes

2 cups coconut milk	1 cinnamon stick
3/4 cup coconut sugar	1-star anise
6 ripe but firm pears	2 lemon rings
2 cups water	

Peel the pears and discard the core. Place the pears, coconut milk, water, cinnamon stick, star anise, coconut sugar, and lemon rings in your Slow Cooker. Cover and cook for 6 hours on Low. Let cool before serving.

Drunken Brioche Pudding

Serves: 6 | Total Time: 6 hours 30 minutes

4 eggs, beaten	¼ cup brandy
2 cups whole milk	½ cup light brown sugar
10 oz brioche bread, cubed	1 tsp vanilla extract

Add brioche bread to your Slow Cooker. In a bowl, combine eggs, milk, brandy, sugar, and vanilla extract until smooth and pour it over the bread. Cover with the lid and cook for 6 hours on Low. Serve and enjoy!

Chocolate & Walnut Bread

Serves: 6 | Total Time: 2 hours 30 minutes

1 cup walnuts, chopped	½ cup light brown sugar
1 cup all-purpose flour	½ cup cocoa powder
1 cup whole milk	1 tsp vanilla extract
3 eggs	¼ tsp salt
¼ cup sour cream	1 tsp baking powder
½ cup canola oil	

In a bowl, beat milk, eggs, canola oil, vanilla extract, and sour cream until creamy. Stir in sugar, flour, cocoa powder, salt, and baking powder until well combined. Fold in walnuts and pour the mixture into your Slow Cooker. Cover and cook for 2 hours on High. Serve.

Pear Crumble with Cocoa

Serves: 6 | Total Time: 4 hours 30 minutes

6 ripe pears, peeled, cored and sliced	
¼ cup light brown sugar	1 tbsp cornstarch

FOR THE CRUMBLE

3/4 cup all-purpose flour	¼ tsp salt
½ cup cocoa powder	½ tsp baking powder
½ cup cold butter, cubed	

Combine pears, sugar, and cornstarch in your Slow Cooker. In a bowl, combine flour, cocoa powder, salt, and baking powder. Put in butter and toss until crumbly, and pour it over the pears. Cover with the lid and cook for 4 hours on Low. Serve chilled.

Spiced Fruit Compote

Serves: 6 | Total Time: 6 hours 30 minutes

2 red apples, peeled, cored and sliced	
½ cup dried apricots, halved	
2 ripe pears, peeled and cubed	
1 pineapple, cubed	1-star anise
1 cup fresh orange juice	1 cinnamon stick
3 tbsp light brown sugar	2 whole cloves

Mix the pears, apples, apricots, pineapple, orange juice, sugar, 2 cups of water, star anise, cinnamon stick, and cloves in your Slow Cooker. Cover with the lid and cook for 6 hours on Low. Let cool before serving.

Chocolate Turtle Cake

Serves: 6 | Total Time: 4 hours 30 minutes

1 cup crushed graham crackers	
6 oz dark chocolate, melted	½ cup mixed nuts, chopped
3/4 cup white sugar	½ cup white chocolate chips
2 eggs	½ cup pretzels, chopped
3/4 cup all-purpose flour	1 tsp baking powder
½ cup butter, melted	¼ tsp salt
½ cup mini marshmallows	

In a bowl, combine butter and chocolate until smooth. Mix in sugar and eggs until well combined. Add in flour, baking powder, salt, toss until well combined. Pour the mixture into your Slow Cooker. Put crackers, marshmallows, nuts, chocolate chips, and pretzels on top. Cover and cook for 4 hours on Low. Serve chilled.

Vanilla Rice Pudding

Serves: 6 | Total Time: 4 hours 15 minutes

1 vanilla pod, cut in half lengthwise	
4 cups whole milk	½ cup sugar
1 ½ cups white rice	2 tbsp cornstarch
¼ cup cold water	1 tsp cinnamon powder

In your Slow Cooker, combine rice, milk, vanilla pod, and sugar. Cover with the lid and cook for 3 hours on Low. In a bowl, whisk cornstarch and water and pour it over the rice. Cover with the lid and cook for 1 more hour on Low. Dust with cinnamon and serve.

Chocolate Cake

Serves: 6 | Total Time: 2 hours 30 minutes

1 cup sugar	4 eggs
1 cup all-purpose flour	1 tsp vanilla extract
¼ cup cocoa powder	1 tsp baking powder
½ cup butter, melted	¼ tsp salt

In a bowl, beat eggs, butter, vanilla, and sugar until creamy. Put in flour, cocoa powder, baking powder, and salt; mix until well combined. Transfer everything to your Slow Cooker. Cook for 2 hours on High. Serve and enjoy!

Simple Tiramisu Pudding

Serves: 6 | Total Time: 4 hours 15 minutes

½ cup mascarpone cheese	2 eggs
1 ½ cups milk	2 tsp coffee powder
6 cups bread cubes	2 tbsp Kahlua
¼ cup white sugar	2 tbsp cocoa powder

Put bread cubes in your Slow Cooker. In a bowl, combine sugar, coffee, Kahlua, mascarpone cheese, milk, and egg until smooth. Pour the mixture over the cubes and sprinkle with cocoa powder. Cover with the lid and cook for 4 hours on Low. Serve and enjoy!

Caramel Custard

Serves: 6 | Total Time: 6 hours 15 minutes

4 cups whole milk	4 eggs
1 cup heavy cream	1 tbsp vanilla bean paste
1 cup sugar for melting	2 tbsp white sugar
2 egg yolks	

Place 1 cup of sugar in a pan over high heat and cook until it gets amber color. Add it to your Slow Cooker and swirl to coat the bottom. In a bowl, beat milk, heavy cream, egg yolks, eggs, vanilla bean paste, and sugar until smooth. Pour the mixture the pot. Cover with the lid and cook for 6 hours on Low. Serve chilled.

Almond Cookies with Chocolate Chips

Serves: 6 | Total Time: 2 hours 45 minutes

½ cup ground almonds	1 cup powdered sugar
½ cup dark chocolate chips	2 egg yolks
1 cup all-purpose flour	1 pinch of salt
1 cup butter, softened	½ tsp baking powder
¼ cup heavy cream	

Add butter and sugar to a bowl and toss until creamy. Pour in eggs, one by one, almonds, flour, salt, baking powder, and heavy cream and mix until well combined. Fold in chocolate chips and transfer it into your Slow Cooker. Cover with the lid and cook for 2 ½ hours on High. When done, remove the lid and let cool before cutting it into squares.

Elegant Butterscotch Chocolate Cake

Serves: 6 | Total Time: 4 hours 30 minutes

1 cup butterscotch chocolate chips, melted	
½ cup whole milk	1 ½ cups all-purpose flour
½ cup butter, softened	½ tsp salt
½ cup white sugar	1 tsp baking powder

Using an electric mixer, beat butter and sugar for 5 minutes until creamy. Put in butterscotch chips, milk, and 1 cup of hot water and pulse until well combined. Add in flour, salt, and baking powder and pulse until smooth. Pour the mixture into your Slow Cooker. Cover with the lid and cook for 4 hours on Low. Serve cooled.

Rum Chocolate Bread Pudding

Serves: 6 | Total Time: 6 hours 30 minutes

6 cups bread cubes	1 ½ cups whole milk
¼ cup golden raisins	½ cup heavy cream
½ cup dark chocolate chips	1 tsp vanilla extract
¼ cup butter, melted	1 pinch cinnamon powder
4 eggs	2 tbsp dark rum

Add bread cubes, raisins, and chocolate chips to your Slow Cooker. In a bowl, whisk butter, eggs, milk, heavy cream, vanilla extract, cinnamon powder, and rum until smooth and pour it over the bread. Cover with the lid and cook for 6 hours on Low. Serve and enjoy!

Cheesy White Chocolate Soufflé

Serves: 6 | Total Time: 2 hours 30 minutes

1 ½ cups white chocolate chips, melted	
1 ½ cups cream cheese, softened	
Butter to grease the pot	1 tsp vanilla extract
4 egg whites	1 pinch of salt
4 egg yolks	

In a bowl, whisk egg whites and salt until it forms peaks. Set aside. In another bowl, mix chocolate chips, cream cheese, egg yolks, and vanilla extract until smooth. Mix in the whipped egg whites. Pour the mixture into your greased Slow Cooker. Cover with the lid and cook for 2 hours on High. Serve and enjoy!

Exotic Grand Marnier Soufflé

Serves: 6 | Total Time: 2 hours 30 minutes

1 large orange, zested
¼ cup Grand Marnier
8 egg yolks
10 egg whites
Butter to grease the pot
¼ cup butter, softened
2/3 cup white sugar
1 cup whole milk
½ cup all-purpose flour
1 pinch of salt

Using butter, grease the pot of your Slow Cooker. In a bowl, combine orange zest and sugar to release the flavor. Place the orange sugar and milk in a pot over high heat and bring it to a boil. In a bowl, beat egg yolks and flour until creamy and transfer it to the hot milk, stirring frequently. Low the heat and cook for 2-3 minutes until thickens, stirring often. Turn the heat off, mix in butter and Grand Marnier. Set aside to cool. In another bowl, whisk egg whites and salt until it forms peaks, add it into the orange mixture, and toss to combine. Pour the batter into your Slow Cooker. Cover with the lid and cook for 2 hours on High. Serve and enjoy!

Apple & Pear Butter

Serves: 6 jars | Total Time: 6 hours 30 minutes

4 ripe pears, peeled, cored and sliced
6 large red apples, peeled, cored and sliced
1 ½ cups fresh apple juice   1 cinnamon stick
1 cup white sugar   4 cardamom pods, crushed
1 cup light brown sugar

Stir apples, pears, apple juice, white sugar, brown sugar, cinnamon stick, and cardamom pods in your Slow Cooker. Cover with the lid and cook for 6 hours on Low. Divide between jars and serve cooled.

White Chocolate & Velvet Brioche Pudding

Serves: 6 | Total Time: 5 hours 30 minutes

½ cup white chocolate chips   3 eggs
5 cups brioche cubes   ½ cup white sugar
2 cups whole milk   1 tsp vanilla extract
1 cup cream cheese   1 tsp red food coloring

Add brioche cubes and chocolate chips to your Slow Cooker. In a bowl, whisk milk, cream cheese, food coloring, eggs, sugar, and vanilla extract until smooth and pour it over the bread. Cover with the lid and cook for 5 hours on Low. Serve and enjoy!

Ginger Pumpkin Cheesecake

Serves: 6 | Total Time: 6 hours 30 minutes

CRUST:

1 ¼ cups crushed graham crackers
½ cup butter

FILLING:

½ cup light brown sugar   4 eggs
¼ cup butter   1 tsp cinnamon powder
1 cup pumpkin puree   1 tsp ground ginger
24 oz cream cheese   ½ tsp cardamom powder

Place butter in a pan over medium heat and cook for 2-3 minutes until golden. Set aside to cool. In a bowl, combine crackers and golden butter until crumby, pour it into your Slow Cooker, and press down on the bottom. Place butter in a pan over medium heat and cook for 2-3 minutes until golden. Set aside to cool. Mix in pumpkin puree, cream cheese, eggs, sugar, cinnamon, ginger, cardamom, and pour it over the crust. Cover and cook for 6 hours on Low. Let cool before slicing.

Tasty Butterscotch Pudding

Serves: 6 | Total Time: 2 hours 15 minutes

1 cup white sugar   1 cup whole milk
1 ½ cups all-purpose flour   1 tsp vanilla extract
½ cup butter, melted   ¼ tsp salt

BUTTERSCOTCH

3/4 cup dark brown sugar   2 cups hot water
2 tbsp butter   2 tbsp golden syrup

Place hot water, brown sugar, golden syrup, and butter in a pot over medium heat and cook for 5-6 minutes until thickens. Set aside. In a bowl, combine butter, milk, vanilla extract, sugar, flour, and salt until smooth. Pour the mixture into your Slow Cooker. Sprinkle with the butterscotch mixture, and cook for 2 hours on High. Serve and enjoy!

Citrus Pudding

Serves: 6 | Total Time: 4 hours 15 minutes

1 ½ cups whole milk   4 egg whites
1/3 cup self-raising powder   1 tbsp lemon zest
1 cup butter, softened   1 tbsp lime zest
1 cup white sugar   2 tbsp lemon juice
3 egg yolks   1 pinch cream of tartar

In a bowl, beat butter and sugar until creamy. Mix in egg yolks, lemon juice, milk, self-raising powder, lemon zest, and lime zest until smooth. In another bowl, whisk egg whites and cream of tartar until it forms peaks, transfer it into the batter, and toss to combine. Pour it into your greased Slow Cooker. Cover with the lid and cook for 4 hours on Low. Serve cooled.

Twisted Selva Negra

Serves: 6 | Total Time: 4 hours 30 minutes

½ cup dark chocolate chips   2/3 cup white sugar
¼ cup cocoa powder   3 eggs
1 ½ cups cherries, pitted   1 tsp vanilla extract
2/3 cup all-purpose flour   1 tsp baking powder
2/3 cup butter, softened   ¼ tsp salt

In a bowl, beat butter and sugar until creamy. Mix in eggs, vanilla extract, flour, baking powder, salt, and cocoa powder. Pour the batter into your Slow Cooker and top with dark cherries. Place ½ cup of water and chocolate chips in a pot over low heat and cook until it melts and smooth. Drizzle over the cherries. Cover with the lid and cook for 4 hours on Low. Serve cooled.

Peanut Butter Cake

Serves: 6 | Total Time: 5 hours 30 minutes

1 cup all-purpose flour	3 eggs
½ cup smooth peanut butter	1 tsp vanilla extract
3/4 cup butter, softened	1 tsp baking powder
1 cup white sugar	¼ tsp salt

In a bowl, beat butter and sugar for 5 minutes until creamy. Stir in eggs, one by one, and vanilla extract until well combined. Add in the flour, baking powder, and salt and mix to combine. Pour half of the batter into your Slow Cooker. Put peanut butter in the bowl and mix until smooth. Pour the mixture into the cooker. Cover with the lid and cook for 5 hours on Low. Serve chilled.

Carrot-Mascarpone Cake

Serves: 6 | Total Time: 4 hours 30 minutes

CAKE:

1 cup crushed pineapple	½ tsp ground ginger
1 ½ cups grated carrot	1 tsp cinnamon powder
½ cup canola oil	1 tsp vanilla extract
4 eggs	1 tsp baking powder
1 cup white sugar	½ tsp baking soda
1 ½ cups all-purpose flour	½ tsp salt
1 ½ tsp ground cardamom	

FROSTING:

1 cup mascarpone cream	½ cup heavy cream, whipped
¼ cup powdered sugar	

In a bowl, whisk eggs, sugar, and vanilla extract for 5-7 minutes until fluffy. Stir in canola oil, pineapple, carrot, cardamom, ginger, and cinnamon powder. In another bowl, strain flour, baking powder, baking soda, and salt. Transfer it into the carrot mixture and toss until well combined. Pour the batter into your Slow Cooker, cover with the lid, and cook for 4 hours on Low. When done, remove the lid and let it cool completely. Using a hand mixer, blitz mascarpone cheese, sugar, and whipped cream until fluffy. Spread the frosting over the cake before serving.

Sweet Potato S'mores

Serves: 6 | Total Time: 3 hours 30 minutes

CRUST

1 ½ cups crushed graham crackers
¼ cup butter, melted

FILLING

1 ½ cups dark chocolate chips	
2 cups mini marshmallows	1 tsp cinnamon powder
2 sweet potatoes, diced	2 tbsp brown sugar

In a bowl, combine butter and crackers until crumble, transfer it into your Slow Cooker, and press down on the bottom. In another bowl, mix sweet potatoes, cinnamon powder, and sugar and put the mixture over the crust. Add marshmallows and chocolate chips on top, cover with the lid, and cook for 3 hours on Low. Serve chilled.

Apple & Caramel Crisp

Serves: 6 | Total Time: 6 hours 30 minutes

6 Granny Smith apples, peeled, cored and sliced	
½ cup caramel sauce	½ tsp cinnamon powder
1 tbsp cornstarch	

TOPPING

½ cup rolled oats	1 cup all-purpose flour
¼ cup butter, chilled	1 pinch of salt

Add apples, caramel sauce, cornstarch, and cinnamon powder to your Slow Cooker and stir. In a bowl, combine butter, flour, oats, and salt and scatter it over the apples. Cover with the lid and cook for 6 hours on Low. Let cool before serving.

Blueberry & Pear Cake

Serves: 6 | Total Time: 4 hours 30 minutes

2 ripe pears, peeled, cored and diced	
1 cup blueberries	¼ cup cornstarch
3/4 cup butter, softened	1 tsp vanilla extract
1 cup white sugar	1 tsp baking powder
3 eggs	½ tsp salt
1 cup all-purpose flour	

In a bowl, beat butter, vanilla extract, and sugar for 5 minutes until creamy. Stir in eggs, one by one, flour, cornstarch, baking powder, and salt. Toss in pears and blueberries and transfer it into your greased Slow Cooker. Cover with the lid and cook for 4 hours on Low. When done, remove the lid and serve cooled.

Pear Butter with Amaretto

Serves: 6 | Total Time: 6 hours 30 minutes

4 lb ripe pears, peeled, cored and sliced	
¼ cup dark brown sugar	1 ½ cups white sugar
¼ cup Amaretto liqueur	½ tsp cinnamon powder

Mix the pears, white sugar, brown sugar, Amaretto liqueur, and cinnamon powder in your Slow Cooker. Cover with the lid and cook for 6 hours on Low. Divide between jars and serve chilled.

Greek Yogurt & Honey Cake

Serves: 6 | Total Time: 5 hours 30 minutes

¼ cup Greek yogurt	1 cup all-purpose flour
½ cup butter, softened	1 tsp baking powder
¼ cup honey	1 tsp lemon zest
½ cup light brown sugar	¼ tsp salt
2 eggs	

In a bowl, beat butter, honey, and sugar for 5 minutes until creamy. Stir in eggs and lemon zest until well combined. Add in flour, baking powder, salt, and yogurt, and toss to combine. Pour the batter into your greased Slow Cooker, cover with the lid, and cook for 5 hours on Low. Let cool before slicing and serving.

Golden Raisin Rice Pudding

Serves: 6 | Total Time: 4 hours 15 minutes

½ cup golden raisins
1 cup white rice
1 cup evaporated milk
½ cup light brown sugar
2 cups whole milk
1 pinch nutmeg
1 tsp vanilla extract

Mix the rice, evaporated milk, sugar, milk, nutmeg, raisins, and vanilla extract in your Slow Cooker. Cover with the lid and cook for 4 hours on Low. Serve chilled.

Golden Butter & Syrup Pudding

Serves: 6 | Total Time: 4 hours 15 minutes

3/4 cup whole milk
½ cup butter, softened
½ cup golden syrup
¼ cup light brown sugar
2 eggs
1 ½ cups all-purpose flour
¼ tsp salt
½ tsp baking soda

Place the sugar, flour, salt, and baking soda in a bowl. In another bowl, combine golden syrup, butter, eggs, and milk until smooth. Fold in the flour mixture and toss to combine. Cover with the lid and cook for 4 hours on Low. Let cool before serving.

Coffee Bread Pudding

Serves: 6 | Total Time: 4 hours 15 minutes

1 cup brewed coffee
6 cups bread cubed
1 cup heavy cream
1 cup whole milk
2 egg yolks
2 whole eggs
½ cup white sugar

Add bread cubes to your Slow Cooker. In a bowl, combine heavy cream, milk, coffee, egg yolks, eggs, and sugar until smooth and pour it over the bread. Cover with the lid and cook for 4 hours on Low. Serve cooled.

Lumpy Pumpkin Cake

Serves: 6 | Total Time: 5 hours 30 minutes

1 cup sour cream
1 ½ cups all-purpose flour
2 cups pumpkin cubes
½ cup canola oil
3 eggs
2/3 cup white sugar
1 tsp baking powder
¼ tsp salt
½ tsp cinnamon powder
¼ tsp ground ginger
¼ tsp ground cloves

In a bowl, beat canola oil, eggs, and sugar for 5 minutes until it doubles the size. Mix in sour cream, flour, baking powder, salt, cinnamon powder, ginger, and cloves. Pour the mixture into your Slow Cooker. Add pumpkin cubes on top, cover with the lid, and cook for 5 hours on Low. Let cool before slicing and serving.

Plum Butter

Serves: 6 | Total Time: 8 hours 30 minutes

3 cups white sugar
6 lb ripe plums, pitted
2-star anise
2 cinnamon stick
4 cardamom pods, crushed
2 whole cloves

Mix the plums, sugar, star anise, cinnamon stick, cardamom pods, and cloves in your Slow Cooker. Cover with the lid and cook for 8 hours on Low. When done, remove the lid, remove the spices, and share between glass jars. Store it in the storage space for late use.

Oat & Coconut Brownies

Serves: 6 | Total Time: 4 hours 30 minutes

1 cup shredded coconut
½ cup rolled oats
¼ cup butter, melted
2 eggs
1 cup condensed milk
½ cup whole milk
1 cup all-purpose flour
½ cup cocoa powder
¼ tsp salt
2 tbsp powdered milk

In a bowl, combine flour, cocoa powder, salt, powdered milk, coconut, and oats. Mix in butter, eggs, condensed milk, and milk until smooth. Pour the mixture into your Slow Cooker. Cover with the lid and cook for 4 hours on Low. Let cool before cutting it into squares.

Buttermilk Cake

Serves: 6 | Total Time: 4 hours 15 minutes

3/4 cup white sugar
½ cup all-purpose flour
4 eggs
1 cup buttermilk
1 tbsp lemon zest
2 tbsp lemon juice
¼ tsp salt
1 tsp baking powder

In a bowl, whisk eggs, buttermilk, sugar, lemon zest, and lemon juice until smooth. Stir in flour, salt, and baking powder until well combined. Pour the mixture into your Slow Cooker. Cover with the lid and cook for 4 hours on Low. Let cool before slicing and serving.

Cinnamon Apple Cake

Serves: 6 | Total Time: 4 hours 30 minutes

6 Granny Smith apples, peeled, cored and sliced
1 box yellow cake mix
½ cup butter, melted
¼ cup light brown sugar
1 tsp cinnamon powder

Add apples, sugar, and cinnamon powder to your Slow Cooker and top with cake mix and melted butter. Cover with the lid and cook for 4 hours on Low. Serve cooled.

Lime Cake

Serves: 6 | Total Time: 2 hours 30 minutes

1 cup buttermilk
1 lime, zested and juiced
1 ½ cups all-purpose flour
1 cup butter, softened
1¼ cups white sugar
3 eggs
1 tsp vanilla extract
1 tsp baking powder
¼ tsp salt

In a bowl, beat butter and sugar for 2 minutes until creamy. Stir in eggs, one by one, vanilla extract, buttermilk, lime juice, and lime zest until well combined. Add in flour, baking powder, and salt and toss to combine. Pour the batter into your Slow Cooker, cover with the lid, and cook for 2 hours on High. Serve cooled.

Sticky Cinnamon Rolls

Serves: 6 | Total Time: 6 hours

1 ¾ cups milk
¼ cup sour cream
¼ cup white sugar
1 cup light brown sugar
½ cup butter, softened

4 cups all-purpose flour
2 eggs
½ tsp salt
1¼ tsp active dry yeast
1 tsp cinnamon powder

In a bowl, combine flour, salt, and yeast. Pour in milk, eggs, sour cream, and white sugar and mix for 10 minutes until smooth and elastic. Let rest covered at room temperature for 40 minutes. Place the dough on a floured surface and roll it into a thin rectangular shape. Rub the dough with softened butter, sprinkle with brown sugar and cinnamon powder, and knead it thinly. Roll the dough as tight as possible and cut them into thick pieces. Place the rolls in your Slow Cooker, cover with the lid, and let rest for another 20 minutes. Cook for 4 ½ hours on Low. Serve and enjoy!

Upside Down Cherry Cake

Serves: 6 | Total Time: 6 hours 15 minutes

1 ½ lb dark cherries, pitted
½ cup butter, drizzled
¼ cup white sugar
1 cup all-purpose flour

1 cup ground almonds
1 tsp lemon juice
1 tbsp cornstarch
¼ tsp salt

Put cherries, cornstarch, sugar, and lemon juice in your Slow Cooker and stir. In a bowl, combine flour, almonds, and salt and scatter it over the cherries. Sprinkle with melted butter. Cover with the lid and cook for 6 hours on Low. Let cool before serving.

Chocolate Lava Cake

Serves: 6 | Total Time: 2 hours 30 minutes

1 cup plain yogurt
3/4 cup whole milk
¼ cup butter, melted
1 cup cocoa powder
1 cup all-purpose flour

1 cup white sugar
2 eggs
1 tsp vanilla extract
2 tsp baking powder
½ tsp salt

Grease the pot of your Slow Cooker with butter. In a bowl, combine cocoa powder, flour, baking powder, salt, and sugar. Stir in butter, eggs, vanilla extract, yogurt, and milk until smooth. Pour the batter into the pot, cover with the lid, and cook for 2 hours on High. When done, remove the lid and let cool before slicing to serve.

Honeyed Chocolate Fudge with Walnuts

Serves: 6 | Total Time: 1 hour 15 minutes

2 ½ cups dark chocolate chips
½ cup chopped walnuts   ½ cup honey
½ cup heavy cream   1 tsp vanilla extract

Toss the chocolate chips, heavy cream, honey, and vanilla extract in your Slow Cooker. Cover with the lid and cook for 1 hour on High. When done, remove the lid, stir in walnuts, and let cool before cutting into squares to serve.

Bizarre Chocolate Cake

Serves: 6 | Total Time: 6 hours 15 minutes

1 cup buttermilk
1 cup dulce de leche
2 eggs
½ cup corn oil
1 cup all-purpose flour

½ cup cocoa powder
1 tsp baking soda
¼ tsp salt
¼ tsp chili powder
1 tsp vanilla extract

In a bowl, combine flour, cocoa powder, baking soda, salt, and chili powder. Mix in buttermilk, eggs, corn oil, and vanilla extract until smooth. Pour the mixture into your greased Slow Cooker. Cover and cook for 6 hours on Low. Spread dulce de leche all over and serve.

Cranberry & Brandy Bread Pudding

Serves: 6 | Total Time: 6 hours 15 minutes + soaking time

½ cup dried apricots, chopped
½ cup dried cranberries   4 eggs
8 cups bread cubes   2 cups whole milk
¼ cup dark chocolate chips   ½ cup fresh orange juice
½ cup golden raisins   ½ cup light brown sugar
½ cup brandy

In a bowl, combine raisins, apricots, cranberries, and brandy and let soak overnight in the fridge. Add bread cubes and chocolate chips in your Slow Cooker. In a bowl, whisk eggs, milk, orange juice, and sugar until smooth. Put soaked fruits and brandy over the bread and drizzle with the milk mixture. Cover with the lid and cook for 6 hours on Low. Serve and enjoy!

Banana Cake with Walnuts

Serves: 6 | Total Time: 4 hours 30 minutes

4 bananas, mashed
1¼ cups all-purpose flour
½ cup canola oil
1 cup chopped walnuts
1 cup white sugar

2 eggs
1 tsp vanilla extract
1 tsp baking powder
¼ tsp salt

In a bowl, whisk canola oil and sugar for 2 minutes until pale. Stir in eggs for 2-3 minutes until fluffy. Pour in vanilla extract and mashed bananas and toss to combine. Mix in flour, baking powder, and salt and toss to combine. Fold in walnuts and pour the batter into your Slow Cooker. Cover and cook for 4 hours on Low. Serve and enjoy!

Pears Poached with Wine Raspberries

Serves: 6 | Total Time: 6 hours 30 minutes

6 ripe but firm pears, peeled and cored
1 vanilla bean, split in half lengthwise
1 cup raspberries   1 cup white sugar
2 cups red wine

Mix the raspberries, red wine, sugar, vanilla bean, and pears in your Slow Cooker. Cover with the lid and cook for 6 hours on Low. Serve chilled topped with the sauce.

Creamy Peach & Apple

Serves: 4 | Total Time: 4 hours 15 minutes

2 ripe peaches, pitted and sliced
2 Granny Smith apples, peeled, cored and sliced
1 cinnamon stick   3 tbsp honey
1 cup fresh orange juice   1 tsp cornstarch
1 tsp orange zest   Ice cream for serving

Toss apples, peaches, cinnamon stick, orange juice, orange zest, honey, and cornstarch in your Slow Cooker. Cover with the lid and cook for 4 hours on Low. Serve cooled with ice cream.

Upside Down Caramel Turtle Cake

Serves: 6 | Total Time: 6 hours 30 minutes

½ cup caramel sauce   ½ cup sliced almonds
1 cup buttermilk   ½ cup pecans, chopped
¼ cup condensed milk   ½ cup cocoa powder
1 cup all-purpose flour   ½ cup light brown sugar
2 eggs   1 tsp baking soda
½ cup canola oil   ½ tsp salt
½ cup crushed pretzels   1 tsp vanilla extract

Add pretzels, almonds, pecans, caramel sauce, and condensed milk to your Slow Cooker and toss to combine. In a bowl, mix flour, cocoa powder, sugar, baking soda, and salt. Stir in buttermilk, canola oil, eggs, and vanilla extract until smooth and pour it over the nuts. Cover with the lid and cook for 6 hours on Low. When done, remove the lid, turn the cake upside down, and let cool before slicing to serve.

Saffron Almond Pudding

Serves: 6 | Total Time: 6 hours 30 minutes

1 cup raw almonds, peeled and soaked overnight
5 cups whole milk   ¼ tsp cardamom powder
½ cup sugar   1 pinch saffron

Using an electric mixer, blitz almonds, milk, sugar, cardamom powder, and saffron until smooth. Transfer everything to your Slow Cooker. Cover with the lid and cook for 6 hours on Low. Serve cooled.

Pumpkin & Pepita Cake

Serves: 6 | Total Time: 5 hours 15 minutes

¼ cup pepitas   2 eggs
1 cup all-purpose flour   1 tsp vanilla extract
1 tsp baking powder   ¼ tsp salt
¼ cup canola oil   ½ tsp cinnamon powder
1 cup pumpkin puree   ½ tsp ground ginger
½ cup buttermilk

In a bowl, combine flour, baking powder, salt, cinnamon powder, and ginger. Mix in pumpkin puree, buttermilk, eggs, canola oil, and vanilla extract until smooth. Fold in the pepitas. Pour the mixture into your Slow Cooker. Cover and cook for 5 hours on Low. Serve cooled.

Cinnamon Pumpkin Bread

Serves: 6 | Total Time: 6 hours 15 minutes

1 ½ cups all-purpose flour ½ cup buttermilk
½ cup almond flour   ½ tsp cinnamon powder
½ cup vegetable oil   ½ tsp ground ginger
1 ½ cups white sugar   1 tsp baking soda
2 eggs   ¼ tsp salt
1 cup pumpkin puree

In a bowl, beat vegetable oil and sugar for 2 minutes until pale. Stir in eggs for 2-3 minutes until smooth. Add in pumpkin puree and buttermilk and toss to combine. Mix in all-purpose flour, almond flour, cinnamon powder, ginger, baking soda, and salt until well combined. Pour it into your Slow Cooker, cover with the lid, and cook for 6 hours on Low. Let cool before serving.

Choco-Banana Bread

Serves: 6 | Total Time: 3 hours 15 minutes

3 ripe bananas, mashed   1 ½ cups all-purpose flour
½ cup dark chocolate chips 1 tsp baking soda
¼ cup butter, melted   ½ tsp salt
½ cup light brown sugar   1 tsp cinnamon powder
1 large egg

In a bowl, combine butter, mashed bananas, sugar, and egg. Mix in flour, baking soda, salt, and cinnamon powder until well combined. Fold in chocolate chips and pour the batter into your Slow Cooker. Cover with the lid and cook for 3 hours on Low. Serve chilled.

Spiced Peach Crisp with Caramel Sauce

Serves: 6 | Total Time: 4 hours 30 minutes

½ cup caramel sauce   2 tbsp light brown sugar
1 cup all-purpose flour   1 tbsp lemon juice
¼ cup cold butter, cubed   1 pinch nutmeg
6 peaches, pitted and sliced ¼ tsp ground ginger
¼ tsp salt

Add peaches, lemon juice, and caramel sauce to your Slow Cooker and toss. In a bowl, mix flour, salt, butter, sugar, nutmeg, and ginger until grainy and scatter it over the peaches. Cover with the lid and cook for 4 hours on Low. When done, remove the lid and serve cooled.

Banana & Cranberry Cake with Walnuts

Serves: 6 | Total Time: 4 hours 15 minutes

2 ripe bananas, mashed   1 cup all-purpose flour
1 cup frozen cranberries   1 cup ground walnuts
2 eggs   1 ½ tsp baking powder
½ cup buttermilk   ¼ tsp salt

In a bowl, combine flour, walnuts, baking powder, and salt. Mix in mashed bananas, eggs, and buttermilk until smooth. Fold in cranberries and pour the batter into your Slow Cooker. Cover with the lid and cook for 4 hours on Low. Let cool before slicing to serve.

Grand Marnier-Hazelnut Pie

Serves: 6 | Total Time: 6 hours 30 minutes

CRUST AND TOPPING:

1 cup ground hazelnuts	1¼ cups all-purpose flour
¼ cup buttermilk	1 pinch of salt
3/4 cup cold butter, cubed	2 tbsp light brown sugar

FILLING:

½ cup sour cream	1 tsp vanilla extract
½ cup white sugar	2 tbsp Grand Marnier
20 oz cream cheese	1 tbsp cornstarch
2 eggs	

In your blender, add the butter, flour, hazelnuts, buttermilk, salt, sugar and pulse until it gets a dough. Divide by half and let chill one half covered with plastic wrap in the fridge. Place the remaining dough on a floured surface, roll it into a thin sheet, and put it into your Slow Cooker, trimming the edges. In a bowl, beat cream cheese, sour cream, sugar, vanilla extract, Grand Marnier, cornstarch, and eggs until smooth and pour it over the crust. Take the dough out of the fridge, and using a grater, grind it over the filling. Cover with the lid and cook for 6 hours on Low. Let cool before serving.

Effortless Chocolate Cream

Serves: 6 | Total Time: 2 hours 15 minutes

1 ½ cups dark chocolate chips

1 cup evaporated milk	2 tbsp butter
1 cup heavy cream	1 tsp vanilla extract

Combine chocolate chips, evaporated milk, heavy cream, vanilla extract, and butter in your Slow Cooker. Cover with the lid and cook for 2 hours on Low. When done, remove the lid and let it cool completely. Use as a filling.

Chocolate Sweet Potato Cake

Serves: 6 | Total Time: 4 hours 15 minutes

2 eggs	½ cup cocoa powder
1 cup buttermilk	1 tsp baking soda
1 cup sweet potato puree	½ tsp salt
½ cup canola oil	1 tsp cinnamon powder
1 cup all-purpose flour	

Grease the pot of your Slow Cooker with butter. In a bowl, combine flour, cocoa powder, baking soda, salt, and cinnamon powder. Mix in canola oil, eggs, buttermilk, and sweet potato puree until smooth. Pour the mixture into the cooker. Cover with the lid and cook for 4 hours on Low. Let cool before slicing and serving.

Choco-Almond Cake

Serves: 6 | Total Time: 4 hours 30 minutes

¼ cup sliced almonds	3/4 cup white sugar
1 cup almond milk	2 eggs
½ cup butter, melted	1 ½ tsp baking powder
1 ½ cups almond flour	¼ tsp salt
½ cup cocoa powder	1 tsp vanilla extract

Grease your Slow Cooker. In a bowl, combine flour, cocoa powder, sugar, baking powder, and salt. Mix in butter, eggs, milk, and vanilla extract until smooth. Pour the mixture into the cooker. Add almond slices on top and cook for 4 hours on Low. Serve chilled.

Big Pancake

Serves: 6 | Total Time: 2 hours 15 minutes

2 eggs	3/4 tsp baking powder
1 cup buttermilk	¼ tsp baking soda
3/4 cup all-purpose flour	¼ tsp salt
2 tbsp white sugar	1 tsp vanilla extract
2 tbsp butter, melted	Maple syrup for serving

Grease the pot of your Slow Cooker with some butter. In a bowl, combine flour, sugar, baking powder, baking soda, salt, remaining butter, vanilla, eggs, and buttermilk until smooth. Pour the mixture into the cooker. Cook for 2 hours on High. Serve drizzled with maple syrup.

Lemon Pie

Serves: 6 | Total Time: 6 hours 30 minutes

CRUST:

1 ½ cups all-purpose flour	1 tsp vanilla extract
½ cup butter, softened	1 pinch of salt
¼ cup white sugar	¼ tsp baking powder
2 egg yolks	

FILLING:

2/3 cup white sugar	½ cup lemon juice
6 egg yolks	1 tbsp lemon zest

In a bowl, whisk butter and sugar for 5 minutes until creamy. Stir in egg yolks and vanilla extract until smooth. Add in flour, salt, and baking powder and toss few times to combine. Put the dough on a floured surface, roll it into a thin circle, and place it into your Slow Cooker, trimming the edges. Combine egg yolks, lemon juice, lemon zest, and sugar in a separate bowl until smooth and pour it over the crust. Cover with the lid and cook for 6 hours on Low. Serve cooled.

Dark Chocolate Brownies

Serves: 6 | Total Time: 4 hours 30 minutes

½ cup dark chocolate chips	1 cup sugar
8 oz dark chocolate, chopped	2 eggs
1¼ cups all-purpose flour	1 egg yolk
½ cup butter, melted	1 tsp vanilla extract
¼ cup cocoa powder	½ tsp salt

In a bowl, combine flour, cocoa powder, and salt and set aside. In a pot with boiling water, place a heatproof bowl, and stir in butter and chopped chocolate until it melts and smooth. Transfer it to a surface. Mix in sugar, eggs, egg yolk, and vanilla extract until well combined and fold in chocolate chips. Pour the batter into your Slow Cooker, cover with the lid, and cook for 4 hours on Low. Let cool before slicing into squares to serve.

Coconut & Cocoa Cake

Serves: 6 | Total Time: 6 hours 15 minutes

2 cups almond flour
1 cup shredded coconut
¼ cup cocoa powder
½ cup coconut oil, melted
4 eggs
1 cup coconut milk
½ cup xylitol powder
1 tsp vanilla extract
1 tsp baking soda
1 tsp baking powder
¼ tsp salt

Put flour, coconut, cocoa powder, xylitol powder, baking soda, baking powder, and salt in your Slow Cooker. Mix in eggs, coconut oil, milk, and vanilla extract until smooth. Cover with the lid and cook for 6 hours on Low. Let cool before slicing and serving.

Coconut Oat Cake

Serves: 6 | Total Time: 2 hours 15 minutes

2 cups oat flour
1 cup coconut sugar
¼ cup cocoa powder
¼ cup butter, melted
1 cup coconut milk
2 eggs
1 tsp vanilla extract
1 tsp baking powder

In a bowl, combine flour, sugar, cocoa powder, and baking powder. Mix in butter, milk, eggs, and vanilla extract until smooth. Pour it into your greased Slow Cooker, cover with the lid, and cook for 2 hours on High. Let cool before slicing to serve.

Pear Cake with Walnuts

Serves: 6 | Total Time: 4 hours 30 minutes

4 ripe pears, peeled, cored and sliced
1 cup butter, softened
1 cup all-purpose flour
1 cup ground walnuts
¼ cup cocoa powder
1 cup white sugar
3 eggs
¼ tsp salt
1 tsp baking powder
½ tsp cinnamon powder

In a bowl, beat butter and white sugar until creamy. Pour in eggs, one by one, and toss until well combined. Mix in flour, walnuts, cocoa powder, salt, baking powder, and cinnamon powder until smooth. Pour the batter into your Slow Cooker and top with the pears. Cover with the lid and cook for 4 hours on Low. When done, remove the lid and let cool before slicing to serve.

Hazelnut & Nutella Bread Pudding

Serves: 6 | Total Time: 6 hours 30 minutes

8 cups bread cubes
½ cup dark chocolate chips
½ cup hazelnuts, chopped
½ cup Nutella
2 tbsp butter, melted
2 cups whole milk
¼ cup light brown sugar
¼ cup dark rum
1 tsp vanilla extract

Add bread cubes, chocolate chips, and hazelnuts to your Slow Cooker. In a bowl, whisk butter, Nutella, milk, sugar, rum, and vanilla extract until smooth and pour it over the bread. Cover with the lid and cook for 6 hours on Low. Serve chilled.

Chocolate Fondue with S´mores

Serves: 6 | Total Time: 1 hour 15 minutes

1 ½ cups dark chocolate chips
1 can (15 oz) condensed milk
½ cup caramel sauce
½ cup heavy cream
1 cup mini marshmallows
½ tsp all-spice powder
Fresh fruit for serving

Combine condensed milk, all-spice powder, caramel sauce, heavy cream, chocolate chips, and marshmallows in your Slow Cooker. Cover with the lid and cook for 1 hour on High. Serve with fresh fruit.

Cinnamon Bread

Serves: 6 | Total Time: 5 hours 15 minutes

3 cups all-purpose flour
1 ¼ cups white sugar
3/4 cup butter, melted
1 cup whole milk
4 eggs
1 tsp vanilla extract
1 tsp active dry yeast
1 ½ tsp cinnamon powder

Using an electric mixer, blitz flour, eggs, ¼ cup of sugar, vanilla, milk, and yeast for 10 minutes until smooth and elastic. Let rest covered for 1 hour until it doubles the size. Place the dough on a floured surface, cut it into 24–30 pieces, and roll them into a ball. In a bowl, combine the remaining sugar and cinnamon powder. Dip each ball in melted butter, then in the cinnamon mixture, and place them into your greased Slow Cooker. Cover with the lid and cook for 4 hours on Low. When done, remove the lid and let cool before serving.

Chocolate Chip & Peanut Butter Bars

Serves: 6 | Total Time: 2 hours 15 minutes

1 cup dark chocolate chips
1 cup pecans, chopped
½ cup butter, melted
½ cup smooth peanut butter
2 eggs
1 cup light brown sugar
1 cup all-purpose flour
¼ tsp salt

In a bowl, beat butter, peanut butter, eggs, and sugar until creamy and smooth. Add in flour and salt and toss until well coated. Pour it into your Slow Cooker. Fold in chocolate chips and pecans, cover with the lid, and cook for 2 hours on High. Let cool before slicing to serve.

All-Chocolate Cake

Serves: 6 | Total Time: 4 hours 15 minutes

1 cup dark chocolate, melted and chilled
½ cup sour cream
1¼ cups all-purpose flour
3/4 cup butter, softened
3/4 cup light brown sugar
4 eggs
¼ cup cocoa powder
1 ½ tsp baking powder
¼ tsp salt

In a bowl, beat butter and sugar until creamy. Pour in eggs, one by one, melted chocolate and sour cream, and stir until smooth. Add in flour, cocoa powder, baking powder, and salt and toss until well combined. Pour it into your Slow Cooker. Cover with the lid and cook for 4 hours on Low. Serve cooled.

Banana Upside Down Cake

Serves: 6 | Total Time: 4 hours 30 minutes

½ cup light brown sugar
2 ripe bananas, sliced

2 tbsp brandy

FOR THE CAKE

1 cup all-purpose flour
¼ cup cornstarch
½ cup butter
3/4 cup sugar
2 eggs

3/4 cup sour cream
1 tsp vanilla extract
1 tsp baking soda
1 pinch of salt

Sprinkle the bottom of your Slow Cooker with brown sugar. Arrange the banana slices all over and drizzle with brandy. Using an electric mixer, blend butter and sugar for 3 minutes until creamy. Pour in eggs, one by one, sour cream, and vanilla and mix until smooth. Put in flour, cornstarch, baking soda, salt, and pulse until well combined. Pour the mixture over the banana slices. Cook for 4 hours on Low. Let cool the cake for 10 minutes. Turn it upside down onto a plate and serve.

Homemade Dulce de Leche

Serves: 4 | Total Time: 8 hours

1 can (14 oz) condensed milk   Water as needed

Poke 2-3 holes on top of the condensed milk can, place it in your Slow Cooker, and pour in enough water to cover 3/4. Cook for 8 hours on Low. Serve chilled.

Raspberry Fudge Cake

Serves: 6 | Total Time: 4 hours 15 minutes

¼ cup raspberry jam
½ cup canola oil
1 cup whole milk
1 cup all-purpose flour
¼ cup cocoa powder

2 eggs
1 tsp vanilla extract
1 ½ tsp baking powder
¼ tsp salt

In a bowl, combine flour, cocoa powder, baking powder, and salt. Mix in canola oil, milk, eggs, raspberry jam, and vanilla extract until smooth. Pour it into your greased Slow Cooker. Cover with the lid and cook for 4 hours on Low. Let cool before slicing and serving.

Plum Pudding

Serves: 6 | Total Time: 8 hours 15 minutes

1 cup mixed dried fruits, chopped
½ cup dried plums, chopped
1 ½ cups all-purpose flour
¼ cup dark brown sugar
4 tbsp butter, softened

½ tsp baking soda
2 eggs
1 cup hot water

Place dried fruits, plums, and hot water in a bowl and let soak for 10 minutes. Meanwhile, mix flour, sugar, baking soda, butter, and eggs in a bowl until smooth. Fold in soaked fruits and water. Pour the mixture into your Slow Cooker. Cover with the lid and cook for 8 hours on Low. When done, remove the lid and serve cooled.

Easy S'more Brownies

Serves: 6 | Total Time: 2 hours 30 minutes

1 ½ cups mini marshmallows
1 cup crushed graham crackers
¼ cup butter, melted and chilled
1 cup dark chocolate chips, melted
1 cup dark chocolate chips
4 eggs
1 cup all-purpose flour

¼ cup cocoa powder
1 cup white sugar
1 tsp vanilla extract

In a bowl, beat butter, melted chocolate, eggs, sugar, and vanilla extract until smooth. Stir in flour and cocoa powder until well combined. Pour the mixture into your Slow Cooker. Add marshmallows, chocolate chips, and crackers on top and cook for 2 hours on High. Serve.

Traditional Cinnamon Rolls

Serves: 6 | Total Time: 6 hours 30 minutes

1 cup light brown sugar
1 cup white sugar
¼ cup melted butter
1 ½ cups warm milk
2 eggs

4 cups all-purpose flour
½ tsp salt
1 tsp active dry yeast
1 tsp cinnamon powder

In a bowl, combine flour, salt, and yeast. Pour in milk, eggs, and butter and mix for 5-10 minutes until smooth and elastic. Let rest covered at room temperature for 1 hour until it doubles the size. Place the dough on a floured surface and roll it into a thin rectangular shape. In a bowl, mix white sugar and cinnamon powder, dust it over the dough, and then knead it thinly. Cut the dough into thick slices and roll them. Sprinkle brown sugar in your Slow Cooker and put in the rolls, cut-face up. Cover and cook for 5 hours on Low. Serve and enjoy!

Citrus Pumpkin Streusel

Serves: 6 | Total Time: 6 hours 30 minutes

STREUSEL:

¼ cup whole wheat flour
¼ cup butter, melted
½ cup rolled oats

1 tsp cinnamon powder
2 tbsp maple syrup

CAKE:

13/4 cups all-purpose flour
¼ cup butter, melted
1 cup pumpkin puree
½ cup fresh orange juice
½ cup light brown sugar
2 eggs

¼ cup maple syrup
1 ½ tsp baking powder
¼ tsp salt
1 tbsp lemon juice
½ tsp baking soda
½ tsp ground ginger

In a bowl, mix oats, flour, cinnamon powder, maple syrup, and butter until well combined. Set aside. In a separate bowl, combine flour, baking powder, salt, baking soda, ginger, and brown sugar. Mix in butter, pumpkin puree, orange juice, lemon juice, eggs, and maple syrup until smooth. Pour the batter into your Slow Cooker and add the streusel on top. Cover with the lid and cook for 6 hours on Low. Serve and enjoy!

Poppy Seed Cake

Serves: 6 | Total Time: 4 hours 30 minutes

1 cup all-purpose flour	2 eggs
1 cup buttermilk	1 tsp baking soda
½ cup fine cornmeal	½ tsp baking powder
3/4 cup butter, softened	½ tsp salt
3/4 cup white sugar	2 tbsp poppy seeds
1 lemon, zested and juiced	

In a bowl, combine flour, cornmeal, baking soda, baking powder, salt, and poppy seeds. In another bowl, beat butter, sugar, and lemon zest for a few minutes. Pour in eggs, one by one, and lemon juice and toss until well combined. Fold in flour mixture and buttermilk, alternating, then pour it into your Slow Cooker. Cover with the lid and cook for 4 hours on Low. Serve chilled.

Lemon Ricotta Cake

Serves: 6 | Total Time: 5 hours 15 minutes

1 ½ cups all-purpose flour	1 tsp vanilla extract
4 eggs, separated	1 tbsp lemon zest
¼ cup butter, melted	1 ½ tsp baking powder
1 ½ cups ricotta cheese	¼ tsp salt
½ cup white sugar	

Using butter, grease your Slow Cooker. In a bowl, combine ricotta cheese, sugar, vanilla extract, lemon zest, and egg yolks until smooth. Mix in the flour, baking powder, and salt. In another bowl, fluff egg whites until it gets peaks, transfer it into the batter, and toss until well combined. Pour the batter into the pot. Cover and cook for 5 hours on Low. Let cool before serving.

Almond Cheesecake

Serves: 6 | Total Time: 4 hours 15 minutes

CRUST:

1 ½ cups crushed graham crackers
½ cup butter, melted

FILLING:

4 eggs	1 tbsp cornstarch
½ cup white sugar	1 tbsp vanilla extract
12 oz cream cheese	½ tsp almond extract
12 oz sour cream	

In a bowl, combine crackers and butter until sandy, transfer it into your Slow Cooker, and press down on the bottom. In a bowl, mix cream cheese, sour cream, eggs, sugar, cornstarch, vanilla extract, and almond extract until smooth and pour it over the crust. Cover with the lid and cook for 4 hours on Low. Let cool before slicing.

Brownies with Chocolate Chips

Serves: 6 | Total Time: 6 hours 30 minutes

1 cup all-purpose flour	3 eggs
½ cup cocoa powder	½ cup white sugar
½ cup butter	2 tbsp dark brown sugar
2 cups dark chocolate chips	½ tsp salt

In a pot with boiling water, place a heatproof bowl and stir butter and 1 ¼ cups of chocolate chips until it melts and smooth. Remove the bowl. Mix in eggs, white sugar, brown sugar, flour, cocoa powder, and salt until smooth. Fold in the remaining chocolate chips and pour the batter into your Slow Cooker. Cover with the lid and cook for 4 hours on Low. Serve cooled.

Made in the USA
Las Vegas, NV
22 November 2021

34883596R00079